❀❀❀❀ THE BETTER PART OF VALOR

MORE, ERASMUS, COLET, AND VIVES, ON HUMANISM,

WAR, AND PEACE, 1496-1535

The
Better Part of
Valor

❈❈❈❈

MORE, ERASMUS, COLET, AND VIVES,
ON HUMANISM, WAR, AND PEACE,
1496-1535

❈❈❈❈

by ROBERT P. ADAMS

❈❈❈

UNIVERSITY OF WASHINGTON PRESS
SEATTLE 1962

This book is published with the assistance from a grant by the Ford Foundation.

TO ALL MY FAMILY

The author hopes that *The Better Part of Valor* will interest both educated readers and students of the English Renaissance—in a word, many who care for a good life. As a study of men and ideas this essay seeks to present, in its entirety, the thought of the greatest early Tudor humanists on war and peace. Life and literature are therefore presented in vigorous interaction.

Completion of this work would have been impossible without sustained encouragement, criticism, and aid. For their friendly thoroughness in criticism of the manuscript at various stages in its growth I am particularly indebted to Professor Douglas Bush of Harvard University, to Professor Emeritus William Haller, of Barnard College in Columbia University, and to Dr. Louis B. Wright, Director of the Folger Shakespeare Library. As those who have sojourned at the Folger Library are well aware, Dr. Wright is a tower of friendly support to toilers in the Renaissance vineyards. Professor Gerald E. Bentley of Princeton University has given support when it was most needed. In addition I am grateful to the Trustees and Director of the Folger Library for several fellowships and grants in aid of research. The American Philosophical Society has generously assisted the progress of the work, as has the University of Washington.

In the interest of heightened readability quotations included in the text have been put into modern spelling. In order to reduce the number of notes but still keep sources clear, abbreviated references have often been placed inside parentheses within the narrative body of the text itself. A list of all abbreviations thus used appears before the text.

Warm thanks are due to the staffs of many libraries: to the Folger Shakespeare Library and in particular to Miss Dorothy Mason; to the Newberry Library and to its rare-book librarian, Mrs. Gertrude Woodward; to the University of Chicago Library; the University of Michigan

Library; Harvard University Library; J. Pierpont Morgan Library; Huntington Library; New York Public Library; and the Library of Congress.

To the editors of these journals thanks are due for permission to make use of materials which, in earlier forms, first appeared in their pages: *Studies in Philology, Papers of the Michigan Academy, Journal of the History of Ideas, Renaissance News,* and *Huntington Library Quarterly.*

R.P.A.

Seattle, Washington

The following abbreviations are used in the text and in the notes.

Adams (1941) = Robert P. Adams, "The Philosophic Unity of More's *Utopia*," *Studies in Philology*, XXXVIII (1941), 45-65.

Adams (1945) = Robert P. Adams, "Designs by More and Erasmus for a New Social Order," *Studies in Philology*, XLII (1945), 131-45.

Adams (1948) = Robert P. Adams, "Pre-Renaissance Courtly Propaganda for Peace in English Literature," *Papers of the Michigan Academy*, XXXII ([1946]-48), 431-46.

Adams (1949) = Robert P. Adams, "The Social Responsibilities of Science in *Utopia, New Atlantis* and After," *Journal of the History of Ideas*, X (1949), 374-98.

AHR = *American Historical Review*.

Allen (1934) = P. S. Allen, *Erasmus* (Oxford, 1934).

Ames = Russell Ames, *Citizen Thomas More and His Utopia* (Princeton, N.J., 1949).

AVM = Amerigo Vespucci, *Mundus novus Letter to Lorenzo . . . de Medici*, trans. G. Northup (Princeton, N.J., 1916).

AVS = *Amerigo Vespucci Letter to Piero Soderini . . . (1504)*, trans. G. Northup (Princeton, N.J., 1916).

BE = *Bibliotheca Erasmiana*, comp. F. Vander Haeghen *et al.* (Ghent, 1897-1907). *BE-A* = *Adagia; BE-C* = *Colloquia*.

Brewer = J. S. Brewer, *The Reign of Henry VIII from his Accession to the Death of Wolsey*, ed. J. Gairdner (London, 1884).

Cal. LP Spain = *Calendar of the Letters . . . and State Papers . . . between England and Spain*, ed. G. A. Bergenroth (London, 1866——). Citations are by volume and number unless otherwise indicated.

Cal. SP Ven. = *Calendar of State Papers and Manuscripts, Relating to English Affairs, Existing in . . . Venice*, ed. R. Brown (London, 1867).

Caspari = Fritz Caspari, *Humanism and the Social Order in Tudor England* (Chicago, 1954).

CDV = *Saint Augustine, of the Citie of God: With . . . comments of Io. L. Vives*, trans. J. H[ealey] (London, 1620).

Chambers = R. W. Chambers, *Thomas More* (London, 1935).

Cromwell = Roger Merriman, *Life and Letters of Thomas Cromwell* (Oxford, 1902).

de Vocht = Henry de Vocht, *Monumenta humanistica Lovaniensia* (Louvain, 1934).

DNB = *Dictionary of National Biography.*

Donner = H. W. Donner, *Introduction to Utopia* (London, 1934).

EAW = *Erasmus Against War,* ed. J. W. Mackail (Boston, 1907).

EC = Erasmus, *The Lives of Vitrier . . . and John Colet,* trans. J. H. Lupton (London, 1883).

ECE = *Erasmus Concerning the Aim and Method of Education,* trans. W. H. Woodward (Cambridge, Eng., 1904).

ECF = Erasmus, *The Familiar Colloquies,* trans. N. Bailey (London, 1725).

ECK = [Erasmus, *The Christian Knight,* trans. anon. (London, 1541)]. *STC* 10482.

ECP = Erasmus, *The Education of a Christian Prince,* trans. L. K. Born (New York, 1936).

EDB = *Érasme Dulce bellum inexpertis,* ed. and trans. Yvonne Remy and René Dunil-Marquebreucq (Berchem-Brussels, 1953).

EE = *Opus epistolarum Des. Erasmi,* ed. P. S. and H. M. Allen (Oxford, 1906-47). References are to epistle numbers unless otherwise indicated.

EMC = Erasmus, *Enchiridion militis Christiani,* [trans. William Tyndale?] (London, 1905).

EN = *The Epistles of Erasmus,* trans. F. M. Nichols (London, 1901-18).

EO = Erasmus, *Opera Omnia,* ed. J. Clericus (Leiden, 1703-6).

EP = Erasmus, *The First Tome . . . of the Paraphrase . . . upon the Newe Testamente* (London, 1548). *STC* 2854.

EPF = Erasmus, *The Praise of Folly,* trans. H. H. Hudson (Princeton, N.J., 1941).

EPF-C = Erasmus, *The Praise of Folly,* trans. Sir Thomas Chaloner (1549), ed. J. Ashbee (London, 1921).

EQP = Erasmus, *The Complaint of Peace,* trans. anon. (Chicago, 1917).

ETC = *Ten Colloquies of Erasmus,* trans. C. R. Thompson (New York, 1957).

Fisher = H. Fisher, *The History of England from the Accession of Henry VII to the Death of Henry VIII (1485-1547)* (London, 1934).

Gee = John A. Gee, *The Life and Works of Thomas Lupset* (New Haven, Conn., 1928).

Giustinian = Sebastian Giustinian, *Four Years at the Court of Henry VIII. Selection of Despatches Written by the Venetian Ambassador, Sebastian Giustinian . . . to the Signory of Venice, January 12th, 1515, to July 26th, 1519,* trans. Rawdon Brown (London, 1854).

Hall = [Edward] Hall, *Hall's Chronicle,* ed. H. Ellis (London, 1809).

Harpsfield = Nicholas Harpsfield, *The Life and Death of Sr Thomas Moore,* ed. E. V. Hitchcock (London, 1932).

Hexter = J. H. Hexter, *More's Utopia* (Princeton, N.J., 1952).

HLQ = *Huntington Library Quarterly.*

Hudson = Hoyt Hudson, *The Epigram in the English Renaissance* (Princeton, N.J., 1947).

Kelso = Ruth Kelso, *The Doctrine of the English Gentleman* (Urbana, Ill., 1929).

Lange = C. L. Lange, *Histoire de l'internationalisme* (New York, 1919).

LB = A. O. Lovejoy and G. Boas, *Primitivism and Related Ideas in Antiquity* (Baltimore, Md., 1935).

LC = Literae virorum eruditorum ad Franciscum Craneveldium 1522-1528, ed. Henry de Vocht (Louvain, 1928).

Lewis = C. S. Lewis, *English Literature in the Sixteenth Century, Excluding Drama* (Oxford, 1954).

LP = Letters and Papers . . . of the Reign of Henry VIII, ed. J. S. Brewer (London, 1862———). Citations are by volume and number unless otherwise indicated.

MC = The Correspondence of Sir Thomas More, ed. E. F. Rogers (Princeton, N.J., 1947).

MDT = More, *The Dialogue Concerning Tyndale*, ed. W. Campbell (London, 1927).

Mesnard = Pierre Mesnard, *L'Essor de la philosophie politique au XVIe siècle* (Paris, 1936).

MEW = More, *English Works* (London, 1557). *STC* 18076.

MEW-C = More, *The English Works*, ed. W. E. Campbell *et al.* (London, 1931-39).

MLE = More, *The Latin Epigrams*, ed. L. Bradner and C. Lynch (Chicago, 1953).

MLR = Modern Language Review.

MUL = More, *Utopia*, ed. J. H. Lupton (Oxford, 1895).

PMLA = Publications of the Modern Language Association.

Pollard = A. F. Pollard, *Wolsey* (London, 1929).

Polydore Vergil = Polydore Vergil, *The Anglica historia . . . 1485-1537*, trans. D. Hay (London, 1950).

Roper = William Roper, *The Lyfe of Sir Thomas Moore*, ed. E. V. Hitchcock (London, 1935).

Smith = Preserved Smith, *Erasmus* (New York, 1923).

SP = State Papers . . . I, King Henry VIII ([London], 1830).

STC = A Short-Title Catalogue of Books Printed in England, Scotland, and Ireland and of English Books Printed Abroad 1475-1640, compiled by A. W. Pollard and G. R. Redgrave *et al.* (London, 1948). *STC* numbers given refer to *STC* books used.

Surtz *PW* = Edward Surtz, *The Praise of Wisdom* (Chicago, 1957).

TLS = (London) *Times Literary Supplement.*

VCD = Vives, *De concordia & discordia in humano genere* [Antwerp, July, 1529].

VCW = Vives, *The Instruction of a Christen Woman,* trans. Richarde Hyrde (London, 1541). *STC* 24858.

VIW = Vives, *An Introduction to Wysedome,* trans. Rycharde Morysine [London, 1540]. *STC* 24847.

VO = *Vivis opera* (Basel, 1555).

VOE = *Vives: On Education,* trans. Foster Watson (Cambridge, Eng., 1913).

VRP = J. L. Vives, *Concerning the Relief of the Poor,* trans. M. M. Sherwood (New York, 1917).

Woodward = W. H. Woodward, *Studies in Education . . . 1400-1600* (Cambridge, Eng., 1906).

CONTENTS

✿✿✿✿ THE BETTER PART OF VALOR

MORE, ERASMUS, COLET, AND VIVES, ON HUMANISM,

WAR, AND PEACE, 1496-1535

CHAPTER ONE

GOLDEN AGE TO IRON PEACE

The most distinguished early Tudor humanists were, of course, Sir Thomas More, Erasmus, John Colet, and Juan Luis Vives. These, with their circle, are the "London Reformers," in R. W. Chambers' happy phrase. Their thought on war and peace reveals how these leaders of the English Renaissance strove to describe, as a model for their age, the outlines of a radically improved social order. Its basic principles were to be drawn from a revitalized Church and from the social application especially of neo-Stoic ideas found in medieval as well as classical sources. By these humanists, at least, no grave conflict between Christian and natural ethics, or between Christianity and natural science, was anticipated. My aim is to present their work, falling between about 1497 and 1530, as a unified whole. When their social criticism is thus viewed, as a lively movement of the Renaissance, it takes on the aspect of a grand campaign of discovery and exploration into a country of the mind. The work of these great friends illuminated the critical deficiencies of the existing society and stimulated both courtly and public acceptance of the goal of social change as rightly the creation of a peaceful good life, a "utopia" according to "reason or nature."

Since it was plain to the humanists that unless wars could largely be prevented, social reconstruction would be well-nigh impossible, much of the London Reformers' literary and political energies went into labors for peace in their time. The resulting propaganda (if the word may be so used) furnishes indeed a signal illustration of the tendency, since the Renaissance, for conscious modification of public opinion and reshaping of society toward an ideal state to be "more important than catastrophe, conquest, or corruption" in effecting social change.[1] Although, to be sure, these humanists failed in their time to achieve a nonviolent reshaping of English society, their ideas on war and peace

3

have become a positive force in shaping modern objectives for social progress. The critique of war and peace whose initial modern pattern was molded by such thinkers as More and Erasmus cannot indeed be ignored except at the risk of losing in literature and history an essential perspective and sense of direction. Without it the spiritual struggle of men for a good life becomes densely obscured, so that there remains in view, as Mesnard wrote, only a "bloody clash of conflicting interests, struggling for power or for bread as though these were ends in themselves." [2]

The vital principle of a society may be found in its visions of a good life and of the ways and means by which the human pursuit of happiness may be made triumphant. Ideas, however, cannot wisely be separated from the men who discover or rediscover them and who, inevitably, are molded by them. An awareness that war was a monstrous folly which could destroy civilization did not, to be sure, dawn for the first time on men's minds at the beginning of the sixteenth century. The rich background of antiquity and of the Middle Ages must be taken into account, however briefly, if only by way of setting the stage for More, Erasmus, Colet, and Vives. For our central story is of one great idea and of the four men who, in the early English Renaissance, were pre-eminently its explorers.

Their concept, to put it with almost deceptive simplicity, was that war is not an action of divine "Providence" but largely a man-made evil which can be minimized, if not wholly eliminated, in a society whose organization is rational and just. The eldest of the four, John Colet, Dean of St. Paul's, pioneered the new humanist criticism on war and peace. His protégés, Sir Thomas More and Erasmus (born a Netherlander), became the most remarkable "English" humanist critics of their age. The work of these older men was in turn carried on, during the 1520's, by the brilliant and bold Spaniard, Juan Luis Vives. By 1535 all were dead save Vives, who had been dismissed in disgrace from England by Henry VIII, and the social criticism most distinctive of the London Reformers' kind of humanism had reached a point of arrest.[3]

The first main act of our drama of men and ideas will properly begin when, at Oxford in 1497, John Colet mounts the stage to undertake a series of critiques upon St. Paul, a series marked by rather striking departures from conventional medieval modes of social and literary criticism. Before Colet thus appears, however, an introduction seems in order—a curtain-raiser, as it were. Certainly in the history of ideas absolute newness is rare. Indeed, out of antiquity and the Middle Ages there came down to the English Renaissance a rich complex of myth, history, and literature bearing upon man at war and at peace. In this chapter a broad sketch is drawn of pre-Renaissance thought on war. "The Waning of Chivalry" (chapter 2) considers more closely ideas current in fifteenth-century England. Thus we may hope more clearly to view the London Reformers as inheritors of the mighty past and as original Renaissance thinkers.

Broadly speaking, the pre-Renaissance history of social criticism on war and peace comprises two famous myths (of the Golden Age and of Prometheus) and proceeds through three grand historical epochs in international relations—the ancient heroic age, the period of the *Pax Romana,* and the Christian era (primitive and medieval), with its ideal of a *Pax Ecclesiae.*[4]

Western man's earliest visions of the origin and function of war in human society are embodied in two of the most haunting and pervasive of all myths, but the social views evident in the Golden Age legend and in that of Prometheus, which seems to have been little current in medieval thought, are largely rival and almost antithetic. On the one hand, the Prometheus myth represents man's earliest condition on earth as the most wretched of all. In this imagined primitive state of nature men lacked all arts and technologies, including of course those of war. Lived in barbarous ignorance, men's lives were brutish, nasty, and short. The Prometheus story celebrates the progress of man upward from primeval backwardness, a progress achieved precisely through the development of arts, inventions, and technical skills. Logically, therefore, this myth presents the rise of war in the world as simply a fact of "progress" like any other. Those who are predominantly allured by this view naturally tend optimistically to identify the achievements of any given culture with its total mastery of useful arts and techniques of production.

On the other hand, those who accept substantially some form of the Golden Age myth tend to regard the history of man's life on earth with profound pessimism. In the golden time, the fancied earliest age of man, he was presumed to have been at his happiest—at peace with his own kind, with the animals, indeed with all nature around him. The Golden

5

Age reveals the pure and ancient dream of a prehistoric paradise, an Eden, a world at peace, to which some Renaissance men, at least, longed to return or which (reading voyager's tales of undreamed shores) they hoped might somewhere actually be found. Poets, historians, and philosophers in antiquity were stirred by the Golden Age ideal and accordingly viewed historical mankind, chronically at war, as representing a profound and ever deepening degeneration. In fact the first period of international relations known to history was one of endless wars in the world of ancient Greece and Israel. In the so-called heroic age, when tribes and states were almost continually engaged in plunder and bloodshed, war was almost everywhere regarded as "natural." Historically nothing is known of a time when universal peace prevailed among primitive men. Ancient social critics, therefore, struggled to imagine by what social processes a presumably once pacific and uncorrupted mankind might have degenerated to the conditions of chronic war known in history.[5]

Pythagoras, Lucretius, Ovid, Seneca, and Plutarch all gave vivid narratives designed to explain war's rise in the world. The commonplaces of this classic social criticism are worth summing up. The Golden Age peace was broken, it was poetically surmised, when men first began to kill animals. Degenerating progressively, men became accustomed to brutality, until they actually learned to enjoy butchery. Eventually even manslaughter and war became habitual and finally were termed glorious. Admiration and applause came to be showered upon bloody conquerors like Alexander the Great, who would once have been regarded as insane homicides. Abusing nature's gifts of wit and inventive powers, men progressively turned their talents to production of ever more terrible weapons for their own destruction. At last the mass insanity of total war became the order of the day, almost universally taken for granted as the natural human lot. While to sane men it must be obvious that war destroys everything that makes life worth living or even tolerable, yet "civilized" mankind seemed incurably addicted to it. When, indeed, men at war were compared with even the most ferocious of the wild beasts, it was evident that men were capable of a matchless depravity.

The Roman Stoics in particular became leaders in such criticisms of man at war. Reasoning that "just" wars are virtually impossible, the Stoics denounced martial "glory" as false. Seneca strongly attacked the kind of fame won by generals obsessed with lust for conquest. Pliny's is probably the most famous of all ancient diatribes upon human misery; and Pliny concluded that man, the only animal addicted to perpetual war upon his own kind, not only is ethically inferior to the most frightful beasts but indeed lives in more disorder and violence than any known animal. Clearly the line of thought which thus described man's degeneration from a supposed Golden Age of peace into the mass depravities of historic times tended to produce a magnificent and dynamic pessimism concerning man's future prospects for a good life on earth. This classical criticism, as with Seneca, found that man was his own worst enemy.[6]

Antiquity offered to some Renaissance humanists, moreover, a historic vision of a kind of golden age—that of Rome under the *Pax Romana* (*ca.* 28 B.C.–A.D. 180). If the first great period in international relations is seen as that of the war-torn "heroic age," the second encloses that imperial Roman phase in which the mighty ideal of a world-wide Roman peace was actually realized. Men of the Renaissance, indeed, tended to idealize above all not so much Greek as Roman history, literature, institutions, culture, and ideals. It is probably fair to say, with Woodward, that early sixteenth-century humanist scholarship did not make possible what would now be regarded as a critical understanding of the actual moral, social, and economic conditions which prevailed either in ancient Athens or in Augustan Rome. This Rome, to humanists like Erasmus, presented a picture of a civilization which had actually achieved a golden age of peace. Glittering through its ruins, that part of the Roman world stood as "the ideal, once realized, of a universal state ruling in peace and justice the entire human race, adorned with arts, letters, and achievements of practical skill, which mankind had lost through barbarism and was then struggling to recover." [7] Unlike the poetic dream of a prehistoric Golden Age, the *Pax Romana* was no myth. Hence imperial Rome offered a supremely important politico-social ideal of law and peace. During the *Pax Romana* there existed (at least comparatively) an age of universal peace, almost the only season of widely extended freedom from war which civilized mankind had ever known in recorded history. Under Augustus, Rome set herself to repress all strife within her vast boundaries and, except for the remote borders, she almost succeeded.

Antedating and paralleling this second or Roman period in international relations is the literary work of the Roman Stoics in which lies prob-

7

ably the beginning of philosophic thought on war and peace. Notably, the Stoics developed a clear consciousness that the human species has a fundamental unity—all men are brothers. At the base of the idea of such human unity lies the conviction that war is fratricide. Fragments of this idea had perhaps appeared earlier, but the Roman Stoics wrought them into a coherent and vital principle. The first expressions of the conviction that men are united as a species, combined with direct anti-war criticism, seem to have appeared among the later Roman Stoics. Thus a strong Stoic humanitarianism, marked by universal compassion and a concern for the welfare of mankind as a whole, gradually came into being. Cicero may first have advanced the significant distinction between just and unjust wars. Seneca was far more sweeping than Cicero in the comprehensiveness as well as the sensitivity of his critique on war. Disdaining the vaunted military glory of great captains and generals, Seneca indeed regarded duty to humanity as greater than that due to the individual. Both Cicero and Seneca attributed to war and its associated evils a large share of civilization's corruptions. Both leaned strongly to programs for social reform. The vigor of the Stoic strain embodied in primitive Christianity as well as the strength of the Stoic revival in the Renaissance gives this Roman social criticism special interest as a force working upon English humanist minds.[8]

The third great pre-Renaissance phase of international relations and of social criticism on war comprises the Christian era, primitive and medieval. Before the decline of the *Pax Romana* as a working ideal, a dynamic primitive Christian antimilitarism came into being. Unquestionably many early Christians held a strong ideal of nonviolence. Its growth was perhaps aided by the extent of agreement between the older Roman Stoic idea of the natural unity of all men with the new Christian concept of brotherly unity between all Christians. Many primitive Christians held to the view that they were ethically restricted to use of the spiritual sword and could never rightly use physical swords, i.e., take part in armed violence and war. There is, however, no clear evidence that St. Paul adopted the Stoic idea that war is a crime against nature and against the bond of mutual responsibility linking all men as members of the human family. On the one hand, St. Paul helped build the doctrine that it is sinful for Christians to shed Christian blood. On the other, he strongly counseled obedience to existing state powers (Rom. 13). Obviously the state might call upon Christians to slay their brothers, thus bringing the two teachings into hopeless conflict.

Indeed, there ensued, before the English Renaissance, fifteen centuries of debate as to whether or no war was "just" for Christians. Probably the very primitive Christian opposition to violence and war was sustained for some time during centuries of struggle and persecution. As the Roman state decayed and as the Church grew stronger, however, the primitive Christian antimilitarism was retained as a minority ideal. Indeed by the fourth century the Church had authorized forcible suppression of pagan rites. Then officially, at least, the antiwar teachings of the earlier Fathers were set aside by the authority of St. Augustine's doctrine that war may be "just" for Christians. St. Augustine, moreover, held that war's cause lay in man's sin and God's answering punishment, or Providence. (It is generally agreed that the medieval Schoolmen took over from Augustine their basic doctrine on war and peace.) [9] Having sanctioned use of force against pagans, the Church later authorized direct violence against heretics. In the seventh century, moreover, the gradual reversal of the primitive Christian antiwar attitude was accelerated by the need for large-scale armed defense against Islam. Insofar as the earliest Christian traditions on war were kept alive from the fourth to the sixteenth centuries, this work may have been done by various heretical sects, such as the English Lollards, inspired by John Wycliffe, in fifteenth-century England. In the realm of ideas, however, it is not strictly necessary to find their vitality derived from continuous life through organized groups or institutions, for sharp wits can always rediscover or reinvent them.[10]

At the height of its power, the medieval Church supported the grand ideal of the *Pax Ecclesiae*. As a practicable social objective, this seemed most nearly within reach between perhaps A.D. 1000 and 1300, when the supremacy of the Church was itself most assured. Broadly speaking, medieval political thought became finally permeated by the Stoic cosmopolitan idea that all men form a single society which is or should be ruled by one Natural Law. This ideal society was Christendom. Hence Dante's idealization of *humana civilitas*, the unity of mankind. Pursuing this mighty goal from time to time, the popes, as universal bishops, strove to suppress both local and international wars. Such efforts, however fantastic they may now seem, occurred as late as the eve of the

9

Reformation; More's *Utopia* appeared when such a Church peace was looked for, in 1516-17.

However unsuccessful were these papal efforts to impose a *Pax Ecclesiae* upon the frequently war-torn medieval world, they emphasized the great ideal and formed a sort of standing testimony that the Church's duty was to maintain peace. Indeed, as Bryce said, they represented "the first serious effort ever made to treat the whole body of Christians as a single ecclesiastico-civil community bound to obey two sovereigns God had placed over them." The medieval Church, to be sure, officially sanctioned the use of force to secure a *Pax Ecclesiae*. Radical sects, from time to time, nevertheless insisted that the true primitive Christian ideal of nonviolence absolutely forbade war to Christians, whose only weapons should be those of the spirit.[11]

Apparently the general medieval intellectual environment did not encourage critical speculation upon basic social reforms which might have reduced the prevalence of war. A major reason for this was suggested by Troeltsch, that the idea of social reform was absent from Thomism. Thus the Middle Ages "created a Christian unity of civilization. . . . This unity . . . however, did not constitute a social reform in accordance with Christian principles." Another major obstacle to critical inquiry was probably the widespread acceptance of the Augustinian view that war, like other evils flesh is heir to, was a dispensation of divine Providence. Medieval political theorists were, indeed, largely content to consider the grand jurisprudential relations of ruler and state, of state and empire. Even John Wycliffe, while declaring that *Lex Dei*, *Lex Naturae*, and *Lex Christi* were equal, opposed war merely on the restricted ground that it was sinful for Christians.[12]

During the fourteenth and fifteenth centuries, tremendous forces were working internationally to undermine and destroy the medieval ideal of a universal *Pax Ecclesiae*. Of one of these forces, corruption, the London Reformers—Colet, More, Erasmus, Vives—like most intelligent men of their age, were acutely aware. The nature of the second force—call it nationalism for lack of a better term—was far less well understood then than now, when hindsight comes to our aid. Who can with certainty stand in a dying world and be positive of the fact? That the old order was desperately sick, More and his friends knew very well. That the malady was to be fatal, they could not know.

Grand in conception, the idea of a *Pax Ecclesiae* became unworkable when the supreme powers, Pope and Emperor, were at swords' points. Rarely in the later Middle Ages were they at peace. Before the middle of the fifteenth century their conflicts had fatally weakened the Empire, while the Papacy had become deeply corrupted by temporal ambitions. The resulting decadence—fascinatingly evident in the notorious Alexander VI (1492-1503) and in the furiously warlike Julius II (1503-13)—appeared likely to destroy all the influences of Christianity upon life in Europe. Erasmus might well wonder what hope remained for Christendom when he saw Pope Julius, at the head of his troops, celebrating a bloody triumph at his entrance into fallen Bologna in 1506.

It is now clear that not only material corruption but the very forces creating modern nationalism (and its concomitant, international anarchy) gradually undermined and destroyed the ideal of a *Pax Ecclesiae*. How far Colet, More, Erasmus, and Vives understood this dynamic of change will appear later. With considerable sureness we can now place the watershed between the Middle Ages and the modern world of nations normally in conflict. It falls between Dante's *De monarchia* (1310-13) and the beginning, by Marsilius of Padua, of his *Defensor pacis* (*ca.* 1324). With its ideal of an imperial peace, Dante's work gave the finest exposition of an already doomed and dying religious and political theory of world government. In contrast, Marsilius in many ways was prophetic of the openly ascendant nationalism made manifest at the Reformation. His approach to the state (says Gewirth) was wholly "economic and individualistic," based on an "entirely secular political concept." The shattering modernity of his criticism on war shows in his view that "peace" is completely "internal to individual states." To Marsilius, the state is at "peace" when "its parts are . . . interacting smoothly" even though possibly at war with other states.[13]

Nevertheless, the old medieval ideal of a unified Christendom and of a *Pax Ecclesiae* persisted in many minds, in the morning of the English Renaissance, even though (as is now so evident) underlying realities no longer supported it, when indeed it had become a kind of myth. It is now no doubt clear that, as a peacemaking power, the Church was breaking down hopelessly at the end of the fifteenth century. Inevitably, one's sense of irony, of a vast social tragedy, is intensified by contemplation of the social drift, the "progress" which, after about 1300, led Europe toward the terrible condition defined by Hobbes in the seventeenth century with his "the natural relation of any two states is war."

That such a breakdown of European culture was possible did indeed occur to the early English humanists who are the focus of our narrative. But their great effort was to help secure what still seemed feasible (in the twenty years before Luther)—the peaceful reconstruction from within of the old order so as to meet newly perceived human needs for social justice. It is we, not they, who are perhaps haunted by our own special form of tragic irony, born of hindsight which lets us perceive (with Duval) that in the new power politics of the Renaissance, broadly speaking, *"La raison d'État finira par se substituter à la notion de la cause juste."* [14] Since the Renaissance, peace has characteristically been a temporary condition imposed by superior force—the iron peace.

　　　　 CHAPTER TWO

THE WANING OF CHIVALRY

Thus far we have viewed broadly currents of ancient and medieval thought on war and peace, flowing toward the English Renaissance. What of the fifteenth century in England? Do those turbulent decades show only the waning of the Middle Ages? Or had a literary tradition of antityrannic criticism preceded and prepared a way for the humanist reformers of the sixteenth century?

Changing English courtly attitudes toward chivalry are mirrored in a variety of literature which is perhaps most appealing today for its reflection of contemporary ideas. Generally it appears that the century after Chaucer produced little or no original thought on war. Rather one senses the slow exhaustion of medieval international idealism and the sometimes wistful relinquishing of hope for a universal Christian peace. Simultaneously, elements of more sharply nationalist ideology begin to appear. From Hoccleve to Caxton most courtly writers paid lip service to the orthodox Catholic conception of war as, on fit occasion, "just" for Christians. Justice itself, however, tended to coincide with prevailing royal expediency, an ironic augury of things to come. Conventional laments deplored the frequent ruin of innocent bystanders in war; and Christian princes were urged to fight the heathen Turk, not their spiritual brothers (Adams [1948], pp. 439-46). The progressive decay of chivalric war, long idealized as man's noblest lay pursuit, may be inferred from the number and intensity of the exhortations which sought to sustain knighthood against collapse.

The gradual weakening of English enthusiasm for chivalrous war may be vividly seen in a group of books produced in England between 1460 and 1489, the best coming from Caxton's press. Mostly these constitute a kind of literary propaganda intended to help restore the vanishing knightly chivalry to what was nostalgically imagined to have been its healthy condition in some vanished day.

The Boke of Noblesse, compiled between 1460 and 1475, is a work of patriotic exhortation. Its anonymous authors strove to encourage and justify as martially glorious a military expedition of Edward IV to renew England's wars with France. Idealized characters are drawn of supposedly typical good soldiers, true captains, and the perfect prince, and war itself is pictured as a valuable school of discipline. A few dark tones are admitted to this idyllic scene. Mention is made of ravage and oppression of the innocent by unpaid or uncontrolled troops and of monstrous injustices sanctioned by wicked captains. These evils, however, are said to be only errors in practice and not inherent in war itself. Fairly typical later medieval views appear, colored with little disillusionment. Thus while doubtless some wars are fought for evil reasons, orthodox piety deplores them. The author accepts the customary medieval distinction between "just" and "unjust" wars, while upholding the conventional medieval ideal of war as a righteous struggle to make Christian justice prevail. He admits, however, that many Christians, with good reason, hold nowadays that war in itself is neither lawful nor just. The question is

. . . whether that wars . . . been lawful according to justice or no. And the opinion of many one would understand that haunting of arms and war making is not lawful, no just thing, forasmuch in . . . war be many infinite damages and extortions done, as murder, slaughter, bloodshedding, depopulation of countries, castles, cities, and towns burning, and many such infinite damages. Wherefore it should seem that maintaining of war is a cursed deed: not due to be maintained.[1]

On the other hand, with far greater enthusiasm *The Boke of Noblesse* then sums up the orthodox theory by which the Church has declared certain wars to be just and approved by God. Of course nothing can be worse than wars of vengeance, greed, or sheer ambition; and it is true that some pious Fathers have urged that Christian men should shun all wars. For all this, everyone knows that our enemies, the French, have often broken the peace. To attack *them* would be no tyranny! (ed. Nichols, pp. 7-8).

This rousing patriotic exhortation was, however, broken by a sorrowful admission that noblemen's sons tend (1460-75) more and more to seek peaceful rather than warlike vocations. This decay of the military profession was profoundly deplored, and all noble readers, "born to arms," were exhorted to train for war according to ancient custom:

But now of late days, the greater pity is, many one . . . descended of noble blood and born to arms . . . set himself to singular practice . . . as to learn the practice of law or custom of land, or of civil matter, and so waste greatly their time . . . to . . . rule among your poor and simple commons of bestial countenance that lust to live in rest [i.e., peace].

How wretched a thing it is, the author wrote to Edward IV, to see such lawyers, "as the world goeth now," more esteemed than stout old soldiers of thirty or even forty years' service (ed. Nichols, pp. 76-78)! In sum, *The Boke of Noblesse* indicates that the old chivalry was already clearly decaying though still cherished by old-fashioned courtiers.

Likewise dear to the English nobility was that war in miniature, hunting. Probably no peacetime sport had more zealous devotees, of whom Henry VIII in his age was only the most famous. Hunting had, indeed, the charms of a martial game, a kind of war (wrote Blades) "which could be pursued in times of peace, and which yet required knowledge, fortitude, and courage." This was the sport which More and Erasmus, after 1509, attacked as inherently brutalizing to humanity. No hint of such hostile views appears in *The Boke of Saint Albans*, printed in 1486, a collection which admirably illustrates contemporary gentlemanly tastes. If, as is probable, Dame Juliana Berners compiled the treatise on hunting, the lady was blissfully unconscious that such sport might be considered a wanton and degrading exercise in cruelty.[2]

No work from the generation just before the London Reformers reveals more brightly than William Caxton's the dominant attitudes toward war. Aware that some strange decadence threatened to overcome the world of chivalry, he strove manfully to revive and perpetuate it through the work of his press. We infer the decay of belief in chivalrous concepts of war from the vigor of the efforts necessary to prop up the collapsing structure.

As though the world that made the crusades possible had not fallen into ruins, Caxton in 1481 urged his readers to ardent belief in a familiar medieval idea—that peace should be made within Christendom, then all should be united against the Turk. To advocate this was his main motive in Englishing *Godefroy of Bologne*, done "to the end that every Christian man may be the better encouraged t'enterprise war for the defense of Christendom, and to recover the said City of Jerusalem. . . . And also that Christian people one united in very peace might emprise to go thither in pilgrimage with strong bond for to expel the Saracens and Turkes. . . ."[3]

Caxton's most impassioned exhortation, that the knights of England restore the health of chivalry, he attached to his translation (*ca.* 1484) of a famous medieval French compilation on war, the *Libre del orde de cauayleria of Ramon Lull* (d. 1315). The decay of the chivalric ideals of war and knighthood in the late fifteenth century could hardly be made more striking than through Caxton's appeal to bring back the good old days when (he believed) war was at its chivalrous best. Clearly he meant the days of King Arthur. Where now (he demands rhetorically) is the Arthurian "custom and usage of noble chivalry" (i.e., war)? What do ye (Knights of England) now but "go to the baynes and play at dice"? Many are even less "honest." He pleads for abandonment of these corruptions. In fact the "noble volumes" telling of Lancelot, Galahad, and others show what knights should be.

For Caxton, historical romance and romantic history went hand in hand. Besides the patterns of conduct exemplified in Malory's *Morte Darthur,* he urged the knights of England to read Froissart's accounts of more recent glorious conquests by Englishmen:

And also behold that victorious and noble king Harry the fifth, and the captains under him . . . and many others whose names shine gloriously by their virtuous noblesse & acts that they did in th'honor of th'order of chivalry. Alas! what do ye, but sleep and take ease, and are all disordered from chivalry.

Caxton then suggested to Henry VII that if jousting were revived and held each year, no doubt the order of chivalry would be restored. In more bitter mood, he harshly compared ancient Roman patriotism with the feeble English love of country.[4]

There is much unconscious irony in Caxton's choice of Ramon Lull's *Le libre del orde de cauayleria* (in a French version) as a goad with which to stir up noble enthusiasm for chivalrous war and knightly good conduct. Nearly two centuries before, Lull had himself lamented the decay of knightly war and longed for the return of its pristine glory. It seems that the alleged golden age of chivalry was always in the remote past, never in the writer's own day. Thus, in early fourteenth-century France, Lull found a horrid discrepancy between contemporary knightly behavior and that credited to those who flourished "in the time in which chivalry began." If current practice were made a guide, "true" knights would be those who "love wars, thefts, and robbery," while, on the contrary, the false—the "evil and wicked knights"—would be those

16

John Colet. Portrait by Holbein
Courtesy of the British Museum

who "pacify and accord the good people" (*The Book of the Ordre of Chyualry*, pp. 44-45).

Caxton, of course, regarded Malory's *Morte Darthur* more as history than what we would now term romance or fiction. His motive in printing it (1485) was above all to give the decadent knights of his day a broad and true mirror wherein to see the age of chivalry at its purest and noblest. His intent was a practical one, to reform noble conduct in war and in society, following the ancient outlines so hauntingly drawn by Malory:

And I . . . have done set it in imprint, to the intent that noble men may see and learn the noble acts of chivalry, the gentle and virtuous deeds that some knights used in those days, by which they came to honour; and how they that were vicious were punished and oft put to shame and rebuke. . . . For herein may be seen noble chivalry, courtesy, humanity, friendliness, hardiness, love . . . cowardice, murder, hate, virtue, and sin. Do after the good and leave the evil.

How radical a revaluation of the past will result from the London Reformers' criticism of war may be suggested by comparing Caxton's simple delight in Malory with the demolishing attack of their disciple, the Elizabethan humanist Roger Ascham, who asserted that the *Morte Darthur* gave delight only to those who enjoyed pictures of plain bawdry and open manslaughter.[5]

Undeterred by failures, Caxton made one more notable attempt to stir the restoration of medieval war's golden age. In 1489, it seems, Henry VII himself saw a need to teach Englishmen how to behave in war. He therefore commanded Caxton to translate and print a remarkable and very popular French work of the early fifteenth century, Christine de Pisan's *Le livre des faits d'armes et de chevalerie*. The King gave the order (and lent Caxton the royal copy) "to the end that every gentleman born to arms and all manner men of war, captains, soldiers, victualers & all other should have knowledge how they ought to behave them in the feats of war." Indeed, said honest Caxton, speaking for himself as critic, he thought it "as necessary a book & as requisite as any may be for every estate, high and low, that intend to the feats of war, whether it be in battles, sieges, rescues, & all other . . . subtleties & remedies for mischiefs." Ironically, the *Feats of Arms* had itself been composed (*ca.* 1408-9) when, as Byles said, "the pure ideals of chivalry had given place to ceremonial observances and extravagant display" [6]—just such conditions as the London Reformers were to find prevailing at the court of Henry VIII after 1509.

Christine de Pisan did more than restate the great commonplaces of medieval thought on war. In comparison with run-of-the-mill thinkers of the fifteenth century, she exhibited a degree of humanitarianism and some sensitivity to the need for at least modest reforms. Her terms are late medieval, but within them she presented consistently "a conception of warfare that is both honorable and, as far as is possible, humane." As for theory on war's lawfulness, she held to the accepted views of St. Augustine and St. Thomas Aquinas. Thus she granted that war had both lawful and unlawful causes; it was just when undertaken on behalf of justice or against oppression and usurpation, although wars of ambition, aggression, and revenge were to be deprecated. Only a sovereign prince might lawfully wage war, and Christine denied the legality of the private wars and feuds which filled medieval history.[7]

Incorporated into Christine's work most notably are ideas from another famous medieval French treatise upon warfare and ethics, Honoré Bonet's *L'arbre des battailles* (*ca.* 1387). In his views on war Bonet was one of the most humane men of his time. Christine agreed with her master in holding that war in a just cause is legitimate, that a warrior's soul was saved if he died in a battle "for to help the right," and that treachery, pillaging, and violence against noncombatants were to be condemned.[8]

Christine de Pisan showed some critical awareness of a growing need for far-reaching social changes in the fifteenth century. For one thing, she had no love of war for its own sake, no feeling for supposed martial glory. On the other hand, she placed what seems to be great stress on a prince's duty to exhaust every possible resource of diplomatic counsel and of arbitration before declaring war. Medieval knights were rarely famous for their love of arbitration and of peaceful compromises. Perhaps with ironic reference to this trait, certainly with rare concern for the hard lot of the common soldier, Christine had the highest praise for her favorite king, Charles V, a master of peaceful diplomacy. With irony she found that what his "right chivalrous" ancestors had lost by war, Charles reconquered with wit and gold, not the blood of men:

And to this purpose verily may well serve for example, the wit and good governance of . . . Charles, the which, not moving from his throne royal in palace conquered again all the lands lost by his predecessors *right chivalrous*.

. . . "It seems to me," said he [in reply to those who objected against paying to recover lands, as unnecessary and unbecoming to a monarch commanding great armed forces] "that what can be obtained with money ought not to be bought with the blood of men." [9]

Caxton, most representative literary man of the late fifteenth century, is strikingly far out of the humanist and Renaissance orbit. His roots are firmly medieval, and he shows virtually no interest in the great social critics of antiquity who furnished power and light to Colet, More, Erasmus, and Vives in the generation after him.

If our sampling is fair, the fifteenth-century writers who appealed to Englishmen simply carried on well-worn medieval patterns of thought on war, unaware of any need for radical changes. Meanwhile the decay of belief in the ideals of chivalry became ever more manifest, despite all efforts at their revival. The whole spectacle shows the waning of a deeply sick or dying world order. Amidst this mass of conventional thought, one man stands out, Sir John Fortescue (*ca.* 1399-1476), Chancellor to Henry VI. English legalists before him made no effort to "give a theoretical analysis of feudalism," the system under which they lived, in its relations to "practical politics," as Plummer observed; but in contrast Fortescue is the first medieval writer who "brings down political philosophy from the clouds to earth by basing his theoretical analysis upon observation of existing conditions." [10] In his *De natura legis naturae* (1461-73), *De laudibus legum Angliae* (1468-70), and in his most famous work, *The Governance of England* (1471-76), he mounted a formidable and distinctly English criticism of the difference between an absolute and a limited monarchy. [11] Where a conventional-minded man like Hoccleve enjoyed idealizing the martial glory embodied in the national hero, Henry V, it is characteristic of Fortescue that he found the basis of the alleged English title to France and the pretexts for making war upon her so flimsy that he disapproved of them (*Governance*, p. 8). It is, I think, significant that Fortescue, like the humanists Colet, More, Erasmus, and Vives after him, had on the whole an intensely practical outlook on contemporary social problems. It has been argued—and is indeed probable—that More knew the social and legal criticism of his predecessor as Chancellor, who was one of his day's outstanding jurists. Moreover, in Mesnard's view, the hard, realistic Fortescuan analyses of kingship had "already become classic" in England by the sixteenth century; and he thinks Sir Thomas More put some of these ideas on the abuses of monarchic powers into Book I of *Utopia*.[12]

In conclusion, it may be said that English pre-Renaissance thought shows no consistent expression of a vigorous, emergent social criticism of war and peace. Rather, the typical writings here touched on suggest clearly that during this period there occurred a progressive weakening and diluting of medieval international and of English chivalric idealism. This enfeebled idealism took the form, in part, of a largely sentimental and often hypocritical lip service paid to the lingering but expiring dream of a universal Christian peace. Nevertheless, it is important to notice that medieval idealism did not entirely disappear, although with the approach of the Renaissance an insular nationalism became more and more dominant in thought on war and peace. Fortescue excepted, no evidence has been found to suggest that a pre-Renaissance literary tradition preceded and prepared the way for the profound and imaginatively penetrating social criticism developed in the early sixteenth century by Sir Thomas More, Erasmus, John Colet, J. L. Vives, and their circle. The absence of such evidence throws the intellectual and moral daring of these humanists, who thought the New Learning should be applied boldly to the construction of a vastly improved, peaceful society, into a truer perspective and more striking relief.

John Colet, who became Dean of St. Paul's (1504-19) and who founded St. Paul's School on humanist lines, was the first of the English new humanists to break away from the traditional medievalist modes of thought on war and peace. At Oxford, beginning with Michaelmas term in 1496, he gave a series of lectures on St. Paul's Epistle to the Romans. They constitute a landmark in literary and social criticism, a turning point in the slow change from medieval to Renaissance ways of thought, feeling, and action in England. Colet, strangely for his time, endeavored no less than to discover the original intent and meaning of St. Paul's teaching for primitive Christians in the first century A.D. Not only his conclusions but his critical methods were virtually novel, scarcely known before him in England, and very little elsewhere. In many ways these lectures, in the long run, "are more important in the history of English literary humanism than the *Utopia* of St. Thomas More, although the latter is sometimes considered as the only work of the early English humanists of European significance." [1]

What conclusions did Colet reach in his first notable criticism of Christian man, of war, and of Christendom itself? To grasp his achievement requires at least a brief résumé of the positions against which he found himself in revolt.

In the first century St. Paul, in Romans 13, counseled a Christian minority in the Roman state upon the meaning and necessity of Christian nonviolence. He gave strong injunctions against disobedience to or violence against the Roman authorities. To St. Paul, Christianity was to be spread to the world, not by bloody iron, but by the sword of the spirit. But what St. Paul said and meant and what the later commentators discovered were his intents and meanings are different things. Upon the work of St. Ambrose (A.D. 340-97) and St. Augustine, the later Schoolmen gradually built up a complex mass of interpretation declaring the roles Christians should play in war. In all this, Romans 13, with its vast accretion of commentary, remained a crucial passage. Thus in the end the Schoolmen who were contemporaries of the London Reformers were able to decide that war, while admittedly filled with evils, was under certain conditions lawful, just, and a righteous method of maintaining Christianity and the Church. Before Colet in England, the most common medieval critical method was to weigh scholastic authorities and established Church precedents.[2]

Nothing was more characteristic of Colet, however, as Erasmus wrote in the first biography of his friend, after Colet's death in 1519, than his intense desire to get at the original "whole doctrine of Christ," separating these original teachings from scholastic commentaries. In the late fifteenth century the Scotists were commonly regarded as subtle, but to Colet they were "dull and stupid and anything but intellectual. For it was the sign of a poor and barren intellect, he would say, to be quibbling about the words and opinions of others; carping first at one thing and then at another, and analyzing everything so minutely. . . . Yet for some reason he was even harder on Aquinas than on Scotus." As for his studies, Colet "eagerly devoured" Cicero and "diligently searched" Plato and Plotinus. Before visiting France and Italy, he had "roamed with great zest through literature of every kind; finding most pleasure in the early writers, Dionysius, Origen, Cyprian, Ambrose, and Jerome." [3]

Christ had said, "Render unto Caesar . . . ," and St. Paul in Romans developed this counsel further. What John Colet sought to do was to discover, among other things, the meaning of St. Paul's counsel on peace and obedience as it was originally given and intended to be understood. It was an extraordinary moment in the history of criticism when Colet took down his Suetonius in order to gain contemporary insights into that Caesar. What is more, Colet compared and contrasted social conditions prevailing in St. Paul's Roman world with those to be found in his own England and Europe.

As one result, Colet was moved largely to repudiate traditional scholastic views on war. He did not find that evil was a good, just, and Christian means for overcoming evil. To him it now appeared impossible that evil (war) can produce good (peace), or be a Christian thing, when the original Christian teaching of nonviolence is rightly understood. To true Christians, those of uncorrupted faith, violence must be absolutely futile in the end, certainly incapable of conveying Christianity to those without it. As Colet came to see it, only through humility and love freely given can evil be overcome in the world. "For it is not by war that war is conquered, but by peace, and forbearance, and reliance in God. And in truth by this virtue we see that the apostles overcame the entire world."

Colet's conception of a good soldier and of true glory won in conquest arose directly out of his critical approach to the problem: "This [i.e., peaceful] kind of contending with evil men was alone used by those first soldiers in the Church, who fought under the banner of Christ, and conquered gloriously." Through the same historical criticism it was made clearer how prudent, under first-century conditions, had been St. Paul's counsel that in the matter of tributes Roman customs should not be defied, lest Roman cruelty and persecution be aroused. For Christians, he emphasized powerfully, not arms but peace alone can conquer: "In this way alone has been introduced whatever light there is in the world. . . . He that sees not this, but fancies that force must be repelled by force, and war by war, and evil by evil, in his unhappy blindness sees no light." However urgently changes in the contemporary Church or state might be needed, Colet's mind was such that to him, if significant reforms were to be achieved, the means must be peaceful. As his biographer, Lupton, observed, these ideas are central: to Colet's mind no idea would have been more disharmonious than to seek change "by violence, or correct evils by measures productive of fresh evils." [4]

The major importance of this humanist advance for English literary and social criticism has recently received some overdue recognition. When Colet discarded the scholastic dialectical method and "adopted the grammatical method of the Italian humanists and the early Patristic writers," says a student of theology, Duhamel, he made an achievement more important than More's famous *Utopia*. To the literary critic Atkins, Colet's methods were not only of a "most unexpected kind" but initiated "a new epoch in literary appreciation," for Colet, and his protégé Erasmus, "were in fact the first to make use of the historical method of interpretation, in advance of their own and many later generations." (Actually, of course, Lorenzo Valla has prior claims to this achievement.) The historian of philosophy, Kristeller, finds Luther's critical approach anticipated:

23

. . . the humanistic study of the Bible and of the Church Fathers led to new interpretations of early Christian thought, that are characteristic of the Renaissance and Reformation period. Thus the attempt to interpret the Epistles of Paul without the context and superstructure of scholastic theology was made by scholars like Ficino, Colet, and Erasmus before it had such powerful and decisive results in the work of Luther.

To Douglas Bush, Colet's lectures show vital "growth of the historical spirit"; while Rowse, the historian of Elizabethan England, finds that "in breaking through the crusted accretions of commentary which the Middle Age had collected and going straight to the meaning of the text, [Colet's work] had an influence in inaugurating the movement for reform in the Church, not less than Keble's Assize Sermon." Perhaps the potential power of Colet's critical approach to transform—humanistically—men's understanding of their world is best defined by McKeon, who observes that the English medieval literary world and that of the Renaissance both possessed the Scriptures as well as many of the same classics: but "to change the manner of reading Aristotle, Vergil, Moses and Paul is to change one's conception of God, nature, man, morals and religion." [5]

Efforts have, of course, been made to explain Colet's great critical advance in various ways, attributing influences upon him to various sources, all possible, none proved. Ficino has attractive advocates. During Colet's Italian travels in the early 1490's, is it not possible that he could have heard Savonarola, whose fiery program for the reform of Florence has been summed up in "four clauses—the fear of God—the common weal—universal peace—political reform"? The English Lollards held antiwar views: could this tendency not have been transmitted to Colet (later once accused of sympathy for the sect, when he preached against Henry VIII's French wars) and through him to Erasmus and Thomas More? [6] When all this evidence is weighed, one truth remains—that unquestionably Colet was the first humanist to begin a new and dynamic critique of war in Renaissance England.

Desiderius Erasmus, second great actor in this drama of ideas, came on the English scene with his first visit to the country in 1499, memorable because from it dated the beginning of lifelong friendships with John Colet and Thomas More. He reached Oxford in October, went up to London in December, and returned to the continent on January 25 of the new year.[7] Colet, of course, had already opened what may be termed a humanist campaign to reshape public opinion on the problem of war and social reform. In the future Erasmus' writing on war and peace was to carry his fame throughout Europe, but in 1499 he was an unknown literary quantity. Should Colet, as an intellectual pioneer, be credited with exerting at this time a decisive influence upon Erasmus, turning the younger humanist's eye to the age's need for a penetrating kind of social criticism?

The question of the extent and nature of the power exerted by Colet upon the youthful Erasmus has been sifted. Indeed at least one scholar has argued against Erasmus' own testimony on his obligations. Hyma would, on the one hand, have us believe that the English humanists had slight influence upon the Netherlander and, on the other, demolish the idea that "Erasmus had a great deal to do with the development of English humanism." [8]

It may help to clear the air to inquire, first, what ideas on war and on his role as a social critic Erasmus had demonstrably developed *before* he first met Colet and More; and, second, whether he had so far crystallized his ideas and sense of purpose that any hypothesis of intellectual leadership by Colet (or for that matter, More) should be abandoned permanently.[9]

Unquestionably Erasmus' youthful environment stirred him to pity the sufferers from the aimless, exhausting civil wars of the Netherlands.[10] Perhaps as early as 1484 he wrote that the time's bitterness made it utterly unsuitable for humane studies: "Are the gentle studies of humanity adapted to this bitter time? Truly Poetry ... is a glad occupation and one that requires peace of mind. Where now is gladness, where tranquillity of heart? Everything is full of bitterness and trouble; wherever I turn my eyes, I see nothing but what is melancholy and cruel." [11] The reaction seems that of a sensitive spectator, not that of a man who had found the desire and the way to make humanistic ideas work to help an age's sickness. A similar bent of mind appeared in his essay *On Contempt of the World* (*ca.* 1487), written after his entrance into the monastery at Steyn, ostensibly to prove that the monastic career was the most pleasant and "epicurean." [12] Its rather incidental reflections of the contemporary scene confirm his earlier recoil from the evil conditions of civil wars. Erasmus' ideas on war at this stage appear to be like those of his friends: aloof from the struggles, they deplored them. Erasmus contemns the world: his friend devises an *Ode* to lament the miseries of the country, overwhelmed by war, poverty, and the plague.[13]

It all sounds a bit like an intellectual game played by bright young monks.

To this point Erasmus appears not only as intellectually detached from practical social criticism but as scarcely aware that his humanism might be set to work to find (as Bush put it) a " 'working ideal for the civilization of the present and the future.' " [14] Consider the seemingly grim realism of a 1489 letter in which he wrote that "for my part . . . there is nothing I hate so much as civil war, to which I prefer peace on the hardest conditions." The stern Ciceronian sentiment was used merely to score a point in a cheerful debate on literary criticism—treated as a witty diversion which parodied the cynicisms of contemporary diplomacy: "Wherefore, if you also prefer peace to war, you will find me indulgent enough provided you accept the terms my heralds will offer you." [15] The sardonic glance at tyranny had no target in particular—in contrast to his frequent practice (and that of other London Reformers) in the great satires written in England after 1505 when associations with More and Colet were close and creative.

Erasmus' *Oration on Peace and Discord Against the Seditious* (ca. 1490), if we first disregard some of its context, seems to prove that by then he had made a long stride toward achieving a social criticism at least aimed toward resolution of society's practical problems. The essay is saturated with ideas either echoed or reworked from Lucretius and Seneca, intended apparently to illuminate the contemporary scene. "I do not find," he wrote, "any subject on which it can now be more useful or opportune to speak" than the necessity for "cultivating peace . . . considering the conditions of our times." He argued that it was not only wicked but a great folly for men to war for temporal possessions. Indeed, as the human body is made, peace and tranquillity are necessities if sanity itself is to last. He advanced the favorite humanist analogy between the body and the social community as living organisms: in both, inevitably, injury (disease, war) in one part creates danger to the whole structure. And he at least touched what later became one of his great themes—the idea of the dignity of man—when he wrote: "No man can maintain his dignity by fighting, not even a heathen, a savage, a barbarian, an idolatrous person, much less a Christian, a member of the clergy, a monk!" [16] The *Oration*'s context, however, has the effect of reducing sharply the idea that it was written as practical social criticism. Not only (as Hyma observed) are conventional sentiments prominent in the

26

whole essay, but Erasmus wrote as an experienced monk who was ostensibly contented with his lot.[17] Call it an exercise piece, its intended audience one other monk. In contrast, when in 1513 he finally found a printer for it, he was living in England and was deeply engaged with More and Colet in a criticism strongly focused upon the actual needs of contemporary society.

Presumably in their letters to him Erasmus' friends expanded upon their common interests. It was thus suggested to Erasmus that the cause of Holland's wars was almost entirely the private jealousies and power lusts of princes (*EE*, 35.50-51). As far as I know, Erasmus made no use of this idea himself until, in England and in association with More (1505-6), he made some translations from Lucian, most particularly from the satires on tyrants, conquerors, and pompous generals, and upon the trifling pretexts so often used for starting wars and for the pursuit of military glory.[18]

Observation of Erasmus' early reading confirms the view that, before he met Colet, he was not moved to solidify a coherent and purposeful form of social criticism. The early correspondence is of course filled with warm enthusiasm for the great Latin writers. Perhaps typical is his praise of Ovid, for instance, because "his pen is nowhere dipped in blood"— that is, he does not delight in sanguinary cruelties (*EO*, III, 1257BC). For a young humanist to read such a popular ancient writer on military strategy as Vegetius was nothing unusual, but his use for his knowledge was merely for practical jokes on a Parisian shrew (*EN*, I, 112, 149). Moreover, I find nothing to suggest that Erasmus had developed, before meeting Colet, an understanding of the historical method of literary criticism. Later, however, after working with Colet and More, he commonly used that method and interpreted the classics in terms of the social criticism which Colet had begun in England, though doubtless antedated by Valla, whom Erasmus praised, in Italy.

Summing things up, before coming to England in 1499, Erasmus had reflected upon man's inhumanity to man, evident in civil wars nearby. His social horizon was as yet little broader than the Netherlands. He had not found a clear sense of purpose as a humanist, had no clear vision of a working ideal of a peaceful social order for the Renaissance, had no special idea as to the literary means by which such an ideal might be brought home to men's minds and bosoms. In short, the record for *ca.* 1480-1500 suggests that he still wanted a sense of vocation as critic and satirist. For confirmation of these conclusions there are the four lines given to the adage *Dulce bellum inexpertis* (sweet is war to those who know it not) by Erasmus in his first book of adages, the *Adagiorum collectanea,* published in 1500 soon after he left England. These four lines, little more than paraphrase, give no hint whatever of the impassioned essay (some fifteen large folio pages) which he was to write under the same heading, in England, for the definitive 1515 edition.[19] My inference is that if Erasmus had absorbed from Colet new ideas on humanist social criticism, he had not yet learned how to use them.

When he became friends with Colet in 1499, the uncommitted Erasmus met a strong personality, a keen mind, a man who already had begun to employ his humanistic ideas to the end of practical social reform. Erasmus remembered his warm, direct appreciation of Colet's "sharp and exact judgement" and came to understand why Colet preferred the original sense of the primitive Christian writers. Fresh from that stronghold of scholasticism, the University of Paris, Erasmus heard Colet in private profess that he considered the Scotists not of peculiar acumen but "stupid fools and anything but ingenious," and he saw Colet's extreme aversion to the poor, sterile, chopping-block arguments of the Schoolmen (*EC,* pp. 21-2). I have already suggested that Colet, in his 1496 lectures on St. Paul, of necessity had to break away from servitude to scholastic doctrine on war in order to arrive at his own position, based on his direct understanding of primitive Christianity. It may be true (as Hyma says) that Colet did not induce Erasmus to "break" with scholasticism in which he had never been seriously interested.[20] What is more vital, I think, is the idea that Colet very probably interested Erasmus seriously in a positive, humanist critique of war and social reform. "When I hear Colet," Erasmus wrote from London in December, 1499, "I seem to be listening to Plato himself" (*EE,* 118.21). When their total twenty-year relationship is weighed, I find it fair (with Renaudet) to regard Colet as, *"pour Érasme, un maître et un directeur de conscience."* [21]

CHAPTER FOUR

APPROACH TO A GOLDEN AGE (1500-1509)

Between 1500 and the accession of Henry VIII in 1509, the English humanists made striking progress toward a full-fledged critique of war and social reform. This movement, after his first contacts with Colet and More, can clearly be seen in Erasmus' work before his next English visit (1505). Separated for the time, these friends pursued converging courses. Now for the first time in Erasmus' work we begin to find what has lately gained some recognition—"its critical aspect, the grim and disillusioned analysis of disintegrating feudalism and rising military despotism." [1] As their story unfolds, eventually it will indeed be possible to reason that these idealists, Colet, More, Erasmus, and Vives, were capable of a realism greater than Machiavelli's in their social and political criticism.[2]

When effort is made to distinguish forms of humanism from each other, it is vital to assess the use made of the classics of antiquity. In 1501 Erasmus annotated an edition of Cicero's *De officiis* and prefaced it with a critical epistle. It is Cicero's insights into life, not merely literary style, that concerned Erasmus. Through reading Cicero one can perceive how vital it is always to be on guard against defenders of such weapons as those which Vulcan forged, to be on guard against admiring such characters as Homer's Achilles or Vergil's Aeneas. For men are at their worst when strength and viciousness are found together, and the fact is that a man is never better defended than by true virtue.[3] In other words, Erasmus praised the study of Cicero because, for one thing, Cicero did not uphold, as models of manhood, classic archetypes of the soldier. This kind of attack will gradually intensify until, by 1517, Erasmus will compare Achilles with Alexander the Great and will find them alike: both "world-robbers," "drunk with ambition," "disasters to humanity." [4] In 1501 Erasmus fired the modest opening gun of a barrage in which other London Reformers would soon join him: its target was the idealization of imperial tyrants, whether by flattering historians or contemporary sycophants.

In 1485 Caxton could seriously offer his age Malory's *Morte Darthur*, hoping to show young noblemen ideal patterns of heroic conduct and to help bring back the good old days of chivalry. Not so Erasmus when in 1501 he wrote his little handbook on Christian conduct, the *Enchiridion militis Christiani*, which became popular all over Europe in the golden years of English humanism, 1509-19.[5] He expanded on the themes of the beastliness and foulness of war, the wretched lot of the soldiers, and the miserable insignificance of their rewards. While in the wars of the spirit the sure prize is salvation, the outcome of ordinary military combat is purely a matter of Fortune's whim; hence men must be mad who join in war.[6] As Colet had done when discussing St. Paul, Erasmus declared that true Christians cannot wage war against each other and yet remain Christians (*EMC*, p. 80). Despite civil laws to the contrary, he urged (again after Colet) that good Christians ought not to use violence against violence (*EMC*, p. 213). It is well known that Renaissance artists heightened sensitivity to beauty in many forms, but the other side of this coin is an intensified awareness of the ugly, the grotesque, and the atrocious and antihuman (as may be seen in the contemporary war paintings of Hieronymus Bosch). Where the painter used color and line, Erasmus used humanist eloquence to represent vividly the distorted, ugly, and evil appearance assumed by angry fighting men (*EMC*, p. 282).

As the London Reformers' critique of war and their work for peaceful reform of the existing society progressed, they directed great energies toward influencing those actually in positions of power. Through the printing press in their generation it became possible almost for the first time to shape public opinion through pamphlets and books, and these too might have some power to move princes. More direct and personal approaches were sometimes possible. At Brussels on January 6, 1504, Erasmus gave an oration, or panegyric, before the Archduke Philip the Fair, who had just returned to the Netherlands from Spain. It has rightly been termed his "first great declaration of principles as to the absolute wickedness and folly of war. . . ."[7] First—an expected gesture, no doubt —he drew a concise picture of a model prince. But then he built an argument that to maintain peace is a royal duty.[8] Vividly he described the miseries which must inevitably attend war, and he urged that, despite existing evils, peace is better than victory. In peace, the arts of living grow, honest learning flourishes, respect for law is sustained, and religion improves mankind; but in war's general calamity all these fall into ruin. As an essential condition for their work (i.e., for the revival of learning), scholars must have peace (*EO*, IV, 536B-538).

Erasmus showed no interest in the idea that to literary genius war furnishes supplies of the inspiring episodes and heroic deeds which, from Homer to Malory, so often gave an impulse to creation. Perhaps the most striking part of the *Panegyricus* is the section which contrasts the virtues of peace with those of war (*EO*, IV, 536B ff.). Erasmus' toughening realism marked his reply to the traditional argument that peace is necessarily enervating to rulers. He held that peace requires not less but greater bravery: in war bravery is far easier, for a rather poor kind of man may show it; but to govern one's spirit, to master desire, to bridle greed—that kind of courage belongs to the wise and good (*EO*, IV, 539A).

Archduke Philip the Fair had built up a rather well-known reputation as a man of arms. In the *Panegyricus*, however, Erasmus represented him to be the embodiment of the peaceful virtues. On the surface it would appear that such praise was at best politic and conventional, at worst insincere and absurd. Should one therefore not agree with those who would dismiss the oration as of no import—merely one of "Erasmus' complimentary writings" (*EE*, I, 396)—and, because complimentary, of no consequence as social criticism?

Erasmus himself explained his tactics when he wrote the letter prefatory to the *Panegyricus* as published. The question was, he thought, how best to persuade a man of actual power (Philip) to choose peaceful rather than warlike courses, presuming such persuasion to be at least possible. Defending himself from charges of falsehood, he cited classic panegyrists and laid down the general principle that (for a man in his position) judicious use of critically selected praise formed one practical means to the desired end: "For there is no such efficacious mode of making a prince better, as that of setting before him, under the guise of praise, the example of a good sovereign, provided you so attribute virtues, and deny vices, as to persuade him to the former and deter him from the latter." [9]

That More and Erasmus began their lifelong friendship during Erasmus' first English visit in 1499 is known, but evidence is sadly thin on More's thought concerning war, peace, and social reform before 1505.

Book I of *Utopia*, it is true, strongly suggests a kind of table talk, focused upon acute problems of the day—poverty, crime, monarchic irresponsibility, and war—that as a youth, between twelve and fourteen, More very likely heard in the household of Archbishop and Chancellor Morton.[10] Through it all runs a deep current of interest in the cluster of practical questions then rising over limited versus absolute monarchy, provoked on the one hand by feudal anarchy, on the other by royal misrule. It would indeed be rather strange if More had not come to know the brilliant analysis of kingship, conceived within a frame of practical politics, which bears the name of Sir John Fortescue, himself Chancellor under Henry VI. How More's mind was shaped by his time at Oxford or while reading law in London after 1496 cannot surely be said.

Probably in 1501, at Grocyn's invitation, More was asked to lecture on St. Augustine's *City of God*. Unfortunately, these lectures at St. Lawrence Jewry, if written, do not survive. It is tempting to conjecture that they contained the germs of the *Utopia*,[11] since in general St. Augustine, like More, sought to conceive of a perfect social order in which all members would be duly subordinated, in which each would be content in his own work, and in which community of goods would exist. (There are, however, striking contrasts between the ideas on war of St. Augustine and More's Utopians.) [12] Almost certainly More's work did further exemplify the growth of that historical spirit, already distinctive in Colet's lectures on St. Paul, which becomes a mark of early English humanism. Stapleton, whose informants had known More, said that More's object was to expound, not theology, but the philosophical and historical arguments of St. Augustine's first few books.[13] During the London Reformers' efforts at revival of ancient culture and reform of medieval ways, efforts persistently to be obstructed by wars and their aftermath, parallels with ancient Roman conditions were not far to seek. With mighty strokes St. Augustine gave his view of a grand cultural drama in which Rome, once the epitome of culture but neglectful of vital reforms, succumbed to degeneracy within until overwhelmed by war from without.[14] Surely the *City of God* can be provocative to a mind inclined to probe patterns of cause and effect in history. How far at this stage, however, More had shaped his own ideas on war and peace remains unsure. In his *Life of John Picus of Mirandola*, a contemporary of Savonarola, he made no mention of that fiery monk's theocratic scheme for reforming Florence and of his preachings upon peace.[15]

32

Before Erasmus' second visit to England in 1505, the fortunes of both Colet and More had altered sharply. In 1504 Colet became Dean of St. Paul's, and, unlike many high churchmen, he began to preach regularly. As Dean during the critical years from 1504 to 1519, Colet's position enabled him to exert strong suasion toward social and religious reforms. Actually the amount of Colet's surviving writing is not great, and by his literary works alone it is hard to explain today the influence he won (by their own accounts) over such men as More and Erasmus, or the respect he gained from Henry VIII. Much of the weight attached to Colet's public acts and reputation arises from the peculiar force of his position as Dean of St. Paul's, where he served as a connecting link between the dying medieval world and the new age. Before Colet's time, indeed, many stirring scenes had taken place around Paul's Cross, that "veritable mirror of mediaeval life and thought," and others had preached on peace there, in medieval fashion, when terrors of pestilence at home were added to those of war abroad. One hears of the late fourteenth-century Bishop Brunton of Rochester, treating of war and the plague, in the "spirit of . . . Savonarola, ever calling men to repent and reform lest worst disasters fall upon them from heaven"—disasters explained as due to man's sins.[16] The early sixteenth century was a time of agonizing reappraisals, in which Colet's part has been ably stated by his best biographer. Not alone as an educational pioneer is he memorable; as Dean of St. Paul's during these years he had a vital hand in an epochal transition of cultures:

He died in the communion of the Church of England as it then was; while yet, by his public expositions of Holy Scripture, and by his avowed opinions on the non-exaction of tithes, on community of goods, on the wealth and secular occupation of prelates, on the unlawfulness of war, the misuse of offerings at shrines and other topics, he was suspected . . . of sympathizing with the followers of Wycliffe.[17]

Colet, then, had prospered, and as Dean of St. Paul's held a position which gave him powerful leverage in work for social reform.

"The golden age of English humanism" [18] (1505-20) unquestionably began, and with it new growth in criticism on war, with More's and Erasmus' translations from Lucian, done together during Erasmus' English visit between 1505 and 1506. This work forms a literary landmark, not only because it prepared the way for the great humanist satire in the *Praise of Folly* and in *Utopia,* but because in it the two friends began one of their greatest contributions to European culture, to "bring irony into literature." [19] Lucian, among others, provided a model for the construction of a racy kind of dialogue which may provide, at a widely popular level, pungent intellectual drama. More than this, in Lucian the humanists found a perfect mine of material for satire on tyrants, on conquerors, on pompous generals, on the trifling pretexts often used to start wars, and indeed on virtually every aspect of the quest for military glory. The *Dialogues of the Dead* especially are so full of antimilitaristic satire that examples are almost too numerous to mention. Three, in précis, may give their flavor and edge:

> From Charon, ferryboatman on the Styx, Hermes demands pay now overdue for conducting shades of the dead thither from the earth. Charon pleads for more delay—there are no bad times on earth just now, no great wars or famine are ravaging it. But he promises quick payment as soon as a war or other calamity occurs, although Hermes suggests it would be better if peace prevailed.[20]

Or:

> Charon's ferry is again the scene. War has apparently occurred, for huge numbers of ghosts crowd up for passage over the Styx. Fearing his old boat will sink under the overload, Charon orders that all their insignia of power, glory, wealth, and earthly pomp be stripped off. A blowhard general in full regalia says he wears it because on earth he won a battle and was awarded prizes for valor by the state. Hermes tells him to leave his trophies on earth, for in Hades there is peace.[21]

Or:

> Diogenes jeers at Alexander of Macedon for his pretensions to divinity. Sarcastically he inquires about Alexander's empire (which of course had been disrupted by struggles for power soon after his death). Alexander ruefully admits that although he was promised a grand burial, he has been a corpse three days and still lies unburied in Babylon. At this Diogenes laughs very heartily.[22]

One dialogue which More translated was the *Cynicus,* then believed to be Lucian's own work. The Cynic presents various arguments in favor of a hard, bare, simple life. He is glad to dispense with most of so-called civilization's luxuries and instead to limit himself to the bare necessities. In so doing one of his main motives is the belief that all human evils—including wars—spring from lust for gold and silver. "For from the desire for these all human evils spring—factions and wars and conspiracies and murders." [23] The idea that a society may be happiest when its economy avoids wasteful luxury and instead seeks to produce what is "necessary" for all men will reappear in *Utopia*. The *Menippus,* also translated by More, brings the cynical Menippus to call upon the ghost of Helen of Troy in Hades. To him it is a matter for ironic astonishment that a mere bare skull should have caused a great war and the deaths of so many thousands.[24] No more than Lucian was More inspired to admiring flights of Marlovian romanticism, of lyric ecstacy over limitless destruction, with butchery serving as a stimulus to eroticism. A humanism differing sharply from More's will be needed to produce

> Was this the face that launched a thousand ships
> And burnt the topless towers of Ilium?

Most acutely relevant to the conditions of Renaissance kingship was the work done on the theme of tyranny. The argument of Lucian's *Tyrannicida* ran thus: "An assassin enters a palace to murder a tyrant, but not finding him in, slays his son and leaves his dagger in the body. The father returning draws out the dagger and slays himself, whereupon the murderer claims the reward of one who has removed a tyrant." [25] To the murderer's declamation More wrote a response, and at his suggestion both he and Erasmus wrote answers to Lucian's arguments in favor of tyrannicide.

In the opinion of these translations' best editor, "More's interest in tyranny was at this time . . . literary, not personal or political." [26] It is very difficult to determine, when a man lives under more or less despotic rule, the point at which his interest in tyranny passes such a delicate line. Had More by 1505, as a social critic, reached a point of commitment, as Erasmus appears to have done by his 1504 *Panegyricus?* For evidence consider his treatment of the theme of tyranny in his Latin epigrams, most of which (said Erasmus in 1519) came from his youth.[27] The best critics have it that More early showed "devotion to the true genius"— "terse, witty, and satirical"—of the epigram. In comparison with Erasmus' efforts in this genre, More's poems leave the scholar's study and bring in a down-to-earth "world of merchants, lawyers, and courtiers." As an epigrammatist, More is most original in handling the topic of kingship, a theme treated in short poems by "no other sixteenth-century poet." He showed intense interest in the differences between tyrants and good kings, but (observe Bradner and Lynch) "it is evident from a reading of this group of epigrams that, whereas the existence of good kings is a theoretical possibility, the existence of tyrants is a present danger." [28] Thomas More already had gained some first-hand acquaintance with his subject in hard reality. As a member of Parliament (1503-4), despite his youth (he was then twenty-six) he had aided in defeat of a proposed rapacious royal subsidy; and as a consequence had been virtually compelled to retire from public life and seek safety in seclusion.[29] On Henry VIII's coronation day in 1509, when a humanist age of gold seemed possible, More addressed to the new king not merely a gracious and poetical set of good wishes but at the same time so bitter an attack upon policies of Henry VII's reign that he later found it difficult to cope with charges of having traduced royalty (*MLE*, p. 143). I think it fair to surmise that by 1505 More had begun to acquire a very practical interest in tyranny, one going well beyond the academic or literary. Finally, these translations from Lucian together with More's epigrams (many built on classical models) brightly illuminate the direction of the new English humanist social criticism as these friends brought Lucianic irony and satire to a focus upon huge follies of their own age, perhaps above all upon tyranny and its addiction to war.[30]

Erasmus returned to England in 1509 as to the most favored of countries, one in which a secure peace would prevail during a historic revival of humanist learning. Between his departure in 1506 and that happy return, however, he spent three years in Italy, and his experience there vividly mirrored the extent of papal corruption and immersion in warfare, under Pope Julius II.[31] The venerable ideal of the *Pax Ecclesiae* seemed to have been replaced in Italy by a new one, the *Bellum Ecclesiae*. The impact of this decadence upon the London Reformers' later work was to be profound, even if Erasmus' testimony comes first.

Indeed in 1506, when Erasmus hoped to pursue his studies at Bologna, Pope Julius II, despite advanced age, was himself leading his troops in an effort to subjugate certain rebel cities, Venice and Bologna among them, and thereby extend his powers. When Bologna was threatened with siege, Erasmus retreated from its university to Florence. Thence he wrote in early November that the turmoil of wars in Italy had brought confusion upon scholarly work (*EE*, 200). After Bologna's fall, Erasmus returned in time to see the conqueror make his triumphal entry amidst gorgeous festive pageantry. So far from delighting him with its splendor, the sight inspired the humanist to revulsion and disgust when he saw, as Smith put it, the "Vicar of Christ celebrating bloody triumphs." [32]

During Erasmus' sojourn in Italy, papal warfare, or plans for it, accompanied by social turmoil, were almost continuous. While Pope Julius planned further wars against the Venetians, Erasmus wrote, studies were at a standstill and the university kept holiday. Anxious to leave, he translated more of Lucian's satiric *Dialogues* to keep busy, and these in mid-November he sent to a friend with his hard ironic opinion of the Pope who emulated the Roman dictator: "For in Italy at present studies are singularly chilled, while wars are hot. Pope Julius fights, conquers, triumphs, and in fact plays the part of Julius to perfection" (*EN*, I, 421).

Clearly the classic figure of Julius Caesar had, in Erasmus' humanist eyes, undergone a devaluation and reassessment no less drastic than he had earlier suffered under the social criticism of some Roman historians, philosophers, and poets widely read in the Renaissance, such as Livy, Lucan, Pliny, and Cicero.[33]

It is possible that Erasmus also witnessed Pope Julius' entry into Rome on Palm Sunday, 1507, amidst pageantries far surpassing any seen at Bologna the year before. Of this show a vivid record was made by a correspondent of Erasmus and a future leading Reformer, Ulrich von Hutten, in harshly satiric verses, *In tempora Julii*.[34] Evidently, in these last years of the old order, not only the London Reformers felt profound revulsion from the decadent papal indulgence in war, whose "glorious" feats, performed by other churchmen as well, stood in such hideous discrepancy with the ideal of a Christian peace. Truly in Europe a Pandora's Box—the idea of a "box" is a witty invention of Erasmus in 1508—only waited to be opened wider to loose "every kind of calamity." [35] Erasmus' hardening criticism of violence and bloodshed in society is further marked during his visit to Rome in 1509. At that time, near the old Vatican, Pope Julius had under construction an arena for tournaments and bullfights, and possibly there Erasmus witnessed and was revolted by a savage spectacle. "I was drawn to it by friends," he wrote, "for of myself I never take pleasure in these bloody games, the relics of pagan antiquity" (*EO*, X, 1754; Smith, p. 113).

We know that while in Rome Erasmus actually composed two orations (now lost) on the proposed papal war against Venice, written for the Pope at the express desire of the powerful Cardinal Riario. One was to favor the war, the other to present the arguments against it. Erasmus said that his heart and best efforts went into the plea for peace (*EE*, I, 37.7-12), but the war, as was virtually a foregone conclusion, was decreed. "A curse on these wars," he wrote to the printer Aldus in 1508, "which prevent our enjoying a part of Italy which pleases me more and more every day . . ." (*EN*, I, 451).

In England, barely a year later, however, a wondrous age of peace and humanistic progress seemed to be dawning with the accession of Henry VIII. The optimism of men like More and Erasmus was almost boundless, and what is more, it had apparently realistic foundations in the known character of the King, in peace policies built up under Henry VII, and in the bold actions by which Henry VIII speedily confirmed a policy of firm justice and humanist liberty of speech. This tremendous surge of optimism is a fact of the first importance for the London Reformers' work in social criticism and reform.

It seemed to many in 1509 that England, with rare fortune, had actually secured in the flesh the practical embodiment of one humanist dream —the ideal prince. Now, doubtless, it is difficult to consider such once-potent figures without the presumption that they were, in their time, imaginative delusions; and that therefore those who put trust in them are proper subjects for either pity or irony. For the early sixteenth century in England, however, the prince himself, good or bad, was the only practicable means through which social change might peacefully be secured. The alternatives were rebellion (seeking some new monarch) or sheer anarchy.

The humanist dream of Henry VIII as this ideal prince, now actually ruling in England, is perhaps nowhere better suggested than in the letter which summoned Erasmus from strife-filled Italy to share in England's fortune. From Lord Mountjoy, one of the King's early favorites at court and one of Erasmus' earliest English patrons, came the invitation, rich with assurances that a veritable new Augustan age of peace and humanist development was dawning in England. What could Erasmus not expect, as one (like Thomas More) already favorably known, almost an intimate, from such a "hero" and "lover of justice and goodness," a king greeted like a "new and auspicious star"—England's "Octavius"?

For what may you not promise yourself from a prince, with whose extraordinary and almost divine character you are well acquainted, and to whom you are not only known but intimate? . . . But when you know what a hero he now shows himself, how wisely he behaves, what a lover he is of

justice and goodness, what affection he bears to the learned . . . you will
need no wings to make you fly to behold this new and auspicious star. . . .
The heavens laugh, the earth exults. . . . Avarice is expelled the country.
Liberality scatters wealth with bounteous hand. Our king does not desire
gold or gems or precious metals, but virtue, glory, immortality. . . . The
other day he wished he was more learned. I said, that is not what we expect
of your grace, but that you will foster and encourage learned men. Yea,
surely, said he, for indeed without them we should scarcely exist at all. What
more splendid saying could fall from the lips of a prince? [36]

Indeed, added Mountjoy, Erasmus' *Adages* (presumably the 1508
edition, "one of the world's most popular and influential books") is so
much approved by the Archbishop of Canterbury, Warham, that one can
scarcely tear it away from him.[37] As Erasmus saw this glorious opportunity (looking back nostalgically from 1531), he hesitated in Rome but
briefly, then hastened to accept this enticing invitation (*EN*, I, 461-63).
Hence the early summer of 1509 found him in England, lodged with
Thomas More at Bucklersbury, where—in a mood of the highest humanist optimism—he wrote the *Praise of Folly*, one of the most popular of
all Renaissance satires and one especially rich in its witty antimilitarism
and social criticism. As far as any man living knew, a great age of peace
and of progress toward a humanistically reformed society was then beginning. Looking back, it is now easier to be wise, to see that Henry VIII's
"pride, his sense of power, his contempt for the foreigner, were qualities
. . . strengthened by all the circumstances of his life." Similarly it is now
easier to find sinister meanings in a burst of his temper in September,
1509, when from Paris came a common envoy to acknowledge his royal
master's receipt of a letter from the young English king, asking for peace
and friendship with France. "Thereupon King Henry took offence, and,
turning towards his attendants, exclaimed, 'Who wrote this letter? I ask
peace of the King of France, who dare not look me in the face, still less
make war on me.'" "In short," wrote the astute Venetian ambassador,
"King Henry holds France in small account." [38]

Humanist hopes for peaceful changes in England were not solely based
on the fact that Henry VIII was a "product of the new age," one who
had grown up in the atmosphere of the Renaissance (Fisher, p. 157).
During the last years of Henry VII's reign it began to appear that a
genuine Tudor precedent and permanent policy of peace was under construction. There is no place here, or necessity, to relate this movement to
Tudor needs to unite and pacify England in the civil war's aftermath.[39]

Not only had diplomatic precedents for peace become apparently firmly established in Henry VII's later councils, but some of his chief advisers were friends not only of peace but of humanism. The chronicler Hall, whose desire was to glorify the Tudors, declared that from 1501 onward Henry VII spared no pains to see that his last years might be spent in civil and foreign tranquillity. The marriage in 1501 of James IV of Scotland to Margaret, daughter of Henry VII, and that of Prince Arthur of England to Catherine of Aragon were designed to cement international peace. In his last years, said Hall, Henry VII "more detested and abhorred intestine and civil war, than death or any thing more terrible." Even the policy of leveling great fortunes was prompted by the aim to insure against civil war, for he was determined to "eradicate and extirp . . . all the causes of unquietness." [40]

An anonymous piece of what might be termed propaganda for Henry VII's peace policies, combined with court and fashion reporting, told the English readers details of Princess Catherine's reception into England in 1501. England was praised as one of Europe's most favored lands and one filled with goodly, devout people. St. Augustine himself brought Christianity to this island and with it the teaching of peace among men, a matter of paramount importance. The author is ironic toward those princes (unnamed) who have "so little pondered" that they hold "the great prize and magnificence of them to be in effusion of blood, strife, and battles." The truth is, peace is "above all things most profitable and necessary." (The Tudors, as everyone knew, had not long been in power.) In proof there stands the historic contrast between the transiency of the Roman empire, attained by "such slaughter," with the "dignity and rule" won by Christian Rome through the faith and "peacefulness" of Peter and Paul. For an instance to show the vanity and brevity of imperial conquests, look at Alexander the Great. Indeed, Christ's own example above all teaches the way to peace. And in their wisdoms the sovereigns of England and Spain have "allowed the sentence of unity and peace to be most expedient." [41] The shaping of public opinion was under way. Finally, in his funeral sermon for Henry VII, John Fisher, Bishop of Rochester, highly acclaimed attainment of domestic and foreign peace as Tudor achievements:

. . . his politic wisdom . . . was singular. . . . Leagues and confederies he had with all Christian princes. His mighty power was dread everywhere, not only within his realm but without also. His people were to him in as humble subjection as ever they were to king, his land many a day in peace and tranquillity. His prosperity in battle against his enemies was marvelous. . . .[42]

But an older ideal—that of common peace between Christian princes, combined with a crusade against the Turks—was cited by Fisher in his funeral sermon for that friend of learning, Lady Margaret Beaufort, grandmother to Henry VII: "She whom I have many times heard say that if the Christian princes would have warred upon the enemies of his faith, she would be glad yet to go follow & help to wash their clothes for the love of Jesu. . . ."[43] More significantly, Lady Margaret helped to place in the royal inner councils a little group of able elder statesmen and friends of humanism who continued for several years as a peace party under Henry VIII. Most notable were Bishop Richard Fox; Bishop Ruthal; Warham, Archbishop of Canterbury, friend and patron of Erasmus; and Bishop John Fisher.[44] Each will have his part to play in this drama of ideas and the humanist struggle for peace and social reform.

During the humanist honeymoon with Henry VIII after his coronation, two royal actions informed the court (and perhaps the people generally) that the King roundly supported justice and an astonishing freedom of speech, at least from a humanist favorite, Thomas More.

First, Empson and Dudley, two of Henry VII's principal tools in the extreme financial extortions of the reign's last years, were impeached and, in due time, found guilty and executed. Ironically, Dudley occupied his days in the Tower with writing *The Tree of Commonwealth*, wherein he offered Henry VIII his unasked counsel upon peace, which he declared was a particular requirement of England because of her dependence upon foreign trade. In fact "Peace" is one of the main "roots" said to be "very necessary" for the tree of commonwealth. "Outward war" (foreign), said he, is a "great consumer of treasure." Good kings need good counselors: let every man "beware what counsel he giveth to his sovereign to enter or to begin war. There are many ways to enter into it, and the beginning seemeth a great pleasure, but the way is very narrow to come honorably out thereof. And then ofttimes full painful, beside that it is very dangerous for the soul and the body." With advice of the council, honorable alliances should be made with potential enemies. At the same time England should not be without "good and sure preparation for war," since this encourages honorable peace; and "in time of peace . . . make good and sure preparation for war." After these things are done, it might not be amiss to aid learning, to aid the universities (badly in need of it), and—with discriminating judgment, of course—give to scholars "the parings of your fruits, connyng [knowledge] to increase." [45] One might conclude that, in his little handbook for a prince's education, even the condemned Dudley thought Henry VIII could hardly do better than to carry on his father's recent and wise peace policy. Here was an idea that a vast number of Englishmen then alive could ardently share.

The temper of the times at the outset of Henry VIII's reign, one seemingly most favorable to both peace and to humanism, is vividly indicated by the quality—and the royal reception—of some congratulatory verses presented by Thomas More to his prince. More, after opposing the will of Henry VII in the Parliament of 1503-4, had been virtually forced to retire from public affairs (Chambers, pp. 87-98). Since he was favorably known to Henry VIII, nothing at first glance would seem more politic than to offer a coronation gift of laudatory epigrams. Some of these express praise for the idealized figure of a good prince. Through many runs the theme that a king's highest triumph is to rule in peace. We hear that, after all, Plato did not feign, for he told truly that after the silver, brass, and iron ages were past, the Golden Age (i.e., of peace) would be renewed. It is, of course, unlikely that Plato ever stated this idea. The point is that More wittily reshaped his materials in order to emphasize to the King the humanist ideal of responsible rule for peace. In *On Two Roses Which Became One* he praised the Tudor house: by firmly joining the warring Roses it had ended the useless strife of the civil war (*MLE*, Nos. 3, 5). So far, no doubt, these epigrams seem safely within the conventions of Renaissance courtesy in poetic compliment.

Strikingly exceptional is the longest of More's five poems on the coronation. It not only expressed patriotic and humanist optimism for peace but went daringly further to mount a bitter attack upon harsh policies of Henry VII. Under the son, as More saw it, England was almost sure of peace: "In the absence of sycophants, your subjects' love and your enemies' fear will hedge you round in peace and safety. As for war beyond the borders—if the French, for instance, join with the Scots—no one is afraid, provided that England is not divided."

The remarkable thing is that Henry VIII "indicated by his impeachment of his father's principal agents, Empson and Dudley, that he would not resent such comments." [46] The measure of humanist optimism in 1509 is reflected in the freedom of More's criticism—a solid example, I take it, of the sweet liberty which Erasmus expected to find in England (*EE*, 253.6-9; *EN*, I, 462).

It is time to examine the antiwar satire in Erasmus' *Praise of Folly*. Should one not first ask, however, why Erasmus of Rotterdam holds so prominent a place in a study of *English* humanist social criticism? As the ferments of nationalism grew, many countries laid their claims to notable scholars, most of all to the widely traveled Erasmus. Was he not a Netherlander at heart, as say those who would minimize the importance of his English relationships? [47] The "purest incarnation" of the Low Countries' genius in the arts of peace and civilization during the period just before the Wars of Religion exploded over Europe? [48] Or none of these but instead above all a cosmopolitan and internationalist—"symbol of the bond that links men of learning across parochial, national, and ideological boundaries"? [49] Something can be said—has been said—for all these views. I choose to side with those who, like A. L. Rowse, emphasize how much of Erasmus' greatest literary work grew out of the time between 1499 and 1517, when his life and work were so closely bound up with Colet and especially with More, with England. "Of this greatest of Europeans, it might almost be claimed that he was half an Englishman," just as Anglo-Saxon countries best appreciate "his humanitarianism, his love of peace and liberty, his lifelong service to international ideals, his spirit of moderation and tolerance in religion." [50] Moreover, Erasmus' criticism of war is an integral part of the humanist thought on social reform which he developed together with Colet and More. And in the 1520's, Erasmus and More helped Vives to come to England as one (said Erasmus) by whom his own name would be overshadowed (*EE*, 1107.6-8).

Erasmus' *Praise of Folly*, famous throughout the Europe of its day, is still well enough known to need little introduction. Perhaps its gaiety and verve can be best enjoyed, however, when it is squarely set at the dawn of what the humanists in England hoped was to be a new Golden Age of peaceful social reconstruction. The whole tone of the piece is bracing, optimistic, and constructive. Like all first-rate satire, it seeks to expose and explode accumulations of human asininities; idiot structures must be blown down (preferably by laughter) to clear the ground—and the air—for new ones better suited to decent human aspiration. Satiric laughter of Erasmus' kind seeks also to clear out pockets of decay, to repair what is worth saving. "Folly," in Erasmus' sense, means, comprehensively, human fatuity—but fundamentally of the curable kinds. Such a satire is possible only at one of those historic moments when the writer, at least, really believes that, if reason is brought rightly to bear, the human animal can yet be brought to live wisely and well, in harmony with his kind and the world around him. Satire grows despairing and suicidal when— as with the older Swift—pessimism overwhelms perhaps writer and readers alike, when man's age-old fatuities have taken on the sinister aspect of massive insanities, and hope for achievement of a rational and humane social order flickers very low. T. S. Eliot's *The Waste Land*, Franz Kafka's *The Trial*, Aldous Huxley's *Brave New World*, Arthur Koestler's *Darkness at Noon*, George Orwell's *Animal Farm* and *1984* suggest this bleak and terrible temper for western Europe in the mid-twentieth century.

It is important to remember the obvious—that in 1509 the London Reformers did *not* know that, just over the horizon, were to come the Lutheran turmoils, the terrifyingly swift collapse of the old medieval order (or what remained of it), and the explosion of Europe into the wars of religion. In the bright England of 1509, almost any good thing seemed possible to achieve, given wit, hard work, and the requisite royal leadership of a nobly Christian prince—Henry VIII. The *Praise of Folly* breathes an air of hope, of toleration, and of critical intelligence eager to be at work creating a peacefully reformed way of life. Whatever one may think of Erasmus as prophet in 1509, no one has ever been able to subject his satire to the fate of *Gulliver's Travels*, which has been turned into an innocently droll fairy tale for children. Like Swift and Thomas More— perhaps like all great humorists and ironists—Erasmus, beneath the mask of laughter, is quite serious.

For our story, the *Praise of Folly* is most fascinating for its trenchant and central satire on war and warmakers, past and present. Within the whole work this forms a structure of relentlessly ironic social criticism, both destructive and constructive. Erasmus was addressing himself to an audience which, if schooled in the quite usual medieval patterns of thought, customarily regarded war (like the plague) as caused by man's sin and God's answering justice, yet at the same time (since St. Augustine) as an action approvable as just and Christian. The accretions of chivalrous romance, moreover, had dressed war in a heroic glamour suitable for one of nobility's most glorious occupations. In startling contrast, Erasmus presented a Christian-humanist image of war and warmakers as beastly, hellish, corruptive of human society, unjust, and unchristian.

44

War is not treated as an incurable form of human folly; it is not in the nature of things inevitable and necessary; it is corrupted men who make it so. The satire was designed progressively to amuse, surprise, shock, appall, and, finally, prompt pensive men to re-examine time-hallowed medieval values and authorities, then—as necessary—to modify and reform them through the right use of reason and the Scriptures.

Erasmus' general method used the personification of Folly as a mouthpiece through which to deliver a witty monologue and commentary upon a wide range of human affairs. Sustained ironic praise is skillfully applied to the manifold absurdities or traditionally established (but potentially alterable and curable) follies of human life. Common patterns of thought and feeling are amusedly held up for inspection in an uncommonly bright humorous light. The opening viewpoint is much like that echoed by Ben Jonson in the prologue to *Every Man in His Humour*, ninety years later. Presented are:

> . . . deeds . . ./ And persons, such as Comedy would choose,
> When she would shew an image of the times,
> And sport with human follies, not with crimes.
> Except we make them such, by loving still
> Our popular errors, when we know they're ill.
> I mean such errors as you'll all confess,
> By laughing at them, they deserve no less:
> Which when you heartily do, there's hope left then,
> You, that have so grac'd monsters, may like men.

The theme of war in the *Praise of Folly* is handled in three main divisions. First, mankind's martial and related proclivities (such as hunting) are ironically lauded as forming part of the general lunacy characteristic of civilization. Next—the attacks growing more specific and coming closer to home—the warmakings of popes and churchmen are treated. Finally, in the criticism of theologians who falsify Christ and the Scriptures to justify war, the whole movement rises to its climax, the grasp tightens, the mood becomes formidable, and that this Christian folly is, in Erasmus' view, "the most important thing he has to say, one cannot well doubt." [51]

To begin with, the satire against war is fairly general, as Folly laughs with amused sympathy at choice varieties of whimsical prejudice and national *amour-propre*. She represents herself to us as the greatest of all inventors, creator of "all noble acts and arts" which cultural historians praise. But of all these noble inventions the first, the greatest, the maddest, and the most profitless to man, was war: ". . . is not war the seed-plot and fountain of renowned actions? Yet what is more foolish than to enter upon a conflict for I know not what causes, wherein each side reaps more of loss than of gain?" How can the carcasses left on the battlefield receive any glory? "As for those who fall, as was said of the Megarians, 'no particulars.'" But is it not always said that wise men are essential for military planning? Call it what it is—"military, not philosophical, wisdom." Of little use would be true philosophy—i.e., concerned with knowing the truth, including how to live well. "Far otherwise: this famous game of war is played by parasites, panders, bandits, assassins, peasants, sots, bankrupts, and such other dregs of mankind." Having thus begun with the semiparadox that wisdom is useless in war, Folly—with droll illustration—concludes that so-called wise men of peace are useless for all practical affairs (*EPF*, pp. 30-31).

From foolishness in general we move toward certain classes of folly large enough to take in the greater part of mankind—for instance, the custom of hunting, in which men everywhere find such joy. Erasmus' satire against hunting is an organic part of the mockery of war. In fact the theme of hunting is bound up with an apparently neo-Stoic theory devised to explain how primitive man may have fallen from the total peace which he enjoyed in the mythical golden age.

As Folly sees such activities as hunting, their general characteristic is that sheer custom has gradually so befuddled mankind that what is, to an objective observer (like Folly!), naturally hideous in itself has become transmuted into sheer joy. In their mutual delights, madmen laugh together. What droll fellows these hunters are! Happy in their delusions (like the ignorant cuckold who "flatters himself in the key of C-major"), as they hunt wild game, they:

. . . feel an ineffable pleasure in their souls whenever they hear the raucous blast of the horns and the yelping of the hounds. Even the dung of the dogs, I am sure, smells like cinnamon to them. And what is so sweet as a beast being butchered? Cutting up bulls and oxen is properly given over to the humble plebeian, but it is a crime for game to be slaughtered except by a gentleman! There, with his head bared, on bended knees, with a knife designed just for this (for it is sacrilege to use any other), with certain ceremonial gestures he cuts just the proper members in the approved order. The company stands in silence, wondering as at some great novelty, although it has seen the same spectacle a thousand times. And if some bit of the animal is handed one of them to taste, he thinks he has gone up a step or so in the ranks of the nobility. And thus with their butchering and eating of beasts they

46

accomplish nothing at all unless it be to degenerate into beasts themselves, though they think, all the while, they are living the life of a king [*EPF*, p. 53].

One wonders whether Erasmus had ever seen Henry VIII, for whom hunting was a passion, at his sport.

Already linked in Erasmus' thought on war are evidently at least three elements. One is that, earlier in history, man's inventive talents were misused by the invention of war itself—with its weapons, technologies, and ceremonies. Second, he observed the pleasure which contemporary men took in that miniature war, hunting. Third, he advanced the idea that, although the hunters are apparently happily unaware of it, what they have accomplished through habitual use of butchery is their own degeneration from the distinctively human toward the bestial. Evidently this reasoning process involves several simple presuppositions: that once upon a time man lived without war and without hunting; that in this earlier condition he lived in a fashion more admirably human, more perfect, than at present (when he unthinkingly enjoys butchery); that man is quite capable of so changing—from an earlier, uncorrupted state—until he is no longer consciously aware either that his tastes and habits are vile, or how vile they are ("the dung of the dogs smells like cinnamon to them"). What we have here seems to be a sketch toward a theory of history and of what might be termed progress. But Folly, through Erasmus' irony, attacks the entire process and holds it up to our view as one of degeneration. It was the ancient Prometheus myth which carried with it admiration for inventors; apparently Erasmus is not (here, at least) impressed unreservedly with the beauties of man's technological progress, including his invention of the art of war. Erasmus will return to the entire theory of history in his greatest piece of war criticism, the *Bellum Erasmi* (1515). Here perhaps it is sufficient to mention only that his efforts, in the *Praise of Folly*, to work out what I have termed a theory of history represent a striking example of his humanism. For he not only absorbed favorite classics (Lucretius, Ovid, Cicero, but above all Seneca and Plutarch), but transmuted them so that they furnished power and light for the English as well as European situation in 1509.[52]

The tone of the satire becomes grimmer when the attack centers upon the warmaking of a degenerate papal hierarchy. The chief target becomes easily recognizable when he devises "an undoubtedly serious criticism of the Church as he had seen it in Italy under Julius II." [53] As he warms to this theme, the irony becomes more brutal and the tension so great that the work almost breaks into outright denunciation. The result suggests the intensity and hard realism which mark the London Reformers' analysis of evil conditions whose reform became daily more vital to Christendom. To the historical method in criticism, Erasmus couples Lucianic irony and his own special form of wit: the result is work distinctive of the Christian humanism then emerging in England.

After a glancing cut at sycophantic courtiers and at kings who ignored the duties of kingship, Folly's satirical eye rested on the great princes of the Church. In general, contemporary cardinals compare badly with the ancient apostles. Why cannot these cardinals muster up enough purity and charity to work for the primitive Christian ends: "teaching, exhorting, chastising, admonishing, ending wars, resisting wicked princes, and freely spending blood—not money alone—for the flock of Christ?" But what can one expect when, as of late, "popes, cardinals, and bishops," after sedulous imitation, have almost beaten the secular princes at their own games? Besides, if they were actually to lead lives of Christian humility and poverty, think of the unemployment that would result! What would become of "all those advocates, promoters, secretaries, muleteers, grooms, bankers, and pimps" who now have steady employment (*EPF*, pp. 97-99)?

The satire in the *Praise of Folly* grows still more intense and destructive when Folly considers the papacy. It would appear from her critique that it was no use looking now for St. Peter's apostolic virtues in the popes. Christian labor?—that "they hand over to Peter and Paul, who have leisure for it. But the splendor and the pleasure they take care of personally" (*EPF*, p. 99). They live in the grossest luxury and, worst of all, are devoted to the vice of war. Indeed their wars to gain and extend ill-gotten wealth have demoralized the Church, whose worst enemies such popes actually are. From them the name of Christ receives scant lip service, but the papal hand is always ready to whip out a sword and "stick it into the guts of his brother." The means which made the primitive Church grow strong—peace and self-sacrifice—are out of date. Nowadays the Pope's main business is to destroy anyone who (doubtless devilishly inspired) would reduce the "patrimony of Peter"—i.e., the vast wealth of the Church. And so they hurry to war: "On behalf of these things . . . they fight with fire and sword, not without shedding of

Christian blood; and then they believe they have defended the bride of Christ in apostolic fashion." To war rush these "most holy fathers . . . and vicars of Christ"! No matter if war is more bestial than human, if it is hellish, if it blights morals like a plague, if it is unjust and the work of criminals, if it is truly unchristian:

. . . nowadays they carry on Christ's cause by the sword. . . . And although war is so cruel a business that it befits beasts and not men, so frantic [*insana*] that poets feign it is sent with evil purpose by the Furies, so pestilential that it brings with it a general blight upon morals, so iniquitous that it is usually conducted by the worst bandits [*pessimis latronibus*], so impious that it has no accord with Christ, yet our popes, neglecting all their other concerns, make it their only task.

Of course the "mob of priests, forsooth, consider it a sacrilege to fall short of their prelates in holiness. O brave! They war on behalf of their right to tithe in the best military manner, with swords, darts, stones and force of arms" (*EPF*, pp. 100-1).

No contemporary of Erasmus' was likely to mistake the chief target of this attack for any but Julius II:

Here [on the war scene] you will see feeble old men [Chaloner expanded this: "so old and wasted, that their bones rattle in their skins"] assuming the strength of youth, not shocked by the expense or tired out by the labor, not at all discouraged, if only they may upset laws, religion, peace, and all humane usages, and turn them heels over head.

Nor will the pope lack "learned sycophants" who will sanction such vile wars with pious texts:

Who will give to this manifest madness [*manifestariam insaniam*] the names of zeal, piety, and fortitude, devising a way whereby it is possible for a man to whip out his sword, stick it into the guts of his brother, and nonetheless dwell in that supreme charity which, according to Christ's precept, a Christian owes to his neighbor [*EPF*, p. 101].

Thus did Erasmus' *Praise of Folly* represent the old Pope Julius who, in Ranke's words, "from the tumults of a general war . . . hoped to extract the fulfillment of his purposes . . . to be the lord and master of the game of the world." [54] Winding up this savage indictment, Erasmus has Folly at once ironically disclaim the slightest intention to "rattle up the vices" of any living Churchman. And of course Folly only praises bad men, whom she likes to eulogize, but she had better say so lest someone think the *Praise of Folly* to be satiric (*EPF*, p. 103; *EPF-C*, p. 69)!

49

The last target of the satire that matters here is Erasmus' treatment of the traditional scholastic interpretation of Scripture by which, since St. Augustine's day, war had been justified. Unmistakably in this work he carried on what Colet had begun in his 1496 lectures on St. Paul at Oxford, using the same historical method in criticism but using it with superior flexibility, insight, and wit. This was deeply serious to Erasmus, and while the irony deepens toward the tragic, the passage tends to abandon the light and jocund tone with which he initiated his high-spirited, humorous mock eulogy of human fatuity.

The literary climax of Erasmus' lifework was to be his edition of the New Testament—the *Novum instrumentum* of 1516—work largely done in England and doubtless in his plans when in 1509 he came to England to live, with every apparent intention of making it his permanent home. In 1496 Colet had searched for the original, primitive meaning of the Scriptures, largely bypassing the scholastic commentators. This whole vital question of biblical interpretation could not very long be separated from the question of a text whose editing would include the latest advances in scholarship.

When in the *Praise of Folly*, therefore, Folly began to cite Scripture to bolster her authority in the world of deluded men, the satire rapidly came to a focus sharply on the question of the biblical authority for terming war to be just. Potentially there were few more explosive subjects for critical investigation; for when this is followed far enough, inevitably one is led to re-examine the basis and justice of power, monarchic or ecclesiastic.

At first Folly seems very pleased; ironically she affects to feel quite at home with these subtle scholastics, so clever and ingenious in reading meaning into the Scriptures. It's no less than "magistral"! Why, these days the "sons of theologues" can prove anything to their own purpose. The secret of their method, it seems, is to pluck out four or five little words "from here and there, even depraving the sense of them, if need be; although the words which precede and follow these are nothing at all to the point or even go against it." In short, by these critical devices (Folly applauds), scriptural precepts are mutilated and abridged, wrenched from their context, and so in the end readily found to mean something quite contrary to the example of Christ's own life. By such methods, indeed, "I pray you . . . tell me, what thing may be too hard for these doctors to bring about?" (*EPF*, p. 33).

For her part, Folly, using the example of Christ's conduct shortly before his death, admits to such stupidity that, to her, it seems Christ meant Christians to shun weapons and violence. Knowing the end to be near, Christ told his apostles to provide themselves with swords as needed in their mission of spreading the gospel. What did this counsel mean? To Folly (who resorts to historical criticism of a simple kind) the meaning is clear enough, in the context of Christ's whole life and teaching. The apostles were to secure and employ "not the sword with which bandits and murderers attack, but the sword of the spirit. . . ." Ah! but not so, says the scholastic expositor. To him (says Folly with some of Erasmus' bitterest irony) it is all quite different. It seems that Christ's injunctions of nonviolence really mean that his apostles should be armed to the teeth with all the latest military weapons. (Updating, Erasmus supplies "muskets.") Similarly the small knapsack of supplies that Christ had in mind is metamorphosed into a whole baggage train of fine food. Nor is such a critic at all disturbed "that He who thus earnestly bade that a sword be purchased, soon after with a rebuke ordered the same weapon to be sheathed; or that no one has ever heard it told that the apostles used swords or shield against the violence of the heathen . . ." though presumably they would have done so had Christ so intended.[55]

The satire ends on a note of serious humor. Is it possible that Christianity itself has some deep "kinship with some sort of folly"? Just ponder the huge discrepancy between Christ's life and those lived by many of his professed modern followers! Many? A majority! And naturally, by majority vote, the minority (who seek to use Christ's whole life as their guide) can easily be declared quite mad. As for Folly, she always agrees with the majority. Why not? They are her faithful devotees. Encouraging readers to "applaud . . . live . . . drink," Erasmus' figure of Folly bids a fond farewell to a world crammed with fascinating lunacies (*EPF*, pp. 118-25).

The *Praise of Folly* (like More's *Utopia*) has often been termed a *jeu d'esprit*, and so it is. But it is much more than that, for it marks a tremendous forward step in social criticism. This is no shaft politely released from some Renaissance ivory tower. It belongs to world literature, true, but the satire's roots run deep into its own time. As critic Erasmus now permanently took his place as a man committed to aiding humanist reforms, not as one outside, a genial spectator, but as a fighter in the midst of a fateful struggle for a better social order, and as one passionately engaged in the great movement of the age.

As criticism, moreover, the work marks an immense growth in the structure of ideas. Summing up, Erasmus put forward five major points about war, points which link his attack to the search for vital reforms of Christendom. First, he argues that war is beastly, that is, more befitting the true, uncorrupted nature of beasts than of men. Here he revives and gives new impetus to the classical beast-man comparisons and analyses. But he is not content merely to echo certain classics, giving the satire a neo-Stoic cast. What he opens out, tentatively, is a critical inquiry into what may be a tragic dichotomy in human nature. Why is man, a creature of such wondrous natural and divine endowments, potentially "a little lower than the angels," seemingly (at least) capable of life ruled by reason and love, prone (as in war) to actions so vile? Why is this creature at times worse than any animal? "A beast without reason," Hamlet will mourn (confronted with another fall from ideal humanity) "would have mourned longer." The whole idea is central in English Renaissance tragedy. But, in the *Praise of Folly*, Erasmus is not content to offer the standard medieval answer, that the cause of this tragic fall is man's sin. Rather, as humanist, he examines intensely man's capacities for irrational and antihuman behavior. Clearly all this involves an implicit theory of what man's capacities for a good life actually are, as well as of means for its realization. This whole complex of thought will be more fully explored in the London Reformers' later social criticism, most fully by More and Vives.

The idea that war is bestial, however, may be a libel on the beasts. Secondly, Erasmus raises the view that war is hellish—"so frantic [*insana*] that poets feign it is sent with evil purpose by the Furies." This carries us toward a tragic perspective exceeding the first. Erasmus, nevertheless, again puts the idea in a humanistic and poetic rather than simply some traditional theological frame. The "devil theory" of historical causation has, to be sure, long had its advocates.[56] Erasmus' way of raising the question invites deep reflection upon the interaction of reason and unreason (or sheer passion and overwhelming compulsions able to topple reason, as when men go berserk with mass-murderous fury) within the nature of man. Shakespeare's plebeians, listening with respect to Brutus' explanation of why he slew Caesar for the good of Rome, seem to be reasonable men. Mark Antony knows the potential vileness of human nature better than the too uncritically stoical Brutus, knows what these same Romans will do in frenzy when he has worked upon them, what unspeakable horrors will be commonplace when this hellish element is released (as perhaps periodically—we might say subconsciously—many men hope it may sometime be) when "Caesar's spirit, ranging for revenge, / With Ate by his side, come hot from hell," is given free play at the most fearful of all Renaissance military commands: "Havoc!" In the *Praise of Folly* Erasmus marks the line of insight which points toward Shakespeare's *Julius Caesar*.

Third, Erasmus advances the idea that war is "so pestilential that it brings with it a general blight upon morals." Thus he suggests the analogy of war and disease. The analogy invites the critical mind to search for causes, prompts again a search into the "nature" of man and the forces at work in his natural environment, an inquiry most imaginatively to be carried out by More in his *Utopia* and by Vives in his latest works.

The fourth and fifth points are closely related in the *Praise of Folly*—that war is unjust and unchristian. Pursuit of both these themes leads toward sharp re-examination, not only of orthodox medieval doctrines of the Church, but of the uses (and abuses) of monarchic and papal powers. Every one of these ideas was potentially dynamite.

To be sure, in the *Praise of Folly*, while these five ideas are all present, some remain in a germinal state. Very probably, at this stage, Erasmus himself had not fully worked out his thought on war and social reform. Nevertheless, as humanist criticism of life, the *Praise of Folly* marks a substantial advance. Barely twenty-five years earlier, in Caxton's work, we moved in a medieval landscape; but now in Erasmus the scene, the very air—the ideas and their attached emotions—all are predominantly distinguished by a changed and Renaissance outlook. The *Praise of Folly*, moreover, appeals for both reflection and action. During the decade to follow, More, Erasmus, Colet, and their friends will (as voyagers of the mind) on the one hand follow out these five ideas and others, discovering many curious ramifications. On the other, being humanists concerned with the search for a good life in both practice and theory, they will be found busy in practical efforts to help design and construct a new social order in England.

In this total humanist effort, every literary and practical talent the London Reformers possessed will be stretched to the utmost. One of the most potent instruments for appealing to men of reason is irony. It has been already suggested that, in their 1505-6 translations from Lucian, More and Erasmus began to bring irony into modern literature. Until now I have used the term "Lucianic irony" to denote this trait, but it becomes inadequate. For, in the *Praise of Folly*, Erasmus demonstrates command of a form of irony distinctive of himself and his friend More, an irony dramatically far advanced over Lucian's.[57] "Erasmian irony" is perhaps the best term available. This irony and its frequent companion, humor, mark much of these humanists' best work in the decade of optimism, after 1509, when a golden age of peaceful reform seemed achievable in England.

The golden age of early English humanism (1505-19) opened out in full splendor with the coronation of Henry VIII and the writing of the *Praise of Folly* in 1509. On the part of the London Reformers, the mightiest effort was to be the search for a working ideal for a peacefully reformed English culture, for the noblest and most practicable designs for a new social order.[1] If, however, the designs could be produced, what chance that the men in power would desire to execute them?

The chances rarely seemed better. Fortune had placed an ideal prince on the throne. Colet, Erasmus, and Thomas More were all very well and favorably known to the young King, so that from time to time they could communicate with him either face to face, or through personal letters, or through friends, or (finally) through published writings (usually giving the King what would now be termed an elegantly bound advance copy). If the men of learning could provide working ideals and designs and if so powerful a prince listened and initiated the labor of their realization in the everyday world, could not a cultural renaissance at least be vigorously begun in England? Given all these conditions, it hardly seems unrealistic of the humanists in 1509 to look forward to a flowering of what Erasmus called the peaceful "genius of this island." Shakespeare's patriotic idealism went to more lyrical extremes as the dying Gaunt brooded on

> This other Eden, demi-paradise,
> This fortress built by Nature for herself
> Against infection and the hand of war,
> This happy breed of men. . . .
> *Richard II*, II.i. 42-45

Yet the London Reformers' ideal and that of Shakespeare are essentially one.

More precisely, Henry VIII seemed to embody the *Christian humanist* ideal of the prince. More and Erasmus, certainly, as their satire shows in copious detail, were aware that contemporary statecraft had produced another ideal, that (to be blunt) of the tyrant, whose literary figure was most brilliantly suggested by Machiavelli. These radically differing concepts of the prince have always, to be sure, been recognized as poles apart; but they are not always recognized as both representing ideals. To More, Erasmus, and Colet, as their concept of kingship is slowly worked out, the Christian prince has a "duty" to rule justly and, as far as possible, at peace; he has no "right" to misrule. To the Italian humanist Machiavelli, the question is: how can the prince succeed as a tyrant? One might say, in his terms, that whatever the prince wants to do and can do, he is naturally entitled to do: he knows no duty to those under him, there are no mutual obligations except those imposed by fear. When specific questions of justice and war are considered, the differences between these two ideals will appear in bold relief. Nevertheless, however unlike, they are not (More is the most acute on this) simply reverse sides of one coin. But all this may best be brought out when we come to the *Utopia*.

Although in 1509 Henry VIII apparently embodied the ideal of the Christian prince, he had not yet been tried in action. The humanists had used their best talents to make their ideal attractive and practical for a young king: positively, as with Erasmus' 1504 *Panegyricus*; negatively, by the satire ridiculing tyrants in the work on Lucian in 1505-6; both, in the *Praise of Folly* and More's coronation epigrams. Moreover, as the humanists recognized—it is the strongest theme in More's epigrams—"whereas the existence of good kings is a theoretical possibility, the existence of tyrants is a present danger" (*MLE*, pp. xxvii-viii). What is more, the image of the king as hero-conqueror had received literary and political glorification aplenty in history, romance, and art (especially, in the Renaissance, sculpture). Which road would the young Henry VIII follow?

Certainly neither the age nor humanist social criticism can be understood and enjoyed unless (as of 1509) we scrap any conception of Henry as a "bestial corpulent tyrant." The fact is that "in every way, physically, mentally, morally, he was the personified ideal" of a good English king.[2] If, as the incarnation of the Christian humanists' ideal prince, Henry VIII embodied a kind of myth, one of the most extraordinary aspects of his ambiguous character is the extent to which, in the eyes of knowledgeable contemporaries, he so long appeared to be devoted to peace. The Venetian correspondence, as late as 1516-17 (i.e., after disastrous English military adventures in France), contains "as many references to the pacific nature of Henry VIII as to the turbulence of Wolsey." [3] Even in 1519, when hopes for an age of peaceful humanist progress were dashed, Henry could still impress his prince-of-peace figure upon the experienced Venetian ambassador:

He was affable and gracious; harmed no one; did not covet his neighbour's goods, and was satisfied with his own dominions, having often said to the ambassador, *"Domine Orator,* we want all potentates to content themselves with their own territories; we are satisfied with this island of ours." He seemed extremely desirous of peace [*Cal. SP Ven.,* II, 559].

In 1509, moreover, there was urgent need for a strong monarch to exert his powers in England. A historian's summary (Fisher, p. 167) of the domestic conditions crying out for treatment reads like a sketch of the topics which More touched in the first book of *Utopia:* "Pauperism, the agrarian question, the regulation of trade and industry, the reform of the church, the improvement of national education, the extension of English influence in Ireland, the elimination of gross scandal and inequality from the administration of justice." Out to the westward, furthermore, incalculable opportunities for profitable new enterprise were catching some English imaginations. Thomas More read Amerigo Vespucci's accounts of his New World travels, and More's son-in-law, John Rastell, soon began to plan the 1516-17 voyage which was intended as the first English attempt to colonize in North America.[4]

The challenge to England to create a renaissance in the arts, moreover, can be suggested by comparing the artistic production of Italy even during the first decade of the century, a time of war and tumult. Leonardo painted the "Mona Lisa," the "David" of Michelangelo was sculptured, Giorgione and Titian received their first major commissions, and Raphael was invited to fresco the halls and colonnades of the Vatican. Unless one excepts the literary production of More and Erasmus, the English scene was "poor and gloomy" by comparison, offering "in the immediate retrospect nothing but the slow and painful exhalation of the long-stored poisons of dynastic strife." A modern historian may nostalgically regret that this first decade also lacked "any reverberation of great martial feats," [5] but this sentiment was shared neither by Edmund Dudley (writing his *Tree of Commonwealth* while awaiting Henry VIII's execution order) nor by the English humanists.

Not only did Henry VIII inherit the outlines of a pacific foreign policy, but he at first accepted the wise elder statesmen chosen for him by his father and by his grandmother, Lady Margaret Beaufort. These men formed a peace party in the inner royal councils, and all, auspiciously, were powerful friends of the new learning. Their leader was Bishop Richard Fox, who from 1509 until his retirement from the King's council threw his weight wholly on the side of peace. In this struggle he was steadfastly aided, as in patronage of humanism, by Archbishop William Warham, by Bishop John Fisher, and in addition by Thomas Ruthal, secretary to Henry VII.[6] The completeness of these advisers' opposition to war was well observed by Luis Carroz, Ferdinand's ambassador to London. "They do not like to be at enmity, or to go to war, with any prince whatever." [7]

On the surface, indeed, English court life between 1509 and early 1511 promised continuation of the peace and "sweet liberty" which Erasmus had expected. The chronicler Hall tells of court pageants, tournaments, Christmas revels, and May games, the most fortunate event of all being the birth of a son to Queen Catherine on New Year's Day, 1511 (Hall, p. 519). Another happy augury was Henry VIII's treaty of peace with the French, concluded in 1510. England was rich and at peace—conditions likely to cheer courtiers and humanists alike. Obviously the London Reformers did not belong to inner court or council circles. In addition to his duties at St. Paul's, Dean Colet was active in founding St. Paul's School, an expression of his search for ways by which the humanistic spirit could be put to practical uses. Presumably Erasmus was busy at Cambridge but, because of the strange two-year gap in his surviving correspondence, he disappears from view until the spring of 1511, when he took the MS of the *Praise of Folly* to a Paris printer. As for More, he was (in Chambers' phrase) "an under-sheriff seeking Utopia." [8]

It now is clear that, seemingly content to leave heavy duties to his council, Henry VIII had concealed ambitions of his own. How much the humanists could learn of Henry VIII's secret diplomacy, we may never know. On the one hand frivolous and pleasure-seeking, on the other adventurous, the young King was delighted with ideas of chivalrous exploits, and eager to wield power for himself. The *Spanish Calendar* (*Cal. LP Spain*, II, xviii-li) shows that almost from 1509 he had been considering the project of a French war. For him the 1510 French peace agreement was a mock treaty. If it was Ferdinand of Aragon who first undertook to tutor Henry, yet the ever-warring Pope Julius II (a chief target of Erasmus' criticism in the *Praise of Folly*) also had schemes afoot inducing him to seek English military aid. If in the royal councils the peace party, led by Fox, for a time prevailed against the war party led by Surrey, Wolsey's entrance into the Privy Council late in 1511 apparently tipped the balance decisively toward war, for he soon secured (said Pollard) "a controlling voice in the government." Wolsey was "nothing if not turbulent," and the plunge into war was doubtless speeded by the "marvellous administrative energy" which he first used fully in preparations for the English expeditions to Biscay in 1512 and into northern France in 1513.[9] The time to begin such a venture publicly was apparently felt to be unpropitious before autumn of 1511, but the scheme for a continental invasion was the King's own.

The tortuous intrigues by which continental powers helped lead Henry VIII into his first war concern our story only insofar as it is necessary to make intelligible the English humanists' reaction to them—that is to the abandonment of peace and the folly of this war. The success of the League of Cambrai was the signal for its dissolution: Pope Julius, having called the French and Germans into Italy to crush Venice, now prepared to call upon Venice to expel the foreigners. Hoping to conquer Navarre, Ferdinand of Aragon joined the papal league. From an English humanist viewpoint (e.g., such as that represented by Hythlodaye, More's principal mouthpiece in Book I of *Utopia* where contemporary European royal follies are satirized), all this had in it precious little to justify England's entering the war. What interests had Henry VIII in Italy or Navarre? In contrast, continued peace with France had the most obvious advantages: peace in the Channel, peace with the restive chivalry of Scotland, even money tribute. And unquestionably war with France would endanger the treaty of "permanent" peace with Scotland and hence the civil peace of England.

In fact, by 1511, all the peculiar conditions which had once enabled England to conquer France had ceased to exist. It was an almost incredible folly for England to "embroil herself in the affairs of the continent." While still formidable in skilled hands, no more was the English longbow a supreme weapon: its practical (if not romantic) value had, to say the least, been spoiled by the creation of artillery (Fisher, pp. 140, 167), however much (shortly before coming to England) the Italian humanist Polydore Vergil might denounce gunpowder as an invention which had destroyed chivalry.[10] If cross-Channel attack had grown vastly less profitable, no one had yet impaired the Channel's efficacy as a "moat defensive . . . against the envy of less happier lands." From an unromantic, a realistic, even a sane viewpoint, "To attempt to recover the lost dominions in France was as wise as to plough the sand or to sow the sea" (Fisher, p. 167).

Henry VIII, however, had romantic aspirations to be a conquering hero. And properly chivalric romance requires that war shall be (or at least appear to be) an action of justice, of honor, and of a kind able to gratify an associated desire for reputation gained through military skill. As seen through the rather ironic eyes of a humanist historian, Polydore Vergil, we may observe how Henry VIII manipulated his council to force agreement that war against France was necessary and noble. "To avoid involving himself in so great a war without an honorable cause . . . ," the King first secretly sent to France an agent bearing an almost certainly unacceptable ultimatum ("fair conditions"). While awaiting the reply, "the good king" summoned his council and "publicly explained how he had been requested by both Pope Julius and King Ferdinand his father-in-law to take up arms in defence of the church." After debate "many came to the conclusion . . . that there was no need to take up arms then" (since England stood to lose more than any possible or likely gains). With this view of the peace party, the King "scarcely agreed," considering it would be "dishonourable to him" not to lend a hand to help end "so great a war" against the church. "Wherefore," concluded Polydore Vergil, "the religious and most valiant prince [*pius et bellicosus*], not unmindful that it was his duty to seek fame by military skill, preferred so justifiable a war rather than peace." When (not very surprisingly) the English ambassador returned with the French rejection of Henry VIII's arrogant terms, "all the nobles, roused by the reply of the French king, came round to Henry's point of view." [11] By a treaty with Aragon on November 13, 1511, England was pledged to attack France in the following April.

Since the young Henry VIII to all appearances "took little pains with the government," [12] it is small wonder that Wolsey, whose wide abilities included a fantastic appetite for work, had early won royal favor. An apparently paradoxical light on them both comes from the nearly contemporary biographer, Cavendish, who said: ". . . and so fast as the other counsellors advised the king to leave his pleasure, and attend to the affairs of the realm, so busily did the almoner [i.e., Wolsey, 1509-11] persuade him to the contrary; which delighted him much. . . ." [13] The paradox is more apparent than real. Advising counselors to "beware" advising the King to begin war, Dudley noted somberly in 1509 that "There are many ways to enter into it, and the beginning seemeth a great pleasure, but the way is very narrow to come honorably out thereof." [14] While taking on himself the hard labor of organizing for a war, Wolsey helped provide Henry VIII with an irresistibly attractive pleasure. The King, at this stage, reminds one a little of Shakespeare's early figure of Richard II, who took such vast delight in the external and theatrical aspects of "chivalry."

The sprightly new martial temper of court life was brilliantly reflected in a pageant designed for New Year's night, 1511/12, at Greenwich. The King himself took part, and the whole proceeding was intended to simulate the gallant progress of the impending war. The theme was conquering England. Only one jarring note of realism intruded: artillery. For the rest (as Hall described it) here was a lovely dream-image of chivalric war at its prettiest:

And against New Year's night was made in the hall a Castle, gates, towers, and dungeon, garnished with artillery, and weapon after the most warlike fashion: and on the front of the castle, was written *le Fortresse dangerus*, and within the castle were .vi. Ladies, clothed in Russet Satin, laid all over with leaves of Gold. . . .

After this castle had been carried about the hall, and the queen had beheld it, in came the king with five other, apparelled in coats . . . spangled with fine gold. . . . These .vi. assaulted the castle; the ladies seeing them so lusty and courageous, were content to solace with them, and . . . to yield the castle, and so they came down and danced a long space. And after the ladies led the knights into the castle, and then the castle suddenly vanished, out of their sights [Hall, p. 526].

One could hardly blame the nobility for enjoying this kind of war, all set to sweet music.

Thanks largely to Erasmus' letters, we can trace in 1511 gradations by which, in humanist eyes, the happy and golden peace (like the play castle in the courtly war game) "suddenly vanished, out of their sights." The atmosphere of early 1511—before, it seems, the humanists had any inkling of war's imminence—appears unmistakably in the spring, when Erasmus (after the startling two-year gap in his surviving correspondence) reappears, cheerfully taking to a printer in Paris the manuscript of the *Praise of Folly*, which became an overnight best seller.[15] The satire, with its plain attack upon corruption and warmongering in the papal court, had circulated in manuscript. It would have been useless to deny its authorship as Erasmus did later with the blistering *Pope Julius Excluded from Heaven*. In a new, prefatory epistle to Thomas More (June 9), Erasmus offered a brief defense of satire as constructive social criticism— as a form of "foolery" that "may be so handled that a reader who is not altogether a fathead may garner more of profit" from it than from the "bristling and pompous argument of some whom we know." Added Erasmian mockery of military glory appears when he cites, as examples of the profitless, one who "paints the glories of some prince," while "another exhorts to the end of making war against the Turks." His own aim, he said, was "to teach, and to warn, rather than to bite"; to devise "pleasure rather than censure"; he had pointed at "no individual by name" (which was technically true), and he had only set out things that are "ridiculous rather than foul" (*EN*, II, 18). The tone of the letter is optimistic, and there is in it no suggestion of coming catastrophe. This, however, was only in June.

War rumors circulated with increasing force between June and November of 1511, carrying with them intimations that England might soon plunge into the continental broil. By August 25, Erasmus noted that the very idea of a possible war was already disrupting trade, not to say raising the price of wine in Cambridge (where he was then recovering from an almost fatal attack of the "sweating-sickness") (*EN*, II, 20). There was something to hope for when the rumor that "Julius the Great [Pope Julius II] is dead" reached him (*EN*, II, 23); but soon it proved false. And the counternote of humanist labors for peace and a good life appeared in Colet's letters that fall, telling of his foundation of St. Paul's School, praising Erasmus' plan of studies (the *De ratione studii*), and wishing he had Erasmus as one of his teachers.[16] In October, however, Erasmus' tone grew rapidly somber and pessimistic; moreover, there were plain hints that some humanists, at least, felt it increasingly unsafe to communicate criticism of the war and the chief actors in it through letters. Andreas Ammonius, Henry VIII's Latin, and Wolsey's private, secretary, was an insider. Writing to him on the fifth, Erasmus said carefully: "Pray let me know . . . whether there is any news of Italian or French affairs that is safely to be trusted to a letter" (*EN*, II, 28). The note of danger is marked again on the sixteenth: he hates to let any "safe" messenger go to London without a letter, for "I . . . want to know . . .

how things go on in Italy, and what the unconquered Julius is doing" (*EN*, II, 28). Ammonius' reply (whose safe delivery to Cambridge took almost a month!) only suggested the scope of the approaching wars: "The Spaniards are almost at open war with the French, and the English, it is guessed, will not remain mere spectators . . ." (*EN*, II, 30). By November 2, Erasmus sensed the approaching "unspeakable shadow" of the disasters of which Italy and Pope Julius were the center, and he saw an Homerically evil omen in the torrential rains which that fall had deluged Cambridge: "Jupiter appears to have listened to the prayers of the man . . . who calls on the rivers, lakes, and pools to weep for the calamities of Italy" (*EN*, II, 38).

Not infrequently in history men in position to initiate wars have nursed the naïve illusion that by the same token they could arrest the process at will. With hardheaded realism Erasmus expressed not merely hatred of war but the grimly accurate prediction that incalculably destructive consequences for years to come must follow from so far-reaching a war, once it had actually begun. It is significant that he still considered Pope Julius II to be the causer of these spreading calamities. (In other words, by inference, had Julius so willed—or should another pope so will—they could be arrested. One perceives that the ideal of the *Pax ecclesiae* still seemed practicable to Erasmus.) If, in late 1511, he had any idea of Henry VIII's true role (or Wolsey's) in promoting England's entrance into war, he was silent upon the point: probably he did not. To Ammonius in private he regretted bitterly that during Pope Julius' recent illness his physician had not dosed him with enough hellebore (i.e., a fatal amount) to "cure his madness for war." Patronage for men of learning declined as the war approached, and in this sense he now began to regret ever having left "smiling Rome": "Your Italian news is anything but agreeable to me, not from love of the French, but from hatred of war. For when we see every day, that the consequences of the smallest raid last for many years, what may we expect, if so momentous a war is once set on foot!" (*EN*, II, 42). Word of the treaty of November 13 pledging England to war with France would presumably have been known to More and Colet in London almost at once and to Erasmus, in Cambridge, not long after. Later he wrote that he had been counting on a cultural golden age in England under Henry VIII when that "Julian trumpet summoned all the world to arms." [17]

Humanist hopes for peace at least in England were thus given a heavy blow. As for the peace party in the royal councils, it had "received a shot between wind and water" (Pollard, p. 17). But a treaty is one thing, its execution another, and hope for peace still breathed faintly. Warham (Erasmus' patron) held out, and implicitly gave warning against the war when he opened Parliament on February 4, 1512, with a grave address on the theme, "Justice and peace have kissed." When Henry earlier proposed the war to his council, he took, of course, the standard medieval legalistic line, that it was arguably just and therefore necessary in the name of piety. Warham's oration first stressed that peace, wisdom, and justice are closely united, while in the second part he reminded Parliament that war was permitted by God only because princes and peoples were sinful.[18] The latter idea shows clearly how this friend of humanism yet had his ideological roots in the old Augustinian doctrine on God, sin, and war. Warham appealed to reason (not to those romantically impelled to seek fame by military skill), before England went over the brink. Nevertheless, the rush to war and martial glory went on apace.

The literary reverberations of this war, evident in humanist social criticism of 1512-14, are considerable. From John Colet we have several notable sermons, one of which survives entire, the other in Erasmus' epitome. From Erasmus, besides his letters (intended largely for publication, as usual with the humanists) there comes his brilliant satire, *Pope Julius Excluded from Heaven,* a long epistle to St. Bertin in early 1514, and finally, his famous *Erasmus Against War*—the *Bellum Erasmi* —written in England and added to the definitive 1515 edition of the *Adages.* From Thomas More we have some rather remarkable antichivalrous epigrams, his unfinished *History of Richard III* with its mordant insights into tyranny, and eventually the criticism on royal abuses of power that burns in Book I of the *Utopia.*

Throughout this body of work, these humanists, with individual differences but with more agreement on basic principles, strove to discern and to make known outlines of a good life—especially for England—and of the practical means, the reforms or new directions in social change, necessary to its achievement. Their deepening common conviction that a good social order must be based on a deeply reformed kind of justice, and that a rationally organized society will be largely at peace (the natural state of man is not necessarily war) led to keen reflections upon existing patterns of law and rule. In turn this effort, stimulated in part by the war events of 1512-14, gradually produced a deepened critique of human nature itself, of man in history, an inquiry less and less confined within the traditional and orthodox God-sin-man-war theory of causation. Without by any means wholly abandoning medieval orthodox ideas, these men struggled toward a contrasting and somewhat radical kind of analysis. Most triumphantly seen in More's *Utopia*, this English human-ist approach treats man (or tends to treat him) as a creature existing in a universe ruled by natural law whose modes of working are knowable to man if he uses rightly his divine gift of intelligence. An effort, heroic if tentative, is made to seek the causes of war, poverty, disease and many other ills the flesh is heir to, not in an inscrutable divine Providence, but in the workings of natural law. (This involves no necessary conflict of religion and natural science: heaven helps those who help themselves by means available.) In this total process of thought these humanists, in their various degrees, employed not only the historical method in crit-icism but what Mario Praz has rightly called (in special relation to More) "the scientific point of view." [19]

Two days after Warham opened Parliament, the Dean of St. Paul's preached probably the most remarkable of all pre-Reformation sermons in sixteenth-century England. The Convocation which heard him, in ad-dition to Wolsey as Dean of Lincoln, would probably have contained about four hundred and forty of the weightiest churchmen in England.[20] Supposedly the object of his address was to have been an attack upon heresies within the Church. Instead, Colet chose the text, "Be ye not con-formed to this world," and boldly attacked abuses and corruptions within the Church itself which cried out for urgent reform.

It seems clear that, in Colet's mind, the needed reform he sought should be effected by wise and judicious but peaceful action beginning from within the Church and with those highest in it. First, four main sources of evil were analyzed together under the head of conformation to the world: devilish pride (i.e., pride of worldly life), carnal concupis-cence, worldly covetousness, and secular business. The second part of the sermon dealt in down-to-earth fashion with practical methods by which the necessary reformation might be brought about. It was under the head of secular occupation that Colet attacked and called for reform of the evil condition (common in late medieval society) under which Christian clergymen had themselves taken to soldiering: "Let the laws be re-hearsed, and the holy rules handed down from our ancestors concerning the life and character of the clergy, which prohibit any churchman from being a merchant . . . or hunter, or common player, or from bearing arms. . . ." [21]

Taken by itself and outside its larger social and literary context, this criticism on war would not carry its rightful weight. In contrast, when the Convocation Sermon is set in its social perspective (and taken as a whole), "More truly, perhaps, than any other single speech or act" it "deserves to be called the overture to the great drama of the English Reformation." [22]

Colet's approach to the need for social change, in this sermon as in his foundation of St. Paul's School, coupled Christian idealism with hard realism. He candidly recognized, as such, degeneracies to which even churchmen had long been complacently accustomed. Can men be moved from age-old lethargy to perceive an idea of a good life? For if those in places of command will lead, beginning with the reforms nearest to hand in their own lives and jurisdictions, then existing laws and practical means lie ready to hand. But the vision must come first.

That the London Reformers' social criticism had *some* impact on its own time might perhaps be inferred from the fact that, as a result of this probing Convocation sermon, the Bishop of London accused Colet himself of heresy—no laughing matter, though Archbishop and Chancellor Warham came to his rescue. [23] But then Bishop Fitz-James, who had long been hostile to Colet and to the new learning, followed up by attacking the Dean directly for his criticism of the impending French war, in which he had publicly declared in favor of an unjust peace over a just war. The effort to destroy Colet with the King himself was, moreover, supported (said Erasmus) by a future bishop, "a very firebrand of war," as well as by another enemy of the new learning who declaimed against "*poets,*— meaning Colet":

[Bishop Fitz-James] . . . tried to excite the Court, with the King at its head, against Colet; having now got hold of another weapon against him. This was, that he had openly declared in a sermon that "an unjust peace was to be preferred to the justest war," a war being at that very time in preparation against the French.
   . . . The noble young King gave a conspicuous token of his kingly disposition; for he privately encouraged Colet to go on without restraint, and improve by his teaching the corrupt morals of the age, and not to withdraw his light from those dark times. [24]

Henry was evidently in a benevolent mood and finding pleasure in playing the humanists' ideal Christian prince.

According to the romances of chivalry, as Caxton interpreted them to noble English readers but one generation earlier, it would seem that not merely reading of chivalric war but the thing itself should rehabilitate knighthood and purify manners. To Henry VIII the French war of 1512 was full of surprises, not to say humiliations, as he followed its progress through the dispatches. The English force, wrote Polydore Vergil, was made up from "the hand-picked flower of men in their military prime . . ." but (alas for romance) "nothing worth recording was done . . . by the important English army." In fact, "the only deed which we can find worthy of record" was the slightly inglorious looting and burning of a "few houses." The Englishmen, doubtless including the King in London with his dreams of martial glory, "took this very badly, because they were keyed up in anticipation of performing some heroic feat all the time the army was away" (Polydore Vergil, pp. 175-83). The expedition which landed on the Spanish coast under the Marquis of Dorset on June 7 was a total fiasco: there was no food, no shelter, and (perhaps worst of all) no English beer—in fact the military arrangements were almost hopelessly inefficient. While Ferdinand, his own purposes accomplished elsewhere, withdrew from the campaign, "the English troops, sweltering idly under the August sun, drank Spanish wine as though it were English beer, and perished in hundreds like flies in the autumn." Finally on August 28, directly violating Henry VIII's commands, the army, in a state of mutiny, resolved to return to England, where it arrived on October.[25] Granting how ridiculous all this made Henry look to Europe's veteran politicians, the historian Brewer (I, 21, 24) nevertheless maintains that then war still had some "chivalrous" aspects, necessary for national greatness. As for Wolsey, chief executive of the campaign, the army—and, one may assume, the English humanists as well as Englishmen more at large—blamed him almost exclusively for its disasters (Pollard, p. 18). Henry VIII could still maintain the public figure of the almost stainless Christian prince.

Stung in his pride and chivalric vanity, and flattering himself that Englishmen fight best under their own king, Henry during the winter of 1512-13 prepared to lead his army into France in person in the spring. He turned a deaf ear to the councilors who thought that "the king in the first flush of his youthful maturity in arms," as Polydore Vergil put it, should not personally endanger himself. Vaingloriously, Henry hoped "by a signal start to his martial knowledge, [to] create such a fine opinion about his valour among all men that they would clearly understand that his ambition was not merely to equal but indeed to excell the glorious deeds of his ancestors" (Polydore Vergil, p. 197).

That a "hurricane of wars" might be dooming the humanistic golden age of peaceful progress, hoped for at Henry's coronation, begins to appear as a theme in Erasmus' letters from the same winter of 1512-13. To be sure, with his old roots in the Low Countries, he had naturally a somewhat more cosmopolitan outlook than More and Colet. From London in the autumn he expressed grief that the Netherlands should be drawn into these wars and his wish that he could safely write what he thought of them. In Britain, to his regret, Fortune had played him false, for promised support of learning largely failed in performance (*EN*, II, 126). To Peter Gillis, More's friend to whom the *Utopia* was addressed, he told his sorrow that general wars, or more precisely "depredations" (*latrociniis*) were nearing the Netherlands while the "dumb Bishops" merely looked on (i.e., did not use their power to arrest the war): "It cannot be expressed how sorry I am, that our countrymen are gradually being involved in war, having been already harried by so many wars, or, to speak more plainly, so many depredations. Oh tongue-tied Divines, oh dumb Bishops, who gaze in silence on these plagues of humanity!" (*EN*, II, 126). Who was more realistic? The King, infatuated with war as a glorious deed? Or the humanist who saw it as organized crime?

Before his disillusionment with the "genius of this island" under Henry led him to seek his fortunes elsewhere, Erasmus (probably in the winter of 1512-13) prepared for the King a gift from which he had expected more through eight days' labor than through all the weary years of toil upon his great edition of Jerome (1516). The gift was a Latin translation of Plutarch's little essay upon ways to distinguish a flatterer from a true friend. "But being suddenly drawn at that time into the hurricane of war by a sort of fatal storm, which then fell upon all Christendom, you had no time, I may well suppose," he wrote to Henry VIII, "to give any attention to literature, when the business in hand could only be conducted with the sword." [26] And in "To the Reader" (January 5, 1513), designed for the 1515 edition of the *Adages*, Erasmus, after kind words for Warham as a patron, was moved to remark how aid to learning had fallen off when the whole earth was catching fire with war (*EE*, 269.89).

By March the exciting bustle and fever of war preparation was intense. After the fiasco of 1512, Wolsey, his career at stake, was enormously busy and determined that the 1513 campaign should be a success. Henry, with swelling "confidence ... in his own great valour" (Polydore Vergil, p. 199), inspired the English nobility to retrieve honor lost the year before. While the army was preparing to embark for France, the fleet, under Sir Edward Howard, was ready to scour the Channel and, perchance, perform heroic feats.[27] Then came bad news—of Pope Julius' death on February 21—bad news at least for the war-hungry king. "The king" (wrote Polydore Vergil, [p. 201]) "received this news with great sorrow, being anxious lest the treaty should collapse and the enormous preparations which he had made for the war should perhaps prove to be in vain." This news, though hardly that of the election of Pope Leo X on March 11, should have reached England within a month. All this may suggest some of the high tensions and crosscurrents at court when, on Good Friday (March 27), Dean John Colet came before the king and preached his extraordinary sermon against the French war.[28]

This sermon, Colet's most advanced statement of his Christian humanist position on war, comes to us only through Erasmus' epitome, given in the first life of Colet (1521). Erasmus, however, not only was living in England in 1513 but had ample opportunity to communicate directly with the great principals in this drama. His account provides internal evidence that he had either seen Colet's manuscript or heard a closely detailed account of it. As for the ensuing private conversation between King and Dean, I surmise that he heard of it directly from Colet himself. The utterly plain straightforwardness of the sermon, even in Erasmus' summary, is notable for its freedom from the peculiar irony characteristic of Erasmus when putting forward his own ideas. In this reporting I have reasonable confidence:

Colet preached a noble sermon before the King and his Court on the victory of Christ, exhorting all Christians to war and conquer under the banner of Him their proper King. For they, he said, who through hatred or ambition were fighting, the bad with the bad, and slaughtering one another by turns, were warring under the banner, not of Christ, but of the Devil. At the same time he pointed out to them, how hard a thing it was to die a Christian death; how few entered on a war unsullied by hatred or love of gain; how incompatible a thing it was, that a man should have that brotherly love without which no one would see God, and yet bury his sword in his brother's heart. Let them follow, he added, the example of Christ as their prince, not that of a Julius Caesar or an Alexander. Much more to the same effect he gave utterance to on that occasion; so that the king was in some apprehension lest the soldiers, whom he was on the point of leading abroad, should feel their courage gone through this discourse [*EC*, pp. 43-44].

Colet's social criticism—here seen at its fullest growth—is built on his own earlier work but it also incorporates ideas from More and Erasmus (e.g., from the *Enchiridion*, the translations from Lucian, and the *Praise of Folly*). Basically, two ideals of the prince are set in sharp opposition: the true Christian prince versus the false Christian prince (with whom may be combined the conqueror-tyrant [Caesar or Alexander], later admired and studied by Machiavelli). For the prince is the central figure in the Renaissance martial drama from which Henry hoped to win chivalric glory during the summer of 1513 in France. Basically, also, Colet set in massive opposition the image of war as seen through orthodox and traditional eyes and the image of war brought forward by the English humanists as they sought a working ideal for a good life for their England. On the one side, again, there is suggested war in theory, on the other (realistically) war more nearly in observable contemporary reality.

Of course according to official Catholic theory and teaching, such a war as Henry VIII's invasion of France (under papal treaty) was just, hence soldierly participation in it was likewise just, for prince and trooper alike. (Moreover a standard article of time-honored Church teaching on war was that the souls of those who die in a just war are assured of salvation.) [29] Not only the Church but secular literature had long supported war: if the Church could decree war to be just, romance upheld it as great and glorious. Thus when traditional romances, or when flattering historians, represented conqueror-tyrants (Caesar or Alexander, the stock types) as great men, then their motives and their soldiers' tended also to appear as noble, their actions as heroic feats.

It appears that, in his sermon before the King, Colet questioned this ancient blended complex of ideas (of both Church and romance extraction) so strongly as to suggest that they contained vast untruth. Erasmus, we noted, spoke of such invasive wars as robbery and piracy (*latrocinium*). Colet grimly asked that men high and low should candidly examine their observable motivations. Is it Christian love that prompts a man to bury his sword in his neighbor's heart? Or is it (to be plain) rather hatred, ambition, love of loot, even delight in slaughter?

At the bottom of Colet's 1513 criticism one can perceive that his fundamental basis of valuation is the same as that set forward in his 1496 lectures on St. Paul and in his 1512 Convocation sermon. That is, against authority and sanction which he took to be corrupt he opposed the example of Christ's life, as made clearer through the historical method in literary criticism. While the sermon threw doubts on the 1513 war's justice, one can see the English humanist working toward a positive concept of justice and of heroism, implied in the idea of the "victory of Christ." In sum, then, before the King, Colet threw the strongest doubts both on this proposed war's Christian justice and on its heroic greatness.

Unlike so many mid-twentieth-century critics, the English humanists were not in the frustrating position of talking to themselves because the men in actual control of power ignored them. On the contrary, Colet's sermon against the French war had such strong impact on so many men that he was called before the King himself. Now, at last, the enemies of the new learning expected his silencing or destruction. (We cannot be sure that this interview took place before Henry heard from his ambassador that the newly elected Pope, Leo X, "will not be fond of war like Julius.") [30] As reported by Erasmus (whose source seems to be Colet himself), the King, to quash "groundless alarm," at once reassured the Dean, approved Colet's "sacred labours," and asked counsel "that we may unburden our conscience of some scruples, and . . . may better discharge the duties of our office." ("I will not," said Erasmus, "repeat the whole conversation, which lasted nearly half an hour.") The King and Colet ended in agreement

. . . upon all points, save only that the King wished him to say at some other time, with clearer explanation, what he had already said with perfect truth, namely, that for Christians no war was a just one. And this was for the sake of the rough soldiers, who might put a different construction on his words from that which he had intended.

Reappearing with Colet before the waiting "throng of courtiers," Henry publicly embraced the humanist, with a perfect speech for an ideal Christian prince: "Let every man have his own doctor, and every one follow his liking; but this is the doctor for me" (*EC*, pp. 45-46).

As far as I can discover, there is no record of another and later Coletian sermon on the justice of war for Christians, although there is what seems to be a literary myth that he delivered a fiery pro-war sermon, shortly after his talk with the King, and "filled all who heard it with martial ardour." [31] More and Erasmus mention no such event, and indeed it is preposterous on its face when set against the lifelong consistency of Colet's character and criticism on war and social reform. For contem-

71

porary evidence there is also a letter which Colet did not live to see, from the continental humanist, Marquard von Hattstein, which particularly praises the Englishman for standing against the currents of "insane violence" of the time when "recently the trumpet of cruel war was sounded," praises him for upholding a true "image of Christ" as showing both the moral necessity and a practical way toward peace.[32] We may possibly surmise, with Allen (*EE*, III, 580n.), that Colet gave some kind of "grudging approval" of the war.

Evidently the English humanists were as one in identifying Julius Caesar as a stock type of the tyrant-conqueror prince at his worst. The most infamous contemporary Julius, however, was the Pope of that name who died on February 21, 1513. We observed Colet's scathing reference to Julius Caesar (i.e., also to the Pope) in his Good Friday sermon against the French war. As for More, his sympathy with this view of Pope Julius and the corruption of papal warmaking is suggested by the inscription to More by Erasmus of one of his most mordant epigrams, *In Iulium II*, probably composed in England either during Julius' last year of life or soon after his death. Erasmus suggests similarities between Caesar and this pope: each broke faith, considered himself virtually a god, and plunged the whole world into war; indeed as tyrants it would be hard to choose between them—their resemblances included even the same diseases and personal vices.[33]

For humanist social criticism, however, the raciest satiric offshoot of Pope Julius' death (probably, like the *Praise of Folly*, written at high speed as it reflects the highest spirit) was Erasmus' ingenious and very funny *Julius Excluded from Heaven*. As Rowse said, "In the comparative freedom of England he wrote, though he never dared to acknowledge, the brilliant, scathing tract *Julius exclusus*, his scoriation of the warlike Pope—a work of the same class in which Byron's *Vision of Judgement* comes." [34] In satiric wit and literary technique the piece shows how Erasmus' powers had ripened since the *Praise of Folly*, for in that *jeu d'esprit* the personified figure of Folly gave only a monologue, which even so at times tended to break into open invective. The *Julius Excluded*, in contrast, develops as a dramatic dialogue between St. Peter, who is guarding Heaven's gates, and the ghost of Pope Julius who, swaggering like a drunken trooper, arrives to find the gates unexpectedly barred against him. Blustering, Julius demands that St. Peter open up and admit him as a matter of right. Recognizing in Julius a precious rascal destined for hell, St. Peter, with ironic humor, draws Julius out to give a candid account of his lifework. The technique allows Julius to convict himself, while St. Peter straight-facedly takes a part somewhat resembling that of a Christian humanist. The satire is too long to quote, but even a précis may give some sense of its flavor and content:

Julius' greatest claim to Paradise is that he has torn up treaties and caused general European wars, satisfying his greed for land and power while causing the savage murder of thousands, many of them innocent of harm. Behind Julius stand rank upon rank of soldier-ghosts, to all of whom Julius had promised heaven's rewards no matter how enormous their earthly crimes.

St. Peter denies that, as the first pope, he ever *rightly* used a bloody sword on Christ's behalf. To him Julius appears to be corrupt and devoid of all Christian virtue.

Julius defends himself by alleging not only that his war methods were not unique but that they had long been traditional with popes. In his own eyes, however, his boast is that he has excelled all popes within memory in sheer bloodshed and creation of mass misery. Revelling in his glory, he gives details of the schisms and wars he has promoted, and in raptures describes his triumphant military entries into conquered Bologna (witnessed by Erasmus) and into Rome itself after the war with Venice. "Scipio and Caesar," he raves, "were nothing by the side of me."

When Julius' despicable tale seems fully told, and St. Peter can endure no more, Julius is witheringly denounced. In contrast with the Christian apostles, whose mission was peace and teaching love of Christ, this brutal, degenerate pope has stormed cities, slaughtered legions, entangled princes and peoples in ruinous wars, and brought schism deep into the Church. And in all this his only motive was sheer greed for wealth and "glory." St. Peter dispatches Julius and his troops forthwith to hell.[35]

Such blistering satire upon papal corruption was, of course, much too dangerous to be openly acknowledged, but on the other hand it was too acute and witty to be kept altogether hidden. At least one manuscript in Erasmus' own handwriting circulated among intimate English friends who shared his views on the folly of war, such as More. Inevitably it became more widely known, and indeed its satiric technique is evident in the famous *Letters of Obscure Men* (*ca.* 1515-16) which marked the revival of satire in Germany, although the *Letters* show nothing comparable to the sustained social criticism on war that is a characteristic of the early English humanists of More's circle.[36] Finally, it is worth noting that the *Julius Excluded* marks at least a brief revival of humanist optimism for peaceful progress in England.

The optimism, at least on the surface, appeared to have some justification in the character of Pope Julius' successor. High diplomatic sources, Henry VIII was soon informed, held it likely that Leo X "will not be fond of war like Julius, will favour literature, oratory, poetry, music, employ himself in building, will not neglect the dominions of the Church, will not enter on any war except from compulsion, except, perhaps, against the infidels." In the spring of 1513, indeed, many either expected or at least hoped that Leo X would help make peace in Christendom.[37] At first, however, he renewed the treaty which gave Henry VIII his precious sense of justice,[38] and the French war went merrily forward as he and the English nobility pursued chivalric glory.

For three months, with all the external trappings of chivalric knighthood, Henry played at the game of war in France. A minor irony of the campaign is that not only Wolsey but those friends of peace and humanism, Bishops Fox and Ruthal, commanded troops (though probably never present at any battles). But then even Erasmus had a small naval vessel named after him. Actually the gains were rather small, considering the vast English expenditures. Tournai and Thérouenne were captured; and at the battle of the Spurs the English routed an already fleeing French army, capturing about two hundred men and six standards, all with little bloodshed.[39] Queen Catherine, without irony but with some justice, wrote to Wolsey on August 13 that the stay-at-homes were more "encumbered" with war than Wolsey was "busy" in France: ". . . they [in England] are all there very glad 'to be busy with the Scots, for they take it for pastime. My heart is very good to it, and I am horribly busy with making standards, banners, and badges' " (*LP*, I, 2162). In due course came September 9 and Flodden Field. Having earlier declined to be enticed from an immensely strong position to a weak one by "a false sentiment of chivalry," the Scottish king, acting on impulse, apparently did just that; and Surrey's English forever broke the Scots' power in this "last great border battle" (Fisher, pp. 186-88). That slaughter evoked exultation from the poet John Skelton (himself something of a humanist) but none from More, Erasmus, or Colet.[40] Late in October, Henry VIII returned home amidst great shows of triumph, pleased with the military glory he had won and apparently eager for further war with France in 1514. In fact he was, at the time, held up as "the type of the Christian warrior, brave, clement, disinterested," not by an English humanist but by an Italian poet who admired the way the English spared the churches of Thérouenne. Other evidence shows that Henry really hoped to reconquer and hold at least some of France, and Londoners believed he "would march upon Paris and renew the fame of Henry V" (Fisher, p. 189). Yet in 1519 even Erasmus could commend Henry's moderation in the conduct of the war (*EE*, III, 580n.). Moderation is, after all, a somewhat relative matter.

Not only in satire but in the epigram did the French war of 1513 have results important for social criticism. The English military fiasco of the year before prompted a French wit to write *De Anglorum fuga,* and, after the panic flight of the French at the battle of Spurs in 1513, Erasmus and More retaliated. Erasmus' elegantly mocking *In fugam Gallorum insequentibus Anglis* is of mild interest.[41] Not so with the work of More, for he is pre-eminent among the early English humanists in the power and critical use which he made of the epigram. And it is quite misleading to view this creative work, like Chambers (p. 113), as merely what a "loyal Englishman" would "naturally" do "when the honor of his country was attacked by a French poet." We would, moreover, miss some of More's sharpest brief insights into chivalric decadence and rising tyranny if we were to toss these poems aside with the damningly faint praise, "not wanting in bellicose ardour." In his best epigrams on the French war More did much more than beat the common patriotic drum.

One might, however, at first glance find little beside the loyal English humanist in some epigrams about the siege of Tournay (the Roman Nervii). During the 1513 campaign, Henry had mounted before Tournay's "iron gates and stone towers" "guns . . . of immense magnitude, enough to conquer by the very sight of them," said the field diary of the Clerk of the Parliaments. Twelve were exceptionally fearsome, for in addition to their huge size, each was "cast with the image of an apostle." Considering the odds, the Tournay city fathers surrendered before the shooting began, and the English entered to enjoy themselves in knightly style (*LP*, I, 2391). In his epigrams More contrasted ironically the fierce resistance of the ancient Nervii to Julius Caesar with the feeble opposition which the modern French had offered to Henry VIII: "Valiant Caesar first conquered you in your might, Tournay, but not without disaster to both sides. Henry, a king both mightier and better than Caesar, has taken you without bloodshed. The king felt that he had acquired honor in taking you, and similarly you yourself felt it no loss to be taken." [42] Had the King himself read this, he might have felt a slight added touch of martial glory. When, however, we reflect upon the humanist critics' identification of Caesar as a tyrant and one who plunged his world into war, it is apparent that More was, in veiled terms, identifying Henry with that figure of the tyrant.

In his set of epigrams of 1513, directed against the French humanist poet Brixius, however, More, rather originally, is at work demolishing prominent elements of an entire outworn epic and romance tradition. What is more, in so doing he operates from a "modern" scientific viewpoint which makes him the first great English historian of the Renaissance.

After the outstanding naval engagement of 1512, Brixius had celebrated in verse the exploits of the French captain Hervé of the *Cordélière* and disparaged the Englishmen who manned the *Regent*. The facts, which were well enough known in England by late 1513, were these: "competing . . . for glory," the ships collided; then, after an exchange of hot fire between English archers and French crossbows, the *Cordélière*'s powder magazine exploded, the ships caught fire, and before they sank, the French captain, in full armor, leaped into the sea where he naturally sank promptly and drowned. As Polydore Vergil said, "Thus the engagement was melancholy for both sides." [43]

More's epigrams on Brixius' account of the episode are written far less in a spirit of bellicose ardor than in one of critical, satiric realism— the spirit of the London Reformers. Douglas Bush observes that Bacon, "in his role of practical psychologist, gave thanks to Machiavelli and others 'that write what men do, and not what they ought to do.' " [44] A like praise is due to More.

More's central target was Brixius' "falsehoods": "In your poem . . . you offer as history that which, since it is not the truth, is not history either" (*MLE*, No. 170). More began by quoting several of Brixius' verses "because some of the following epigrams make fun of them." Captain Hervé, as Brixius imagined him, stood on the deck heroically alone: missiles thick as hail flew at him, but with his shield he cleverly forced them to rebound upon those who had fired them (No. 172). Still holding the marvelous shield, he rushed forward to slaughter the English, while wielding simultaneously in the other hand no fewer than four weapons (No. 173). Finally Brixius, in the best medieval romance tradition (and hoary conventions of the classical epics loom behind), had represented the dying captain (presumably after jumping from his doomed ship but before the weight of his armor sank him) as delivering himself of a long prophetic speech. In this he foretold that a foster son of Apollo (i.e., a poet, Brixius) would give eternal fame to him and to the French navy (No. 176). In other words, as Hudson (p. 52) humorously observed, "Brixius represents himself as writing *Herveus* practically by request of its hero."

The English humanists' attack upon the nonsense which the English Renaissance inherited from the degenerate world of romantic chivalry is, indeed, an integral part of their social criticism. We may recognize the bracing spirit which in France will motivate much of Rabelais and which, later in sixteenth-century England, will underlie some of Falstaff's realistic and antiromantic humor directed against the idea that it is automatically glorious to die in battle. ("Food for powder, food for powder," says Sir John of his scarecrow troops, "they'll fill a pit as well as better.") The Morean satiric spirit has more in common with Sancho Panza than with the vainglorious Don Quixote.

Suavely ironic, More wrote of Hervé's alleged marvelous deeds:

All this is beyond the reach of understanding. How could one man fight with so many weapons, and that while one arm was burdened with a shield? Unyielding nature herself contradicts this battle. I think that in this passage [*MLE*, Nos. 172-73] you [Brixius] have omitted something. For when you represented heroic Hervé fighting indiscriminately with four weapons and a shield, perhaps the fact slipped your mind, but the reader ought to have been informed in advance that Hervé had five hands [No. 174].

Even funnier and more devastating, perhaps, is the image evoked by the second ironic suggestion More put forward, to solve the problem if the reader were so hardhearted (or hardheaded) as to disbelieve in the idea of five hands:

You wonder how Hervé could carry shield, sword, spear, javelins, and ax and fight with all of them, too. Well, his right hand is armed with the merciless battle-ax, his dire left is equipped with a sword all its own. At the same time he boldly holds (with clenched teeth) in his mouth the javelin and the spear to take the javelin's place. And because missiles thicker than wintry hail

77

threaten his head, on his head he wears his shield. . . . And so, as he rushed against the enemy, he was a strange monster . . . [*MLE*, No. 175].

Finally, More raised the innocent-seeming question; "Where did [Brixius] learn what his poem tells?" Again "unyielding nature herself" gave More the answer: "In your poem . . . you offer as history that which, since it is not the truth, is not history either" (*MLE*, Nos. 170, 176).

More's satire against Brixius reveals strikingly his humanist conception of both valid poetic and historical truth. In both regions of the mind he implicitly appeals for a common standard (which does not mean that they are identical). In neither does a writer have a right or privilege to insult either "unyielding nature" or the readers' intelligence. His criticism carries with it the idea that a good writer's duty is to tell the truth about what men actually do and (implicitly, in broad context) the idea that only when such truth is known and assimilated can desirable social reform be practicable. Once more, he was at work seeking a "working ideal for the civilization of the present and the future." [45]

As I see it, More (like Erasmus) was opening a vital way toward a literary growth whose flower came only, belatedly, in the last decades of the sixteenth century. Then, in their diverse ways, Sidney, Shakespeare, and Ben Jonson resumed the struggle to unite art and good sense. Sidney mocked the feebleness of stage romance's improbabilities; Shakespeare exposed the nature of tyranny in play after play; and Jonson invented a critical, satirical comedy in the hope that audiences which had graced the monsters of romantic fiction might be moved to like men. Nor is this new humanist spirit of critical realism necessarily fatal to all romance, as Shakespeare's best work so delightfully proves.

Henry VIII's second campaign in France had just enough success to induce him and Wolsey to prepare for a third in 1514. The vainglorious King's response to the sinking of the *Regent* in the sea fight with the *Cordélière* was characteristic, namely, to have built a ship greater than ever seen before in England and to name it *Henrie grace de Dieu*. Leo X took the lead for peace, however; Henry was willing to be content with the glory he had won; and Wolsey, who had organized and financed the war, jumped on the bandwagon and "openly claimed the credit" for the new "perpetual" peace made with France during the winter of 1513-14.[46] The results of this secret diplomacy, however, were not made public until the peace was signed on July 10, 1514.

For the English humanists, as for the general public, the winter of 1513-14 was a troubled one, colored by expectations that war with France would be resumed in the spring. As nearly as it can be dated, More's *History of Richard III*, which he apparently laid aside to work on the *Utopia*, emerged from this time (Chambers, pp. 115-16).

Both the epigrams against Brixius and the *Richard III* nakedly expose what were once acceptable and even widely lauded images of human greatness. More did not attack Captain Hervé as a person. Rather he satirized in outline the archetype of the chivalric hero, one of the most prominent concepts of human greatness thrown up by the Middle Ages. One might go further and say that, in some degree, More satirized the chivalric hero as chauvinist, one filled with blind, absurd devotion to an obsolete cause, with exaggerated and vainglorious patriotism. This attack on certain forms of heroism and patriotism is not nihilistic, it is selective and critical, born of a probing inquiry into the right uses and the abuses of the monarchic powers which set the English *Regent* and the French *Cordélière* originally on their collision course. Out of this inquiry emerged reformed or new images of greatness, of heroism, of patriotism—some fresh ideas on the meaning of legitimate sacrifice for a country's welfare.[47]

What was the utility of history to Sir Thomas More as he pushed forward in exploration of such concepts? The *History of Richard III* is certainly "as much an onslaught on tyranny as are some of More's epigrams" (Chambers, p. 116). In his epigrams on the coronation of Henry VIII, More exuberantly greeted the golden age of peaceful progress at its outset. With Henry's debut, "peace, ease, joy, and laughter have returned" to England. Enjoying solid peace at home, England need fear no "wars beyond the borders—if the French, for instance, join with the Scots, no one is afraid, provided that England is not divided." As for danger of civil strife between "powerful leaders," Henry's "nod" will put a stop to that (*MLE*, pp. 140-42). In a word, in 1509 More felt that a united England could ably resist joint attack and invasion by the Franco-Scottish alliance. The events of 1512-14, however, exhibited to the world not a united England rising to heroic necessity and defending herself against external aggression but an

Henrician England itself invading France, seeking martial glory in what the humanists felt was largely an unnecessary war, whatever its trumped-up pretexts.

The most persistent and original theme (i.e., original for the sixteenth century) in More's epigrams, many of which were done between 1509 and 1519, is exposure of the essential nature of tyranny. Some twelve of the most piercing and grim of these poems treat some phase of this idea. In his use of the classics More thus revealed once again the quality of his humanism, the power and understanding for present use that he had gained from his readings in antiquity. Let *On an Iron Statue* illustrate (here he adapted from the Greek Anthology): "To you, the king who ravaged the world, they set up a statue of iron—as far cheaper than bronze. This economy was the result of starvation, slaughter, the clash of arms, and destitution. These are the instruments by which your lust for wealth has brought ruin to all." [48]

In his *Richard III* More drew a basic contrast between two types of princes—the relatively just king versus the tyrant, Edward IV versus the Machiavellian Richard of Gloucester. Edward he represented as "a king of such governance and behaviour in time of peace (for in time of war each party must needs be other's enemy) that there was never any Prince of this land attaining the crown by battle, so heartily beloved . . ." (*MEW-C*, I, 399). Edward further appeared as "in peace just and merciful, in war sharp and fierce, in the field bold and hardy, and nevertheless no farther than wisdom would, adventurous. Whose wars, whoso well consider, he shall no less commend his wisdom where he avoided than his manhood where he vanquished" (*MEW-C*, I, 400). In other words, More did not automatically attack Edward as abusing his royal powers for having been at war, for war cannot always be avoided. But Edward sought to avoid unnecessary wars and to create the conditions of justice upon which a Christian peace might be based.

In contrast, the portrait that More drew of the ruthless and megalomaniac Richard is that of a tyrant who is permanently engaged in total war with the world. A man of great abilities, he recognized the validity of only one principle: self-interest. "None evil captain was he in the war, as to which his disposition was more meetly than for peace. . . . Friend and foe was muchwhat indifferent: where his advantage grew, he spared no man's death whose life withstood his purpose" (*MEW-C*, I, 402). At the dramatic core of the piece as it stands is the greatly sinister oration in which Buckingham offers the citizens the hideous alternatives of civil war or subjection to the tyrant, while reminding them that "the common adventure of open [i.e., civil] war, what about getting of the garland, keeping it, losing and winning again, it hath cost more English blood than twice the winning of France" (*MEW-C*, I, 441).

More's Richard is a tragic figure of large proportions: he is not inhuman or a monster but rather represents the horror that is realistically possible when a man of genius, but one who follows no mandates of love or law but only his compulsive and limitless criminal ambition, violently abuses monarchic power and becomes a despot, ruling by terror. In his vision of Richard's death, More went far beyond mere gratification of Tudor patriotic cultists' pleasure in a choice bit of vicarious slaughter, pleasure sweetened with moral virtue since Richard stood as the arch-villain opposed to the virtuous hero of the future Henry VII. More shows us a world far removed from the realm of chivalric grandeur such as the poet Brixius hoped to represent in his poetic vision of Captain Hervé's death. What More did was to express his critical humanist understanding of the death appropriate and necessary for a man more depraved than any wild beast: "[He perished] . . . as ye shall hereafter hear, slain in the field, hacked and hewn of his enemies' hands, harried on horseback dead, his hair in despite torn and tugged like a cur dog" (*MEW-C*, I, 451).

This, says the English humanist, is the way a tyrant should and did end—not in a false blaze of chivalric glory. As historian and as a student of tyranny More worked rather in the spirit of Julius Caesar's Stoic critics than in that of either Caesar himself (as his own historian) or his idolaters. As for the significance of the *History of Richard III* as the initiation of modern historical writing, or for its impact upon Shakespeare's drama of tyranny, or for its value as a classic of Renaissance English prose—all these are perhaps now too well known to require comment.[49] It seems most probable, however, that More broke off its writing with a feeling that it was too dangerous to be continued, and evidently he did not even intend that the Richard III fragment of his projected history should be published in his lifetime.[50]

During that uneasy winter of 1513-14, while More secretly set down his insights into a tyrant whose whole life was spent in a kind of total war upon the English people, Erasmus in March wrote a critical letter to Antony of Bergen, Abbot of St. Bertin (*EN*, II, 120-25). Evidently it was intended to reach many of the leading statesmen whose cooperation was requisite in order to attain a general peace (the Abbot's influence with Prince Charles, with Maximilian, and with the English nobility is mentioned). It is a remarkable letter, whose main argument is that Europe's rulers, for very practical reasons, should recognize that to effect and maintain a general peace is solidly in their own self-interest. Erasmus proposed that, when the issues at stake were well understood, it would be feasible to settle them through arbitration conducted under the joint administration of the Pope and the highest officers of the Roman Church. Erasmus does seek to evoke practical moves toward peace from the men in power, as a Christian duty; but the bulk of the letter appeals to realistic, dispassionate examination of the evidence, contemporary and historical. Along the way, Erasmus put forward a very daring concept of the rights and duties, the defensible interests, of a prince and his people.

One might say that the letter is implicitly addressed to any prince who might at the moment be considering whether to continue or to begin war upon his European neighbors. Let us, said Erasmus in effect, examine some rather obvious points. First, it is plain that in war humans display actions worse than the wildest brute beasts, who fight only occasionally and without arms (except claws, teeth, and so forth): men, however, have perverted their intelligence by devising ingenious machinery for human slaughter. One must wonder what drives men (seemingly rational beings) to such chronic madness. Second, in actual fact to achieve so-called success in war a prince must hire professional soldiers, depraved men who are the "scum of the earth." Once hired, however, these men spread their corruption everywhere, committing crimes against any likely victim nearby: thus the prince who hires them becomes a "slave" to them out of "anxiety to be revenged on others." Third, the facts are that war does not pay—not when all the costs are realistically counted: does not pay in money, in blood, or in true glory. And history shows that many princes, having begun avoidable wars, ended by losing all they had through revolution (this idea Erasmus rather implies than spells out: "I say nothing of the revolutions of states, which cannot take place without the most disastrous results"). Fourth, a prince who is tempted to make war for his rights as a sovereign may be on thin ice, so to speak. For when the legal rights of a ruler are balanced against the (unwritten) duties—i.e., against the rights of the people—then it is almost impossible honestly to justify a prince's waging war. (Erasmus throughout is clearly thinking of invasive war deliberately begun, not of self-defense.) While some Catholic authorities have sanctioned war as just, Erasmus finds their weight far overbalanced by the authority of Christ himself, of the Apostles, and the primitive Church fathers.

Fifth, suppose that a European prince asserts what he takes to be a legally perfect "title" to rule a disputed country—that he (as Erasmus proposed) submits it to arbitration by Church powers—and that he wins their decision but the other side refuses to obey and yield possession of the country? Erasmus makes a far-reaching suggestion: that by accepting a government, the common people gave their "consent"; that if they so peaceably consented (i.e., are satisfied with the ruler they have, even if his legal "title" is weak), then the people have a right to be left in peace and a prince has *no* right and would be most unwise (counting the economic costs) to insist upon a "title, perhaps unfounded after all." If the prince does not have to govern an enlarged kingdom, he is free of that much added burden.

Sixth (and last), Erasmus asks: in fact, speaking plainly, what are the so-called "rights" and "justifications" most often now in use? Do not some (relying on recent Church authority rather than Christ's teachings) "savour of a Christianity already becoming degenerate"? Are not some princes really criminals, whose crimes against "humanity" are praised by sycophants? And if you "look a little closely, you will find that it is generally the private interest of princes that give occasion to war." Is this "consistent with humanity"?

Several points are perhaps especially notable in Erasmus' letter to St. Bertin. One is his return, with stronger emphasis, to comparison of men and beasts at war. (Rather lightly he had touched this in the *Praise of Folly*.) Another is the hard realism of his argument that war does not pay when all the costs are counted.[51] These costs must include the degradation of slavery to soldiers, "this scum of mankind," to "cut-throats, gamblers, whoremongers, the meanest hireling[s]." They must include all the "crimes . . . committed under pretext of war, when as they say, in the midst of arms, laws are silent. . . ." The cost includes all the aftermath of this outburst of subhuman action—

"this moral contagion cannot but last for many years, even when the war is over." The candid prince must include in the cost "the lives and blood of so many thousand men." "And yet the greatest part of the mischief affects those who have no part in the fighting. The advantages of peace reach everybody; while in war for the most part even the conqueror weeps. . . ." Further notable is Erasmus' recognition that many princes are tempted to war by the "desire of glory." But he appeals grimly to the consent of sane humanity: ". . . that is no true glory which is mainly sought by wrongful acts." The far-distant growl of democratic revolution may be faintly heard in his following remark: "It is much more glorious to found, than to overthrow, states; but in these days it is the people that builds and maintains cities, and the folly of princes that destroys them." Has history some practical utility for would-be Renaissance empire builders? "With how much blood was the Roman empire raised, and how soon did it begin to fall!" [52]

To St. Bertin, Erasmus is perhaps most piercing in his discussion of the rights of kings. He lived, one might remember, in an age of despotisms:

But you will say, that the rights of sovereigns must be maintained. It is not for me to speak unadvisedly about the acts of princes. I only know this, that *summum jus*,—extreme right, is often *summa injuria*,—extreme wrong; there are princes who first decide what they want, and then look out for a title with which to cloak their proceedings. And in such great changes of human affairs, among so many treaties that have been made and abandoned, who, I ask you, need lack a title [*EN*, II, 123]?

Finally, there is just one kind of war that Erasmus seems slightly unsure about, as he notes how "pious authors" have sanctioned some wars, such as those in which "the peace of Christendom is defended against the invasion of barbarians" (*EN*, II, 124).

When he wrote the St. Bertin letter in the spring of 1514, however, Erasmus had already begun to think that his plan to make his lifelong home in England—England of humanism's hoped-for golden age— might have to go by the board. Ominously, he notes to St. Bertin how

. . . preparations for war are quickly changing the genius of the Island. . . . Moreover, while every island is in some degree a place of banishment, we are now confined more closely than ever by war, insomuch that it is difficult even to get a letter out. And I see, that some great disturbances are arising, the issues of which are uncertain. I trust it may please God mercifully to allay this tempest in the Christian world [*EN*, II, 121].

When Erasmus wrote the St. Bertin letter, the issue of continuing the war with France still hung in the air. The humanist critic's deepening and toughening realism shows in an episode which came to his mind again long afterward. It seems that Pope Leo X had sent a secret nuncio to London to help negotiate a peace between England and France, and early in June the papal ambassador, Canossa, dined with Erasmus, who had been kept in the dark as to the political identity of the Italian visitor. Erasmus asked his host, Ammonius (the King's Latin secretary), what truth might be in the current rumor that such a papal agent had really been sent? Had the Pope asked his advice, remarked Erasmus, he would *not* have counseled proposing a permanent peace at that time. His reasons may surprise some who have thought of him as an impractical dreamer. What is needed, he said, is a truce. As armies now are, to make peace suddenly after a bitter war is impractical for one grimly down-to-earth reason. For while the monarchs treat of peace conditions, the soldiery—at the very "smell of peace" (*odorem pacis*) are stirred to far worse deeds than in war itself! [53] As in the St. Bertin letter, when Erasmus thought of a good life, a good state, he gave the rights of princes no such supremacy that the rights and welfare of humanity, of the common people, could be ignored. "For my part, whatever fortune I have is in England," he wrote to St. Bertin, "but I would willingly resign it all, on condition that a Christian peace might be established between Christian sovereigns" (*EN*, II, 125). But the "genius of the island" was evidently changing as Henry VIII and Wolsey pursued dreams of martial glory, and in the same week that Erasmus wrote to St. Bertin, men in Europe had begun to speak of "the overgrown power of England" (*LP*, I, 2707).

On July 10, 1514, however, a "permanent" peace with France's aged King Louis XII was worked out, accompanied by rites full of "harmony, ceremony, tranquillity and blessed peace," in all of which Wolsey "gloried exceedingly" (Polydore Vergil, p. 225; Pollard, p. 19).

Erasmus came to England at the coronation of Henry VIII prepared to share in and to help create a golden age of humanism, one in which the new learning might be employed in designs for a new social order, a good life, for England.[54] By the spring of 1513, however, he had evidently begun to explore possible plans for leaving an island which (to him) was taking on some aspects of a prison, an island in which the expected "sweet liberty" as well as practical support from patrons all seemed to be seriously diminishing, the opportunities for literature and learning contracting month by month. If the outlook in England seemed to be growing ever more dark, on the other hand he had been invited to the court of Prince Charles, and he put out feelers in many directions. As far as aid for learning went, the suspension of the war effort did not mean that the talents in Henry's government were turned toward aid for social reform in England. Nevertheless, in May of 1515 we find Erasmus writing to a possible continental patron, and still the young Henry holds the figure of the noble prince, the "kindest of kings," who has—as it were—been drawn into wars by external circumstances and the idealism with which he supported Pope Julius' military ventures. (It is also true that this letter shows an extreme caution and circumspection, written so that if it came to Henry's own eyes [it was actually published at Louvain in 1516], it would appear undangerous.) No one man in particular is blamed (not Henry, not Wolsey) for England's plunge into wars: diplomacy here finds the cause in the "perversity of the times":

[Decline in support for learning in England] . . . has come to pass, not so much by any breach of faith on their [patrons'] part as by the perversity of the times. The King himself, who is the kindest of kings . . . has been carried away by the tempest of wars bursting suddenly upon us. With such spirit and zeal did this pious and generous young prince engage in the contest which he thought necessary for maintaining the dignity of the Roman Church. So also . . . Lord Mountjoy . . . has been so overwhelmed with the burdens of war, that he has given us more love than help [EN, II, 185].

We have perhaps seen clearly enough how the English humanists tended to regard Pope Julius II as the chief instigator of this "tempest of wars" but also to find in Julius a symbol of papal corruption and imperial folly. Is Erasmus saying that Henry VIII, in the innocence of youth, was duped by this pope?

Erasmus, of course, had some practical reasons for needing to spend time abroad in Basel, since only printers such as Froben (of whom there were then none in England) could produce such complex books as those on which Erasmus had so long labored in England: e.g., his edition of the New Testament in Greek, his edition of St. Jerome, and the vastly enlarged *Adages* which was to become one of the sixteenth century's most popular and influential books. The most famous man of learning his age had produced quietly went forward with plans to leave England. There has been modern debate as to whether or no humanism in England suffered an "arrest" under Henry VIII.[55] In the simplest sense, the progress of learning is arrested whenever a great (or even humble but devoted) man of learning is frustrated and gradually deprived of whatever is essential for his work, or whenever such a man is diverted from use of his greatest talent to mere administrative routine (the fate, in part, of More after he took government office). No more than other men could the humanists eat the air, promise-crammed. As he laid plans to leave England, Erasmus seemed to have awakened from the dream of peaceful humanistic progress which in 1509 had promised to become reality, "of an age that was really golden and isles that were happy," before "that Julian trumpet summoned all the world to arms. . . ."[56]

CHAPTER SIX

THE GENIUS OF THE ISLAND: DESIGNS FOR
A NEW SOCIAL ORDER—ERASMUS' AGAINST WAR (1515)

Although between the coronation of Henry VIII in 1509 and the "permanent" peace with France, made in July of 1514, England was impelled into a needless storm of war, in contrast the years between this peace and the strange diplomatic event of June, 1520—the Field of the Cloth of Gold—appeared to the humanists to be at last the time for a great flowering of the "genius of the island," in Erasmus' happy phrase. Now, if ever, it seemed that designs for a new order might well have their most practical impact upon social change.

These are the years when the great promise of the English humanist group came to its most triumphant literary achievements as well. From Erasmus there came, first, the definitive edition of the *Adages* (1515), with the powerful attacks upon abuses of monarchic power that he had worked out in England. From Thomas More there came the great *Utopia* (printed in December, 1516), one of the works which most decisively marks in England the watershed between the medieval and modern worlds. Erasmus in 1516 brought out his *Christian Prince,* which now stands in such formidable and ironic contrast to Machiavelli's *Prince* (also written by 1516 but not published until after the downfall of the Medicean tyranny which it was designed to bolster). From Erasmus in 1517 came the *Complaint of Peace Ejected from all Countries.*

In 1510, with his foundation of St. Paul's School, Dean John Colet had for the first time in England established the education of youth along humanistic lines. Then in 1517 that leader of the peace party in Henry VIII's early councils, Bishop Richard Fox, set himself against further participation in, as he himself said, "the intolerable enormities" of war, and instead, with the founding of Corpus Christi in Oxford, began the permanent establishment of humanism in that university. In 1517 the philosopher, More, finally agreed to enter the everyday service of his Christian prince; and while in April of that year Erasmus left England, his return to share in the work of creating the new social order seemed likely enough (as late as 1526 Wolsey renewed the invitation).

Then in October of 1518 Wolsey stage-managed his grandiose Treaty of Universal Peace, which led Erasmus to rejoice that the golden age might be coming after all but to mourn that he was too old to enjoy it. True, in 1516 an obscure German monk named Luther first communicated with Erasmus (*EE*, 501), and, on October 31, 1517, just eleven months after More dated the introductory letter in *Utopia*, the German nailed up some theses for debate, on a church door in Wittenberg. At the moment almost no one could have seen in this episode any formidable portent. In the favored island of England a tempered humanist optimism for peaceful social reform lasted at least until the diplomatic hypocrisies at the Field of the Cloth of Gold.

Finally, is was just after this brilliant chivalric spectacle that More and Erasmus met one already favorably known to them, the rising young humanist from Spain, Juan Luis Vives, whom both joined in bringing to England as a man who (said the age's most famous scholar) would in time overshadow the name of Erasmus (*EE*, 1107.6). With the arrival in England of Vives, as it were in lieu of Erasmus, the last principal actor in our Renaissance drama of ideas will have come on the stage.

So much by way of preview. Returning to the moment when peace was a great reality, in late 1514, let us trace the flowering of the genius of the island, perhaps best of all seen in humanist designs for a good life.

Between the summer of 1509 and July of 1514, except for the 1511 visit to Paris to arrange the printing of the *Praise of Folly*, Erasmus was at work in England. From August, 1511, to January, 1514, he was established at Cambridge, very busy with his editions of St. Jerome, Seneca, and Plutarch, with the monumental and daring edition of the Novum Testamentum, and with a greatly expanded version of his best-selling *Adages*, through which he poured his ranging learning and wit into pungent explication of and commentary upon quotations largely from the classics of antiquity. The growth of Erasmus' book of *Adages*, indeed, has rightly been described, by the greatest of Erasmian scholars, P. S. Allen, as typical of his lifework between 1500 and 1515.[1] Clearly

89

this lifework was inseparably bound up with early English humanism. He had undertaken the project for a vastly expanded revised edition by 1511 (*EE*, I, 521), and the prefatory letter was dated at London on January 5, 1513. The most remarkable and original of all the additions are the long essays in criticism of monarchic abuses of power, particularly in needless wars, and on needed reforms in states. The composition of these enlarged or new essays may safely be placed in England, between 1513 and 1515, with the bulk of the most famous, now known as *Erasmus Against War*, probably done in the winter of 1514-15.[2]

Three pieces concentrate upon royal misrule, and these are slashing critiques of tyranny—of the rights of rulers versus the assumed rights of the people under them. They are "The king and the fool are born such" (No. 1301), "The beetle attacks the eagle" (No. 2601), and the *"Sileni Alcibiadis"* (No. 2201). To Preserved Smith (p. 200), these express "a bitter hatred of monarchy . . . such as is hardly found elsewhere save in the French monarchomachs of St. Bartholomew and the Revolution." I should rather say that Erasmus, like More, had become acutely and realistically aware of what was rotten and in need of drastic reform in historical and contemporary monarchy. Unlike Machiavelli, whose handbook on how to succeed in tyranny was intended for the private use of Lorenzo de' Medici, the English humanists addressed themselves, with constructive as well as warning intent, to such kings as Henry VIII, who they passionately hoped could and would rule as Christian princes. *Their kind* of humanism thus sought practical ways by which the wisdom of antiquity and the Middle Ages could be employed to create a good life for their own time.

"The king and the fool are born such" (*Aut regem, aut fatuum nasci oportere*) develops a line of criticism touched on in the *Praise of Folly* in 1509—that is, of the hideous and all-too-common folly by which princes come to power, not merely unskilled in the difficult but teachable art of wise and just rule but actually encouraged by corrupt guardians to inflict ruin on mankind, as though a king could do no wrong. To summarize his argument:

In all ancient and modern history Erasmus recalls but one or two princes whose "signal folly did not inflict ruin on mankind." But perhaps most of the blame is mankind's own: only skilled pilots are allowed to guide ships, but ships of state are guided by pilots who have mostly never been trained in the most honorable and difficult of sciences, that of government.

But this vicious custom has been too long established to be easily altered: "Do we not see that noble cities are erected by the people and destroyed by princes? that a state grows rich by the industry of its citizens and is plundered by the rapacity of its rulers? That good laws are enacted by representatives of the people and violated by kings? that the commons love peace and the monarchs foment war?" (*EO*, II, 106C).

Erasmus does not find the trouble's roots to lie in congenital evil or original sin. A main source of princely corruption lies rather in the lack of sound education of princes for just government, a fatal defect which is channeled into war by the vicious counselors with whom rulers are typically surrounded:

The guardians of a prince aim never to let him become a man. The nobility, battening on public corruption, endeavor to make him as effeminate as possible by pleasure lest he should know what a prince ought to know. Villages are burnt, fields are devastated, temples pillaged, innocent citizens slaughtered, all things temporal and spiritual are confounded, while the king plays dice or dances, or amuses himself with fools, or with hunting or drinking [*EO*, II, 109D-110B].

Obviously this bitter indictment is not a simple characterization of Henry VIII and the war party in his councils. No one, I believe, ever accused Henry of being effeminate. The key contrast is rather implied by the problem, what is—rightly speaking—a "man"? (This whole humanist question was greatly to agitate the imagination of Shakespeare in a long series of histories and tragedies.)

Far more scathingly satiric is "The beetle attacks the eagle" (*Scarabeus aquilam quaerit*), which was completely new in the 1515 *Adages* (*BE-A*, p. 91). Apparently the satires of both Aristophanes and Lucian helped to power Erasmus' driving attack (*EO*, II, 869AB, 870F). In the first edition of 1500, done after his earliest visit to England, there was an adage, *Cantharus aquilam querit*, based on an Aesopian fable which told how a beetle, to avenge an insult, "cast the eagle's eggs out of the nest"—in other words, "do not provoke an angry and proud man with abuse" (Allen [1934], p. 62). The new comment began as an essay on impotent envy, then turned into seven and a half large folio pages of harshly antimonarchical satire on the heraldic devices of kings. Now in 1513-14, after closer acquaintance with Henry's and Wolsey's first war adventures, the theme suggested to Erasmus the inequality of the struggle between helpless subjects and a mighty monarch who was oblivious of owing duties to the governed, except "when in leisure moments he gives thanks to God 'who subdueth the people that is under me.'" In epitome this is his argument:

> Perhaps there once were just princes such as the philosopher-kings whom Plato pictured as ruling his ideal kingdom (i.e., the *Republic*). But in actual history scarcely one or two approach the ancient model. As for recent and contemporary rulers, they are almost unspeakable.
>
> How wretchedly they are mistitled! Typically the kings called "most serene" are those who perpetually trouble the world by their insensate wars; they are called "most Catholic" when utterly ignorant of Christ; "most illustrious" when plunged in abysmal ignorance; "gods" or divine when they are scarcely even worthy to be called men or human; "most invincible" who are always defeated. Believing that the wealth of all the people is their own royal treasure, all their thoughts are for laws, treaties, and wars designed to aggrandize the royal coffers. Things sacred and profane are indifferent to them.
>
> Like eagles, kings feed upon the "entrails" of lesser birds (i.e., their people's blood and treasure), seizing it rapaciously. The odious physiognomy of the eagle fits him to be a symbol of the kind of king who is most common. The eagle, like a human tyrant, with savage cruelty tortures its prey subtly and at length (*EO*, II, 873AE).

But upon further reflection, it appears that the king is more depraved than the eagle:

> If one reflects on the ruses, stratagems, schemes, and artifices with which evil princes are equipped to despoil the people—fiscal laws, amendments, false pretexts, pretended wars, denunciations, family alliances, it seems that the eagle is not worthy to bear the name of king (*EO*, II, 873AE).

Nevertheless, although the beast-man comparison is imprecise, it is satirically apt:

> The eagle is the image of a king, for he is neither beautiful, nor musical, nor fit for food, but he is carnivorous, rapacious, a brigand, a destroyer, a solitary, hated by all, a pest to all, who, though he

can do more harm than anyone, wishes to do more harm than he can [*EO*, II, 875F].

Running through these essays as a major theme is the idea that needless war is one of the evil prince's crowning follies.

Even more exacerbated is Erasmus' denunciation of war-mad princes in the essay on *Sileni Alcibiadis,* also new in the 1515 *Adages* (*BE-A*, p. 91). This does much more than discourse on the deceptiveness of appearances. In epitome:

> It refers to Socrates, a Silenus hideous to behold but a temple of the virtues within; and the thought suggested its contrary, the men whom that age knew only too well, popes and bishops, kings and nobles, lapped in pomp and circumstance and holden with pride in the plenitude of their power, but inwardly contemptuous of their subjects and careless of God's poor (Allen [1934], p. 64).

The whole essay is energized by a strong republican spirit, startling in an age of despotisms. Consider the hard realism with which Erasmus put forward definitions of just war and of peace as in fact understood by many contemporary rulers. "Just war" exists when princes join in robbing the peoples (i.e., with open violence); when they only conspire to the same end, they call it "peace." [3] The only good prince is said to be he who recognizes and executes his duties as a ruler. As for the use of war machines, Erasmus doubts (as in the *Praise of Folly*) that any sincere Christian can call such weapons "spiritual swords" and thus rightly use them against heretics and others. How can infidel Turks ever be convinced that Christianity is valid when they observe how the Christian "brothers" incessantly shed each other's blood in war? And he attacked the authority of Aristotle on matters where Christ's wisdom is ethically superior (*EO*, II, 772C-8C). Let priests, surely, fight only war of the spirit and avoid "the furious and rumbling business of tyrannous war," as the Tudor translator put it (*STC* 10507, D5r).

Of all the criticisms on man, war, and society in the 1515 *Adages, Erasmus Against War* is unquestionably the most remarkable. This piece is one of the highest points of the English humanist struggle for peaceful social change toward a good society—in the accurate sense, a utopia. As late as the 1513 edition, Erasmus' remarks on *Dulce inexperto bellum* used but four lines, but for the great work built up while in England and while in his closest creative relation with More and Colet, ten large folio pages were required.[4] For some years he had contemplated writing a systematic essay on war, and one such (now lost) was still in manuscript (1513-15), but this seems to have dealt mainly with the question whether "good" Christians might slay Turks,[5] a point of minor weight in his discourse on *Dulce bellum inexpertis* (sweet is war to those who know it not).

Its argument falls into two balanced major divisions, indicative of the dual but harmonious entity of early Tudor Christian humanism. (More exactly, there are about eight parts of humanist criticism to five that offer restrictedly Christian reasoning.) No conflict is implied between the two, however, for Erasmus harmonizes his reading of the classics, especially those of Roman Stoicism, with his reading of Scripture and the history of Christianity. In both sides Erasmus uses a much more sophisticated form of historical criticism than did John Colet in his 1496 lectures on Romans.

Before offering any detailed treatment of *Bellum Erasmi*, it may be useful to suggest the over-all structure of the piece very briefly. First, then, the humanist side. His basic premise seems to be that war is a man-made violation of uncorrupted man's true nature as a reasoning creature, potentially capable of living at peace with his fellows and his natural environment. He assumes that (as in the Stoic account of the rise of war) early man once lived in a substantially uncorrupted, rational, and happy state of peace. (He does not, however, assume that this good life lacked the pleasure of learning: no more than Seneca does he admire the noble savage ideal.) After disruption of the original state of peace, if one traced man in history down to the Christian era, a degenerative process worked until finally offensive war became chronic in society. This tragic degeneration, furthermore, had continued to the sixteenth century and would be intensified in the future unless wise men could change the downward course of human history, this sorry tale of progress and catastrophe. But Erasmus assumes that powerful rulers have a choice and that further massive man-made calamities are not inevitable. The ultimate question is, what practical actions can be taken which hold some solid promise of reducing war and creating a stable peace, now and for the future? The humanist side of his critique therefore has three stages: analysis of man's potentially peaceful nature, a theory of historical change, and concrete proposals for a good and peaceful social order (*EAW*, pp. 1-33, 48-54).

The Christian side of his argument balances the humanist part. Here his basic premise is that war is a violation of uncorrupted Christian man's true nature, whose model must be Christ's own life. Therefore war is virtually always unjust. Analyzing history, he maintains that as long as Christians followed the example of Christ and the Apostles, they took no part in armed strife. But, like the pagans before them, Christian men and official Christianity itself underwent gradual corruption, a process extending to the sixteenth century and exemplified in such war-making popes as Julius II. This corruption is, however, man-made and not inevitable in the nature of things. Therefore the ultimate question for the actual rulers in church and state (unless they desire to continue the corruption of war) is, what practical actions can be taken within the existing social structure in order to reduce wars and achieve a good, peaceful life at least among all Christians (*EAW*, pp. 34-47, 55-64)? In *Against War* Erasmus not only brought to sharp focus his earlier social criticism but very greatly strengthened it. Thus he produced almost the classic new humanist treatment of the theme, a treatment with which More's *Utopia* will be found in powerful agreement.

> . . . What is a man
> If his chief good and market of his time
> Be but to sleep and feed? A beast, no more.
> Sure, He that made us with such large discourse,
> Looking before and after, gave us not
> That capability and godlike reason
> To fust in us unused.
>
> *Hamlet*, IV.iv. 33-39

What is a man? *Erasmus Against War* begins with a eulogistic description of man's typically peaceful nature before he became corrupted, at some prehistoric time as echoed in poetic accounts of civilization's rise, accounts which some Roman Stoics treated as quasi-historical. Erasmus glorifies this unspoiled archetypal man as a reasonable creature with incalculable potential for a good life. First, man, unlike the carnivores, has no natural weapons, such as formidable teeth or claws. The very design of the human body indicates it was meant for peace. At birth, man alone is so helpless that he would perish without tender care (*EAW*, pp. 5-6). Nature brought forth man alone of all animals "wholly dedicate to be benevolent, pleasant, friendly, and wholesome to all other" (i.e., of his species) (*EAW*, pp. 15-16). But Nature's supreme gift to man was the

95

reasoning power which gives him ability to recognize and enjoy his unique talents for living in harmony with his own kind:

Nature not yet content with all this [i.e., with the gift of a benevolent social instinct], she hath given unto men alone the commodity of speech and reasoning: the which things verily may specially both get and nourish benevolence, so that nothing at all should be done among men by violence [*EAW*, p. 8].

So strong are the natural drives to love and care for, speak and reason with one's fellows that only a man who desired to abandon humanity and turn beast could long endure loneliness. But Nature has done more than endow man with reasoning power possessed by no other animal: Nature has given man curiosity, the desire to know, that underlies all civilized arts:

. . . yet nothing would be pleasant without a fellow: except a man would cast off all humanity, and forsaking his own kind would become a beast. Besides all this, Nature hath endued man with knowledge of liberal sciences and a fervent desire of knowledge: which things as it doth most specially withdraw man's wit from all beastly wildness, so hath it a special grace to get and knit together love and friendship [*EAW*, p. 8].

Moreover, Nature originally endowed (uncorrupted) man with the impulse basic to all altruism—pleasure in helping others: "Finally [Nature] hath endowed man with a spark of a godly mind: so that though he see no reward, yet of his own courage he delighteth to do every man good: for unto God it is most proper and natural . . . to do everybody good" (*EAW*, p. 8). Thus swiftly Erasmus evoked the image of human life in a quasi-historical ancient golden age, when men lived in essential harmony with their fellows within the human family.

With a sudden transition Erasmus then presented a savagely brilliant description of this same creature, man, in his present-day corrupted state, slaughtering his fellow men, ravaging the innocent, zealously laying in fiery waste whole towns and countrysides. The shock technique is not a trick. Erasmus well knew how people grow accustomed and deadened to familiar horrors. If language driven by the most intense conviction could crack this habituation to man's brutality to man, breaking down a tyranny of custom, he would have effected a breakthrough vital to his purpose in *Against War*. "Behold with philosophical eyes the image of man on the one side, and the image of war on the other side" (*EAW*, p. 5)—but these butchers and these victims alike once had all the ideal and godlike capability of archetypal uncorrupted man:

96

Imagine . . . that thou dost behold two hosts of barbarous people, of whom the look is fierce and cruel, and the voice horrible; the terrible and fearful rustling and glistering of their harness and weapons; the unlovely murmur of so huge a multitude; the eyes sternly menacing; the bloody blasts and terrible sounds of trumpets and clarions; the thundering of the guns, no less fearful than thunder indeed, but much more hurtful; the frenzied cry and clamour, the furious and mad running together, the outrageous slaughter, the cruel chances of them that flee and of those that are stricken down and slain, the heaps of slaughters, the fields overflowed with blood, the rivers dyed red with man's blood. . . . Verily, this tragedy containeth so many mischiefs, that it would abhor any man's heart to speak thereof [*EAW*, p. 10].

The comparatively "light and common" hurts he hardly mentions—whole countrysides set ablaze, thefts, rapes, old men butchered, churches robbed, "all things confounded"—not to speak of the inescapable horrors that accompany that chivalric princely ideal, "the most happy and just war of all." The aftermath spreads crime and corruption, for "Out of this fountain [war] spring so great companies of thieves, robbers, sacrilegers, and murderers" (*EAW*, pp. 10-11)—obviously ready to put their bloody skills to work. No wonder grammarians think the word "*bellum*" has its origin in "*Belva*," a brute beast! Erasmus declares, however, that man-at-war is viler by far than any known or conceivable wild animal (*EAW*, pp. 10-13).

One favorite neo-Stoic humanist way of probing into the tragedy of the human condition was through extended comparisons of men with beasts. For of course, in the traditional scale (or chain) of creation and being, man at his noblest held (as Hamlet put it) a place "a little lower than the angels," while the brute wild creatures were supposedly far, far below him.[6] Paradoxically, as things now stand, reasoned Erasmus, it is unfair to compare beasts and men—unfair to the beasts, that is—for men in war show an ethical depravity, a kind of conscientious cruelty and murderous ingenuity that puts them in a tragic class of vast dimensions, quite alone.

First of all, beasts of the same species (e.g., lions), however fierce and cruel, rarely fight each other. But no beast is more wild, cruel, and hurtful to his own species than man.

Second, at war beasts use motives and methods which appear to be ethically superior to man's, because they seem more natural, hence more honorable than civilized men's motives and techniques. For instance, beasts fight from hunger, or when hunted to death, or to protect their young; and in combat they use only their natural weapons and armor. In contrast, depraved modern men fight for the most trifling causes—a vain title, childish wrath, a wench, or pretexts even more to be scorned. What is more, in the art of war men have depraved their divine natural gift of reason in ways contrary to nature for cruel and corrupt ends. For instead of fighting with nature's weapons—teeth and bare hands, as the animals do—men employ innumerable devilishly invented machines and strategies in their wars.

Third, as a rule beasts fight only in single combat, in which at most one or two are wounded; while many animals agree lovingly together. Men, however, fight ceaselessly and by the hundred thousand in organized masses according to the "art" of war (*EAW*, pp. 13-14). It would be ethically better, he thought, to have men fight, as cannibals do, from motives of hunger rather than, as now, from mere customary hatred and with more-than-fiendish cruelties and inventions. If Nature could view her most wonderful creation, man, would she not wonder how the being originally alone brought forth to be peaceful, reasonable, and benevolent toward his kind had become thus degraded (*EAW*, pp. 14-17)? (In Lucian's *Menippus*, which More translated, the pagan philosopher looked down from the moon in wonder at the perpetual wars of that supposedly rational creature, man—wars endless and senseless as those of flies.)

As a humanist, how did Erasmus account for the historical degeneration of man? Using what seem to be largely Stoic sources, he offered a coherent explanation of the rise of war from its social beginnings to the founding of empires. Throughout his account harmonizes with the Stoic theory that the good life is that lived according to nature and that happiness consists of or depends largely upon protecting and maintaining a healthy state of mind in which the irrational elements in human nature (the passions) are kept under control by right reason. His account, while of great interest, can only be sketched here.

The first stage found man living naked in the woods at the world's beginning. There were no walled towns or weapons and, except for peril from wild beasts, men were happy. "Sorely grieved and destroyed" by wild beasts, men first made war upon them, but in self-defense only, not for pleasure. (Hence war began with the rupture of a primitive peace between men and animals.) The greatest captain then was he who could best defend men against wild animals, for it seemed to these men "most equable" (i.e., naturally just) to defend themselves against unprovoked attack. Hence Hercules became a god. When, however, it was held an honor to defend men against the beasts, young men began systematic hunting. "These were the first slaughters that men used; these were their spoils and robberies." Initially skins of slain beasts were only hung up as victory tokens, but soon use was found for the skins as winter clothing (*EAW*, pp. 18, 23). (Customs, however, can gain a tremendous hold over men, and on this theme Erasmus wrote an invective quite in the Senecan vein.)

The second stage in war's rise began when man, now used to killing wild beasts, gradually forsook his earlier vegetarianism. Thus he found additional utility in slaughter and, worse, now found pleasure in cruelty which would formerly have horrified him. But custom dulled sensibility: soon no horror was felt at flesh-eating, and rising new generations ceased to find in it matter for comment or revulsion. Human degeneration accelerated its pace, as gluttony tyrannized over men who had quite forgotten that formerly they took animal slaughter to be a cruel deed. Now in cold blood not only wild but harmless and amiable household beasts began to be slain for food. As yet, however, manslaughter had been considered a crime of unthinkable horror.

The third stage found manslaughter becoming respectable and even rising to the status of a profession. Erasmus hazards that such vicious passions may perhaps be controlled and evil opportunity denied them (*EAW*, p. 20), but once evil passions are loosed in man, they tend to inundate and overwhelm all virtue. In the third phase of degeneration from the golden age men were prompted by wrath to slay their fellow men, as they had slain beasts. At first this cruelty of man toward man happened only between isolated individuals, and only the simplest weapons were used: clubs and stones. However, it soon became accounted "no small colour of equity" for a man to slay an enemy who had wronged him. Praise outright was soon after this given for slaying "violent and mischievous men" in general. Nor did single combat long continue to be the style. In time men banded together to combat other bands simply for petty spoils, "and what is now robbery was then war" (*EAW*, pp. 20-21). Still only the simplest and crudest weapons were in use.

Then followed a gradual but continued improvement in weapons technology. After his degeneration had gone on for a time, man's reason— fraught for good or ill—worked him evil as his inventive genius produced ingenious devices for slaughter. When custom had won its acceptance, this too was called honorable. Although war was now more cruel than formerly, it was still mainly defensive; some courtesies and conventions (such as truces for burial of the dead) were respected; and a rude code governed fighting.

The last stage saw the formation of empires. As offensive wars of greed and conquest developed, man's progressive degeneration proceeded with frightful rapidity. Such wars became a characteristic instrument of tyrants. In the process all the original virtues of uncorrupted man (in his natural state) disappeared. Benevolence, kindness, humanity—all were discarded. Now uncontrolled evil passions, combined with perversely inventive reason, spurred the degradation of man. Finally all thought of the original, simple, relatively equitable (i.e., defensive) motive of war was forgotten. Spread then throughout the world were huge numbers of savage men devoted solely to the murder of strangers, not for personal hate or revenge, but merely for hope of gain. Even this was at last termed honorable. Out of this historical process, said Erasmus, empires rose in the world, and since then man has almost continually been at war with his own kind (*EAW*, pp. 22-23). This last stage, continued, is that in which he found contemporary Europe.

After this passionate explanation of war's rise in the world, Erasmus put forward his grim definition of modern war as no better than common murder, robbery, and massive lunacy—although many gentlemen find all these things very amusing:

War, what other thing is it than a common manslaughter of many men [*multorum commune homicidium*] together, and a robbery, the which, the farther it sprawleth abroad, the more mischievous it is? But many gross gentlemen nowadays laugh merrily at these things, as though they were the dreams and dotings [*deliramenta*] of schoolmen, the which, saving the shape, have no point of manhood, yet seem they in their own conceit to be gods. And yet of these beginnings, we see we be run so far in madness [*insaniae*], that we do naught else all our life-days . . . [*EAW*, pp. 23-24].

Erasmus' argument had now reached its third main stage. Practically speaking, what is to be done in the present day? Suppose you are right so far—intelligent Renaissance princes, noblemen, or common soldiers might have asked him—what of it? We must deal realistically with man and war as they *now* are. Is the situation really as bad as you (Erasmus) say it is? Is it not, in counterargument, obvious that war pays huge rewards

—in personal and national economic gain (loot, tribute, and so forth), in sweet revenge, in empire building?

Placing ethical considerations to one side, Erasmus took the bold position that enlightened self-interest alone, at all levels in society (apart, of course, from the debauched professional soldiery to whom war is a way of life) must, when the problem is examined with full candor, conclude it to be impossible that war can be a profitable method of settling disputes. Indeed, men must be truly insane who, after reckoning in advance (as rational men presumably should) the costs in blood and gold, yet plunge of their own free will into offensive war: "And so at last shall appear, how great madness it is, with so great tumult, with so great labours, with such intolerable expenses, with so many calamities, affectionately to desire war: whereas agreement might be bought with far less price" (*EAW*, p. 25).

His practical proposal is that leaders on both sides, as rational men pursuing self-interest, should count in advance *all* war's costs. When this is done, wisdom will dictate settling disputes quietly by arbitration. (It should, of course, be kept in mind that Erasmus was thinking of disputes among the various Christian nations of Europe primarily.) When full accounting is made of costs, all military triumphs turn out to be Cadmean: everyone suffers ruin. It is surely obvious that mankind is the victim of countless unavoidable natural evils (cf. Hamlet's "natural ills that flesh is heir to")—earthquakes, lightnings, great floods, and the ever-present "mortal pestilence," for example, not to speak of the new diseases that constantly appear. In contrast, war is a man-made calamity and one worse than all the others combined.[7] Furthermore, it is entirely practical to prevent most wars, provided men in places of power use right reason. When men might have the practical and real pleasures and profits of peace, how can they be in their right minds when they actually seek such a monstrous and avoidable calamity (*EAW*, p. 31)?

Does war profit nobleman and common soldier alike? (As for the economic costs, England by 1514 had begun to know full well the French war's huge price.) Erasmus stressed the damage war often does to the nobility who usually supported it (e.g., the near-annihilation of the Scots nobles at Flodden in 1513). He also spoke to the common men who, hoping for gain, take up soldiering. What price gain and glory? After a spell of physical wretchedness and abuse, they have at last a fine choice, that between cruel slaughter or being slaughtered:

What is he that can reckon all the incommodious life that the most foolish soldiers suffer in the field? And for that worthy to endure worse, in that they will suffer it willingly. Their meat is so ill that an ox of Cyprus would be loath to eat it; they have but little sleep, nor yet that at their own pleasure. Their tents on every side are open to the wind. What, a tent? No, no; they must all the day long, be it hot or cold, wet or dry, stand in the open air, sleep on the bare ground, stand in their harness. They must suffer hunger, thirst, cold, heat, dust, showers; they must be obedient to their captains; sometimes they be clapped on the pate with a warder or truncheon: so that there is no bondage so vile as the bondage of soldiers. Besides all this, at the sorrowful sign given to fight, they must run headlong to death: for either they must slay cruelly, or be slain wretchedly. So many sorrowful labours must they take in hand, that they may bring to pass that thing which is most wretched of all other [*EAW*, p. 32].

As for material gain from war, on full balance it is an illusion. For a tenth of its cost in capture through war a flourishing town may be built peacefully. Ironically, in conquest a town is first destroyed, then rebuilt (*EAW*, pp. 32-33).

Yes, the soldiers admit, war is costly. But how sweet is revenge—*that* hurts our enemy. So? said Erasmus, quite apart from the savagery and inhumanity involved, what does this sweet revenge cost? Before you can hurt your enemy, you must first do great harm to your own people. What makes you think, moreover, that you are certain to achieve even such a Pyrrhic victory? History shows that mere chance—"Fortune"—rules battles everywhere, and only a madman would risk so much on Fortune's whim (*EAW*, pp. 32-33).

Finally, what about the modern value of war for purposes of empire building? (The early Tudor humanists lived, after all, in a time when the lust for modern imperial aggrandizement was in its infancy.) Acidly, Erasmus indicts the classic types of the empire builder as insane world robbers—men whose interests were criminally opposed to those of the vast majority of humanity. Some relative praise may nevertheless be given even to an Alexander the Great, for such ancients were ethically superior to their modern apes (e.g., they used ethically superior [simpler] weapons, they warred only for grand causes, and sometimes they spread benefits of a superior civilization in the train of conquest). The modern Christian princes surpass the ancient imperialists in vile, witty brutalities; and they simply leave desolation in their wake:

Xerxes doted, when he led out of his own country that huge multitude of people to make war upon the Greeks. . . . Who will deny that Alexander the Great was mad also? He, the young God, wished that there were many worlds, the which he might conquer—so great a fever of vainglory had embraced his young lusty courage. And yet these same men, the which Seneca doubted not to call mad thieves [*furiosos latrones*], warred after a gentler fashion than we do: they were more faithful of their promise in war, nor they used not so mischievous engines in war, nor such crafts and subtleties, nor they warred not for so light causes [*frivolis titulis*] as we Christian men [*pseudochristiani*] do. They rejoiced to advance and enrich such provinces as they had conquered by war; and the rude people, that lived like wild beasts without laws, learning, or good manners, they taught them both civil conditions and crafts, whereby they might live like men. In countries that were not inhabited with people, they builded cities, and made them both fair and profitable . . . and with a thousand other commodities they helped the life of man. So that then it was right expedient to be overcome. Yea, and how many things read we, that were either wisely done, or soberly spoken of them in the midst of their wars. As for those things, that are done in Christian men's wars they are more filthy and cruel than is convenient here to rehearse. Moreover, look what was worst in the heathen peoples' wars, in that we follow them, yea, we pass them [*EAW*, pp. 42-44].

When we recall More's and Erasmus' 1505-6 work on Lucian's satires on the tyrant, as well as the antityrannical theme so strong in More's epigrams, it appears that these humanists had already drawn for the English Renaissance the outlines of the tyrant-overreacher tragedy.

Because earlier humanist social criticism, beginning with Colet in 1496, dealt with increasing emphasis on the idea that between Christians war was profoundly unjust, the Christian side of Erasmus' argument in *Against War* can be dealt with more summarily than the humanistic. The humanist part of the essay traced the rise of war until it had become the chronic condition of pagan mankind. Historically, Erasmus maintains, Christ himself defined the essential Christian way of life. Charity, humility, poverty—to suffer and to love—all these and only these Christ enjoined upon Christians. This, in contrast to military victory, was the true "Victory of Christ." "So he reigned, so he warred, so he overcame, so he triumphed" (*EAW*, p. 35). Christians are all brothers, and therefore between them war is parricide. True, in pre-Christian times the original "bond of nature" became so perverted that war's madness became usual, but the pagan example cannot serve for true Christians:

But admit that either foolishness, or wrath, or ambition, or covetousness, or outrageous cruelty, or else (which I think more like) the furies sent from hell, should ravish and draw the heathen people to this madness. Yet from whence cometh it into our minds, that one Christian man should draw his weapon to bathe it in another Christian man's blood? It is called parricide, if the one brother slay the other. And yet is a Christian man nearer joined to one another than is one brother to another: except the bonds of nature be stronger than the bonds of Christ. What abominable thing, then, is it to see them almost continually fighting? [*EAW*, pp. 33-34].

Like Colet, who was led by use of the historical method in criticism toward the same conclusion, Erasmus based his whole argument—flying in the face of the dominant orthodox position of the late medieval Roman church—on the ultimate authority on the good life for Christians, Christ's example, asserting that in Christ's life there is nothing that "breathes not of peace." The fathers of the primitive church, such as St. Jerome, whose works Erasmus edited while at Cambridge, rightly understood Christ's teaching on war. "All the true Christian writers," said Erasmus, support this ideal; and in an international community based on it war is as though hand and foot of one body fought each other (*EAW*, p. 35).[8] Hence the duty of truly Christian popes to strive for and maintain peace in Christendom (the ideal of the *Pax Ecclesiae*) (*EAW*, pp. 63-64). In sum, for uncorrupted *Christian man* peace is the natural state and war is a violation of his original nature.

Then, as on the humanist side of *Against War*, Erasmus, by a witty device, offered beside this image of Christians at peace the reality of his own day. Imagine the arrival on earth from outer space of a philosopher who learns with delight that the planet is peopled by a brute-creature, man, who possesses a godlike power of reason and whom Christ has taught to love. What is this wondrous creature's favorite occupation? asks the happy philosopher. And he is dumfounded to learn that man lives in almost continual war with his fellows, that in war he is more depraved than any other animal, and that the Christians are so far from exhibiting higher ethical standards than the pagans that they overmatch them in military savagery (*EAW*, pp. 37-39).

How, then, did Erasmus explain the degeneration of Christians from the antiwar ideal held by Christ and practiced in the primitive Church? Briefly, he blamed scholasticism—and with it the gradual substitution of Aristotle's authority, as well as that of civil law, for the authority of Christ's own original teaching. A summary will show his reasoning:

Pagan learning was first used by orthodox Christians only to refute heretics who argued from pagan "philosophers, poets, and orators." Soon, however, "brawling disputations" exceeded all bounds. Worse, Aristotle was received "into the midst of divinity" (i.e., theology), and in time his authority became reputed almost holier than that of Christ himself. "For if Christ spake anything that did little agree with our life, by interpretation with Aristotle it was lawful to make it serve their [the scholastics'] purpose." "And we endeavour . . . to glue fast together the decrees of this man [Aristotle, but also, by inference, Aquinas] and the doctrine of Christ, which is as likely a thing as to mingle fire and water together."

Second, Christians accepted a "gobbet of the civil laws," because equity seemed to be in them. But the civil law is not that of Christ, for civil law defends only civil rights—the legality, according to precedent, of violent defense against violent attack. Obviously, however, civil law approves much that is disallowed by Christ's own teaching. Most crucially, lawyers "praise war as a noble thing, so it be just."

Third, scholastic sophistries have made men forget that Christ's teachings, including those against war, were designed to show the practical way to a good life. The interminable commentaries of logicians, philosophers, and lawyers have by now so defiled "all the doctrine of Christ" that a lifetime would be hardly enough to wade through them to come at Christ's direct teachings. Anyway, the man who approached Christ through such commentators would be fully infected with corrupt worldly opinions before he arrived at the destination. At best a conventionally trained schoolman will apply the true Christian doctrines, not to life itself, but rather to the minds of earlier writers! By now the pollution of pure Christian ethics with scholastic sophistry has gone so far and become so rooted in the universities that the schoolmen think it a "heinous deed" for a man to study the Scriptures "which hath not buried himself up to the hard ears in these trifles, or rather sophistries of Aristotle" (*EAW*, pp. 39-42).[9]

This degeneration within scholasticism was, moreover, accompanied by corruption proceeding from popes ambitious for wealth and temporal power. (The example of Pope Julius II was too notorious and recent to require emphasis.) Events speak loudly enough: "What stormy rumblings, what tearings of leagues, and what piteous slaughters of men have we seen ourselves within these past few years?" (*EAW*, p. 42).

Erasmus had now brought both the humanist and the Christian sides of his argument in *Against War* to the present. The last main section of *Against War*, therefore, is concerned with the joint responsibility for peace or war of the highest authorities in the state and in the church. Erasmus examines and refutes in turn the validity of the six principal pretexts for "just" war between Christian nations. The first four may be summarized:

1. To the claim that war was allowed in the Old Testament (and by inference should be as "just" in the sixteenth century), Erasmus replied that the Jews were not Christians and that Christ bade Peter put up his sword.

2. For this last reason he also repudiated the time-honored orthodox theory of the two swords, one "temporal" and the other "spiritual," by which for centuries the Church had justified armed violence against heretics and war against infidels.

3. Erasmus met squarely his opponents' arguments based on the authority of key patristic writings or canon law. Tersely he said that the fathers who held war "just" for Christians were few compared to those "which were before them, which in their writings persuade us to flee war . . . ," while many of the pro-war writers were of a later period when Christ's own doctrine "waxed cold." Even St. Thomas Aquinas' authority was rejected in favor of Christ's own.

4. Is not war socially beneficial because it punishes evildoers? Erasmus asserted it were better that a handful of criminals should go unpunished than that innocent thousands suffer untold injury. For the social benefits of war can possibly accrue only to a few "vengeable thieves, hired soldiers, and strong robbers, and perhaps . . . a few captains"—very likely those who craftily helped provoke war so as to get employment (*EAW*, pp. 48-49).

His fifth point was dynamite: is it not certainly true that princes "must fight for their right"? (Here Erasmus touched an idea which was to be pivotal in antidespotic controversy for centuries to come.) Like More in the first book of *Utopia*, Erasmus noted realistically that whenever princes desired to make war, quasi-legalistic pretexts were never known to be lacking (e.g., that used by Henry VIII to justify war against France in 1512). His main argument here is of amazing boldness, for it goes to the very root and justification for kingship itself. First he observed that it was unmeet for him "to dispute overboldly of prince's matters . . . though I might do it without danger . . ." (*EAW*, p. 50). It is worth remembering that he lived when tyrant-kings customarily claimed divine sanction and virtual immunity from earthly judgment for their deeds, like Shakespeare's Richard II.

In brief, he declared that, unlike brute beasts, all men are "free by nature." Princes gain power only by the "consent of the people" (a familiar Stoic idea). If this power is abused, as through needless wars, the people have a right to demand it back again. In other words, kings have no "right" to injure their people or, more broadly, humanity at large; for such a right could only be justified by the untrue assumption that the common people, like beasts, have no human rights of their own. His indictment of evil princes to some degree fitted every king in Europe when he declared that only sheer trivialities were the prime cause of the incessant contemporary wars and manslaughters:

We call that a dominion, which is but an administration. The power and authority over men, which be free by Nature, and over brute beasts, is not all one. What power and sovereignty you have, you have it by the consent of the people. And if I be not deceived, he that hath authority to give, hath authority to take away again. Will ye see how small a matter it is that we make all our tumult for? The strife is not, whether this city or that should be obeisant to a good prince, and not in the bondage of a tyrant; but whether Ferdinand or Sigismund hath the better title to it, whether that city ought to pay tribute to Philip or King Louis. This is that noble right, for the which all the world is thus vexed and troubled with wars and manslaughter [*EAW*, pp. 50-51].[10]

Even supposing that princely powers to make war are really as absolute as princes now believe, what truly wise king—one who stopped to reckon the certain losses as well as the uncertain gains from a proposed war— would fail to grasp the fact that military triumphs are like lawsuits which destroy the sought-after prize before it can be enjoyed? The benefits of peaceful arbitration are practical and solid. Most titles have something dubious in their history. Bloodshed to change them, when the community as it is ruled is prosperous, is evil and stupid because any newly established title is itself uncertain in this world where all things change—"at the scornful pleasure of fortune they roll to and fro, as the waves of the sea." Hence there is truth in the (Ciceronian) idea "that unjust peace is far better than righteous war" (*EAW*, pp. 50-54).

The sixth and last major orthodox justification of war had long sanctioned strife of Christians against infidels—e.g., the contemporary Turks. While not disapproving outright, Erasmus thought even such wars ethically dubious. (Here he seems to reflect the basic Stoic idea that all men are brothers.) At bottom, he declared, "if we set aside the title and sign of the Cross, we fight Turks against Turks" (*EAW*, pp. 55-56).

Those who, like the London Reformers, seek practical ways to reshape social patterns must naturally recognize the momentum of existing human motivations. Grimly Erasmus scrutinized some major contemporary psychological drives, seeking answers to the urgent question: why do Christians now make wars? The first recalls Stoic speculation on the idea that human nature may have inherent latent defects that make a life of reason difficult if not impossible. Says Erasmus, as for the foolishness and malice that stirs many men to make war, it is a thing "more to be lamented than reasoned." Traditional education is at fault; for young inexperienced men join in wars from sheer foolhardiness as a result of reading untruthful narrative "histories, written of some foolish authors. . . ." Experienced older men (flatterers, lawyers, even divines and bishops), for their own reasons, have urged young men to go to war. As ever, would-be tyrants stir up war the more readily to abrogate laws and seize power. Finally, many men hurry to war to find what they take to be true glory. But to Erasmus glory won through manslaughter is evil and false. If men desire true glory, it is to be had in peace: "It is a thing much more magnificent and glorious to save than to destroy; much more gay and goodly to build a city than to overthrow and destroy a city." And even if a Christian prince were to win a war "prosperously," with whom must he share this martial glory but with barbarous mercenary soldiers, "the very dregs of all men living," "if we must needs call such . . . monsters men" (*EAW*, pp. 57-60).

Let Pope Julius have the false glory resulting from his years of war, accompanied by "great decay" in the church. Through the peace now (i.e., 1514-15) restored to Christendom, "Leo shall get more true glory" than was ever won by his predecessor (*EAW*, pp. 63-[65]). Thus he ended the essay on an optimistic note.

In effect Erasmus' *Against War* was an open letter, addressed to Pope Leo X and to all the great Christian princes of Europe. When he wrote, the grand medieval fabric of church and state relationships still appeared to exist. Obviously it was in shockingly bad repair, but it was not clearly beyond reconstruction. From the viewpoint of More, Erasmus, and Colet, engaged as they were in a sustained effort to induce those actually in power to initiate and carry through peaceful reforms leading toward a good life, optimism seemed justified. These critics blamed Pope Julius II, not Henry VIII or Wolsey, for England's war with France in 1512-13. Now, however, the pacific Leo X, in July, 1514, had proved that a truly Christian pope could arbitrate between warring princes and induce them to make "permanent" peace. Thus the supreme ideal of the *Pax Ecclesiae* still seemed to be practicable. Erasmus' *Against War* was a most gallant, passionate, and shrewdly reasoned effort to bring Europe's leaders to their collective Christian senses while there was yet time to make the vital necessary reforms in church and state upon which enduring peace could rest.

The late spring of 1515 was thus a time of joy and wonder for the English humanists—and a time of intense literary creativity. Erasmus had gone to Basel in August of 1514 to see the *Adages* through the Froben printing house (*EE*, I, 521n.), a work completed by mid-March of 1515, after which he left for England (*EE*, II, 67n.). By May 7 he was in London again, with his work on the Christian prince "in hand." Although the sketchiness of material support for his scholarly work still induced him to look abroad for more substantial aid, he blamed the "perversity of the times" for this falling off, while Henry VIII (almost as in 1509) still enjoyed the status of the almost ideal Christian prince:

The King himself, who is the kindest of kings . . . has been carried away by the tempest of wars bursting suddenly upon us. With such spirit and zeal did this pious and generous young prince engage in the contest which he thought necessary for maintaining the dignity of the Roman Church. So also . . . Lord Mountjoy . . . has been so overwhelmed by the burdens of war, that he has given us more love than help. . . . Now that, by the labours of Pope Leo, peace is restored to the world, my position is much improved. . . .[11]

Meanwhile Thomas More, during intervals of waiting while engaged with Cuthbert Tunstall on the King's commercial peace mission to Flanders, was—as nearly as has been determined—writing the second book of the *Utopia*, which describes the good life developed in that fortunate isle after the wise beginnings originally made by a great prince.[12] Finding that More was at Bruges, Erasmus wrote cheerfully to Peter Gillis there that "the two most learned men of all England are now at Bruges" (*EN*, II, 205-6). Wolsey himself seemed kindly disposed toward humanism: on July 9 Tunstall wrote to him that " 'Master More at this time, as being at a low ebb, desires by your grace to be set on float again' " (*MC*, p. 16). On May 21 Erasmus elaborately congratulated Pope Leo on his glorious work, through which "by a sudden revolution a worse than iron age was turned to gold," a letter which the Pope received with evident great favor.[13] Although More had not yet decided to enter Henry VIII's service wholly, the "kindest of kings" exerted great magnetism at this time of peace. On February 18, 1516, Ammonius wrote to Erasmus that "More is now returned home from his friends in Flanders, having fulfilled his mission with great credit. He now haunts with us the smoky chambers of the Palace" (*EN*, II, 243).

Furthermore, the brilliant renaissance in England was beginning to receive notice abroad. Erasmus' *Christian Knight* of 1504, with its relatively mild attack on the folly of war, began in 1515 to be widely popular.[14] Erasmus' far-reaching correspondence had the effect of making known throughout Europe the great talents at work in England.[15] A Louvain humanist, humorless and unpenetrated by Erasmus' irony and social vision, had attacked the *Praise of Folly*, suggesting that instead Erasmus should write a "Praise of Wisdom." With confidence, in the bright October of 1515, More wrote in reply a spirited explanation and defense of his friend's satire.[16]

Perhaps even more remarkable was the reception of Erasmus' *Adages*, with their blistering attacks upon monarchic abuses of power through needless wars. The leading French humanist, Guillaume Budé, probably meaning to refer to Erasmus' recently printed edition of the Novum Testamentum, had expressed surprise, as Erasmus put it, that he "employed so much ingenuity in slight and subtle discussions . . . which were treated as matters of serious importance." Replying, Erasmus chose deliberately to misunderstand, for he cited proudly, as "trifles" then highly praised by important men, almost all the scathing antiwar and antimonarchical criticisms in the *Adages*, including "The king and the fool are born such," "Sileni Alcibiadis," and his essay "Against War." Of course, he said ironically, "what we have said upon the proverb, 'the beetle and the eagle,' was merely an ingenious jest." "Still," he wrote with emphasis, "these trifles, however slight, I certainly prefer to any of the productions of Darkness." [17] From the exchange we infer that English social criticism was most distinctively a product of the humanist approach of Colet, Erasmus, and More, and that their ideals were by no means always meaningful to those of another breed.

Considering only the period until Erasmus' death in 1536, the demand for what he had to say on war and monarchy appears to have been phenomenal. First, the complete *Adages* (a huge folio which he drolly termed a "tiny work"—*opere minuto*) had seven printings. Froben knew a best seller when he had one, and in early 1517 he began to print *Bellum Erasmi*, the *Sileni Alcibiadis*, and the *Scarabeus* as separate pamphlets. *Against War* alone ran through thirteen editions, printed in nine cities as other printers took up the good work. There were also translations into German (1519, 1520) and into English (1533-34).[18]

Taking it all in all, it is clear that a climate of opinion strongly favorable to the new social criticism was apparent by late 1515 or early 1516.

With More and Erasmus, after 1505-6, a recurrent theme is that while good kings are a theoretical possibility, tyrants are an ever-present danger. Again and again their satire exposes the maleducation of future kings— the customary process by which the young prince is corrupted and brought up to be either irresponsible or a potential tyrant.

Clearly, to the English humanists, the education of the prince was crucial, for by it inevitably a good life in the commonwealth would be either enhanced or ruined. The results of their reflections emerged in reformed programs for education, first of the prince himself, then more broadly of the leaders under him.[1] In the great criticisms in the *Adages* Erasmus bitterly attacked abuses of power, particularly in the form of needless and unchristian wars. Since he attributed to the princes the power to make or avoid war, in a sense Erasmus had attacked the results of vile education among princes. This much was destructive criticism.

In his famous *Education of the Christian Prince*—the *Institutio principis Christiani* (Basel, May, 1516)—Erasmus turned to a positive approach. He had the treatise "in hand" by May 15, 1515, after his return to London (*EE*, 334.170). In January, 1516, he was appointed Councillor to Charles, the sixteen-year-old prince who had just succeeded to the throne of Spain, and it was to Prince Charles that he dedicated the book after his return to Basel by March (*EE*, II, 161n., 205-8). The *Christian Prince*, written in England and a part of English humanist literature, was presented to Charles after Erasmus' appointment.[2] It is a distinguished and (in comparison to Machiavelli's *Prince*, also done by 1516) curiously neglected element in what Chambers (p. 121) happily termed "the wonderful year of Erasmian reform," although he dismissed Erasmus' book in one sentence as "a passionate plea for peace, arbitration, mercy to the poor, the fostering of learning—but, above all, for peace."

Not infrequently Erasmus' *Christian Prince* receives rather short criti-

Erasmus. Portrait by Holbein
Courtesy of the Louvre

cal shrift on the grounds that he was a cloud-borne dreamer, incurably given to offering impossibly idealistic advice instead of realistic counsel based upon a sound estimate of what human nature really contains. When not accused of woolly-headedness, he is said to pursue his ideals of humanity and correspondingly to disregard everyday realities.[3] Insofar as his social criticism in the *Christian Prince* does not attempt to deal with specific problems of politics, the charge is of course true. On the other hand, this was not his intention in the work, which rather tried to offer some basic, time-tested principles for the guidance of the prince in making day-to-day executive decisions. I should rather agree with Preserved Smith (p. 198) that "His essay was above all practical," based on his wide reading and on his "own observations of the needs of his country." If attacks on Erasmus (or on the English humanists generally) are based on the premise that they put vastly too much stock in the educability of man and in his potential capacity for a life of decent reason, one might counter—religion apart, what else is there to hope for?

Underlying the *Christian Prince* are certain premises or assumptions that are generally not stated when it is discussed. Machiavelli's *Prince* is best understood against the background of Florentine politics. Erasmus' essay is perhaps better understood against the background of the *Pax ecclesiae* which prevailed when he wrote. These appear to be some of his main assumptions: (1) that Pope Leo X, an experienced statesman and a good pope, had in fact arbitrated between the princes to end the English-French war of 1512-13; (2) that the "fatal storm" of war had primarily been caused by the corrupt Pope Julius II; (3) that at least some princes of Europe, including Henry VIII, had proved by accepting peace that they believed in the *Pax ecclesiae*—in other words, they had behaved more like true Christian princes than not; (4) that no irreversible catastrophe had yet taken place which made peaceful reform within state and church impossible.

Others of his main premises apply more narrowly to the sixteen-year-old Prince Charles of Castile and the Netherlands for whom it was prepared: (1) that before Charles lay a fateful choice, to which he had not yet committed himself—to become a Christian prince *or* to become a tyrant; (2) that Charles had power (free will) to choose between these courses if the differences between them were made unmistakably plain; (3) that Charles, at sixteen, was not yet corrupted by tyrannic ambition; (4) that Charles was sane and capable of rational, dispassionate thought and action; (5) that Charles was accessible to such communications as Erasmus'—i.e., had not yet been cut off by a screen of self-protecting, corrupt counsellors; (6) that Charles was a Christian and that he desired to be a good Christian prince first, a good national or imperial prince second.

Finally, Erasmus assumed that the cause-and-effect patterns which human history had repeatedly shown to exist still were valid in 1516. In other words, the entire past history of kingship was relevant to the problems of contemporary government. This does not imply that Erasmus thought the past an infallible and comprehensive guide to the solution of today's problems, but rather that where past human experience *was* demonstrably relevant, only an idiot would disregard it.

Erasmus had strongly in mind a parallel between Alexander the Great (tutored by Aristotle at fourteen) and Charles (at sixteen tutored by Erasmus). Again and again in the *Christian Prince* the history of the tyrant Alexander was quietly held up as an appalling example of one who inflicted needless suffering on his world. Even in the prefatory letter Erasmus struck a novel note: Alexander used his wit, plus vast bloodshed, to build his short-lived empire; but you (Charles) may need to use your talents—peacefully, it is hoped—"in the voluntary cession of part of yours, which it may be better not to retain." [4]

In other words, the Christian Prince begins with and maintains a keen, practical interest in the real and present danger of 1516, renewed outbreaks of tyranny. Erasmus did not attempt to provide for Charles a complete résumé of the art of government. Smith (p. 197) observed that Erasmus was unconcerned with questions typical of medieval political writing (and for that matter, never studied politics "thoroughly"). What Erasmus does, in eleven short chapters, is to boil down certain essentials of the good prince (and government which seeks the greatest peace and prosperity for the greatest number of the people) as opposed to the tyrant (with his schemes of imperial war and conquest, or rule which treats human beings like brutes). This is not the place for any extended critique of the essay, in which, actually, Erasmus puts forward as exposition a great many of the ideas which More wove into the imaginative pattern of a humanist romance in the *Utopia* (see *ECP*, pp. 128-30). In a sense, to be sure, the entire piece is social criticism, but I wish particularly to stress insights into peace and war.

Having in the prefatory letter touched on the world disaster that was Alexander the Great's mania for imperial war, Erasmus in his first chapter compared at some length tyrants in history with good (generally peaceful) rulers (*ECP*, pp. 157-67). It is evident, I think, that what the humanist tried to do was to deglamorize (if the word is permissible) tyranny, by showing (in an age when the thirst for fame was a peculiarly powerful motive for princely actions) [5] how odious was the reputation that in time inevitably accrued to evil kings, frequently cursed even while they lived. On the other hand, Erasmus was well aware that idealistic youth delights in rising to meet the challenges of a noble career. Negatively, then, his problem—in writing for Prince Charles—was to denude the tyrant role of all possible air of true nobility, honor, or glory. Positively, therefore, his effort was to represent the career of the Christian prince as one potentially filled with challenge and excitement, one through which a talented ruler might win in his lifetime and after his people's profound admiration. It is, then, the Christian prince who will surely win lasting and true fame, glory, and honor, for "True honor is that which follows on virtue and right action of its own will" (*ECP*, p. 148). In effect, Erasmus said, from the verdict of history—that the tyrant's reputation is that of a terrible criminal against humanity—there is no appeal. Only from sycophants and corrupt men can the tyrant expect praise even in his own lifetime.

The *Christian Prince*, however, was directed to the sixteen-year-old Charles. Obviously, whatever his potential, he was not *then* a tyrant. True, as suggested by the adage "The king and the fool are born such," there is such a thing as congenital incapacity, but this too did not apply to Charles, who was a youth of great promise. No more was the potential frightfulness of the future Alexander the Great manifest when at fourteen he began to be tutored by Aristotle. To become an evil king required a process of change by degrees. With tyranny as with the beginning of war, as Dudley wrote in 1509, "There are many ways to enter into it, and the beginning seemeth a great pleasure, but the way is very narrow to come honorably out thereof."

Hence the special importance which humanist social criticism attached to flattery, the subject of the second chapter in the *Christian Prince*. (Hence also, in the first edition of 1516, the essay to Charles was followed by a reprinting of Erasmus' 1504 *Panegyric* and by his 1512-13 Latin translation of Plutarch's essay *On how to tell a flatterer from a friend*, dedicated to Henry VIII but which that king was too busy to read during wartime.) Obviously Erasmus was not attacking all flattery, for he used it himself, as he observed in the letter prefatory to the *Christian Prince*. In this context what he, like More in *Utopia*'s first book, did seek to expose in its true colors was the kind of flattery which poisons the young prince's mind and, in short, incites to tyranny and war. Such flatterers may be of two kinds: men and books. (It is, no doubt, characteristic of humanist thought on education that great importance is attached to early reading and the images of a "good life" formed through literature.) In this context Erasmus attacked the unguided reading by such inexperienced young future rulers as Charles of books which "incite to tyranny":

A boy that is wild and impetuous by nature would easily be incited to tyranny, if without forewarning he should read about Achilles, Alexander the Great, Xerxes, or Julius Caesar. But today we see many a one taking delight in the tales of Arthur and Lancelot . . . which are not only about tyrants, but are also very poorly done, stupid, and fit to be "old wives' tales" [*Arcturis, Lanslotis, & aliis id genus fabulis delectari, non solum tyrannicis, verum etiam prorsus ineruditis, stultis & anilibus*], so that it would be more advisable to put in one's time reading the comedies . . . of the poets instead of nonsense of that sort [*ECP*, p. 200].

Erasmus' third chapter, on "The Arts of Peace," tries to suggest concretely that there *are* great, challenging, and honorable arts of peace. These are the enjoyable arts which build rather than destroy cities, which preserve and strengthen civilized living rather than create havoc and death. The art of war he attacks as worthy of condemnation together with all arts which deprave humanity (*ECP*, pp. 205-14). Sane men are not taken in by outward shows: "Who thinks a prince great just because he is adorned with gold and precious stones?" (*ECP*, p. 209). To set this terse chapter in its full original context perhaps one should recall the immense Renaissance fascination, especially in Italy, with the idea that war was itself, like the state, potentially a work of art.[6]

Since, as he said, he had elsewhere written on war (i.e., his *Against War*, which he evidently desired should serve as a companion piece to the *Christian Prince*), he wrote only a concise final chapter "On Beginning War" (*ECP*, pp. 249-57). (Curiously enough, he did not write on the difficult problem of ending wars, unless one counts his eighth chapter, "On Treaties" [*ECP*, pp. 238-40].) Quite consciously Erasmus deviated from the traditional patterns of advice to princes, in which sections on the making of peace were balanced by those on the art of war.

Characteristically, like the other English humanist social critics, Erasmus sustained the major thesis that offensive war was not only almost invariably unjust but that, in terms of ruggedly practical self-interest, it was disastrously unprofitable when all the costs were taken into account. (As far as I know, none of the London Reformers ever questioned the justice of repelling invasion.) Erasmus' Christian prince will never initiate war against other Christians, nor even rashly against the Turks (i.e., while his prince may help repel Turkish invasion, he will be very slow to mount crusading attacks). Before undertaking *any* war, he will exhaust every means, especially arbitration, for avoiding it. If the prince holds the ideal of human dignity strongly, he will consider well the differences between beasts, for whom to prey upon each other is natural, and men—born for good will and peace. Repeatedly the humanist urged that the prince should in advance with the utmost realism weigh the cost and calamity of even the most "just" war, taking careful estimates on the slightness of sure gains and the certain enormity of losses. Particularly the prince will weigh the degrading and dangerous wartime necessity (as things then were) for dependence on the barbarous dregs of humanity who are the mercenary soldiers, professional paid killers. Not that war can always be avoided; but if fought it must be, Erasmus advises that campaigns be so conducted as to shed as little Christian blood as possible. For in itself war is not only usually unwise and profitless, it is necessarily inhumane and tragic. If Plato called war between Greeks "sedition," what can we term it between Christians? Again, but more briefly than in his *Against War*, he refuted traditional justifications for war. He granted that theoretically some wars may be just, but in his own lifetime he could scarcely cite a single one whose cause had not been criminal ambition, lust, ferocity, wrath, or avarice. As for glory, he proposed that the Christian prince should accept as both real and practical a higher concept of heroism than that of corrupt chivalry: "Let the good prince always lean toward that glory which is not steeped in blood nor linked with the misfortunes of another. In war, however fortunately it turns out, the good fortune of one is always the ruin of the other. Many a time, too, the victor weeps over a victory bought too dearly" (*ECP*, p. 254).

Does not mankind suffer, he asked, from sufficient unavoidable calamities without inflicting upon itself one worse than all others, war? He recognized, as a real and growing current form of mass irrationalism, surging hatreds of pure nationalism as a force making for war:

But now practically every Angle hates the Gaul, and every Gaul the Angle, for no other reason than that he is an Angle. The Irishman, just because he is an Irishman, hates the Briton; the Italian hates the German; the Swabians, the Swiss; and so on throughout the list. . . . Why do these stupid names do more to divide us than the common name of Christ does to unite us [*ECP*, p. 255]?

It is characteristic of English humanist optimism that, even as late as 1516, Erasmus evidently believed that, given enough good will and through using the wisdom which was available, the national princes of Europe still had it in their power to choose, whether to restore the better parts of the old internationalism, or to encourage a tide of warring nationalist hatreds.

Although between the abortive attack on France in 1513 and the early 1520's the English did not again attempt continental invasion, a series of events, beginning in early 1515, conspired to undermine English humanist optimism for continued peace in Europe. At the same time, solid hopes grew that at least in England a golden age of peaceful social reform and progress would develop under Henry VIII and Wolsey. The great English leaders are implicitly excluded from the pessimistic views which Dean John Colet wrote to Erasmus on June 20, 1516: "You have done well in writing on the *Instruction of a Christian Prince*. How I wish Christian princes would follow good instructions! Everything is upset by their mad follies. I am very desirous of having the book; for I am sure that like everything else of yours, it will turn out perfect" (*EN*, II, 286-88).

The *Christian Prince* appeared in Basel in May, but on April 1 Erasmus' own deepening pessimism on European affairs, as well as hope for England, was expressed to Warham, Archbishop of Canterbury, one of the leaders in the peace party in Henry VIII's early councils. To Warham Erasmus dedicated part of his Cambridge accomplishments, his edition of St. Jerome—one of the early Fathers who "in their writings persuade us to flee war" as unjust. Warham, at least, he could praise for his efforts to induce monarchs to turn from senseless and needless war to the mighty, imperative work of building an age noble in the arts of peace:

Would that all our princes were disposed, as you are, to put an end to the tumult of war, as mad as it is miserable [*ut omissis insanissimis pariter ac miserrimis bellorum tumultibus*], to turn their minds to making their age illustrious by the arts of Peace, and to kindle by adequate rewards the zeal of the learned. . . .[7]

What were these princely follies and tumults, as mad as they were miserable, which undermined humanist optimism for peaceful social reform on the continent?

Some grasp of events between July, 1514, and the printing of More's *Utopia* in December, 1516, is required to make humanist criticism intelligible and its objectives clear.[8] In 1514, although Henry VIII and many of the English nobility were by no means sated with chivalric glory, the intervention of Pope Leo X apparently effected a French peace. On January 1, 1515, however, the nineteen-year-old Francis I succeeded to the French throne. Not only younger and more rashly adventurous than Henry VIII, Francis by his upbringing had been even more strongly predisposed to regard war as a noble, heroic, and chivalrous adventure. The romances of the Round Table had helped to exalt his juvenile imagination, and, like Henry, he had a vast devotion to all kinds of violent exercises, hunting, masquerades, and tournaments. From an early age dominated by women, his character combined sensuality and capriciousness; by turns he was weak and authoritative. "Dreaming of fair feats of prowess," he found his romantic desire for chivalric glory and power first attracted by the prospects in Italy. While Henry began his "golden age" reign with three years of peace, Francis I plunged into invasive war within nine months. Thus through his triumph at Marignano (September 13, 1515) he first tasted the heady joys of being adored and feared as the most knightly and powerful prince in Europe.

The repercussions of Marignano upon Wolsey and Henry VIII were profound and immediate. While the battle had shattered the myth of the Swiss mercenary soldiers' virtual invincibility, it also subjected the Pope to French domination. Wolsey's policy, from his rise to his fall from power, has been (as Pollard showed brilliantly) mistakenly characterized as an attempt to keep in England's hands the "balance of power." Although his motives often puzzled his contemporaries, he "consistently followed a papal policy and was led by personal interest [his desire to become pope] in the same direction." "Marignano was a far more resounding blow than all the English victories of 1513, and there seemed no way of counteracting its effects." Without aid from Spain, the Netherlands, or the Pope, renewed direct English invasion of France seemed impossible even to Wolsey. On the other hand, while half of Henry's royal patrimony had gone in the French war of 1512-13, half remained, plus whatever could be extracted from the English people.

Without consulting Parliament, Wolsey devised a scheme. The King's counsel, including those friends of humanism, Warham and Fox, were "mostly adverse to it." Younger men like Tunstall and Thomas More "deplored the adventure," all to no avail. The scheme required much secret diplomacy. A huge English subsidy was to be raised and used to "bribe Maximilian and the Swiss to renew the contest against Francis I and his Venetian allies." (Ironically, on October 24, 1515, Thomas More, then returning from his peace mission to Bruges, near Calais met Richard Pace, who had been secretly sent to purchase for England the services of Swiss mercenary troops [*LP*, II, 1067, p. 282].) Pope Leo, however, made his peace with the French at Bologna in December, 1515. Then in the following spring the English-financed expedition against Francis was a splendid fiasco. Meanwhile in January Ferdinand of Aragon died, leaving his dominions to the Prince Charles who Erasmus hoped would become not a tyrant but a Christian prince. By April the Pope sent to London a nuncio who was charged to "negotiate a general peace between the princes of Christendom, or, at the least, a four years' truce. . . ."[9] In July, Charles, seemingly having weighed the cost and calamity of war, however "just," made what Pollard called an "ignominious peace" with Francis at Noyon. In late October, from London where (as the Venetian ambassador rightly reported) not Henry VIII but Wolsey "led the dance," Giustinian (I, 319-20) suggested to his masters the wisdom of making Wolsey a "great offer, or gift" to avoid further war, for he "being quieted, the whole turmoil would cease. . . ." That friend of humanism, Bishop Tunstall, in late December expressed to the ambassador his great desire to have an end of these wars. Moreover (although Giustinian [II, 25-26] suspected that the English lords desired their continuance), the Duke of Norfolk told him "that the whole of this kingdom wished for a general peace. . . ." In addition Norfolk desired pacification in Christendom in order that the rising Turkish menace might be met with a united European resistance.

How much the humanists, even More (who was closest to the court), knew of all these secret maneuverings is almost impossible to say. "The truth of the war preparations," as Pollard noted, was kept very secret. Outwardly England had been at peace since late 1513 or early 1514. In June, 1516, brushing aside the idea that the English-financed league was "*against* any one," Henry could blandly assert that " 'I content myself with my own; I only wish to command my own subjects; but, on the other hand, I do not choose any one to have it in his power to command me, nor will I ever suffer it' " (Giustinian, I, 237). To modern historians Henry VIII would perhaps in time appear as a "Nero-Tartuffe," Mesnard (p. 147) observes, but with England at peace, during the time when More wrote his *Utopia*, Henry seemed, compared to his predecessors and in his own right, "a prince charming and a paragon of virtue."

Put summarily, such was the broad pattern of events between the "permanent" Franco-English peace of 1514 and the appearance of More's *Utopia*, which was sent in manuscript to Erasmus on September 3 and printed at Louvain by December, 1516 (*EN*, II, 381).

The *Utopia*, then, appeared when England was at peace and when a rather well-tempered humanist optimism existed, based on the hope that, at least in England, peace might continue and that a golden age of social reform might yet be possible. This optimism, one surmises, endured until the Field of the Cloth of Gold in 1520.

As we have it, the *Utopia* stands as a unified work of art, comprising what may be called the Dialogue of Counsel (Book I) and the Discourse (Book II) which sets forth a romantic account of the remarkable commonwealth which More's narrator, Raphael Hythlodaye, had ostensibly seen for himself while voyaging to the New World. The best analysis of its composition indicates that most of Book II was done in Flanders after May, 1515, and the rest of the work finished in London after More's return that autumn (Hexter, p. 26). More's work was done, therefore, after Erasmus had already completed his sharp criticism on abuses of monarchic power in the *Adages* and had his *Christian Prince* "in hand" (i.e., completed or essentially so). To establish this sequence is to suggest the high degree of unity developed in the London Reformers' social criticism (see *ECP*, pp. 128-30).

Like all notable works of art, the *Utopia* is and has always been a focus for lively critical dispute. All efforts to ascertain More's meanings have, to be sure, been complicated by his masterful wit, humor, and pervasive irony. Both popular and scholarly debates, however, have largely centered upon the Discourse itself, for Book I—the Dialogue of Counsel— is by no means equally mysterious. Perhaps More's critics might be able to agree on only one thing: that his "piercing analysis, in the first book . . . of the social and economic troubles of England, remains a famous document of social history" (Caspari, p. 56). Since Book I is a dialogue in which More himself contends with his fictional creations, the globetrotting Hythlodaye and with others, readers naturally have sought to discern what were More's personal opinions. Clearly, however, the most important artistic function of the Dialogue was to prepare the reader for his induction into the imaginary New World state of Utopia itself.

The criticism of war in *Utopia* begins in the two realistic and dramatic discussions of sore contemporary social problems in England and western Europe which comprise Book I. One is a treatment of the causes of corrupt government, together with comment on princes, good and evil. The other part of the Dialogue centers on justice, the causes of vagabondage and theft, and generally on the social causes of crime against property and persons. In both sections matters relating to war are touched on, but attention is mainly focused upon economic and administrative maladies affecting the state as a whole and in its international relations. Finally the Dialogue ends with Hythlodaye's tantalizing assertion (which More met with skepticism) that all these social evils, as well as others not specifically mentioned but bound up with them in Renaissance Europe, could be eliminated from the state if property were held in common. He promised, moreover, to prove as much in his account of the Utopian commonwealth which he had seen in the New World. Such are the broad outlines of Book I.

Some details concerning war deserve closer notice. In the Dialogue, More (in a way then threshing out with himself a similar question), delighted with Hythlodaye's wisdom, urged the philosopher to enter a prince's council, as Plato had advised must be done if commonwealths were to attain felicity (*MUL*, pp. 34-40, 79-114). Replied Hythlodaye, Plato's advice would be futile in the face of contemporary realities. Typically nowadays a prince, while young, is rapidly corrupted by vicious counselors who instill in him their own lust for power, regardless of the hideous damage and suffering inevitably inflicted upon the common people when their schemes were executed. All this evil advice, furthermore, is based upon the unquestioned assumption that the king can do no wrong. Chivalric war is all their glory:

For first of all, the most part of princes have more delight in warlike matters and feats of chivalry (the knowledge whereof I neither have nor desire) than in the good feats of peace: and employ much more study, how by right or by wrong to enlarge their dominions, than how well and peaceably to rule and govern that they already have [*MUL*, p. 38].

Hythlodaye sums up the counsel which, if honest and candid, he would feel compelled to give to a king who was eager for martial glory and about to embark on invasive war. What good would it do, he asked More, to tell such a corrupted king that the outcome of war depends on the whim of Fortune? That the people give the king his authority and that hence he has no natural right thus to abuse it? That just government is a duty inseparable from right kingship? In reply, More was obliged to admit that, kings being what they were, it would be useless to offer such advice to a typical contemporary European sovereign. The adviser would simply be thrown out (*MUL*, pp. 87-104).

The Dialogue's discussion of crime (to which we shall return) deals, among other things, with causes of theft, with this conversation set in the context of a postwar wave of crime. Hythlodaye emphasized strongly two discernible causes, both man-made. One was land enclosures, undertaken by greedy capitalists, as we would say now, which drove men out of their homes and into wandering beggary, into starvation, and at last to theft or murder (since either had the same punishment, death). Second, he identified frequent wars as a cause of crime. For wars, with their concomitant maintenance of mercenary professional soldiers, inevitably produced large numbers of trained thieves and more vicious criminals, because theft and war are inseparable (*MUL*, pp. 47-57).

Another major cause of crime, directly related to war, was the maintenance by noblemen of idle serving men, supposedly to fight the nation's wars as needed. When these men are finally cast out, destitute, they have little choice but to "starve for hunger, or manfully play the thieves." Besides, said Hythlodaye (here there is a solid touch of English realism, perhaps echoing Sir John Fortescue's critique of monarchy), such idle retainers in any event do not make as good soldiers in a pinch as stout English handicraftsmen! [1] As for the veteran who returns home crippled for life, he is useless for honest work and, when desperate, virtually certain to turn criminal—and More evokes the grim image of events which were taking place about the time when John Colet was delivering his Oxford lectures on Romans:

Nay . . . first of all, I will speak nothing of them that come home out of war maimed and lame, as not long ago out of Blackheath [June, 1497] filed, and a little before that out of the wars in France: such (I say) as put their lives in jeopardy for the weal public's or the king's sake, and by the reason of weakness and lameness be not able to occupy their old crafts, and be too aged to learn new: of them I will speak nothing, because war like the tide ebbeth and floweth. [2]

Thomas More and Shakespeare's braggart soldier, Falstaff, touch hands but without seeing eye to eye, across the century. Falstaff, cynically scanning his miserable band of recruits, cheerfully characterized them as "Food for powder, food for powder. They'll fill a pit as well as better. Tush man, mortal men, mortal men." But Falstaff is more romantic and hopeful than More in his view of the future for the few who return from the wars: "There's not three of my hundred and fifty left alive; and they are for the town's end, to beg during life" (*I Henry IV*, V.iii.38).

A key idea of the humanist social criticism (already seen working in the minds of Colet and Erasmus) appears in the Dialogue's broad discussion of justice and the causes of crime. More's fiction made Hythlodaye a dinner guest of Cardinal Morton, More's youthful guardian and friend. There a cunning, traditionally minded lay lawyer hotly defended "strait and rigorous justice," including death for all thieves. When pressed, however, he was forced to admit that, despite the harshest infliction of the penalty which he asserted would cure the evil, thieves were never more numerous in England. Hythlodaye's treatment of this question is, I think, a historic landmark of humanist social criticism. First, he declared that such crime would not be reduced, much less eliminated, unless its true causes were searched for and reduced or, if possible, eliminated—a line of action which he thought more profitable than the cruel but futile course of savage punishments, however "great and horrible." The lawyer's counterthrust was in the powerful Augustinian tradition: the cause of such criminals' evil-doing is perfectly clear, for they could earn honest livings "if they would not willingly be nowght [i.e., evil: *ni sponte mali esse mallent*]." Thus seen, the cause of crime is in the sinful, corrupt makeup of the criminal. Nothing practical can be done about such sin but to mete out justice to the evildoer (*MUL*, p. 45).

With Hythlodaye's reply, to use a naval metaphor perhaps suitable to an age of intellectual as well as geographical exploration, a historic cape of the mind was turned, one which divides the medieval from the modern world. In it we may see at work that scientific spirit for which More stands pre-eminent among the humanists.[3] Not for a moment does Hythlodaye agree that sin is the basic cause of crime. Instead in his analysis such social evils as crime, poverty, and war are all man-made. These are *effects*, which can be traced to their man-made sources, if men will but use their wits rightly. In other words, these causes are within the power of the human mind to discover. Then the social processes by which these causes produce their necessary effects can be studied. Finally, the most practical (or, as we would now say, scientific) way to cure such a social symptom as crime or war, insofar as it is curable, is to take the necessary realistic action required to alleviate or eliminate the ascertained cause. As I understand it, this is Hythlodaye's reasoning. The suggestion with which the Dialogue ends—that *the* cause of all remediable social evils in Europe lies in failure to hold property in common, as the Utopians do—was, I think, misleading, if taken as the sole clue to the meaning of the Discourse which was to follow directly, but certainly it was well calculated to lead the capitalistic reader onward into that humanist romance and satire.

No one, I believe, questions that his *Utopia* is More's most triumphant contribution to the English Renaissance, indeed to world literature. As a political romance it is to be classed with Rabelais' *Gargantua and Pantagruel* as "a masterpiece of humanist criticism of man and society." [4] After agreeing on so much, its interpreters fall into the liveliest kind of differences as to More's intentions and as to the work's significance, although very few doubt that, as books go, it is still a living force. A critical view of the handling of war and peace in Book II—the Discourse—may be aided by a swift review of some principal approaches which have been made to it, for it is the picture drawn of a good life in Utopia that is most controversial.

It may be that most of these modern critical difficulties are of recent manufacture, for, insofar as we can judge, they did not trouble More's contemporaries. More had feared that Tunstall, as a busy diplomat, would have no time for such "trifles" as *Utopia*. By early 1517, however, in the highest good spirits he wrote to Erasmus that Tunstall's "judgement about our Republic, so frank, so complimentary, has given me more pleasure than an Attic talent" (*EN*, II, 442-43; *MC* 84-85). From Antwerp in late February Erasmus advised a friend to look out for the *Utopia* "whenever you wish to be amused, or rather I should say, if you ever want to see the sources from which almost all the ills of the body politic arise . . ." (*EN*, II, 503). Within three months of its publication, Erasmus desired a corrected text for a second edition (*EE*, 545). In late July, Budé, the great French humanist who took Erasmus to task for such "trifles" as *Against War* and *Sileni Alcibiadis*, wrote to More's young humanist friend Thomas Lupset a long commendatory letter, which was printed in both editions of 1518 (*MUL*, pp. lxxx-xcii). As for Henry VIII, however, there is no certainty that he ever read the *Utopia*.

Because of More's deep engagement in the 1520's with Henrician power politics, with the struggle over the rising Lutheran movement and, later, with the fatal issue of the King's divorce, it has never been possible, if it were desirable, to separate interpretation of the *Utopia* from its author's life. Hence some have been baffled by numerous alleged inconsistencies between the good life shown in Utopia and More's own character. One way out has been to assert that More's personality was full of psychological conflicts and contradictions so that Utopia necessarily lacks unity. This view takes the work to be only a vivid "Renaissance daydream," notable for its display of realistic imagination but filled with logical lapses best attributed to More's "characteristic humor." [5] Seeming political and religious paradoxes in the Discourse have, however, perplexed even scholarly editors and left doubts as to More's central purpose in describing Utopia.[6] Even the work's best editor, J. H. Lupton, is baffled and shocked that More made his Utopians so utterly lacking in chivalry in war though generally they are ethically scrupulous in fulfilling social obligations. Repellent and incomprehensible, to him, are such standard Utopian practices as destroying enemy navies by "translating" shore beacons, or their effort to shorten wars by procuring the assassination of hostile princes.[7]

Approaching the *Utopia* from angles almost as varied and complex as the work itself, recent scholarship, however, has strongly tended to discover in it the significant unity of a great work of art and criticism. Perhaps it may be impossible ever to reach an agreement on any single view, but this again means that this humanist romance is still alive, since such an agreement would mean it had fallen into the tomb of art. One major line of criticism (the one which to me seems most dubious) seeks violently to create a principle of unity for the Discourse by imposing one devised by the critic himself (e.g., by assuming More to have been a proto-Marxist).[8] In opposition are ranked those who, from one viewpoint or another, perceive an internal form of unity. A. W. Reed argued carefully that a high degree of consistency and integrity runs through the Discourse as well as through More's official and personal life.[9] R. W. Chambers' fine *Thomas More* (pp. 226-27) strongly emphasized a curiously neglected basic idea, that in the Discourse More showed how he thought that "enlightened and righteous heathen ought to behave." Representing, not defending, all Utopian practices, More pictured the Utopian citizens as "heathen philosophers, and, as such, guided solely by the light of reason," a viewpoint with which I strongly agree.[10] H. W. Donner, in perhaps the most attractive introduction for the general reader, treats the *Utopia* as a work of great current topical interest and the Discourse itself as an eclectic romance whose "implied criticism of society" lies in "the description of a commonwealth whose institutions appear ideal by means of the contrast it presents to the conditions actually prevailing." Such an approach tends, of course, to emphasize topics which are now of greatest interest.[11] To J. H. Hexter the sin of Pride is the key to the work.[12] Fritz Caspari, finding Plato's *Republic* to be More's "most important inspiration and prototype," temperately emphasizes in Utopia the "rule of virtue, achieved through humanistic training." [13] Basically agreeing with Chambers, Father Edward Surtz finds the *Utopia* to be "essentially a humanistic document aimed at the Reformation of Christendom." As far as the conduct of war goes, More "paints a picture which he knows the Christians of Europe will abhor." He represented "an ideal but pagan world." [14]

Because evidently More owed much to Plato, there has been a recurrent tendency to conclude that he intended to picture Utopia as an "ideal" republic, in approximately the same sense as ideal applies to Plato's imaginary state. Plato, I take it, did construct an ideal republic, in the sense that, substantially turning his back on human limitations (e.g., in his dream of incorruptible guardian-rulers), he escaped the bounds of reality. Hence perhaps his *Republic* has influenced certain poets more than it has practical politicians. The title page of *Utopia*'s definitive 1518 edition read *De optimo reip.* [ublicae] *statu* . . . (*MUL*, p. lxxvi), with *optimo* meaning apparently, as in Cicero's *Republic* (ii.23.41) "of or belonging to the best." What was meant, I think, was that the Dialogue would represent "the best state of a republic" in the sense of the best practicable, or optimum form, when the limitations of known human nature are taken realistically into account, as More does take them. (Machiavelli's *Prince* might, in an antiutopian sense, be termed "ideal" in that it seems based on the inverted, antihumanitarian premise that most, if not all, men can practically be reduced to abject submission to a tyrant). As a social critic More, like Colet and Erasmus, had highly practical intentions, namely, to produce what may be termed designs for a new social order, requiring peaceful humanistic reform within England (Adams [1945]). We would hardly need Erasmus' comment to know that More based his image of a possible good life, as well as his diagnosis of existing evils calling for remedy, on England. As Chambers (p. 125) observed, "the remarkable thing about *Utopia* is the extent to which it adumbrates social and political reforms which have either been actually carried into practice, or which have come to be regarded as very practical politics." [15] Hexter (pp. 63-64) thinks that "More surpassed the usual limits and limitations of traditional social satire and of humanist social criticism" and that since More prescribed realistic remedies for social evils, he "is not in the humanist tradition at all." If just, this criticism would apply equally well to Colet, to Erasmus, and (a bit later on, in the 1520's) to J. L. Vives. It should be evident, however, that this comment does not really fit the kind of humanism developed by these London Reformers. Indeed a valuable study might be made to discriminate between kinds of humanism.

The need for such discrimination, and an opportunity for an improved critical concept of More's social criticism, may be suggested by a brief comparison of Utopian war practices with those found in some of his known or probable sources. Had More any controlling principle in selecting or rejecting available materials, or, for that matter, in his own witty inventions?

That More owed much to Plato has long been apparent.[16] Particularly with regard to war, however, there are radical differences between them.[17] Plato presented war as a school of virtue for which hunting was good practice (as in the Middle Ages), and his professional soldiers form a military elite, one of the two highest ruling classes. The Utopian citizens (a sharp distinction is drawn between freemen and bondmen or slaves), however, regard war as a school of unnatural cruelty and hunting, when pursued for pleasure, as an inhumane debauchery. The Utopians in fact abhor professional soldiers as such; and they regard the Zapoletes (i.e., the Swiss), who were mercenary soldiers by free choice, as more depraved than the most savage beasts. Plato's ideal citizen is a soldier (or guardian), and the healthy city in his ideal Republic is very much an armed camp. As for the Utopians, despite their abhorrence of a professional military class, every one, including women, must be trained for national defense. Plato's soldiers are forbidden to hear music (demoralizing), to engage in commerce (degrading), or to do manual labor (reserved for congenital slaves). In Utopia, however, music is encouraged for all as is learning, trade is honored if it aids the public good, and necessary manual toil is honored as well. The professional soldier who enjoys war would have been highly esteemed in Plato's Republic, but in Utopia he would have been regarded as insane and either made a bondman or destroyed as of incurable criminality. In all this there seems a good deal that More did not owe to Plato.

Is it probable that the germ of the idea for the Discourse came from St. Augustine's *City of God*? True, in general St. Augustine had tried to conceive of a perfect social order in which all members would be duly subordinated, in which each would be glad of his own work, and wherein community of goods would exist.[18] But it would be rather difficult to trace the Utopian's views on war to St. Augustine. For Augustine considered war to be a divine punishment for sin and laid great stress on the weakness and sinfulness of man. As we have seen, moreover, during the Middle Ages Augustine's authority became decisive in determining the concept of war as "just" for Christians to wage upon heretics. In contrast, the Utopian freemen regard war as a man-made evil, they glorify man's reason and his large measure of freedom of will, and they never use force to compel any peaceful dissenter to agree with a central authority.

What did More's social criticism possibly owe to recently published accounts of New World travel? [19] His fictional narrator, Hythlodaye, had been "in company with Amerike Vespuce, and in the iii last voyages of those iiii that be now in print, and abroad in every man's hands" (*MUL*, p. 27). Very likely More did draw from these letters ideas for the basic structure of the Discourse (an imaginary travel) and two specific points—that the New World savages regarded gold with contempt, and the observation that they "live according to nature, and may be called Epicureans rather than Stoics" (*MUL*, p. xxxviii).

We have seen that when Erasmus, in his *Against War*, treated war's mythical origins, he was moved to consider characteristics of human nature in its presumed prehistoric pacific and uncorrupted state. In Vespucci's travel letters More came upon a first-hand description of primitive man himself, coexisting with European civilization but possibly still living in a state of nature, certainly unspoiled by previous contact with a decayed European culture. Through Vespucci, therefore, More laid imaginative eyes upon what the eighteenth century would perhaps have called the "noble savages." In short, the travel accounts invited comparison of ancient golden age myth with modern reality.

But how noble and peaceful were the New World savages? Vespucci's letter has many fine touches concerning war.[20] True, the savages did not seem to be leading the perfectly happy life of nature (such as Pythagoras, Ovid, Lucretius, and Seneca had eulogized). Nevertheless, in many respects they were less depraved than the civilized Europeans, and they seemed to be living in an only slightly corrupted state of nature. Physically, life was simple: feathers were wealth, there was no trade, and "they . . . are contented with what Nature gives them," setting no value on gold. As for religion, no evidences of ritual or dogma were found, and they were identified as "Epicureans" (*AVS*, p. 9). The savages' wars fascinated Vespucci. The New World did not, indeed, reveal a warless golden age, for while some tribes were perfectly peaceful (pp. 19, 26), others at times cruelly and wantonly attacked them (pp. 12-13, 20-21, 36). The savages' notions of a just war furnished a strong contrast to Catholic Europe. There were no wars of greed for land or rule; instead the savages fought to avenge murders or (as cannibals) for food. A crude sort of natural justice seemed moreover to prevail; there were no written law codes and indeed very few disputants (pp. 6-7). This natural harmony between men was reflected in the practice of holding much property peacefully in common (p. 9). Even with respect to the art of war, savage practices contrasted ironically with those of the Europeans. New World weapons were technologically crude and simple, and no metal weapons were seen. Combat was cruel but simply hand-to-hand, and there was no complex military organization (pp. 6-7). The peaceful savages were terror-struck by a cannon's report, and probably were little comforted when the Europeans "reassured them by telling them that with those weapons we slew our enemies" (p. 17).

It is uncertain whether More knew Vespucci's *Mundus novus* (1504), which tells of the third voyage and generally corroborates the first account. The savages described are even more peaceful than those who appear in the Soderini letter, but still they waged war "without art or order" occasionally.[21] The Europeans were amazed to find the savages "so like beasts" that they made no effort to protect their bodies against enemy arrows. Learning rapidly, the savages promised to abandon these customs which the Europeans, apparently without irony, regarded as depraved.[22] It is probable that More's reading in such voyage narratives stimulated critical comparisons of contemporary European society with a life "lived according to nature." Obviously, however, the cultured Utopian social order is unlike the New World savages', despite some borrowing of details.

We are still searching for some idea of a critical principle which may have guided More in the design of the Discourse and therefore in his social criticism. It has been asserted that once he had chosen the literary form of an imaginary travel in the contemporary New World, then many matters of great interest (such as the Utopian religious-political philosophy) were "imposed on More by the literary mould." Except for the Utopian lack of Christianity (until Hythlodaye brought the Gospels in his travel kit), More is alleged to have used carte blanche, save that he "could only ascribe to the Utopians such customs, laws, and institutions as conceivably might prevail on the other side of the world in his own day." [23]

This view of More's artistic purposes and methods begs an important question. The early sixteenth-century reader had long been accustomed, in romances and in medieval travel narratives, to believing in the real existence of the wildest fantastic natural impossibilities. Such tales as Sir John Mandeville's were immensely popular, not least for their realistic descriptions of monsters and other strange beings. The gullible public, "lacking both knowledge and criticism, swallowed them whole" (Donner, p. 16). Christopher Columbus himself was influenced by Mandeville.[24] Shakespeare's rogue Autolycus, almost a century later, found a public still ready to believe in comparable romantic nonsense: "Here's one [a ballad], to a very doleful tune, how a usurer's wife was brought to bed of twenty money bags at a burthen! . . ." Cries Mopsa: "I love a ballet in print a-life, for then we are sure they are true" (Winter's Tale, IV.iv.263-67). If he had chosen, More could have out-hoaxed the reading public and the author of "Mandeville" himself. But in his approach to the design of a good life in Utopia, an antiromantic critical principle is at work. He specifically parodied Mandeville when he described the strange country of the Polylerytes—"talkers of much nonsense" (MUL, p. 65; Donner, p. 89). More's satiric attitude toward the superstitious rubbish common in romances appears finely in the Dialogue. Speaking in his own person, he says that, while questioning

Hythlodaye about his travels, he and Peter Giles "were nothing inquisitive" about "monsters, because they be no news. For nothing is more easy to be found, than be barking Scyllaes, ravening Celenes, and Laestrygones, devourers of people, and such like great and uncredible monsters." Instead the humanists eagerly questioned Hythlodaye about what would be truly romantic, truly fantastic—"to find citizens ruled by good and wholesome laws, that is an exceeding rare and hard thing" (*MUL*, p. 33). Perhaps this brief glance at More's possible indebtedness to, as well as Utopia's sharp differences from, such obvious sources as Plato, St. Augustine, or contemporary voyage narratives, indicates the need for a unified idea of his methods and purposes in constructing his imaginary state, whether it is regarded as a humanist romance cast in the literary form of an imaginary travel, as social criticism aimed at reform of Christendom, as optimistic satire (like Erasmus' *Praise of Folly*), or, finally, as tragic satire.

It is hardly surprising that Book II of *Utopia* has both puzzled and delighted centuries of readers. Throughout the Dialogue preceding it they had enjoyed themselves in realistic surroundings with which anyone acquainted wtih traditional English social satire would have been reasonably familiar. When Hythlodaye began his Discourse of Utopia, however, More artfully plunged his readers without warning into an ingeniously but logically imagined state, whose superficial resemblances to Christian Europe were quite deceiving. So different is Utopia from contemporary Europe, indeed, that the average European would there be only a bondman (slave), while most European princes and noblemen, such as those Hythlodaye denounced in Book I, would be executed for the same reasons as were dangerous wild beasts. Even the humanist philosopher Hythlodaye was obliged to endure probation before he could be accepted as equal to the humblest Utopian freeman. Only gradually, and when one perceives the coherent philosophy underlying all major aspects of Utopian life, do the startling differences between Europe and Utopia become comprehensible. Then it becomes apparent that while in Europe the power of custom has enabled the ruling princes to regard themselves as sane when they are quite corrupt and mad, in Utopia every freeman, which includes rulers, is a philosopher whose life realistically exemplifies the idea that happiness and a good life for the community result from living strictly according to "nature" or "reason," although paradoxically the Utopians at the same time pursue pleasure. In other words, they have a Stoic ethic and an Epicurean psychology.

The course the present writer has followed to discover how far the imaginary commonwealth of Utopia and More's social criticism is represented with artistic coherence has been to examine with some care the central religious-political philosophy to which all Utopian freemen subscribe. It is not enough to perceive, with Chambers (p. 227), that these citizens are guided entirely by the "light of reason." Machiavelli could have said as much for his prince. The question becomes, what is meant by reason? It then gradually becomes apparent that the Utopians' guide is *uncorrupted* reason or nature, a concept that itself cries out for clarification. The basic principles of the Utopian philosophy are worked out in a delightfully thorough and imaginative way, and in this work More shows finely how he combined the humanistic and the scientific spirit. Once this central philosophy is perceived to be at the basis of the Utopian way of life, it is not too difficult to show that all the major features of that life are logically expressive of it—e.g., community of property, planning of agriculture and industry, of city and country life, marriage and population control, the system of justice and government, penology and slavery, education, war, and religion itself (see Adams [1949]). In order, therefore, to make clear More's Utopian social criticism, we need to set forward at least an outline of the Utopian religious-political philosophy. When this is done, his treatment of source materials will be intelligible. We should then be better able to enjoy the Utopian commonwealth for its quality, not as a monster of whimsical pseudoromance or escapist fiction but as a masterfully coherent work of art which throws into dazzling satiric relief the actual man-made ills as well as the potential beauty and humanistic progressiveness of a peacefully reformed Renaissance England.

The Philosophic Unity of Utopian Life—a Short View

The unity of the freeman's life in Utopia appears best when its major aspects are seen to be a logical, internally consistent development of one basic idea. This is that uncorrupted men will and do "by nature" [25] (that is, by the natural law of their being—human nature) actively prefer to live "according to reason" for the sake both of maximum personal happiness and for the common good of all. The freemen *must* (to retain full citizenship) subscribe only to two absolute ideas:

that man's soul is immortal, and that after death every one will be rewarded or punished in proportion to his merits. These postulates the Utopians adopted pragmatically as well as on religious grounds. That is, they cannot be proved by material evidence but are the most practical known basis on which to construct a good life for the greatest number of people. Within the bounds of these limitations or assumptions, More then proceeded, wittily and realistically, to imagine a good society. In Utopia the natural causes of such chronic man-made European social evils as poverty, crime, and war are attacked at their roots in irrational and vicious custom. In every respect, I think, the Utopian conceptions of value—religious, political, economic, esthetic—together with the operating practices and institutions which realize these values, are those approved as necessary for the achievement of happiness here and now, both by reason and by the test of experience during the seventeen centuries required to evolve the Utopian society out of initial conditions closely resembling those still prevalent in Renaissance Europe.

The original practical steps toward this end had to be taken by a wise absolute monarch, Prince Utopus, who used his power to begin building the Utopian republic. First he made Utopia, once part of the continent nearby, an island. Thereafter steps were continuously taken to protect the slowly built-up good life within it from known sources of corruption and unreason, whether within human nature itself or in external conditions. For one thing, a quarantine was put upon free invasion of Utopia by vicious customs as well as men who continued to flourish in states nearby. From these essential beginnings the Utopians began to enjoy an increasingly good life, one lived still subject to death and natural catastrophes (storms, plagues, and so forth) but lived by men in harmony with their fellows and with the natural environment. In Utopia destructive fear is at a minimum.

The Utopian philosophy is founded upon certain basic premises concerning the divine powers in the universe and concerning human nature itself. While God or Nature (the terms are interchangeable) cannot be known by human reason directly, the divine intent can be known through God's handiwork, of which man, the beasts, and the entire natural environment are and have long been open to acute observation. In man's nature (without qualification, this means always "uncorrupted") are apparent several mighty gifts of the divine creator. The first is man's godlike reason: the Utopians believe that man was divinely intended to live "according to nature," being then ruled by "reason," in the sense of uncorrupted right reason. Hence the Utopians delight, as scientists, in perceiving natural law working everywhere in the universe—a pleasure no beast could know. While the Utopians think their religious philosophy to be the truest possible "unless any godlier be inspired into man from heaven" (*MUL*, p. 211), both natural science and the historical records of human experience on earth are ways by which the Utopians hope gradually to increase their understanding of the divine universal virtue (or Nature). This desire, too, is distinctively human, possible only to man, who is distinguished from the beasts by his faculty of reason.

No less important than reason is Nature's great second gift to man. The Utopians take it to be man's natural capacity for and strong inclination toward a close-knit and loving family and communal social life. Again as compared with the beasts, man is distinguished by his power of mutual benevolent solicitude for the common welfare. Moreover, both these natural gifts—reason and the power of love—urge man to live happily himself yet at the same time to help others to happiness "in respect of the society of nature" (*pro naturae societate*) (*MUL*, pp. 190-91). Furthermore, the Utopians generally agree that the divine Nature, as the world about man makes evident, is a "most tender and loving mother" who benevolently has given life and made available the material necessities which men use to attain their happiness (*MUL*, p. 174). Since Nature's benevolence to man is so apparent, the Utopians generally deduce that "the merciful clemency of God" takes no "delight in blood and slaughter"—that is, it would be illogical for the benevolent creator of life to enjoy its destruction. Hence the Utopians abhor all bloodshed as contrary to nature and as cumulatively destructive of the "clemency" which is the "gentlest affection of our nature" (*MUL*, p. 158). (All of these ideas, incidentally, are found emphasized in the thought of certain of the later Roman Stoics, such as Seneca.)

Finally, the distinctive Utopian social practices are determined, not only by man's two great gifts from the divine nature, but also by the singular Utopian form of Epicureanism. For Epicureans they are, since pleasure is identified as their *summum bonum* (*MUL*, pp. 188-211). In practice, however, certain highly ingenious restrictions are rigidly put upon this concept. For the freemen, guided by uncorrupted right "reason" with the common welfare always in mind, agree in a careful division of pleasures into those which are "true and honest" and those which in effect are counterfeit. The basis of this vital distinction comes from the Utopian religious philosophy. Since it is assumed that the divine nature planted in man the master drive to live in harmony with his species, ruled by reason, the Utopians conclude that only those pleasures which are (i.e., "by nature") "true, good and honest" and which are known to enhance (or at least not damage) the good life should be desired by or permitted to the citizens. (Evidently individual preference for a socially destructive pleasure would become prima-facie evidence of insanity!)

They reason of virtue and pleasure. But the chief . . . question is in what . . . the felicity of man consisteth. But in this . . . they seem almost too much [i.e., from Hythlodaye's Catholic viewpoint] given . . . to . . . defend pleasure; wherein they determine either all or the chiefest part of man's felicity to rest. And . . . the defence of this . . . opinion they fetch even from their grave . . . and rigorous religion, without the which they think reason of itself weak and unperfect. . . . But . . . they think not felicity to rest in all pleasure, but only in that pleasure that is good and honest [*bona atque honesta*]; and that hereto, as to perfect blessedness, our nature is allured and drawn even of virtue [*naturam nostram ab ipsa uirtute pertrahi*]. . . . For they define virtue to be life ordered according to nature . . . and that he doth follow the course of nature, which in desiring and refusing things is ruled by reason [*MUL*, pp. 187-90].

But what constitutes true pleasure? How practically can it be distinguished from clever counterfeits? Indeed, how is this eccentric Epicureanism, which incorporates the Stoical definition of virtue, related to the whole Utopian philosophy? [26]

First, all Utopian freemen agree that the nature of true pleasure, like the taste of vinegar or honey, is objectively fixed and beyond man's power to alter. To uncorrupted men true pleasure is "by nature" pleasant. One might say that it is "universal and immutable in thought, feeling, and taste." Esthetically it is universally valid. In Utopian practice, furthermore, there are strong suggestions also that, for those of unspoiled nature, true pleasure has always been immediately known, understood, and enjoyed as such. To the Utopians it makes no difference that to a sick person vinegar may taste like honey. For they perceive that man himself can deteriorate, can grow sick in nature until he is no longer guided by "right reason." In fact, as they perceive is common in their neighbor countries which resemble Renaissance European states, it is not only possible but inevitable that men who indulge in counterfeit pleasures, contrary to right reason, will in time become so corrupt, so dominated by perverse custom, as to be no longer able to distinguish the counterfeit from true, natural pleasure. In any event, to the Utopians the willful choice of pleasures which have been historically identified as injurious to the individual and to society serves as prima-facie evidence that such a man has become of corrupt nature. The well-known fact that the passions or senses may be stirred by the counterfeit (e.g., when men who enjoy hunting slay animals happily) does not make such pleasures "true," "good and honest"; rather the Utopian is confirmed in his judgment that the individual who enjoys such things is corrupt (or sick): ". . . though the common sort of people [i.e., in Europe] doth take them [hunting, dicing, hoarding gold, and so forth] for pleasures, yet they, seeing there is no natural pleasantness in them [*illi tamen quum natura nihil insit suaue*], do plainly determine them to have no affinity with true and right pleasure." That the senses are stirred by the counterfeit makes no difference: "For not the nature of the thing [*non enim ipsius rei natura*], but their perverse and lewd custom is the cause hereof. . . . Howbeit no man's judgement, depraved and corrupt, either by sickness or by custom, can change the nature of pleasure, more than it can . . . the nature of other things" (*MUL*, pp. 201-2).

Thus the Utopian philosophy provides that the freemen follow pleasure in their pursuit of happiness, each for himself, but at the same time every form of sensual stimulation must have won the approval of uncorrupted right reason. And on this last point the individual's own view is not shown as decisive, for now right reason expresses the common consent of the great body of sane men and women, the *consensus gentium*. The criteria applied in choosing or refusing pleasures, as either true or counterfeit, are clearly derived from the Utopian concept of God's purposes for man on earth. God or nature, they reason, intended man to develop a good life here and now, one in which his divine gift of reason would guide his choice of pleasures so that these would simultaneously delight the individual and strengthen, or at the worst not injure, the bonds of reason and affection which hold the community together in a "strong league," not of lawyers' terms, but of "love and benevolence."

In everyday practice the Utopians are shown as judging pleasures to be socially acceptable or to be prohibited by use of several criteria, all of which reflect More's realistic analysis of man in history. First of all, the record of trial and error which is their 1760 years of history represents wisdom accumulated by painful, extended inductive observations. In a word, the Utopians take a humanist view of the utility of history as not just an exciting or boring narrative, but as a sort of laboratory record of actions and their social effects, of progress or catastrophe all depending upon what actions men chose to take, each action having inevitably its necessary effects. Furthermore the Utopians in practice tend to find a possible pleasure to be forbidden (as counterfeit) when it appears clearly contrary to "right reason" or man's best "nature." Relatively new pleasures might well be forbidden if their observed aftereffects actually prove injurious to one of the distinctive human qualities, above all the powers of reason and mutual love, upon whose healthy preservation the entire Utopian society of "nature" depends. What of pleasures previously unheard of? It seems that they are presumed innocent until demonstrated guilty. There is in Utopia a genial assumption that, barring evidence of a pleasure's actual antisocial effects (which, it is true, might appear in time), all pleasures are good and honest. For "no kind of pleasure [is] forbidden, whereof cometh no harm" (*MUL*, p. 166).

One point certainly requires some explanation, namely, the paradox by which More describes his Utopians as following two kinds of highest good, kinds which had for many centuries been assumed to be not only antithetic but irreconcilable. Like the Stoics, the Utopians are devoted to virtue, justice, the common welfare of their state, and—when feasible—to the welfare of humanity. At the same time, like the Epicureans, they consider pleasure to be the main desire of human beings. How is it possible at once to be wise sages (with passion under control, not erased) while reveling as porkers in Epicurus' sty? One sees why some of More's critics have inclined to think him merely joking in his ironic, seemingly inconsequential way. But a reasonably careful study of Utopian philosophy will show that, according to the premises underlying the Utopian commonwealth, More was strictly logical when he described the freemen as pursuing both virtue and pleasure without insoluble conflict.

In explanation, consider that More quoted the accepted Stoical definition of virtue—the one all Utopians accept—from Cicero himself, citing *De finibus* pointedly in the earliest editions (*MUL*, p. 187 ff.).

Certainly then we may assume that More was aware of Cicero's famous attack upon the Epicureans as antisocial men who refused to be governed by "natural law" or virtue; and indeed, from the Stoic viewpoint, Cicero even flatly asserted that devotion to sensual pleasure was incompatible with moral rectitude.[27] Is it possible to resolve the paradox that the Utopians follow virtue and pleasure at once?

On the one hand, More, like Erasmus, admired the philosophical ethics of the later Roman Stoicism as closest to the original Christian ethics. He observed, nevertheless, with his characteristic realism, that in everyday life as well as in recorded history, most men everywhere actually sought pleasure before virtue, justice, and the common welfare. In short, he saw that while the Stoic social values were finer, the Epicurean theory of social motivation was more practical. Wittily, in his satire, More provided a restraint which enabled the Utopian freemen to be, as it were, simultaneously Stoics as well as Epicureans. For in the Utopian republic all *antisocial* pleasures—that is, all pleasures which the lessons of history have proved to be destructive of the bond of nature between men—are absolutely forbidden to all citizens, under the terrible penalty of loss of citizenship (i.e., becoming a bondman or slave). For instance, while the Utopians are beefeaters, no freeman is allowed to butcher oxen, and if he were to take pleasure in butchery, he would be treated as insane, a status intermediate between being a citizen and being a bondman (many who in the twentieth century are punished by prison, as criminals, would be treated as sick in Utopia). No freeman takes pleasure in hoarding gold, in conspicuous waste, in hunting, or (though at times it may be necessary to protect the good life) in war. Briefly, then, while all healthy or innocent pleasures are free to the citizens, pleasures which can corrupt or destroy societies are forbidden. Hence, one might say, a sound state of health is forcibly maintained in the public mind, just as nowadays citizens may be forcibly restrained from enjoying themselves by polluting the source of a public drinking-water supply. Since it is obvious that the only pleasures which will remain after this process of critical censoring is complete will be those which are either innocent and harmless or socially beneficial to the commonwealth (like the joys of marriage or of natural science), it necessarily follows that the Utopian citizens can consistently pursue both pleasure and virtue at the same time. Among the Utopians toleration does not extend to those sometimes attractive vices which tend to destroy the republic.

The Utopian republic, although in many ways very attractive when compared to Renaissance Europe as suggested in Book I through the Dialogue, is of course in many others rigorously righteous. Certainly few twentieth-century men or women would be at ease in it, but this proves nothing. This imaginary state, like other great works of art, was not designed for our physical residence or, for that matter, residence by More's contemporaries. The Utopian commonwealth represents a grand satiric construction, a "mirror" not merely for a magistrate but for all Englishmen. Considering the tough realism of the satire, it seems wildly funny that "we go on using the word 'Utopia' to signify an easy-going paradise, whose only fault is that it is too happy and ideal to be realized" (Chambers, p. 125). *Utopia*, like the *Praise of Folly*, is best seen as a work of art which belongs not only to the English but also to the Continental Renaissance. Both satires range over the broad reaches of European civilization; both hold up life ruled by reason and compassion for the welfare of the whole people in ironic and sometimes tragic contrast to the patterns of contemporary life. True, Utopia itself is an island state; but then the new age of humane culture, of which More, Erasmus, and Colet dreamed in 1509, was to begin in England. How these humanists conceived the classics should be used in the reformed culture they sought also emerges more clearly. It appears that they commonly thought of the hoped-for new order, not as a rebirth of ancient civilization, but as a new and original creation which should incorporate much from the most recent age, yet would be potentially as different from it as Utopian culture was from that of contemporary Europe. Surely this English humanist vision of a new and rationalized good society leaps far beyond the intellectual confines of the tight little isle, and it thus embodies an international and cosmopolitan concept of the Renaissance.

Indeed, More set forward one of the great shaping ideas of modern free societies which aim at peace—the ideal of utopian progress. This is the concept that communities are capable of advancing slowly in a positive and desirable direction, that this change can continue indefinitely in time and is within the control of man rather than simply dependent on Providence, and that, ultimately, as J. B. Bury wrote, "a condition of general happiness will . . . be enjoyed, which will justify the whole process of civilization." [28] Obviously the state of Utopia does not embody More's own complete Christian humanist idea of a good life, for to him this would require that the achievements based on wise use of reason and nature be joined to those of a purified Catholicism. (When Hythlodaye brought the Scriptures to the pagan Utopians, they found essential harmony between original Christian teachings and their own philosophy of nature.) But the Discourse of Utopia may be regarded as a complete picture of a good life. And the Discourse itself adopts the humanist premise that, under requisite safeguards, men are by nature capable of a rational life lived in harmony with both human and external nature. (The Utopians never, as so many moderns do, seek to "conquer" nature—itself a war concept.) On the other hand, the treatment of human nature in Utopia does not itself imply such a belief in spontaneous and congenital human rationality or goodness as to suggest that some sudden social change can overnight establish a rule of peace and justice forever. The Utopian good life is, in many respects, a hard and plain one. In material things the Utopians carefully restrict production and consumption to what is necessary. They avoid all luxury and waste (conspicuous consumption), since history had shown these to be roads to social corruption. Thus their communal life is marked by Utopian rather than Baconian progress, for, although rich, they are not enslaved to what has been called a pig economy in which all are stimulated to limitless production and consumption of material goods (Adams [1949]).

The idea of Utopian progress could not have been conceived, let alone taken seriously as defining attainable goals for western society, until several formidable ancient traditions had been at least partly overcome. The first of these was the persistent medieval belief that the world was in its senile dotage and man degenerate, that the Golden Age occurred long ago and that the world's end was imminent, all of which prompted the heavy pessimism about man's future which pervaded much Renaissance thought.[29]

Utopian progress, moreover, involved an idea that applied natural science can be used to advance human happiness. But there had to be a "rehabilitation of nature" before natural science could be advanced as an instrument of social progress. It had to be proved that the experimental study of natural phenomena was not a criminal probing into a realm of forbidden and Mephistophelean knowledge which leads to diabolism or atheism, as with Marlowe's Doctor Faustus. With this mighty advance in ideas, the name of Sir Francis Bacon and the *Advancement of Learning* will, of course, always be associated. Actually, however, Thomas More put forward the same essential argument a century before Bacon, in the *Utopia*, where "natural philosophy (i.e., science) is considered, not as 'conjuring,' involving a pact like that of Faust and Mephistopheles, but as something acceptable to God and even a part of religious duty." [30]

Furthermore, a new and dynamic conception of human happiness had to appear, gradually to replace the static idea of older cultures, illustrated, for instance, in the last cantos of Dante's *Divine Comedy*, which represent supreme bliss as contemplation and love, combined at the highest intensity but with perfection achieved and nothing remaining to strive for.

Finally, man had to arrive at the conception, as represented in Book II of *Utopia*, that the problems of existence and of the pursuit of happiness on earth are in man's own hands for solution, and not simply in those of Providence. All four of these prerequisites for an idea of Utopian progress were represented by More a century before Bacon set out his sumptuous but radically different vision of science's power to improve man's lot on earth (Adams [1949], pp. 374-76).

It is time to examine the criticism of war in the Discourse of Utopia. Basically, More's criticism of war through his picture of the good life in Utopia amounts to a massive onslaught upon several kinds of tyranny. One—the more obvious—is the tyranny of evil and corrupt men, exemplified by the ruling powers and their supporters in states near to Utopia, states which of course closely (and even at times identifiably) resemble those actually existing in Renaissance Europe. The other form assumed by tyranny is more subtle and pervasive: it is the tyranny of vicious custom over men's minds and social behavior. As satire, the *Utopia* is especially powerful because it cannot be taken as merely negative. On the other hand, neither does it eschew realism for romanticism, and escape, like Plato in the *Republic*, into a never-never land of secular saints and permanent, static subjection to them of the human majority. Evidently, when Utopia is taken by itself as a representation of a good life, More has rejected both the ideas that agonizing social evils (e.g., poverty, crime, war) result from congenital sinfulness or corruption in human nature itself, and that a good life should automatically emerge (as Rousseau may have felt) if only all civilization could be stripped away and man left in a condition of presumptive primitive anarchy.

The Utopian freemen emphatically are not "noble savages." In his positive picture of a good life in Utopia, as an alternative available to men in the Renaissance (most of all to Englishmen), More recognized certain inborn human qualities which distinguish men from beasts—above all the power of reason and the power of love. In Utopia every practicable means is used positively to insure that every man capable and willing shall achieve happiness through living in harmony with his own nature and with the human family as a whole. Positively each freeman from birth is ceaselessly educated toward this end, partly through example, partly through conscious inculcation of ideals of honor and glory common to all citizens and admired because they strengthen the good life for all. For these purposes, the coexisting neighbor states serve as a sort of living museum of the follies and insanities of which human nature is potentially capable. (Examples would be acceptance of the idea that the king can do no wrong, the worship of tyrants, or pride in possession of wealth beyond human needs.)

Since the *Utopia* is too rich to be examined in detail here, let us concentrate upon several critical examples, first, of the attack upon vicious custom and false ideals of honor and glory. In context of the whole Utopian philosophy, More appears to have accepted as valid the neo-Stoic account (such as Erasmus gave in his *Against War*) of the process by which man's inborn talent for reason and love can become, by gradual degrees, corrupted. This appears in his treatment of butchery and hunting. As the Utopians see it, to learn from childhood to take pleasure in systematic cruelty certainly, in time, corrupts human nature and, finally, prepares men to enjoy (or take for granted) killing their fellows in war. While most Utopians are beefeaters, since meat is found necessary to give strength for the work they think right by man's nature (*MUL*, p. 282), such necessary slaughters are strictly forbidden to freemen and are instead assigned only to the bondmen, who are already depraved and who are bondmen as long as they prove incapable of a life of reason and mutual affection. *All* Utopian freemen oppose sacrificial slaughter, since they believe that Nature (or God), as a benevolent mother, has no pleasure in blood (*MUL*, p. 293). Freemen may not even witness butchery, and only prepared meat is brought into the city: "For they permit not their free citizens to accustom their selfs to the killing of beasts, through the use whereof they think that clemency, the gentlest affection of our nature, doth by little and little decay and perish" (*MUL*, p. 158).

The custom of hunting, so vastly popular in More's England, and esteemed as practice for war, was held by the Utopians in even greater revulsion than butchery. For hunting, while necessary, they thought to be the "lowest, vilest, and most abject part of butchery." Neither their God nor they, godlike in natural gifts at birth, find "true pleasure" in slaughter. They declare that there is no (uncorrupted) "natural pleasantness" in such killing, and that it can be enjoyed only by a man who is so degraded (beastly) as to savor bloodshed. Hence, hunting, "as a thing unworthy to be used of free men, the Utopians have rejected to their butchers, to the which craft . . . they appoint their bondmen." The passage, though a bit long, should be quoted to illustrate finely how vicious custom comes to tyrannize over men born with no love of cruelty:

For what delight can there be, and not rather displeasure, in hearing the . . . howling of dogs? Or what greater pleasure is there to be felt, when a dog followeth an hare, than when a dog followeth a dog? For one thing is done in both, that is to say, running, if thou hast pleasure therein. But if the hope of slaughter, and the expectation of tearing in pieces the beast doth please thee, thou shouldest rather be moved with pity to see a silly innocent hare murdered of a dog . . . the innocent of the cruel and unmerciful. Therefore all this exercise of hunting, as a thing unworthy to be used of free men, the Utopians have rejected to their butchers . . . their bondmen. For they count hunting the lowest, vilest, and most abject part of butchery . . . and do kill beasts only for necessity. Whereas the hunter [i.e., as in More's England] seeketh nothing but pleasure of the silly and woeful beast's slaughter and murder. The which pleasure in beholding death they think doth rise in the very beasts, either of a cruel affection of mind, or else to be changed in continuance of time into cruelty, by long use of so cruel a pleasure [MUL, pp. 199-202].

Only "lewd and perverse custom" causes some men to think differently. In contrast to common practice in More's Europe, Utopians are not brought up conditioned to find true honor or glory in such pursuits.

Underlying these Utopian views of butchery and war is evidently a specially intense form of the humanist comparison between man and the wild beasts. The passage just quoted on hunting, however, indicates that when men have gradually become depraved and habituated to cruelty, the power of custom, coupled with the depravity of the natural gift of reason, now adapted to the art of killing, makes such men worse than any beast can possibly be. This insight, revived by the English humanists with great satiric force, is related to the ideal concept of the good life of which uncorrupted man is potentially capable even when, as by definition in the state of Utopia, lacking Christianity.

More's satire on human folly perhaps reaches its greatest and most tragic height in his attack upon the addiction of despots and their supporters to needless war. At the end of Book I, Hythlodaye offered the thesis that when the broad European scene was viewed candidly, it revealed nothing less than a conspiracy of the rich few to oppress the great body of the people (*MUL*, p. 303).

Erasmus, in the criticism expressed in the adages cited earlier, and in his *Christian Prince*, threw nearly total doubt on the justice of almost all wars initiated by princes in his lifetime. He identified needless invasive wars as the characteristic instrument of tyrants in history. As for his own time, he could hardly cite a war whose cause had not been ambition, lust, ferocity, wrath, or avarice. In other words, the tyrants of the Renaissance, when it came to war, were if anything worse than those of antiquity. What Erasmus in effect had done (and at times, as in "The king and the fool are born such," explicitly) was to stress a fateful split between the interests of the decadent Renaissance princes and the common people: "the commons love peace and the monarchs foment war."

In his treatment of war in *Utopia*, More carried this idea logically forward toward its necessary extreme. Not that he attacks monarchy per se, for in the wise humanist Prince Utopus the greatness of just rule was exemplified. In some sides of Utopian warmaking, the aim is evidently to protect the island of sanity and reason from invasion by corruption and injustice from without. In undertaking war without their borders, however, the basic Utopian perception is that the common people in foreign lands, while of course not untainted by long-sustained vicious customs and false ideals of honor and glory, are basically far saner than their princes, who are virtually all tyrants of the worst breed: "For they [the Utopians] do no less pity the base and common sort of their enemies' people, than they do their own; knowing that they [commoners abroad] be driven and enforced to war against their wills by the furious madness of their princes and heads" (*MUL*, p. 259).

In the Utopian concepts and practices of war, More's social criticism goes far beyond that implied by presenting (as Donner put it) "the description of a commonwealth whose institutions appear ideal by means of the contrast it presents to the conditions actually prevailing" in the neighbor states which closely resemble Renaissance Europe. The Utopians, when war is unavoidable, employ it either to protect or to enhance, first, the good life in the island, second, Utopian justice and the rights of common humanity as opposed to the interests of tyrants and their equally criminal supporters abroad. True, at every point Utopian theory and practice does contrast sharply with that actually prevailing in More's day —conditions such as were acidly sketched in his first book. But More was not working out an academic exercise: underlying the whole work lies the conviction that, given the necessary leadership of a wise prince, England was itself capable of becoming a utopia—but Christian, not pagan. Politics to More was the art of the possible.

Let us consider the Utopian concepts of war and its glory, of treaties, of conditions which may make war just, and of the art of humane war.

The Utopians, evidently, do not regard the natural state of man as peace—only the natural state of uncorrupted and rightly educated man, which is the basis of their good life. Even below butchery and hunting in the scale of bloody depravities which man may, by the power of custom, come to enjoy, is such war as their neighbor princes conduct. In view of the Utopian philosophy, war of this kind is the worst of man-made evils and the ultimate in group depravity. If no true pleasure or glory can be won through butchery or hunting of beasts, it follows logically that no true honor or glory can be gained through war. Only "lewd and perverse custom" makes foreign warmakers think so: "War or battle as a thing very beastly [*rem plane beluinam*], and yet to no kind of beasts in so much use as it is to man, they do detest and abhor; and, contrary to the custom of almost all other nations, they count nothing so much against glory, as glory gotten in war" (*MUL*, p. 243).

Abroad, as noted, the Utopians perceive that the bulk of humanity agrees but is driven to war against its will. More's satire does not indict all mankind, as Swift's sometimes seems to do in *Gulliver's Travels*. But the Utopians perceive that custom has produced abroad a class of men who actually revel in war—the mercenary soldiers such as all corrupt princes employed. To the philosophic Utopians these men are not merely deplorable. Rather, like their masters, they represent the depths of utter depravity to which men can fall when they have utterly perverted Nature's greatest gifts to all men—reason and the power to love. Whereas among uncorrupted men everywhere, the "bond of nature" and humanity prompts humans to aid each other, these men's pleasure and business is in manslaughter, legalized as just war by the tyrants who employ them. For a few pence a day, they change sides, and while at their trade will cheerfully murder their own fathers or brothers. Habitual cruelty has so debauched these men that it would be useless to capture them and attempt to educate them, as bondmen in Utopia, for a life of reason. These professional soldiers, as a class, form a body of aids to tyrants. For foreign wars, therefore, the Utopians hire these mercenaries for gold, with two purposes in mind: to secure military victory and to exterminate as many of them as possible. "Now the Utopians pass not how many of them they bring to destruction. For they believe that they should do a very good deed for all mankind, if they could rid out of the world all that foul, stinking den of that most wicked and cursed people" (*MUL*, p. 255). Those who survive are duly paid. So much for one type of military glory common in Renaissance Europe.

To the Utopians, war is only justified when it protects the good life for all their citizens, not the interests of any special minority. This has a bearing on the satire concerning international treaties, which in More's Europe, as among the Utopians' neighbor states, were commonly made only to be broken on some pretext when princely warmakers wished to resume their sport. In the Utopian republic, all sane men recognize the humanitarian bond of nature which links the uncorrupted in ties of common affection within the human family. The atheist is held to be not only insane (in the Utopian sense) but potentially a danger to others, since—having discarded the certainty of impartial justice after death—he is restrained only by fear from injuring other men (*MUL*, pp. 274-75). The Utopians, to whom the bond of nature is league and treaty enough, regard foreign princes in a similar light. What corrupt prince, who does not respect the bond of nature and humanity, will let words deter him from injuring others when it suits his tyrannic will?

As touching leagues, which in other places between country and country be so oft concluded, broken, and renewed, they never make none with any nation. For to what purpose serve leagues, say they? As though nature had not set sufficient love between man and man. And who so regardeth not nature, think you that he will pass for words [*MUL*, pp. 238-42]?

Of course, adds the ironic Hythlodaye, in Christian Europe treaties are always inviolate.

As pagan philosophers living according to reason, the Utopians find only two kinds of war to be naturally just: (1) those which protect the good life in Utopia itself, where all citizens have the common welfare at stake; and (2) wars which extend some measure of this good life abroad, where, in contrast, the common peoples' desire for peace is generally opposed to the desire for war of corrupt princes or tyrants and their supporters. With other justifications for war, including some long held officially to be just in More's Europe, they will have nothing to do.

One kind of war which the Utopians regard as naturally just is that made to repel imminent attack. It is remarkable that, although the Utopians abhor foreign professional soldiers and indeed war itself, every able-bodied Utopian who is willing—men, women, and children, working as a family group (i.e., the unit most closely bound by "nature")—is perpetually trained for war (*MUL*, p. 258). But the Utopians do not wait for invaders to bring ruin and disease into their island: "If any prince stir up war against them, intending to invade their land, they meet him incontinent out of their own borders with great power and strength. For they never lightly make war in their own country" (*MUL*, p. 265).

The second motive for "just" Utopian war illustrates the common unity of interest and nature which exists in the island state. A Renaissance prince might have made war had some highly regarded nobleman been slain abroad. But the Utopians will make war to avenge the execution abroad of the humblest freeman. Within the bond of nature all are equally precious, so "that they would not be willing to change [exchange] any of them for their adversary's prince" (*MUL*, p. 251). Regardless of whatever foreign (i.e., corrupted) legal process may have preceded the execution, the Utopians take revenge upon the wrongdoers' entire nation—unless the offenders are handed over to the Utopians for punishment by death or slavery (*MUL*, p. 246).

The third motive for "just" Utopian wars—offensive action to gain land for colonization—has long attracted the most attention and perhaps caused the most confusion among modern readers. Chambers (pp. 140-41) reasoned that here More wished to deliver "a side-blow at the state of Europe in 1516, and to censure wars waged at the whim of, and for the personal aggrandizement of, autocrats like Francis I, or Henry, or Wolsey." This is, I think, only part of the satire's point. In seeking unoccupied land for a population which would otherwise overburden that already cultivated and available, the Utopians follow reason to protect a good life "according to nature." Experience has taught them that cities and the supporting countryside are happiest when of the optimum size in relation to available natural resources (*MUL*, pp. 119-36). Suppose the population passes the "due number"? First, a peaceful proposal is made to a neighboring state which has directly contiguous, unoccupied ground, that simply as much land as is required—no more—shall be ceded, for use by the Utopians to build a new city. The Utopians are famous for their skillful agriculture, which can make land formerly insufficient for its few occupants now support them plus the Utopian emigrants in heightened prosperity. Furthermore, the erstwhile foreigners gain the privilege of Utopian citizenship at once. Where the interest of the common people is admitted (i.e., as opposed to some prince's claim to a "title"), the proposal is usually accepted at once. If, however, it is refused, then the Utopians consider that the law of nature justifies them in conquering simply as much unused land (a gift of Nature, in their philosophy) as needed (*MUL*, pp. 154-55). But—in contrast to various Renaissance princes—they never embark on schemes of unlimited imperial expansion which are simply designed to change titles from one prince to another.

More does not simply satirize traditional imperial land-grabbing: positively he advances an alternative concept which is based upon the implicit principles that the rights of the common people are superior to the rights of traditional princes and that the most fundamental right of human beings is to that share of a benevolent Nature's gifts to all men (earth, water, and so forth) which are requisite for man, through wise labor, to create for himself a good life. These three kinds of wars, then, the Utopians find "just" as required to protect the good life in their island homeland.

The second major class of wars which the Utopians will wage as "just" extends some measure of this good life, or at least its kind of republican justice, abroad. The conduct of these wars expresses consistently the cosmopolitan and humanitarian Utopian view that all men belong to one human family and that potentially all belong to one "society of nature." In these wars the Utopians sacrifice treasure and blood, not in their national interests merely, but for the welfare of all humanity. First, they will wage war, if necessary, to aid oppressed friends to gain true justice or to redress loss of money after wrongs have been inflicted in enemy nations under false pretenses of justice or through invasions for plunder. If a Utopian merchant abroad has suffered unjust loss merely of money, their only action is to embargo trade with the entire nation where the incident occurred. If, however, a friendly nation's merchants have sustained unjust money loss abroad, then the Utopians will make war to secure redress for them. Secondly, out of "natural" pity and compassion the Utopians sometimes volunteer their military aid to deliver a people from bondage to tyranny. The Utopians require, however, that they be consulted while the wrongs are "new and fresh" (*MUL*, pp. 243-46). In other words, the Utopians apply a kind of statute of limitations, in contrast to the common practice of Renaissance princes who, wishing a pretext for a war of aggrandizement, often dug up some ancient injury which they now loudly proclaimed required avenging.

Finally, let us consider the remarkable Utopian art of humane war. More's handling of this topic constitutes one of the most mordant parts of his satiric attack upon remediable social evils and upon decadent contemporary statecraft. Apparent earlier, in his satire upon the French poet Brixius in epigrams written in 1513-14, was More's application of a critical and scientific realism to the absurdities of the arts and ideology of chivalric war. Now in the Discourse of Utopia he developed this critical approach in a devastating way. As in all else they do, his Utopians approach war as rational and uncorrupted men, gifted with reason and the power of love, not as beasts. They seek to preserve where possible the lives of their good freemen and all others abroad who are not so hopelessly corrupted that their deaths will serve the good of common humanity. The antichivalric Utopian art of war is, in effect, premised upon the idea that chivalric honor, glory, and falsely heroic war methods serve the interests only of a small class of decadent men, all corrupted by vicious custom: tyrannic princes and some of their noble supporters. (As for the professional mercenary soldiers, the Zapoletes, we have already seen that the Utopians regard them as depraved murderers who richly merit extermination.)

Machiavelli has fascinated many by the way in which he applied reason, or *realpolitik*, to the support of his tyrant-prince. The Utopian art of war, one might say, applies a kind of witty *realpolitik* against tyranny of both decadent men and ideas as embodied in traditional chivalry. The Utopians well know that the common people abroad generally desire peace but that they are "driven and enforced to war against their wills by the furious madness [*furiis agi*] of their princes and heads" (*MUL*, p. 250). Since to the Utopians war is the absolute antithesis of the good life according to Nature and reason, they bend every effort to attaining victory with a minimum of bloodshed (mercenary soldiers excepted), and, when victory has been attained, to administering a just, merciful peace in which they seek to prevent the recurrent rise of the tyrannies and injustices which mainly caused the war in the first place. Throughout the Utopian art of war appear their humane, antiromantic, antichivalric, and antityrannic ruling ideas of true honor and glory.

First, soldiers must be selected, if war must be, and to this job the Utopians apply a graduated scale of reason. While the Utopians themselves, of course, regard lust for gold as unnatural (insane), they see realistically that outside their good state many are so corrupt as to be ruled by avarice "so that there is no manner of act nor deed that gifts and rewards do not enforce men unto" (*MUL*, p. 249). Accordingly the Utopians accumulate vast stores of gold for use in wartime (*MUL*, p. 172). First of all therefore they hire mercenary soldiers abroad to fight Utopia's battles, which they gladly do, since the Utopians pay the best wages. Next they hire somewhat less corrupted (i.e., nonprofessional) soldiers from their friends and others. Only last of all do they use their own philosopher-citizens, any one of whom they value more than an enemy prince (*MUL*, pp. 252-55). Even then no man is forced against his nature to fight, although all are honored who do. Most notably, "according to reason," every fighting Utopian, since he is linked by a bond of nature to all others but especially to his own blood kinsmen, goes forth to war in a family group. (By inference, next to a family would stand its direct neighbors, and so forth.) The contemporary mercenary soldiers would even kill fathers or brothers for gold and regard this presumably as the normal chance of war. But to the Utopians one of the greatest forms of dishonor is to abandon a close relative:

And in set field the wives do stand every one by their own husband's side. Also every man is compassed next about with his own children, kinsfolks, and alliance. That they, whom nature chiefly moveth to mutual succor, thus standing together, may help one another. It is a great reproach . . . for the husband to come home without his wife, or the wife without her husband, or the son without his father . . . [*MUL*, p. 258].

The broad Utopian strategy in war follows from their rational humanitarianism and hatred of tyranny. It is to use whatever means reason can devise to end the war with victory but with a minimum of cruelty to and bloodshed by the common people of the enemy as well as their own. If reason and love are nature's greatest gifts to man, as distinguished from the brute beasts, then reason and love should be used in the art of war to the utmost. Logically therefore, the Utopians have no epithet more precise than "beastly" to characterize traditional European chivalrous war practices and "glory" which depended on brute force and at times gloried in promiscuous slaughter (e.g., Flodden Field in 1513):

They be not only sorry, but also ashamed to achieve the victory with bloodshed, counting it great folly to buy precious wares so dear. They rejoice . . . if they vanquish . . . their enemies by craft and deceit. And for that act they make a general triumph and, as if the matter were manfully handled, they set by a pillar of stone in the place where they so vanquished their enemies, in token of the victory. For then they glory, then they boast and crack that they have played the men indeed, when they have so overcome as no other living creature but only man could—that is to say, by the might and puissance of wit. For with bodily strength (say they) bears, lions, boars, wolves, dogs, and other wild beasts do fight. And as the most part of them do pass us in strength and fierce [i.e., "animal"] courage, so in wit and reason we be much stronger than they all [*MUL*, pp. 247-48].

Utopian tactics follow logically from their broadly humane strategic view of war's nature and purposes. Completely avoiding bloodshed of their own people when possible, they may "translate" shore beacons on their island so that approaching enemy navies may be wholly wrecked with ingenious ease. Generally every advantage is taken of the natural defenses of the island's topography (*MUL*, p. 117). "It is hard to say whether they be craftier in laying an ambush or wittier in avoiding the same" (*MUL*, p. 260). They use great cleverness in devising defenses, armor, and military machinery, all intended to hasten the end and lessen the bloodshed of the war (*MUL*, pp. 260-62). Neither in battle nor in victory do the well-disciplined Utopians forget that they fight only for justice or to free from oppression common men, who have been forced by criminal leaders to be their enemies. Conditioned and educated from childhood to find no true glory in bloodshed and to believe that Nature's gifts were intended to benefit all men, the Utopians (unlike many Renaissance European soldiers, especially mercenaries) never break ranks after victory with a violent rage for slaughter or plunder. All who surrender freely are well treated: as bondmen they may even in time be re-educated so far as to become freemen themselves. The Utopians, thinking a bond of nature unites common men, never plunder, burn, and destroy almost at random (as did many Renaissance armies, to friend or foe alike). When a besieged city is captured, those who encouraged prolonging resistance (i.e., adding to needless bloodshed) are put to death promptly. Common soldiers are enslaved (in the Utopian sense). But the mass of the people go unharmed, because the Utopians feel that not they but their princes were guilty of injustice:

Truce taken with their enemies for a short time they . . . so faithfully keep that they will not break it . . . though they be thereunto provoked. They do not waste nor destroy their enemies' land with forragings, nor . . . burn . . . up their corn . . . thinking that it groweth for their own use and profit. They hurt no man that is unarmed, unless he be an espiall. All cities that be yielded unto them, they defend [cf. the English wanton destruction of Thérouenne in 1513]. And such as they win by . . . assault, they neither dispoil nor sack, but them that . . . dissuaded the yielding up of the same, they put to death. The other soldiers they punish with bondage. All the weak multitude they leave untouched. If they know that any citizens counselled to yield . . . up the city, to them they give part of the condemned men's goods . . . [*MUL*, p. 263].

The cost of the war is finally levied against the conquered whose injustice and tyranny caused it, but the Utopians administer their just peace mercifully and seek to spread their good life abroad. Thus they rarely demand payment of all the tribute. Again, they send some of their best citizens to live in the conquered country, to give, of course, an example of the good life and to encourage the conquered people to make utopian progress (*MUL*, p. 263).

At the actual point of direct close combat, when this proves unavoidable, the Utopians are particularly formidable, both because of their high training in the very chivalry and feats of arms which they despise as a source of honor and glory, and because of their union in philosophy and religion. They fight and, if they must, die according to reason and nature. First, no man need doubt that survivors in his personal family will be well cared for by all his fellows, joined as they are virtually into one family by the bond of nature and education. Furthermore, the common Utopian faith assures reward after death according to one's merits:

The wholesome and virtuous opinions, wherein they were brought up even from their childhood, partly through learning and partly through the good . . . laws of their weal public, augment . . . their manful courage. By reason whereof they neither set so little store by their lives, that they will rashly . . . cast them away; nor they be not so far in lewd [ignorant] and fond love therewith, that they will shamefully covet to keep them, when honesty biddeth leave them [*MUL*, p. 258].

Perhaps, however, no Utopian war tactic—that is, no element of the social criticism on war in *Utopia*—has provoked more mixed response than the idea of shortening war by purchasing the assassination of the enemy leaders or, that failing, seeking them out for first killing in actual battle. When war begins, the Utopians cause to be offered throughout enemy country very great rewards in gold to anyone who kills the enemy prince and other key leaders. For it is these evil men, not the common people, that the Utopians count to be their chief adversaries. The Utopians, however, are guided by reason and abhor needless bloodshed: therefore the reward is doubled if enemy leaders are delivered over alive. The same doubled reward is given to the leaders if they desert to the Utopians. Since by inference the foreign peoples are well aware, living as they do under tyrants who oppress the common people with needless wars, that among them there is little unpurchasable honor, virtue, or justice (i.e., not every man but every *corrupt* man has his price), the enemy ranks are apt to be rapidly broken by mutual mistrust. Certainly More pointed his deadly attack on decadent chivalrous codes clearly enough. Outside Utopia, where many are still subject to the tyranny of an evil custom (or idea), this assassination-or-surrender scheme is widely regarded as base and cruel, not to say "cowardish." The Utopians, however, think that to defeat or destroy tyrants is truly glorious and honorable, for they have at heart not the tyrant's comfort but the welfare of the oppressed common people—humanity:

And their promises they perform faithfully without any fraud. . . . This custom, of buying and selling adversaries, among other people is disallowed, as a cruel act of a base and cowardish mind. But they [the Utopians] in this behalf think themselves much praiseworthy, as who like wise men by this means dispatch great wars without any battle. . . . Yea, they count it also a deed of pity and mercy, because that by the death of a few offenders the lives of a great number of innocents, as well of their own men as also of their enemies' be . . . saved, which in fighting should have been slain. For they do no less pity the base and common sort of their enemies' people than they do their own, knowing that they be driven and enforced to war against their wills by the furious madness of their princes and heads [*MUL*, pp. 250, 259].

Finally, in actual battle, bands of picked young Utopian men strive first to slay the enemy captains and thus win more quickly (*MUL*, p. 259).

Many questions leap up concerning tyrannicide as represented in More's state of Utopia. It seems quite clear that, on grounds of their own philosophy as applied to war, the Utopians themselves regard such action as just. May their ideas well be identified as "More's own"? This is highly dubious: as Hexter (pp. 50-51) has observed, both More's irony and his chosen imaginary-travel form make it "unresolvably uncertain"—if we use only the *Utopia*—what his personal views were when he wrote it. Father Edward Surtz, in his *Praise of Wisdom* (pp. 290-91) considered, from a Catholic viewpoint, whether both More and his Utopians sanctioned only "legitimate tyrannicide." Regretfully he felt obliged to reject this idea, though finding it "tempting in its simplicity and in its exoneration of More and the Utopians." First, he found the passage's "realistic" tone against it, "in its appeal to the venality of the agents. Second, if More had intended to excuse and defend the behavior of his Utopians, he would have been much more careful to make clear that the rulers among their enemies were viewed as tyrants and hence worthy of death."

In comment I would say that, as far as the Utopians are concerned, More's satire could hardly have made more clear the Utopian view that those who oppress the common, peace-loving people with needless wars of foreign invasion are indeed unbearably oppressive and merit death, unless their surrender alive can be achieved. After all, both More and his book demand their 1516 setting. When he wrote, More lived under a Henry VIII who may well have seemed to the English humanists, certainly comparatively, to be an almost ideal Christian prince. Yet nonetheless there was then no mistaking the real absolutism of his monarchic power. We need not be surprised that the humanists, from Colet in 1496 to More in 1516, did not even more sharply identify oppressors as tyrants worthy of death. The wonder is rather that they felt able to be so free critically during the golden age of English humanism.

If we look broadly at the entire *Utopia* as humanist social criticism, its great power and significance stand probably in its representation imaginatively of a good life and just rule, with a wealth of detail touching a great variety of everyday practical forms of life, as a potentially practicable alternative to existing dog-eat-dog patterns. It offered, not a fantastic dreamworld of "ideal" perfections, but a concrete vision of a good life perhaps attainable for at least one part of humanity, a part favored by Nature in its islandic position, but even more in its relative freedom from corruptions and tyrannies seemingly endemic on the continent nearby. Even for its own time, the *Utopia* can be dismissed to the realm of the fairy tale only if one presumes the realistic impossibility of such a people, whatever its genius, finding even a single wise monarch—a Prince Utopus—capable of initiating the creative process by which a benevolent despotism can evolve into a republic wherein the good of all, not the interest of a privileged few, is paramount (cf. Hexter, pp. 59, 98).

To the humanists the period reaching from the opening of 1517 to the
Field of the Cloth of Gold in 1520 was one of great accomplishments
and greater expectations. Its theme, up to Wolsey's Treaty of Universal
Peace in late 1518 was "the whole kingdom wishes for peace." Then this
turned (in Erasmus' phrase) to "perhaps the golden age is coming after
all."

With the publication of the *Utopia* in December, 1516, the critical
structure of humanist ideas on war and peace was virtually completed.
The drama was ready for a new turn. Nor could its outcome be foreseen.
True, to the humanist critics it had become apparent that a deep decay
had penetrated medieval Christendom, a decay capable of exploding into
international anarchy and spreading wars capable of destroying all practical possibility for peaceful reconstruction of the old order along new
and Renaissance lines. Modern critics who view the idea of revolution
with favor are apt to condemn the early Tudor humanists for not being
"of the sort to inspire mass enthusiasm on a revolutionary scale." Were
they either too visionary or too unrealistic to meet the needs of their
time? "Even More, who had a far deeper insight than Erasmus, and
was centuries ahead of his time in his vision of social reform, seemed positively anxious to dissociate his speculations from any idea of their practical use." [1] This view mistakes the men and their age. In early 1517 the
most practical humanist strategy available certainly was to attempt, by
every possible means, to influence the existing princes, like Henry VIII,
to undertake the duties of just rule for the common welfare. This was
indeed the only course of wise action then available. Henry might in
time become a tyrant, but he still held high esteem as a generally great
and good Christian prince.

As 1517 opened, the visible evidence suggested that perhaps at last
the great princes were coming round to grasp the wisdom of the very

peace ideal whose hard, realistic necessity the humanists had urged for years. At London in late December, 1516, the Venetian ambassador heard that friend of humanism, Bishop Tunstall, express great desire for an end to the wars in Europe; while the Duke of Norfolk told him that "the whole of this kingdom wished for a general peace," and Norfolk further hoped all Christendom would unite to meet the very real and rising danger of Turkish invasion (Giustinian, I, 237).

Even the conduct of Francis I of France indicated that, after one adventure in pursuit of chivalric glory, he might turn toward rule as a just, peaceful Christian prince. The singular battle of Marignano (September 13-14, 1515) gave Francis an apparently complete triumph, yet in its aftermath, when nothing hindered the war's expansion deeper into Italy, he too showed a desire for peace. In Antwerp Erasmus had taken up residence for a few months of his rather nominal duties as a Counselor to Charles, Francis I's potential enemy, and from there on February 21, 1517, wrote to Francis to eulogize his evident will to desist from further war and instead to help build a permanent peace among all Christian princes. In an age when great men were extravagantly eager to establish claims to perpetual fame, Erasmus' tactic was to emphasize strongly that by his peacemaking Francis would achieve forever the reputation of a truly heroic, noble sovereign. He wished that his own literary genius could do justice to such a king, among the glories of whose reign he numbered especially "that divine blessing of peace which has been restored, chiefly by your efforts, to the Christian world." [2] To a friend, on February 24, Erasmus wrote to suggest not only that *Utopia*, then beginning to sell throughout Europe, was based on England, but that in it could be seen treated "the sources from which almost all the ills of the body politic arise" (*EN*, II, 503).

Grand indeed is Erasmus' vision, set out in a letter of February 26, of the progress in the arts of civilization then imminent, given the requisite peace and encouragement needed for the release of long-pent-up human talents. It must be remembered that the humanists felt that their first great work for the new age should be to recover at least the degree of knowledge possessed by antiquity before its own culture was overwhelmed by war. But the English humanists, at least, had built up even more far-reaching designs for a new social order now possible—given peace and tolerably responsible kingship, all of which seemed now at hand.

At the present moment I could almost wish to be young again, for no other reason but this, that I anticipate the near approach of a golden age; so clearly do we see the minds of princes, as if changed by inspiration, devoting all their energies to the pursuit of peace. The chief movers . . . are Pope Leo, and Francis . . . of France. . . . When I see that the highest sovereigns of Europe, Francis . . . Charles . . . Henry of England, and the Emperor Maximilian have all set their warlike preparation aside, and established peace upon solid . . . foundations, I am led to a confident hope, that not only morality and Christian piety, but also a genuine and purer literature may come to renewed life of greater splendour; especially as this object is pursued with equal zeal in various regions of the world. To the piety of these princes it is due, that we see everywhere, as if upon a given signal, men of genius are arising and conspiring together to restore the best literature. . . . Why should I say more? Everything promises . . . the happiest success [EN, II, 505-8].

True, at work behind the scenes of secret diplomacy there were evidently still sinister forces, whose startling results appeared from time to time. Only a week later (March 1) Erasmus wrote grimly to More. On the bright side he already wanted revised copy for a new edition of the *Utopia* as soon as More could send it. On the other hand, suddenly the fields near Antwerp were filled with mercenary soldiers, led by the Emperor Maximilian. What—except new outrages upon humanity—it meant, was beyond Erasmus' ken:

The Emperor, generally in want of arms, is now here with a retinue splendidly armed, and the fields are full of bands of soldiers, but whence and in whose name they come, is not known. What a wretched country this is, with so many vultures knawing at it; and how happy they might be, if the communes were united among themselves [EN, II, 514].

These, as we know, were the mercenaries whom Henry and Wolsey had financed with a huge English gold payment to continue the war against France after renewed English invasion proved impossible. Fortunately for peace but unfortunately for English dreams of chivalric glory, the wily Maximilian saw the light of reason (i.e., French gold), and outfoxed his English ally by agreeing with Charles and refusing to renew the war. Instead he joined the peace of Noyon (Pollard, pp. 111-24). Thus exploded Wolsey's scheme for reconquering France with the Emperor's aid. On March 5, 1517, moreover, Pope Leo X issued a Bull imposing a five-year truce on the rulers of Europe, coupled with the hope that soon a joint expedition would be made against the Turks.[3] In private fact, Henry and Wolsey made peace with France only because they were forced to do so by the desertion of their allies. Publicly, however, with the English rulers, the papal Bull seemed to carry great weight.

For once Wolsey sensed accurately what the humanists had seen for years, that not just the whole of England but almost the whole of Europe desired peace. Balked, like Henry VIII, in schemes for war, the Cardinal, rarely without an ingenious expedient up his sleeve, set out in the spring of 1517 to achieve a superb victory of peace. At once he set in motion the secret diplomacy whose eventual public climax was to be a fantastic Treaty of Universal Peace. In the end, as Pollard observed (p. 114), "It is one of the most striking tributes to [Wolsey's] versatility and diplomacy that he should have received so much of the credit, at the time and in the eyes of posterity, for the pacification of 1518." Giustinian (I, 320) had only given credit where credit was due: "he being quieted, the whole turmoil would cease." The maneuvers and countermaneuvers, many behind the scenes, leading to this treaty occupied much of 1517-18. Even More was not privy to Wolsey's operations, although throughout 1517 he became ever more closely attached to Henry's court. Meanwhile rumors of peace and war, waves of optimism and pessimism, swept Europe and are reflected to us through the humanists' criticism.

As the slow English spring came on in 1517, Archbishop Warham, a power for peace and always Erasmus' best patron in England, longed for Erasmus' conversation to make his retirement more pleasant (*LP*, II, 2, 3046). Leaving no work for peace undone, before leaving Brussels in April Erasmus hastily wrote to Pope Leo X to congratulate him upon his effective work for peace. Leo, he thought (and in obvious contrast to Julius II), was building "undying trophies" through restoring "truly Christian piety, which in many ways has fallen into decay," "learning of the best sort," and "the public and lasting concord of Christendom, the source and parent of Piety and Erudition." He congratulated "this our age—which bids fair to be an age of gold, if ever such there was" (*EN*, II, 521-22). Then he came over to England for what we now know (although he certainly did not) was to be his last visit. Grimly he reported to More (May 30) a conversation he had recently had with an unnamed cardinal who "openly inveighs against the French with all the frankness of a Switzer. . . ." Far worse to him were reports current that Charles and the Emperor Maximilian had after all failed to agree and that renewal of war (against France) seemed likely. With pleasure he told how Tunstall had read the 1516 reprint of the *Panegyric* (1504) which glorified the prince skilled in arts of peace, and admired it. As for Tunstall himself, he was "glad that his part in the puppet-show [*peractam fabulam*] is ended at last"—(i.e., that he need have no more hand in war).[4] If only, the good old Bishop wished, Erasmus would stay in England (*EE*, 572)!

One remarkable event, at which Erasmus and every English humanist must surely have rejoiced, took place that spring, when in March Bishop Richard Fox founded Corpus Christi College at Oxford and thus began the permanent establishment of humanism in that university.[5] The story, a moving one, shows how fused in these men's eyes had become the practical problems of establishing just peace together with vital and long overdue reforms in religion and education. It also reveals clearly how, in the first part of the sixteenth century, medieval and Renaissance ideas were intertwined. Richard Fox (1446/7–1528), Bishop of Winchester, like More's youthful patron, Cardinal Morton, rose through the civil wars to power with Henry Tudor, afterward Henry VII. Fox sought peace within and without the realm throughout his long official life. Indeed, he was a leader in the peace party within the Council which young Henry VIII inherited from his father.[6] Wolsey had himself been Fox's secretary, but when Wolsey rose to power and royal policies turned toward adventures in war, the old Bishop was eased out of politics by his former aide. Long a patron of humanists, Fox turned his wealth and energy to furthering the New Learning, but not without some persuasion, since his first idea, as Hall tells, was to found at Oxford a "house of monks" (or, as Allen noted, for "the young monks of St. Swithun's at Winchester, studying at the University"). Bishop Hugh Oldham changed Fox's mind, after his own project of enlarging Exeter College proved too much for him alone. He got together with Fox and convinced him that a greater service to church and commonwealth would result if they pooled their resources and established a new college for strengthening humanism:

Now these two bishops conferring together, what manner of house they should build, and to what end and purpose, Bishop Fox was of the mind and determination to have made the college for religious men. But Bishop Oldham . . . said unto him: "What, my lord, shall we build houses, and provide livelihoods, for a company of bussing [buzzing?] monks, whose end and fall we ourselves may live to see? No, no, it is more meet, a great deal, that we should have care for the increase of learning, and for such as who by their learning shall do good in the church and commonwealth." To this

Bishop Fox at length yielded . . . and since . . . the same college hath been and is the nurse of many good scholars.[7]

A few weeks later, despite his age, Fox received from Wolsey a summons to drop his episcopal work and to take part in an expedition to Calais. Evidently he scented a scheme for possible renewal of war, and he refused. Already, he wrote, he had had too much of the "enormities" of war, and too little time for penance remained:

I have determined and, betwixt God and me, utterly renounced the meddling with worldly matters, specially concerning the war or any thing to it appertaining. Whereof for the many intolerable enormities that I have seen ensue by the said war in time past, I have no little remorse in my conscience. . . . And now, my lord, to be called to fortifications of towns and places of war or to any other matter concerning the war, being of the age of LXX years and above, and looking daily to die—the which if I died, being in any such meddling of the war, I think I should die in despair—; no marvel, my lord, the premises considered, if this my present vocation to such matters trouble not a little my spirits. I fear that I shall not, by reason thereof, be in such quietness that I shall dare say mass these next v or vi days.[8]

In 1510 John Colet founded his St. Paul's School on humanist lines, as I take it in part to provide a practical alternative to a pattern of education, both formal and informal, which had in the past helped prepare future leaders to find "glory" in chivalric war. Fox seems finally to have made a similar decision; indeed he followed Colet, by founding grammar schools on his manor at Taunton (1522), and in his town of Grantham (October 2, 1528) only three days before his death.[9]

During the late spring and the summer of 1517 an uneasy kind of peace persisted, crossed with rumors of war's renewal—that is, of another outbreak of the princes' classical folly. As early as 1496, when John Colet began in England a new and historical kind of literary and social criticism, he used his Suetonius in an effort to determine the original context for St. Paul's counsel of obedience to Christians living under Roman rule. On June 5, 1517, Erasmus dated the preface to his edition of Suetonius' *Lives of the Caesars*. Now Erasmus drew grimly realistic parallels between forces which caused the decay of ancient Roman civilization and those at work in Renaissance Europe. Princes, he thought, might learn both good and evil lessons of experience from Suetonius, especially concerning the inherent instability of empires founded by war. He found a direct causal relation between the Roman use of mercenaries, the expansion of civil wars (analogous to wars within Christendom), and the eventual collapse of the Roman world center before barbarian invasions from without (like the then-threatening Turkish invasion). Erasmus argued that when, under evil rulers in decadent Rome, an insatiate passion for military glory prevailed, the real power in the state came to be "in the hands, not of the senators, not of the Roman citizens, but of the mercenaries." After Roman social corruption became well enough advanced, the barbarian hordes were irresistible, and the ancient Roman empire was doomed. When once thus extinguished, not the glory but only the name of Roman civilization could be restored by the medieval popes.[10]

Clearly with the development of the historical method in literary criticism, there emerged a general concept of the utility of history itself. Since Roman civilization under the *Pax Romana* represented to the English humanists nearly the ultimate in man's achievement before their own age, they tended especially to set the two cultures in comparison. Thus history became more than a mirror for the individual prince; it became a mirror of patterns in world civilization. During the years 1517 to 1527, the Turks mounted a military advance, by surges, moving toward the heart of Europe. As we see in Erasmus' comment on Suetonius, the parallel between the pattern which led to ancient Rome's downfall and the contemporary threat to Christendom was stunningly obvious. There was, therefore, a grand and tragic irony in that, just as the Renaissance seemed ripe for a great forward movement, the Christian princes, blind to the consequences of their insane wars for national glory, were apparently well on the way to a repetition of the classic Roman debacle. Broadly speaking, one result of the humanist social criticism thus appears in work toward definition of a philosophic theory of progress and decay in the history of civilizations.[11]

In the uneasy July of 1517, Erasmus wrote to More that while he found Louvain "full of snarling. . . . In England I am afraid of disturbances and have a horror of slavery" (*EN*, II, 576). And by that July he completed one of his most widely read criticisms on war and peace, the *Complaint of Peace, Unwanted and Ejected from all Countries.*[12]

With the publication of the *Complaint of Peace* as a small quarto, a new phase in the humanist criticism of man and society may be marked. It appears to show conscious recognition of the potential power of the press as an instrument for reaching and reshaping what we now call public opinion. For example, when Erasmus first published his essay *Against*

War in 1515, it appeared in the midst of a huge and expensive volume of the *Adages,* whose very cost limited its circulation. In April, 1517, however, Froben put it into quarto form, and as a pamphlet it appeared in thirteen editions, printed in nine cities, by 1530. The *Complaint of Peace* sold even more widely: between 1517 and 1529 no fewer than twenty-four editions are known (ten in 1518 alone), including translations into French, German, and Spanish.[13]

Thus a battle between ideas was waged. Humanist criticism worked, both positively and negatively, to change men's minds—satirizing, analyzing, seeking to discredit outworn and catastrophic ways of thinking about war, while on the other hand aiming to persuade an age, beginning first with its leaders, to accept and practice the newer Christian humanist ideal.

By late 1516, the kind of flashing optimism that marks much of the *Praise of Folly* had vanished from the English humanist outlook, replaced by a tougher mood. Probably the last words written in the *Utopia* were More's own concluding speech: "So must I needs confess . . . that many things be in the Utopian weal public, which in our cities I may rather wish for, than hope after" (*MUL,* p. 309). One senses by early 1517 an awareness that the time was growing very late for peaceful reform, although the need and opportunity had never been more great and challenging. The tone of the criticism of war grows grimmer, not despairing but as of men aware that their society may well be standing on the brink of some enormous but still possibly avoidable tragic catastrophe. The moment resembled our own today.

So with Erasmus' *Complaint of Peace,* whose composition had been provoked by the spectacle of the warmongering of a few evil men (*EN,* III, 89-90). In it he largely dropped the use of the ironic and satiric approach of which he, like More, was a master, but which leaves many readers unused to it wondering exactly what was meant. The *Complaint of Peace* presented the personified figure of Peace, delivering a reasoned, passionate discourse—a sustained appeal to men as rational beings and also as Christians. It was a direct effort to induce men to see a crucial truth—that they were the victims of the tyranny of unsound ideas and corrupt men, and that practical alternatives did indeed exist. He used, of course, the whole body of criticism which the English humanists had built up. He exposed and analyzed the social dynamics making for renewed wars, and he kept steadily in focus what might realistically be done to effect a creative escape from a vicious, circular social pattern.

His arguments (as in his own *Against War*) are addressed to the enlightened self-interest of both princes and the common people, and to the conscience of those who had been stirred by corruption in the Church.

The *Complaint*'s first half dealt with matters of practical self-interest (cf. Machiavelli's *realpolitik*). Erasmus began by restating the fundamental idea that the uncorrupted nature of man is utterly opposed to the nature of war.[14] Thus he implicitly denied the despairing premise that "the natural state of man is war" and denied equally the premise that war is the result of some cause, such as sin, now inseparable from the human condition. All men on earth, whether Christian or Turk, are of one species, united by the very fact of their human nature (*EQP*, pp. 56-62, 78). This elemental fact, the basis of all modern humanitarianism means that nationalism is largely a folly, contrary to reason. Declaring that nations are only names, he denounced as irrational the idea of so-called natural enemies (pp. 58-61). National honor, as viewed by the eyes of reason, is a hideous form of folly if its pursuit leads to war (p. 68). This much formed a general analysis of a tyranny of unsound concepts, with positive counterideas advanced in their stead.

Then, as in *Against War*, he put forward his strong argument—seemingly aiming particularly at those who have the most wealth to lose through war—that invasive war does not pay. By any halfway complete financial and human accounting done in advance, it will be made quite clear that war can be conducted only at a loss, never at a profit. It is a delusion that war pays. This argument supports his assertion that even in pure selfishness the plain duty of a wise king is to rule in peace (*EQP*, pp. 46-53, 63-72). Even if absolute material self-interest were all a prince had to consider, any peace is preferable to the most "just" invasive war (pp. 44, 66-70).

What, as he saw it, were then the dominant causes of war? One was certainly the ungoverned passions and the unreason of many men (*EQP*, pp. 15, 43-46). This alone, however, he thought insufficient to have caused the contemporary wars between nations. Far more influential and decisive was the depravity of many modern princes, a condition not caused by sin but typically by bad education and a corrupted court environment. For one thing, princes are stirred to needless (tyrannous?) war through the greed, deceit, and artifices of vicious advisers. In addition, during their early education as well as later on princes are persuaded to seek war through rashly chosen or unwisely read literature, such as romances or histories which represent a war career as noble and honorable (pp. 56-58).

In the *Complaint of Peace* Erasmus' arguments drawn from Christian thought, or from comparisons of Christian and pagan civilizations, roughly parallel those in his *Against War*. He pictured to his Catholic readers the horror that even rationally ethical atheists would feel toward contemporary man, were they to visit Europe and perceive, in broad panorama, the Christian nations perpetually attacking each other on the most trivial pretexts (*EQP*, p. 72). (Swift, misanthropically perhaps, achieved this effect when he made his Gulliver boast of European statecraft to the King of Brobdingnag, only to be denounced with disgust as evidently a member of a race of odious vermin.) Extensively he compared ancient pagan and modern Christian civilizations, only to conclude that the moderns were ethically far the worse (pp. 29-45). Even in extreme decadence, when chronically mad with the rage for martial glory, ancient Rome was better than Christian Europe, for at least occasionally Rome enjoyed peace (pp. 70-73). As he had reasoned that war is absolutely a violation of (uncorrupted) man's human nature, Erasmus argued that war is a violation of the good life intended by Christ (pp. 16-20, 35-44). Therefore between Christians war is inescapably more vile than between the heathen, for it breaks both the natural unity of all men as a species and the higher unity which should bind men together within Christendom (pp. 10, 58).

No such summary of ideas can hope to convey the passion and conviction with which Erasmus mounted this appeal to the princes and peoples of Europe to return to Christian sanity. This work was, for him as for the English humanists, no mere intellectual diversion—a mere playful throwing-about of brains. He evidently hoped it might still be possible to awake his age to seek the causes and the practical means to reduce or arrest one of the raging but man-made plagues of the time. In the *Complaint of Peace* he renewed with particular fury his ridicule of a tyrannic idea which custom had made seem normal, necessary, and even glorious —the paid profession and the "celebrated art of war," in which he found man's distinctive powers of reason put to the utmost perversion. This, he said, is the art in which the "best" soldiers are the most savage and depraved men—"butchers of the human race" (*EQP*, pp. 39, 63-66).

It is often said that the Christian humanists believed in the idea of human perfectibility. Less noticed, perhaps, is the intense realism with which their analysis of human nature stressed the social processes by which this potentially noble creature may become so corrupted and hardened by custom that he may either at best be useful to society, though himself incapable of a good life (as in the Utopian form of slavery), or at worst may unsentimentally require destruction, like a dangerous wild beast, for the good of humanity. Grimly Erasmus speculated as to whether or not man really is a rational creature (*EQP*, pp. 2, 9). Perhaps in human nature itself there lies hidden some tragic flaw, illustrated in action by man's sinister propensity for war; but if so, at least let Europeans fight the Turks, not fellow Christians (p. 62). Nearly a century before *Hamlet* it appears that these humanists had isolated from the welter of worldly circumstance the essentials of the English Renaissance's central tragic response to life, based upon a most highly intensified perception of the appalling and ironic gap between man's promise and his performance. Hamlet muses: "What a piece of work is a man! how noble in reason! how infinite in faculties, in form and moving! how express and admirable in action! how like an angel in apprehension! how like a god! the beauty of the world, the paragon of animals . . ." (II.ii.315 ff.).[15] But this insight must be set against that of Queen Gertrude's wantonness: "A beast that wanted reason would have mourned longer." Were she a beast, where would be the tragic mystery? There would indeed be no occasion for tragedy at all. The haunting question is not merely why the noble human being mourned no longer but why she did not retain power for a life of virtue and harmony. Yet in the end the effect of both *Hamlet* and the *Complaint of Peace* is similar—one not of despair but of tempered hope for humanity.

Erasmus left England in April, 1517, but with no evident idea that he might not return at some propitious time. On September 9 he wrote to both Henry VIII and Wolsey. Partly his purpose was to proffer presents previously tendered but overlooked in wartime. His major aim was like that which More urged upon Hythlodaye as the best way to advise princes, namely, "to handle the matter wittily and handsomely for the purpose; and that which you cannot turn to good, so to order it that it be not very bad" (*MUL*, p. 100). To Wolsey he mentioned the King's evident inability to consider the gift (Erasmus' Latin translation of Plutarch's essay *On the Distinction between a Flatterer and a Friend*), "which . . . I may well suppose that in the turmoil of war [1512-13] he has not found time to peruse." Yet "now that tranquillity has been long established," he understood that Henry "has come back to literature . . . and that he converses from time to time with books,—not indiscriminately, but chiefly with such as convey lessons of piety and royal wisdom" (*EN*, III, 48-51). Such expressions at times inspire a fine ridicule, as when Erasmus' *Christian Prince* is viewed as "one song" which had to be sung "for a promised lifetime of suppers" (Hexter, p. 103). What Erasmus meant by literature fit for a great prince is vividly clarified by his letter to Henry, which not only praised him for his interest in serious books on statesmanship but contains what I take to be one of the earliest humanist attacks on the idea that princes, if they read at all, should relax with a romance:

Thus you are very far from agreeing with persons who think that princes of the highest rank ought of all things, to keep clear of serious or philosophic study, and that, if books are taken in hand at all, nothing should be read but amusing stories, scarcely good enough for women, or mere incitements to folly and vice [*fabulas meraque stulticiae ac viciorum irritamenta legi oportere*] [*EN*, III, 45-46].

The intended point is clearly the same as that made, in a similar context, in the *Christian Prince* (*ECP*, p. 200). He grants that such tales may be amusing. The humanist objection is here that when a prince reads nothing but old wives' tales, he gains no skill from the past for his present duty of wielding power for good and may, on the contrary, well be stimulated to use his powers for evil.

The uneasiness and tension which the humanists felt late in 1517, as war and peace rumors circulated, is captured by More in the letter of October 7 in which he thanked Erasmus and Peter Giles for their portraits, recently done by the Flemish master Quentin Massys: "if future ages preserve any love of the fine arts and if savage warfare does not obliterate the arts, then what a price posterity would pay for this picture!" (*MLE*, p. 242). That autumn, as he had been before, More was engaged in dreary commercial litigation for the King. From Calais on October 25 he wrote drily to congratulate Erasmus on so handling his affairs as not to be, like himself, so "involved in the busy trifles of Princes; and you show your love for me by desiring that I may be disentangled from such matters, in which you can scarcely believe how unwillingly I am engaged . . ." (*EN*, III, 102-3). Just six days later—almost a year after the dedicatory letter in the *Utopia*—an obscure monk of Wittenberg nailed up on a church door some theses for debate. Probably at that moment More had never heard of Martin Luther, whose first communication to Erasmus (*EE, 501*) had been made only in 1516. The time was later than even the humanists were aware.

Erasmus carried on the critical attack upon books which incite men of power to folly and vice when (November 4) he wrote the preface to an edition of Quintus Curtius' eulogistic *De rebus gestis Alexandri Magni*. He could not recommend the life of Alexander, in the manner of Polemon in 1587, "for the profit of those that practise arms and for the pleasure of such as love to be harmless hearers of bloody broils" (*STC* 20090, title page). Rather he delivered a slashing attack on the kind of "greatness," the false and corrupting heroic ideal, which he found embodied in Alexander's terrible career. By his interpretation the classical biographer became a humanist mirror, not only for magistrates but for all readers. That is, he treated this piece of history as a practical means whereby, without repeating the same errors, men might now see the dreadful results of abuse of power on a grand scale. From Quintus Curtius would-be imperialists may discover what fate awaits them and their people. He mocked the idealization of such imperial tyrants by flattering historians. So far from being admirable and a model for kings to imitate, Alexander was, as the English humanist saw him, on the whole a frightful example of a "world-robber," a king "drunk with ambition," no less a disaster to mankind than Homer's Achilles. What good was it to "this solid globe"—i.e., all humanity—to be thrown into bloody confusion "to please one young madman?"

And yet, after straining every nerve to portray a sort of exceptional and inimitable sovereign, what else have they [historians like this] described but a world-robber, occasionally mad, but everywhere successful? For indeed he was not more dangerous, when overcome with wine, than drunk with anger or ambition; and in proportion as the rashness of his unruly temper was followed by success, the more mischievous was he to humanity. For my own part, I have no more liking for the Alexander of the Greek historians, than I have for Homer's Achilles. Both the one and the other present the worst example of what a sovereign should be, even if some good qualities may seem to be mingled with so many faults. It was, forsooth well worth while, that Africa, Europe and Asia should be thrown into confusion, and so many thousands of human beings slaughtered, to please one young madman, whose ambition this solid globe would have failed to satisfy. It is well, that this living Plague, too much indulged by Fortune in everything else, was denied the gift of longevity.[16]

No such feeling that renewed outbreak of war and tyranny could endanger the cultural revival was apparent in high places as 1518 opened, just before the Lutheran agitations broke out. Erasmus' first major social criticism was the *Moriae Encomium*, dashed off in high spirits at More's home in 1509. Now (as he wrote on January 2, 1518) Pope Leo X had "read the *Moria* through, and laughed over it. . . . And yet there is not a set of men whom I treat with more bitterness than Popes!" (*EN*, III, 209). (It is not known whether or not Pope Julius II ever read the *Praise of Folly*.)

Although general peace negotiations outwardly seemed the order of the day, the humanist critic was by this time too hard-bitten to be overly optimistic. Temporary peace existed—but on what foundations? On March 5, Erasmus wrote to More his sharply satirical opinion of the current diplomacy. He saw the "Pope and a few Princes" as "playing a fresh comedy." Ironically he reported upon a set of absurd injunctions to stay-at-home wives which had been issued to emphasize the seriousness of the proposed holy war against the Turks. Beneath the bright surface mockery runs a grim undertone, for the "comedy" of the princes and the pope had usually turned out to be the tragedy of the common people in their age:

The Pope and a few Princes are playing a fresh comedy, under pretext of a tremendous war against the Turks. Poor Turks—we Christians must not be too hard on them! This is a matter, too, in which wives are concerned. All husbands under the age of fifty and over twenty-six are to take arms, but meantime the Pope forbids the wives of the absent warriors to indulge in luxury at home. They are to abstain from elegance of attire, not to wear silk or gold, nor any jewels, to make no display, not to drink wine, and to fast every alternate day, that God may speed their husbands while they take part in so sanguinary a war. And if there are any husbands who are detained at home by necessary business, their wives are nevertheless to follow the same practices that they would have had to observe if their husbands had gone to the war. They may sleep in the same room, but in different beds, and not a kiss is to be exchanged, until this terrible war has been successfully concluded. I know that this will be annoying to many wives, not sufficiently weighing the importance of the matter in question; though I am sure that your wife, with the wisdom and piety that she possesses, will readily obey.[17]

For More's information, with the same letter he sent a copy of Luther's theses, while deploring the violence of German polemics (*EE*, 785.37). With more bluntness, if possible, he wrote also to John Colet, denouncing the pretense of a crusade as just one more cynical move in papal power politics. "The pretext is now put forward of a war against the Turks, when the real object is the expulsion of the Spaniards out of Naples, since the Pope's nephew Lorenzo [de'Medici] lays claim to Campania on account of his marriage with the daughter of the King of Navarre. If such disturbances are to continue, it would have been better to submit to the dominion of the Turks, than of these Christians!" (*EN*, III, 298-99). Even more bitterly on March 13 he wrote to a friend, Rhenanus, on how high tyranny had now "reached its climax, Pontiff and Kings treating the people, not as men, but as cattle to be bought and sold!" [18]

What solid hope could men have, when, as in the spring of 1518, talk of peace and that of war's renewal eddied like the winds? On February 15 old Bishop Fox warned Wolsey that if war was intended for England, some defenses were "too feeble"—"Our manner is never to prepare for the war [until] our enemies be light at our doors." [19] Two days later Giustinian visited Wolsey and heard of busy French war preparations, perhaps for an invasion of Spain and Flanders; while Henry VIII, not to lag behind, was putting ships and militia in readiness for combat (*LP*, II, 3954). Yet on February 21 Wolsey's agent at the court of Charles wrote that "the acceptable time is near" for a peace treaty, and after that an "expedition against the Infidels will soon follow" (*LP*, II, 3964). Whatever military noises Henry and Wolsey might make, in 1518 peace had finally become a practical necessity: ". . . the treasure left by Henry VII had been largely depleted, and financial prudence as well as papal precept" counseled the making of a peace (Pollard, p. 132).

At some time during the first three months of 1518, apparently, More finally decided to enter the King's service wholly, where before he had served on occasional commercial missions. He had long hesitated to do so, for many reasons, most ably explored by Mr. Hexter, and it seems clear that one force which tipped the balance was the fact that the rulers of England had established a policy for peace.[20] Part of More's difficulty in making the decision was suggested by his hard agreement with his creation, Hythlodaye, in *Utopia*'s first book, when Hythlodaye realistically objected that the contemporary prince was so war-mad that he would listen to no counteradvice:

For first of all, the most part of princes have more delight in warlike matters and feats of chivalry (the knowledge whereof I neither have nor desire) than in the good feats of peace: and employ much more study, how by right or by wrong to enlarge their dominions, than how well and peaceably to rule and govern that they have already [*MUL*, p. 38].

All that is known of More's ideals suggests his agreement with the English peace policy which outwardly prevailed between 1514 and 1518, and there is no evidence to suggest that at this time he was in any position to know what went on to the contrary in Wolsey's secret diplomacy. "As to your being attracted to the Court," Erasmus wrote More (*ca.* April 23), "there is one thing that consoles me: you will be taking service under an excellent Prince. But there is no doubt that you will be carried away from us and from Literature" (*EN*, III, 369). To that friend of humanism, Bishop Tunstall, he wrote the next day that consolation for More's enticement to court might be found in that, "with so many learned men ... it may seem not a Court, but a temple of the Muses. But meanwhile there is nothing brought us from Utopia, to amuse us; and he, I am quite sure, would rather have his laugh, than be borne aloft [like a Roman senator] on a curule chair" (*EN*, III, 361).

What did Erasmus mean when he surmised that, although at Henry's court there were many learned men, More would "be carried away from us and from Literature"? The hope of the London Reformers was that Henry would indeed prove to be a great Christian prince who would begin and sustain peaceful reforms in English Renaissance society. In this context what Erasmus meant by "Literature" is suggested, I think, by his letter to Henry (September 9, 1517) in which he praised the King for reading, not only trifles, but works of serious value to princes, i.e., just kings rather than tyrants (*EN*, III, 45-46). In other words, Erasmus feared that More would, at court, be deprived of his power of incisive social criticism.

The English humanists and particularly More, as Chambers (p. 154) saw their function at court, were to play the role of "missionaries" who sought to " 'prepare the hearts and minds of the contracting sovereigns' " for peace. Although it is very difficult to tell just how far, under Wolsey, More knew the secrets of foreign policy,[21] he seems generally to have been assigned to routine tasks requiring an expert diplomat. While the Cardinal dominated the King's council, I do not find that Henry asked and accepted More's advice on matters of war versus peace. The ease-loving King seems to have relied on Wolsey's great talents, and Wolsey often kept details of secret diplomacy even from the very council of which More was a member. Between April and September of 1518, for instance, Wolsey was busy negotiating for his Treaty of Universal Peace. What did More know of these affairs? When on September 18 the Venetian ambassador, a man More respected, pumped him for information by expressing congratulations for a peace agreement which had not yet been concluded, More told him that Wolsey " 'most solely . . . transacted this matter . . . and when he has concluded, he then calls the councillors, so that the King himself scarcely knows in what state matters are' " (Giustinian, II, 216). As far as I know, More was telling the truth of his situation as councilor.

During the summer of 1518 the communication lines of secret diplomacy hummed with negotiations for peace in Europe and a general war against the Turkish invaders. How thinly buried were national suspicions is suggested by Wolsey's preliminary treaty draft of July, which provided that "none were to hire the Swiss [mercenaries] against the other" (*LP*, II, 4357). The humanist critics' mixed mood of optimism and pessimism is perhaps suggested by Erasmus' letter of August 14, 1517, written as the preface to the 1518 edition of his *Christian Knight*.

Originally the *Christian Knight* (1504) put forward, for a new age, an alternative to the medieval chivalric ideal. Now, in a time of "such great darkness" and "such great troublous ruffling of the world," Erasmus set out the new edition including "certain fragments of mine old study." [22] The humanist critics' desire, not just to talk to each other, but to reach toward wide influence on their age is evident. There is need, he said, for a plain, brief, simple guide on essential Christian principles for the "unlearned and rude multitude." Now that preparation is made for war against the Turks, he hoped it would profit all men, not just a few. But, supposing that not all Turks are killed and that some are captured, how shall Christian principles be communicated to them? Surely not by the "cumbrous, lextricable [*sic*], subtle" works of Occam and Scotus, especially when the learned schoolmen appear in "fierce disagreements." Practically speaking, if the Turks can be won over to a Christian life it will only be by pure example. False ideals—"ambition and desirousness of honor . . . more than ever any tyrant did use" will not serve. If they are not shown examples of a truly Christian life, "It shall sooner come to pass that we shall degenerate . . . into Turks ourselves, than that we shall cause them to become Christian men." He hoped that Pope Leo X would set such an example, "unless the great trouble and rage of worldly business pluck him . . . another way" (*ECK*, A4^v-6^v).

Imaginatively, anticipating the twentieth century, he proposed trial of a pamphlet war to convert pagan minds "before we . . . try them in battle." Not, however, with "threatening epistles or with books full of tyranny," but rather with those full of the Apostles' own "fatherly charity." Because the Biblical language is difficult, he proposed trial of a plain "collection and sum of Christ's philosophy," gathered out of the "pure fountains of the Gospel." Thereby, he hoped, the Turks might "perceive that they have gotten fathers, and not tyrants. . . ." When he first wrote the *Enchiridion* he had in mind only to help the "common people of Christendom," who seemed—like many of their pastors and princes—to be "in opinions . . . corrupted." "And in such great darkness, in such great troublous ruffling of the world, in so great diversity of men's opinion, whither should we fly for succor than to . . . the Gospel?" How unfortunate would men now be if Christ had not left "some sparks of his doctrine" but only the expiring "coals of men's fantasies" (*ECK*, A6ᵛ-8ʳ).

Wistfully he offered an almost Dantesque vision of a reformed Christendom, in a metaphor of three circles. Christ is at the center; in the first circle are churchmen, in the second, princes, and in the third are the common people. Should war "rise suddenly," the bishops' work should be to halt it by arbitration; but "if that cannot be brought to pass, by reason of the great storms of worldly business," let them at least try to cut it short with a minimum of bloodshed (*ECK*, B2ʳ-B4ʳ).

He saw acutely how rough is the path of the social critic who attempts to expose a corrupt but long accepted custom (i.e., a tyrannizing idea). Nowadays, "If a man should dissuade from such war . . . which now of long time hath been used . . . he should be noted by and by of the pick-quarrels [as] one of those which think that no war is lawful for a Christian man." "And yet he is not suspected . . . of heresy, which doth provoke . . . men to battle, & bloweth the trumpet thereunto for every trifling matter" (*ECK*, B8ʳᵛ). Indeed, it is now the man who proposes at least trying peaceful conversion rather than war upon the Turks who "is suspected, as though he affirmed not to be lawful, for Christian men to withstand the Turks, when they invade us." If, however, a priest "be a dicer, a fighter, a brawler, all unlearned, drowned and wrapped in temporal business, all given to the evil service of evil princes," no fault is found with him (*ECK*, Ciʳ-C3ʳ).

Finally Wolsey had the stage all set for the signing of his grandiose

Treaty of Universal Peace on October 2. This amazing document was ostensibly to seal perpetual peace among all Christian princes, after which Christendom was supposed to unite in a crusade against the Turks.[23] For Wolsey it was another splendid scene in the drama of his rise toward his ultimate goal—the papacy. Well understanding these secret objectives, "knowing him to be greedy of glory and covetous of praise," the Venetian ambassador congratulated Wolsey on September 24. How much greater was Wolsey's accomplishment and honor than that of the Pope himself!

> . . . for that the Pope had laboured to effect a quinquennial truce, whilst his lordship made perpetual peace; and that whereas such a union of the Christian powers, when joined by the Pope, was usually . . . concluded at Rome, this confederacy had been settled in England, his Holiness, nevertheless, being its head [Giustinian, II, 219].

Four days later Henry VIII gave public audience at Greenwich to the French ambassador and to Campeggio, the papal legate; and the Bishop of Paris "delivered a grave and elegant oration in praise of the peace and confederacy which had now so long [three years] prevailed" between England and France (Giustinian, II, 221).

Wolsey stage-managed the actual signing of the treaty on October 2 and the following eight days of speeches and celebrations as a spectacular piece of living theater, in which he was one of the great stars. Even the humanists had a minor part in the show: the signers included More, Tunstall, and Mountjoy, Erasmus' first English patron (LP, II, 4469). The public proclamation of the treaty was set for St. Paul's for October 3, but Dean John Colet, now old and sick, did not occupy his pulpit; and Wolsey himself sang the mass. Richard Pace, the King's secretary, gave the dignitaries a short oration on the peace. Bluntly, the chronicler Hall (p. 594) laid less emphasis on any ideas the speech contained than he did on the fine dinner served soon afterward at the Bishop's palace. Pace's oration, unlike that of the Bishop of Paris, survives: it is almost an epitome of Christian humanist social criticism, omitting the indictment of tyranny. Since now all the Christian princes were conducting themselves as though they had, as one, accepted the humanist critique on war as correct, I imagine More enjoyed the speech very much. Pace congratulated the sovereigns on having in actual practice replaced the worst of evils with the greatest of good things—peace perpetual. Citing St. Paul and Isocrates, he contrasted briefly the human condition under war, with its mass of crimes, and under peace with justice, certainly very acceptable to God. Human nature itself triumphs best in peace, as both Isocrates and Christ have taught. The art of war, on the other hand, he attacked as a hellish invention (*diabolicum plane inuentum*) productive of calamity, a condition better befitting beasts than reasoning man. In peace, on the contrary, all that is good in human genius flourishes. Turning from this critical résumé, he touched briefly on the present danger of imminent invasion of Europe by the Turks, to repel which the Pope wanted a crusade. Naturally he praised all the assembled kings individually, but Wolsey came right behind Henry VIII and the Emperor, and before the King of France and the papal legate, in Pace's order of compliment. And he closed with an expression of the common desire that the peace should be truly perpetual.[24]

The diplomat Giustinian (II, 224), by his emphasis, implied ironically that what the orator said by no means represented the essential concern of the assembled princes: he dismissed it as polite ("elegant and grave"), but gave elaborate descriptions of the entertainments of the day. From Paris a little later, however, the rising young English humanist, Thomas Lupset, wrote Pace that "the speech you delivered after the treaties has been remarkably pleasing to the learned men here" (Gee, pp. 6, 297-98). Lupset's implied sympathy with the humanist critique on peace and war is of some interest as showing the impact on the rising younger men of the work done by More, Erasmus, and Colet above all. He was, indeed, one of the first Englishmen of the Renaissance to be brought up in the new learning, one of the first younger men to express humanist educational convictions, and was among the leaders in revolt against the old curriculum at Cambridge (*ca.* 1512) (Gee, p. 49).

Obviously, sharp social criticism had no place in Wolsey's show. Even the seasoned diplomat Giustinian was dazzled when he went on October 5 to Wolsey's "most sumptuous supper, the like of which, I fancy, was never given either by Cleopatra or Caligula; the whole banqueting hall being so decorated with huge vases of gold and silver, that I fancied myself in the tower of Chosroes. . . ." It must have been an exhausting week of almost continuous spectacle. On the tenth the faithful Giustinian, still up and about notwithstanding these epic revels, traveled to Greenwich for "entertainments . . . consisting of stately jousts, and banquets, and comedies; pageants of such a sort as are

177

rarely seen in England" (II, 224-28). In such a fashion, Wolsey—his eye ever on the papal tiara—turned to his own good account what Pollard (p. 115) called "the hush before the storm."

But there was not a storm cloud in the sky. Bishop Fox, who had been eased out of politics by Wolsey and who had recently founded Corpus Christi at Oxford, rejoiced, both as statesman and as Englishman, that at last peace policies, which the humanists had steadily advanced as required for England's practical needs, had prevailed. He wrote happily to Wolsey on October 30, giving credit where credit was due, no matter what the inevitable few carping objectors might say against the peace:

And none Englishman gladder than I of this honorable and profitable amity and alliance with the realm of France. I doubt not there be some *inuidi et maliuoli obtrectatores*; but undoubtedly, my lord, God continuing it, it [the peace] shall be the best deed that ever was done for the realm of England; and after the King's highness, the laud and praise thereof shall be to you a perpetual memory.[25]

For old Dean Colet, for Erasmus, and for Thomas More, the signing of this great Universal Peace probably seemed to justify the hard, rough work of criticism which they had striven to accomplish: to help bring the men in actual power, the princes, to see and act on the wisdom of creating peaceful designs for a new social order. One small horizonal muttering, caught by the sharp ear of the humanist historian, Polydore Vergil (p. 251), would not quite fall to silence. "Neighboring peoples," he said, suspected uneasily that the treaty was by no means intended to be fully executed. "Thus the princes in our own day are accustomed to pledge their faith one to another, which however they but rarely keep, afterwards producing many excuses to mitigate their offence."

The space between Wolsey's Treaty of Universal Peace and the Field of the Cloth of Gold (June 11, 1520) appears as the twilight of early Tudor humanism's golden age. Ironically, at the time it appeared in an almost opposite light. From the first, the London Reformers' designs for a new social order had depended for practical success upon the availability of a virtuous Christian prince, and by late 1518 England seemed to have found not one but two, Henry VIII and Wolsey.

The theme of praise for the peaceful accomplishments of "our England" runs through much of Erasmus' correspondence for 1519.

In February, when recommending the brilliant young Spaniard, Juan Luis Vives, as a tutor for Prince Ferdinand, then about sixteen, he held up "our English court" as a model (*EE*, 917.10-12). In May he sent to England a whole flight of letters—to Henry, to Wolsey, to various prominent courtiers. As he saw it, the world was at last waking out of a "long, deep sleep." Henry's court was itself a university, and under him the long-desired golden age of law, order, universal peace, and revived learning was coming to be reality. Wolsey and Fox at Oxford, John Fisher at Cambridge, were establishing great new colleges to foster the revival of learning. The only drawback Erasmus could find in all this was that he was perhaps too old to enjoy this brave new world.[26] As he wrote to Sir Henry Guildford, always close to the King, Henry VIII himself is the ideal Christian prince. Who is more assuredly skillful in matters of war, more sagacious in establishing laws, more keen-eyed in council, more vigilant in quick repression of abuses, more diligent in choosing judges and officers, more able in making a royal treaty (*EE*, 966.34-38)? There can be no doubt of the import of these letters: Erasmus would gladly have returned to England if suitable arrangements had been made for him (*EE*, III, 587n.).

It is quite clear that at this time Erasmus, the most cosmopolitan and widely traveled of all the English humanists, saw England (as More did, implicitly, in his island of Utopia) as the country favored in its genius above all others in Renaissance Europe. His letter of May 18 to Wolsey, realistically, used very much the same language as did the one to Henry himself. As Chambers (p. 168) saw it, Erasmus was expending hopeful flattery in a good cause: "The time had come for the triumph of learning, the defeat of obscurantism, the reform of the Church by reason and scholarship. And if, at the price of a little astute praise, the great Cardinal could be persuaded to concentrate his enormous power upon these things—the Golden Age might come after all." The point is, rather, that the praise was already solidly deserved because Wolsey was even then apparently engaged exactly in this great work (Hexter, pp. 146-55). Erasmus simply praised the Cardinal for the actual accomplishments which the humanist critics had long urged the men in power to perform.

Indeed "our Britain" was to be congratulated for possessing Wolsey, who was even then administering swift and simplified justice, reforming abuses in the Church, and inviting erudite professors to the English universities with fine salaries. Referring to the gift to Oxford of six readerships, Erasmus declared that for this all Britain owed Wolsey an obligation. The Cardinal, moreover, collected libraries assiduously and fostered all the learned languages. But the climax of his notable achievements was the great peace of October, 1518, for while the Pope himself thought only of a five-year truce, Wolsey treated for peace perpetual. Not only was England at peace, but the country had escaped the atrocities of war. Surely for such triumphs Wolsey should be happier than Alexander the Great, and immortal fame awaited him if he could use his power to induce the sovereigns of Europe to follow his example. "I see, I see a truly Golden Age arising, if that temper of yours shall prevail with some proportion of our sovereigns." Ominously, however, now that the stormy name of Luther had begun to crop up frequently, he felt it wise to explain carefully to Wolsey that Luther was a stranger to him and that he had read only a few pages of his work.[27]

In the mellow atmosphere engendered by Wolsey's superb theatrics surrounding the Treaty of Universal Peace of October, 1518, it was planned that Henry VIII and Francis I would meet later in personal interview as a public symbol of their friendship. Preparations for this encounter, however, were interrupted in January, 1519, by the death of Maximilian and the ensuing contest for the Empire. Charles V was elected on June 28 amid popular acclamation, thus preparing the cockpit of Europe for the rivalry of three young princes (Henry, Francis, and Charles) which, as we now know, was to dominate Europe beyond Wolsey's and the London Reformers' time (Pollard, p. 118). If we judge by their surviving correspondence, the English humanists felt no such alarming prospect to be near. Consider the first biographical sketch of More—Erasmus' letter to Hutten of July 23. Erasmus still regretted that Henry had "dragged" More into his court and still saw More as "anxious to escape it" (cf. Hexter, pp. 138-55). Nevertheless, the humanist character of the men with whom Henry had surrounded himself, together with the constructive work being done by Henry and especially by Wolsey toward peace and social justice were major compensations: "But as this excellent monarch was resolved to pack his household with learned, serious, intelligent and honest men, he especially insisted upon having More among them . . ." (EN, III, 387-402). Under Wolsey many needed reforms within the Church in England were proceeding, but as yet this movement had taken on little or none of the color of violence already rising in Germany.

From the humanists' viewpoint, no doubt the golden age seemed on its way, not beginning with an imaginary pagan prince Utopus but with an existing Christian prince, Henry VIII, who at last understood the genius of his island. Consider the critical portrait of Henry drawn in Giustinian's secret dispatch of October 10, 1519, in which the keynote was the King's extreme desire for continued peace. After speaking of Henry's free and liberal manners, his great strength, his passion for hunting, and so forth:

> He was affable and gracious, harmed no one; did not covet his neighbour's goods, and was satisfied with his own dominions, having often said to me, "Sir Ambassador, we want all potentates 'to content themselves with their own territories; we are satisfied with this island of ours.' " He seems extremely desirous of peace. He is very rich. His father left him ten millions of ready money in gold, of which he is supposed to have spent one-half in the war against France [1512-13] ... [*Cal. SP Ven.*, No. 1287].

The keynote was essentially the same as that sounded by the King to Giustinian in June, 1516 (when More was preparing the final manuscript of *Utopia*): "I content myself with my own; I only wish to command my own subjects; but on the other hand I do not choose to have any one ... command me." [28]

Within the circle of the London Reformers, there was doubtless sadness at the death on September 16, 1519, of the intrepid and imaginative man, John Colet, who had blazed the trail for all their criticism of man and society.[29] At long last, however, it seemed that many of Colet's ideals of peace and church reform were coming to be realities.

A literary tempest-in-a-teapot in early 1520, however, suggests that these humanists by no means felt that the recently established peace was as solid as its façade might indicate. This broil shows curiously that the newly arrived golden age presented novel, tender, and potentially explosive conditions, in which the English critics desired not "To wake our peace, which in our country's cradle / Draws the sweet infant breath of gentle sleep" (*Richard II*, I.iii.132-33). And in the midst of it all, we perceive More himself growing sensitive to new limits for his criticism—a partial loss of freedom of expression formerly used to treat such royal follies as needless war. There seems to be even some humanist awareness that forthright criticism might, in a new climate of opinion, be so handled by enemies as to cast very dangerous doubts on the critic's loyalty to the king.

All this appears in the course of a little, hot, and at first seemingly inconsequential literary wrangle between More and the French poet Brixius (Hudson, pp. 52-58). More had a certain genius in the epigram, and his favorite concern was the difference between a good king and a tyrant. He had already turned his satiric wit upon the bogus romantic hero figure which Brixius had drawn of the naval captain, Hervé, after the war of 1513. When the epigrams were printed, the uproar grew rapidly bitter. Outwardly all was simple enough, had national tensions not been so high. More had given Erasmus authority for the publication of his epigrams, and the sellout of the *Utopia*'s first edition created the opportunity. By May 30, 1517, Erasmus had sent both his and More's epigrams to Basel, where they appeared in the second and third editions of *Utopia* (March, December, 1518) (*EE*, 584.15). Evidently More's satiric shots at Brixius had circulated in manuscript, however, for as early as July or August of 1517 Erasmus knew that Brixius was contemplating an attack upon More and begged him to refrain.[30] But by December, 1519, Brixius' *Antimorus* was in the press; and by March, 1520, copies had reached Paris, Basel, and More himself in London (*EE*, IV, 217n.).

Brixius struck shrewdly. More could have met snide aspersions on his language by corrections in later editions; he could have ignored Brixius' insulting suggestion that evidently More had never heard that the epic has its own poetic conventions; he could have ignored the question—would he (More) call Virgil and Homer "liars," as he had termed Brixius?

What More could not ignore, however, were Brixius' insinuations that when More's epigrams were looked at carefully by Henry VIII, that King might possibly find reason to doubt his courtier's loyalty. In the hectic joy of Henry's coronation in that long-ago 1509, More *had* presented to the young King himself epigrams which both praised Henry VIII and were sharply critical of his father's policies. (Whether Henry ever read them, I do not know.) Much water had flowed under London Bridge since then. If, in 1520, the *Antimorus* were brought to the King's eyes, how would he respond to Brixius' sardonic observation that More was transparently guilty of impudently insulting the father while praising the son (" '*Mori impudentia, dum filium laudare instituit, patrem vituperantis.*' ")? [31]

In the More-Erasmus letters during the outwardly peaceful spring of 1520, it is quite evident that both were alarmed at the introduction of the King's name in this fashion. While protesting the folly of imputing disloyalty to More, they are, as Chambers said (p. 191), "clearly uneasy." To Erasmus, More got off (March-April) a very long letter, in which he admits that some of the epigrams are more rash than he would now write—but how bad-mannered to hold up against him, in this time of peace, the poems written years ago amidst the tumult of war! He still thought it a joke that Brixius seriously represented Captain Hervé as a military prodigy. But would Brixius like to ruin me by this talk of treason and Henry VII? (*Quam seditiose calumniatur me lacerare parentem Principis!*) And he outlined to Erasmus the reply he had in mind, by which he would try to laugh the whole thing off as an ill-timed revival of old trifles, while reminding his readers positively of the great fact that England and France were at peace (*EE*, 1087.219). More's proposed title is droll—it tells the entire content of the essay: "Epistle . . . against . . . de Brie, who, because seven years ago More composed in sport a few epigrams against his book in which he attacked England with slanderous lies, now, in the midst of profound peace between the English and French, only six weeks before the meeting of the princes of those countries, has published a book against More, defaming that author with stupid and bitter railing." [32] Obviously More thought that if a 1520 reader took in the viewpoint suggested by this title, his battle would be more than half won.

For his part, Erasmus (April 26) urged More to keep a dignified silence rather than make such a cutting reply. When there are so many barbarians to fight, it is tragic for men of good letters to brawl. And as for what More had written about the King's father in 1509, it will surely not be held against him now. Erasmus' hope was to patch things up quietly on both sides (*EE*, 1093).

Apparently More, however, felt it unwise to remain altogether silent, lest he seem to give assent to Brixius' accusations (even if true!). What he did was a bit curious, but as a defensive operation not stupid. He wrote the reply (*MC*, p. 86)—but time was of the essence, should the original charges of Brixius come to Henry VIII's ears. Therefore

More had the piece printed at once, in London, by Pynson—a rather unusual procedure for him at this time. One copy he sent to Erasmus, another to Peter Giles. Pynson sold five publicly; then More stepped in and bought out the remainder (*EE*, 1096.117-23). More's choice of a London printer, instead of those in Basel or Louvain who did the *Utopia*, coupled with his quick buying up of the edition, suggests not that he felt a need to get a reply into Brixius' hands but that he felt a very urgent need to protect his own position at court. Having thus replied, in a fashion, to his French accuser, he seems to have been quite willing to suppress this literary war at a point strategically advantageous for himself.

More met with Erasmus at Calais (probably June 30) and showed him a copy of the *Epistola ad Brixium* (*EE*, 1184.21-22); and Erasmus himself had public conversations with Henry and Wolsey, although this is all one knows of them (*EE*, IV, 296n.). As far as is known, Brixius' aspersions on More caused no trouble between him and the King; and More even added new epigrams, joking at Brixius (but not about tyranny), to the December, 1520, edition of his *Epigrammata*.[33] The whole episode suggests how little it took to ruffle the deceptive surface calm of the brief time of peace, beneath which currents of great danger still flowed.

The golden age of peace and social progress swept on to the interview with Francis I, projected in London in October, 1518, but delayed, especially by the contest for the Empire. After Charles V won election, Wolsey's policy of adherence to the papacy in politics drew him at first gradually toward an alliance with Charles. Meanwhile the outward pretense of friendship with France was maintained. Finally the historic meeting between Henry VIII and Francis I was staged, amidst truly amazing chivalric pageantry, near Calais in mid-June of 1520, at the Field of the Cloth of Gold.[34]

The Field has been precisely characterized by A. F. Pollard: it was not only "the last and most gorgeous display of the departing spirit of chivalry; it was also perhaps the most portentous deception on record." [35] Only the brilliance of the scenes, not the profound insincerities, appeared on the surface. Thomas More crossed the channel in the King's train, but to him, as usual, was appointed the job of serious, prosaic bargaining about foreign trade. The elaborate ceremonies all expressed the theme of perpetual peace. Even the royal tents were hung with mottoes reinforcing this idea. Over and over again the sovereigns vied in declaring their deep concern for the peace of Christendom. Henry VIII himself delivered a brief oration in praise of peace, although no one bothered to record its text.[36] To wind up the colorful humbug, when all the jousts and feastings were over, Wolsey sang mass in a chapel erected as by magic during the night. And afterward Richard Pace, the King's secretary and one active in promoting the new learning, spoke briefly, "saying that such a divine service had been performed to the glory of God, and . . . beseeching Him of all his infinite goodness, to be pleased to render this peace . . . perpetual." [37]

After his return to England, Bishop John Fisher, who had recently founded at Cambridge his college to aid the new learning, preached a sermon on the peace in which he struck the note of great and unaffected rejoicing which was felt through almost all England. He could imagine no finer example of virtuous worldly joys than these solid evidences of peace in Christendom. "Was it not a great thing within so short a space [1518-20], to see the three great Princes of this world . . . showing their power? . . ." "Such harmonies, such dalliance, and so many pleasant pastimes. . . . These assuredly were wonderful sights for this world and as much as hath been read of in many years done, or in any chronicles . . . heretofore written, and as great as men's wits . . . could devise and imagine for that season." The good Bishop, however, saw a warning to human pride in the quick tempests that marred the Field's ending. Great storms of dust, rain, and thunder arose so "that scantly one might see another. . . . Sometime when men would longer have disported them at the jousts, came the night & darkness upon them, and interrupted their pleasure." [38]

The astute Venetian diplomat, Giustinian, was probably far better informed on the real meaning of the Field of the Cloth of Gold than was Thomas More, the King's councilor. "These sovereigns," he wrote (September 7, 1520), "are not at peace. They adapt themselves to circumstances, but hate each other very cordially" (*Cal. SP Ven.*, III, 119).

> After that it were once come to that point, and the world once ruffled
> and fallen in a wildness, how long would it be, and what heaps of
> heavy mischiefs would there fall, ere the ways were found to set the
> world in order and peace again?—Thomas More, 1528

Superficially, in midsummer of 1520, after the Field of the Cloth
of Gold, Renaissance England exhibited superb peace and the reality
of social progress. Nevertheless, as sometimes happens long before
an approaching hurricane in human affairs, occasional mighty ground
swells began to appear, lifting into an ominous surf pounding the shores
of England.

The teapot-tempest of the More-Brixius literary quarrel was after
all but a tiny ruffle in the Golden Age peace. The quarrel's soreness,
however, did not merely fade away. Rather it was soon eclipsed by
unexpected and far more ominous forms of social strife, which threatened all humanist hopes for a rule of reason and justice, and not only
in England. The symptoms are apparent in Erasmus' last allusion to
the More-Brixius squabble (February 16, 1521). On the one hand he
had the warmest praise for a rising young Spaniard, Juan Luis Vives,
whom both he and More hoped to bring to England to carry on their
kind of humanism. On the other hand, he wrote somberly to Budé,
"this Lutheran tempest tears away the arts" (*EE*, 1184.25).

More's own sense of a fateful contraction of the political space and
time available for humanist social criticism in England appears soon
after the Field of the Cloth of Gold itself. "Cautious and guarded"
(*caute ac circumspecte*) is the new keynote, apparent in his discussion
of proposals to publish not only a third edition of his epigrams but to
add, in the humanist fashion, his letters, many of which, like Erasmus'
own, contain very piercing observations on war, peace, and other matters
in living controversy. At the Field of the Cloth of Gold, More had

met the great French classical scholar, Guillaume Budé, who soon made a friendly proposal for joint publication of their letters. But More wrote (*ca.* June, 1520) that "now I see it would be safer to wait awhile . . . in my remarks upon peace and war, upon morality, marriage, the clergy, the people, etc., perhaps what I have written has not always been so cautious and guarded that it would be wise to expose it to captious critics [*calumniatoribus*]." [1]

Had More felt equally cautious and guarded in 1515-16, he might have written but very likely felt it too dangerous to publish Book I of *Utopia* itself, with its passionate indictment of contemporary tyranny, as in 1513-14 he wrote but never published his *Richard III*. A further sense of caution about politically sensitive utterances appears in More's censoring of his own text prepared for the December, 1520, edition of his epigrams. True, he retained the first, in which at Henry VIII's coronation he had praised the brave new Christian prince while disparaging some of his father's policies. Kept in print also were his classic series of generally ironic comparisons of good kings with tyrants in antiquity. But he suppressed what might seem obviously still no more than a patriotic Englishman's view of the Scots' crushing defeat at Flodden Field: "While dutiful Henry with victorious armies reclaimed you, France, for the Roman Pontiff, behold! James, King of the Scots, was wickedly trying to take by armed force the kingdom of the Britons" (*MLE*, p. 237). Had Henry VIII read this in early 1521, why should he not experience anew a heady sense of chivalric pride? But the epigram concluded that it was surely God's will that James "perished amid the slaughter of his men." Evidently, as Bradner noted, the reasons for this suppression were political: the epigram was written in wartime by a private citizen, as More still was when it was printed first in the golden age atmosphere of 1518. Now in late 1520 he was not only a court official but "was becoming a person of national importance." [2]

There may be a sharper explanation possible, set in terms of intensifying dangers for the humanist social critic at the court in late 1520. The great theme of More's epigrams on kingship, as well as Book I of *Utopia*, is the same: good kings are a theoretical possibility but tyrants are an ever-present danger. To the English humanists, tyranny's masterpiece was the destruction of humanity through needless (invasive) war, such as the Scots' invasion of England. But More had stressed that divine justice was well served when a *contemporary* (not antique) tyrant "perished amid the slaughter of his men." I take it that More suppressed this epigram in late 1520 because he had begun to sense a growing danger of despotism in England. After 1520 he wrote no more epigrams on tyranny; he had begun to breathe it distinctly with the daily air.

Events of early 1521 throw a grim light on such matters. The King had no heir, and there was a growing anxiety about the succession, what with the Wars of the Roses so fresh in memory. The first head to go over this anguished matter was that of the Duke of Buckingham. A few weeks before More's own appointment (May 2, 1521) as under-treasurer, the Duke was suddenly arrested. On May 17 he was executed. Thus began that terrible series of "judicial murders" which was to last for over a quarter-century and to end only with Henry's death (Chambers, pp. 191-92). So serious, indeed, were the disaffections aroused in London over the Duke's beheading that on July 9 Thomas More was sent to suggest to the Court of Aldermen that " 'all the harness [battle gear] of the City should be brought to certain places in the City, so as to pacify and please the King.' " [3]

More himself dared to express his tragic revulsion from this act of tyranny only in *The Four Last Things,* written *ca.* 1522 and containing some of his most vigorous English prose, but evidently not intended for publication in his lifetime. His theme was the loathsomeness of death; the essay is really part of the extensive Tudor literature on the art of dying. Who, he asked, would not rather pity than envy a great Duke, before whom so many men "kneel and crouch . . . and at every word barehead begrace him," if they knew certainly that

. . . lately detected to the King, he should undoubtedly be taken the morrow, his court all broken up, his goods seized, his wife put out, his children disinherited, himself cast into prison, brought forth and arraigned, the matter out of question [i.e., his conviction a foregone conclusion], and he should be condemned, his coat armour reversed, his gilt spurs hewn off his heels, himself hanged, drawn, and quartered . . . [*MEW-C,* I, 21-22, 482-83]?

Juan Luis Vives, the fourth and last of the great actors in our drama of Renaissance ideas, is about to make his appearance on the English stage. He makes his entrance late in the show, but we can at least suggest that there was nothing accidental about his coming to England, for he was already well and favorably known to both More and Erasmus when, after the Field of the Cloth of Gold, he first met them face to face, probably at Bruges in late August of 1520.[4] That these three great humanists were drawn together is not surprising, for by a convergence of minds they had already come to share much of the same idealism and the same realism in criticism of man and society.

These tendencies may be marked from Vives' earliest published work, a little dialogue on *Iesu Christi triumphus* (1514).[5] By that time, however, he had very probably already been influenced by the work which had come from England, beginning with that of Colet in 1496 and perhaps reaching to Erasmus' scathing satire, *Julius Excluded from Heaven*. Already Vives was skeptical about rather than delighted with Caesarian heroism. In the dialogue, several young scholars, together with their master, Caspar Lux, gather to examine an old miniature depicting the Triumph of Caesar. Lux remarks sharply, " 'How much more excellent if the subject had been Christ, our *optimus Maximus*, instead of Caesar, a man by no means good!' " It appears from the dialogue that Vives had already begun to turn against traditional acceptance of war as glorious.

Vives' friendship with Erasmus began at Brussels in 1516-17, and by the latter year he was known to More by reputation.[6] Vives may have been drawn toward More by their common interest in Pico's philosophy. Vives' little *Fable about Man* (1518) makes direct use of Pico's concept that human dignity comes from man's potential ability to share "with God alone the power to do all things." Vives imagined man in the role of archmime, enacting before the assembled gods all parts, tragic and comic. Appearing as a moral satirist, man took the "shapes of a thousand wild beasts," representing the passions, as in the classical tradition.[7] More's Utopians found no practical use in scholastic logic: Vives' *In pseudodialecticos* (1519) drove home the idea that, as an all-sufficient end in itself, logic was useless.[8]

Vives continued to rise in English humanist esteem before the meeting with More and Erasmus. By February 13, 1519, Erasmus had come to regard him so highly that he recommended him as a tutor for Prince Ferdinand, while upholding as a model "our English court" (*EE*, 917.10-12). During the heat of the Brixius trouble, More expressed to Erasmus his pride that, although in Brixius he had an enemy, leading humanists, including Vives, praised him (*EE*, 1087.351-55). While preparing for the Field of the Cloth of Gold, More commented to

Erasmus at some length on Vives' work as among the best then coming from the Louvain scholars, and he particularly praised Vives' recent *In pseudodialecticos* (*EE*, 1106.15-81). More was delighted at the way in which the brightest younger men were working with the spirit and ideals which he shared with Erasmus. Replying in June, Erasmus—not one to throw such praise about carelessly—agreed with warmth, and saw Vives as one who in time would overshadow his own name (*EE*, 1107.6-8).

For Vives the direct meeting with the two English humanists, after the Field, was a long step toward England (*LC*, p. xlix). Off and on since 1518, Erasmus had been working on a proposed complete new edition of St. Augustine for Froben's press at Basel. Now, in the fall of 1520, a turning point in his career, Vives was induced to undertake the *City of God*, which was projected as the first volume, doubtless because of its great early popularity as a printed book (with twenty-four editions before 1500) (*EE*, 1309n.).

It is hardly surprising that at this stage of the Renaissance many thoughtful men were drawn to St. Augustine's great apology in vindication of the early Christian Church and of Christianity. The *Civitas Dei* itself was written when, after centuries of imperial follies and tyrannies, the center and symbol of the ancient world culture collapsed in a storm of war. The humanists were inclined to find in ancient Rome, before the barbarian invasions, the epitome of the highest culture known in western world history before their own age; and when they studied the disastrous failures in leadership which helped bring Rome to ruin, they set them in parallel with the follies of princes in their own time. As for More's interest in the *City of God*, this dates back to his own 1504 lectures on it; and since these are lost, Vives' commentary (that of a humanist sharing ideals very close to More's) is probably as close as it is possible to come to More's own work. I judge that from the outset Vives planned to dedicate the edition to Henry VIII and thus make it his bridge to a secure position in the English humanist world of court and university. His comments on St. Augustine were written at various stages between January, 1521, and July, 1522, and they provide many successive insights upon Renaissance man and society.

With a possible bright future in view in an England ruled in peace and humanist progress by a great Christian prince, Vives set to work; and by January 1, 1521, he had the first book of the *City of God* finished (*EE*, 1309n.). St. Augustine (*CDV*, I, vi) had reasoned that the bloody savageries characteristic of pagan soldiers after the capture of cities (as of Rome) were customary, "and wherein they were moderated, it was through . . . Christ." Vives noted that such savage customs had indeed existed in the pre-Christian era, and he quoted in illustration Quintilian's superb and terrible description of the sack of a city. Vives' own grim comment resembles that of More and Erasmus upon the depravity of contemporary professionals at war:

Now these things came thus to pass, because the soldiers (as they are a most proud and insolent kind of men, without all mean and modesty) have no power to temper their avarice, lust, or fury in their victory: and again, because (taking the town by force) if they should not do thus for terror to the enemy, they might justly fear to suffer the like of the enemy.[9]

St. Augustine (*CDV*, I, xx) dealt with "some sort of killing men, which notwithstanding are no murtherers," i.e., with lawful exceptions to Christ's "Thou shalt not kill." Vives had no quarrel with lawful justice when it was truly just, not inhumane savagery wearing a cloak of justice:

The Jews . . . waged wars; but . . . by God's express command. But if they were counted godly that to please God (though against natural humanity) [cf. More's Utopians] afflicted his enemies with war and slaughter: truly then cannot we [i.e., nowadays] but be held the most ungodly of the world that butcher up so many thousand Christians against the express will of God [*CDV*, p. 30].

As we have noted, during the Middle Ages St. Augustine's authority became decisive on the question of war's justice for Christians. Consider, however, Vives' remarks on praise (*CDV*, I, xxiii) of the Roman general, Regulus, for not committing suicide to avoid capture by the enemy. Observing that St. Augustine praised the Christians for excelling the Roman in his highest virtue, Vives wrote sharply that Augustine "makes fighting as far from Christian piety, as religious humanity is from barbarous inhumanity" (*CDV*, p. 34). These were the most sharp criticisms on Renaissance man at war written by Vives by the beginning of 1521.

While England appeared to be peaceful, in the heart of Europe began to rise turbulences from which the fortunate isle could not escape. On February 16 Erasmus saw that "this Lutheran tempest tears away the arts." At the same time he looked forward with pleasure to Vives' future success in England, where his talents would surely gain recognition from "our Maecenases" (*EE*, 1184.14-26). Then Luther came before the Diet of Worms in April to make his uncompromising defense. The storm was rising. More's climb in the court world was marked in May by his appointment as undertreasurer, but the month also brought Buckingham's swift execution. By May, also, Henry VIII had answered Luther's *Babylonish Captivity of the Church* with his *Assertion of the Seven Sacraments,* and—a year and a half after Dean John Colet's death—in St. Paul's churchyard smoke curled upward from bonfires of Luther's books, while Bishop John Fisher went to Colet's old pulpit to denounce Luther's errors (Chambers, p. 193). Although More was evidently being drawn deeper into the King's service, Erasmus hoped wistfully (June 11) that as the undertreasurer's post was pleasant, honorable, and involved little work, More would have time left for humanistic concerns (*EE*, 1210.10-11). England was, nonetheless, still the promised land of peaceful social progress. On July 10, Vives wrote hopefully to More of his project to settle there, if maintenance could be found. More anticipated pleasure in Vives' conversation, and the Queen herself had already bestowed some bounty upon Vives as a learned countryman (*EE*, 1222.15-23).

Vives' sharing of critical values with the English humanists is even more evident in his commentary upon St. Augustine's Books II-VI, completed between February and July of 1521 (*EE*, 1309n., 1222). One might think Erasmus himself were writing praise of More as man and as critic, and the attacks on empire building and on war as legalized robbery. St. Augustine argued that pagan philosophers' wisdom is "weak and bootless," not only because the pagans lack divine authority but also because "the examples of the gods are greater confirmation of vices in men than the wisemen's disputations" are bracing to virtuous action. First Vives cited Plato's exclusion of poets from his Republic "because their fictions of the gods give examples very prejudicial unto the honesty of their readers, as, their wars, thefts, seditions, adulteries, and such like." Then he quoted Thomas More's translation of Lucian's satiric *Calling up of the Dead* to sharpen the point:

I (saith he [Menippus]) being a boy, and hearing Hesiod and Homer singing of seditions and wars, not only those of heroes and demi-gods, but even of the gods themselves, their adulteries, rapines, tyrannies, chasings out of parents, and marriages of brethren and sisters; truly I thought all these things both lawful and laudable . . . [*CDV*, pp. 56-7].

It was in association with this criticism of ancient and modern ethics that Vives gave his warmly personal praise of More's virtues, including his "unmoved loyalty" (*CDV*, pp. 56-57)—rather specific than (as Chambers [p. 177] saw it) "general adulation."

As congenial to Vives' critical temper as it was to Erasmus' and More's was the question, "Whether happy and wise men should account it as part of their felicity to possess an empire that is enlarged by no means but war?" (*CDV*, IV, iii). St. Augustine himself satirized the inherent brittleness of such states, although he found that many men give great thanks for them. Before agreeing, he would like to make a historical inquiry:

Seeing you cannot shew such estates to be any way happy as are in continual wars, being still in terror, trouble, and guilt of shedding human blood, though it be their foes': what reason then or what wisdom shall any man shew, in glorying in the largeness of Empire, all their joy being but as a glass, bright and brittle, and evermore in fear and danger of breaking?

Even Vives' brief comment, taken in context with those of More and Erasmus, not only points his thorough agreement but again suggests the debts of these humanist social critics to the Roman Stoics, as well as to the primitive Christian Fathers who opposed war as unchristian: "Wherefore Jerome thinks that Stoicism commeth nearer to Christianity, than any of the Sects beside it" (*CDV*, pp. 149-50).

Like his English friends, Vives perceived that most contemporary wars were forms of tyranny, of legalized robbery. St. Augustine (*CDV*, IV, iv) advanced the theme, "Kingdoms without justice, how like they are to thievish purchases" (i.e., stolen goods). Vives fastened his comment to thievish—and supported the criticism as currently applicable:

The world . . . is bathed in floods of mutual blood. When one alone kills a man, it is called a crime, but when many together do it, it is called a virtue. Thus, not respect of innocence, but the greatness of the fact, sets it free from penalty. And truly fighting belongs neither to good men nor thieves, nor to any that are men at all, but is a right bestial fury, and therefore was it named *bellum*, of *bellua*, a beast.

With obvious approval Vives quoted the classically savage and witty reply of a pirate, whom Alexander the Great asked: "What wickedness moved him to trouble the whole sea with one only gally-foyst?" "The same," replied the pirate, "that makes thee trouble the whole earth." And Vives added, for good measure, Lucan's epithets for Alexander: "a happy thief of the earth," and "earth's fatal evil" (*terrarum fatale malum*) (*CDV*, p. 150). Thus Vives wrote between February and July of 1521.

While England seemed at peace that summer, in eastern Europe the mightiest military machine of the age was moving, as the Turks advanced into Hungary. No one more than Erasmus was aware of the senseless violence of most contemporary war, and he still hoped for a golden age of progress, at least in England. In a letter to Pope Leo X (August 31) he again insisted that the original Christian teaching was everywhere based on peace and conciliation, and that it nowhere said that war is lawful between Christians. Now, however, he observed that it was extreme to consider *all* war forbidden among Christians, since there are evil men who must be restrained (*EE*, 1232.50-55). As he wrote, on August 29, Belgrade was falling to the Turks—the Renaissance counterpart of the Goths who had overwhelmed ancient Rome in St. Augustine's day.

By July the leading English critic of tyranny and its reckless passion for invasive wars, More himself, could have had no doubt of his anomalous position as the King's servant. At home England still enjoyed Wolsey's perpetual peace of 1518. Wolsey, however, was at Calais and Bruges, with More in his train, on a mission of intrigue. While pretending to arbitrate between Francis I and Charles V, he was in fact busy scrapping the treaty of "universal" peace with France whose permanency had been so chivalrously elaborated at the Field of the Cloth of Gold during June of 1520. Before this, as far as I know, as a royal councilor More had been kept in the dark on Wolseyan diplomacy. Now, however, the King, on July 24, ordered his secretary, Richard Pace, humanist friend of More, to acquaint the new and younger men with affairs: ". . . where as old men doeth now decay greatly within His realm, his mind is to acquaint other young men with his great affairs, and . . . to make . . . Sir Thomas More privy to all such matters as your Grace shall treat at Calais." [10] The King himself was indeed delighted with the prospect of renewed French wars, and he desired Wolsey's opinion on "a secret device of his own" for the "high and great enterprise" of destroying the entire French navy (*LP*, III, 1440). By a secret treaty with Charles (Bruges, August 25), England was to aid the Emperor against France and to share in the presumptive spoils. Probably the contrasting hopes of most Englishmen at home were expressed by an otherwise undistinguished law student who wrote to Lord Darcy at Calais that he trusted "Wolsey will bring peace home" (*LP*, III, 1669).

Meanwhile English efforts to combat Luther were intensified, and More was involved. By October the King bore the new title of *Fidei defensor*, and, to Luther's violent reply to Henry's *Seven Sacraments*, More—as "William Ross"—penned his strong counterattack. There was nothing inconsistent in the stern realism of the author of *Utopia*, either in 1516 or in 1521 or later, in dealing with willfully violent or revolutionary men, as More thought Luther to be. In the state of Utopia any freeman might peaceably and reasonably try to persuade his fellows to any social change he liked, but if he took to violence (and rhetoric can be a form of violence) he was forthwith deprived of freedom of speech and, if he persisted, he might even be made a bondman or put to death (*MUL*, pp. 268-74). By late 1521 the Lutheran tempest, to the humanists in England, had begun to appear as a very dangerous form of violence.

The pretense of friendship with France was continued until November 24, when Wolsey "threw off the mask." Once again England was set for invasion of France, and the hoped-for humanist golden age of peace went glimmering. Beyond it all there was for Wolsey the enthralling lure of the papal crown, and for Henry VIII there was once again his old fond dream of castles in France (Pollard, pp. 124-26).

A flash of insight into More's opinion of this latest effort to renew the medieval chivalric dream of reconquering France comes from words uttered long after, when he was prisoner in the Tower and an Aesopian fable was repeated to him. He knew it only too well, for when war and peace were discussed in the council under Wolsey, "some thought it wisdom, that we should sit still & let [Charles and Francis] alone." To justify his war, Wolsey used this same fable. It seems that some ancient wise men knew that soon a rain would fall and turn all it wetted into fools. Therefore they retired into a cave until the showers were over, expecting then to lord it over the unwise. The fools, however, though wet, were a majority, and they gave the wise men a good beating "to take their conceit out of them." "And so, said his Grace, that if we would be so wise that we would sit in peace while the fools fought, they would not fail after to make peace and fall at length upon us." "I trust," said More, with his peculiar irony, "we never made war but as reason would. But yet this fable . . . did in his [Wolsey's] days help the king & the realm to spend many a fair penny" (*MEW*, p. 1436). More, however, was ignorant of the special bait which induced Wolsey again to plunge England into war: the Emperor Charles had shrewdly taken up and surpassed the French promises to " 'make Wolsey pope' " (Pollard, p. 126).

The incredible folly of this latest English excursion into France was obvious not merely to the humanists. In 1521, both French and imperial critics expected England to "hold aloof and make her profit out of the loss the combatants inflicted on one another" (Pollard, p. 126). Perhaps More's view of this latest English martial lunacy may be surmised in part from his state of Utopia, based as it was on contemporary England. It was no accident that Utopia was imagined to be a strongly defensible island and that the Utopian citizens were so well trained in arms that they could afford both to hate and despise war. Although in 1521 the English were a small nation, four times outnumbered by the French, many times more by Charles V's subjects, the Machiavellian doctrine that neutrality is dangerous to small states did not fit England. Just before the French war of 1521-23, that great ambition of the Tudor dynasty, a united England, was almost realized. If so, Englishmen need fear invasion no more than the Utopians, even if an invader could have accomplished the feat of landing on her shores. Despite the invention of firearms, still relatively crude, the English longbow remained a relatively potent weapon, capable in skilled hands of dispatching ten arrows a minute at two hundred yards. On the other hand, it might seem that the experience of 1512-13 would have taught England, had the humanist concept of "reason" (cf. More's ironic "we never made war but as reason would") prevailed, that if the costs were to be realistically counted in advance, as Erasmus so often urged, the English were too few in number and lacked the trustworthy allies needed to make any major imperialistic impression on the continent. They could, as More once said to Roper, win a few "castles in France"—"ungracious dogholes" said Cromwell bluntly in the Parliamentary debates of 1523. But whatever costly gains were made in France could neither be held nor extended. In the end, when diplomatic flourishes were over, they had to be let go for a small fraction of their conquest's heavy cost. As Chambers said (p. 165), for England "European war was futile. There was neither danger to be averted nor advantage to be gained." Under certain conditions of absolute necessity, More's Utopians made war, but to them the 1521-23 adventure into France would have appeared to be a worse than bestial folly—indeed, an act of tyranny.

At Bruges in August, 1521, Charles V had told Wolsey that he would help him secure the papacy whenever the next vacancy came. Unexpectedly Leo X died on December 2, and Wolsey's grandest ambition seemed within reach. Then the Emperor's tutor was elected instead (January 9, 1522) and became Adrian VI. Now, of course, it is evident that Wolsey had been elegantly double-crossed by Charles. To the disappointed Wolsey, Charles V apologized, declaring that his ambassador at Rome had been instructed to advocate only Wolsey's claims (Pollard, pp. 126-27).

We may assume, then, that by early January of 1522 More, Erasmus, and Vives, as well as a great many English and Frenchmen, knew that war was imminent. Erasmus, refusing to despair, appealed to Charles V (January 15) in dedicating to him a *Paraphrase of Matthew*. (Charles was to visit England that spring to work out plans for the war upon France.) War might be near, but at least it had not yet begun. Erasmus urged Charles to play the "True Emperor" who is a "defender of the Gospel," in implied contrast to a false emperor, a corrupt monarch. "Meet it is," wrote Erasmus, "not to be ignorant what manner thing it [the Gospel] is . . . which one taketh armour to defend. . . . Much less apt things do they bring unto you, that give you great gifts of precious stones . . . of lusty fierce horses, of hounds, and of rich hangings, that come out of far strange countries." The humanist critic, aware of the storm rising in Christendom, hoped that the imperial conscience might be reached before new outrages were inflicted upon humanity:

It may please [you] from time to time to have it in your remembrance, that no war there is upon so just and lawful causes taken in hand, nor with so good moderation executed, that draweth not after it an hugie [*sic*] heap both of abominations, & . . . miseries; yea, and remember also the greatest portion of all the harms to light in fine upon persons both guiltless and also unworthy the same.[11]

Here was a terse reminder to one at the summit, asking the Emperor in effect: are you sure you have counted in advance *all* the costs of this

197

adventure? And characteristically, Erasmus' critical eye was upon the welfare of the common people.

Three months later Erasmus produced a sharp-edged new instrument for use in the humanist's battle to drive home to their age the folly and injustice of typical needless wars. The new weapon was found when he set about producing a new edition of his *Colloquies*, brought out in March by Froben's press. Years before, he had written some little conversations—brief dramatic dialogues—for use primarily by school-boys learning their Latin. After a former student printed some of these without permission in 1518, Erasmus protected himself by printing an authorized edition amidst the golden age peace of 1519. Now by 1522 he had perceived that the *Colloquies* might, in the spirit of his and More's translations from Lucian, of his own *Julius Excluded from Heaven,* and of *Utopia*'s first book, serve a double purpose. As examples of racy speech they could also work as splendid and potentially far-reaching vehicles for social criticism. Between 1522 and 1533 there were a dozen new editions, and in each he introduced new pieces or sharpened up the old in the light of contemporary events. Even in translation the style is surprisingly racy, flexible, and easy, often sauced with broad humor and cutting satire upon follies and madness of the time, above all those of the great princes in Church and state, but now more and more broadly reflected in their disastrous effects upon the common man, who could hardly hope to escape the widespreading ruins of the wars of princes. The colloquies have the added value, for a broadly popular audience, of shortness, variety, and (like the best literature produced by the humanists) of both topical and universal appeal as part of the continuing struggle for men's minds and for peaceful reforms in Renaissance society.

Of a Soldier's Life (*Militaria*) was the most lively addition to the March, 1522, printing.[12] Erasmus' intentions are perfectly apparent from the outset. Through his dramatic voices in the dialogue he takes the part of a witty realist, a Renaissance Voltaire stinging the conscience of Europe, destroying the customary complacencies of princes and their peoples, and, what is more, reaching out to touch every soldier not utterly corrupted. (It may be remembered that John Colet's 1513 sermon against the French war stirred Henry VIII's fear that such criticism might dampen the troops' enthusiasm and conviction of war's "justice.") Generally speaking, the *Colloquies* which satirize war aim to strip from the military profession any shreds of tawdry glamour possibly remaining from the world of medieval chivalry.

The eighteenth-century translator, Bailey, rightly saw the purpose of *A Soldier's Life*: to so "lay open" the everyday realities of a military career "that youth may be put out of conceit of going into the army." As the mercenary soldier, now returned from seeking his fortune, speaks, he himself reveals the famous art of war as actually one of thievery and inhuman butchery of fellow-Christians. Hanno ("stay-at-home") encounters an old acquaintance who has lately been to the wars. Under acute questioning, Thrasymachus ("bold-in-fight") candidly tells an unvarnished tale which turns out to be not a romantic résumé of heroism, glory, and honor, but a sordid relation of actual or witnessed crimes against common humanity, friend and foe alike.

The narrative is not without its touches of dreadful comedy. Why does the youth who of his own free will went to war with such swift eagerness now return "limping home? . . . You, a soldier, that would out run a stage if an enemy were at your heels?" "The hope of booty made me valiant." Ah! so now you're rich? Unfortunately, no: he has no plunder, only "empty pockets," although he is loaded heavily enough with sin, having seen more in the campaign than in his whole previous life. Well, as you see it now, why do men enlist as soldiers? "In truth, I can think no other, but that they are possess'd [insane], for if the devil were not in them, they would never anticipate their fate" (i.e., hurry to meet death, which will come for you). Since you saw it, how did the battle go? "I don't know, in all the confusion," and as for those ex-soldiers who tell you "every circumstance to the life . . . [they] lie confoundedly." You're limping—how did you get your wound? As for that, when he ran away in a fright, he hit his knee on a stone. What about making restitution for what you admit you have stolen? To this the soldier says bitterly, "That's made already . . . to whores, sutlers, and gamesters." It seems from what you say that you've committed sacrilege: what of that? "There's nothing sacred in hostility, there we neither spare private houses nor churches. . . . They say there's no satisfaction to be made for what is done in war, for all things are lawful there" by the "law of arms."

Driven into a corner after this confession of criminality, the soldier admits: "that law [of arms] is the highest injustice; it was not love of your country, but the love of booty made you a soldier," but he believes "very few go into the army with any better design." Hanno, thoroughly disgusted, offers the savage comfort that "it is indeed some excuse to be mad, with the greater part of mankind." Weakly the trooper argues that he has "heard a parson say in his pulpit, that war was lawful," and that it is honorable for every man to "live by his trade." (We can almost hear that fat coward and thief, Sir John Falstaff, defending himself to Prince Hal: "Why, Hal, 'tis my vocation, Hal. 'Tis no sin for a man to labour in his vocation" [*I Henry IV*, I.ii.116-17].) Crushingly Hanno replies that "pulpits are indeed the oracles of truth," and asks, "A very honorable trade indeed to burn houses, rob churches, ravish nuns, plunder the poor, and murder the innocent?" To which the soldier haplessly replies: "Butchers are hired to kill beasts, and why is our trade found fault with, who are hired to kill men?"

Belatedly, Erasmus' imaginary soldier is a bit worried about his chances for salvation (cf. Doll Tearsheet's question to Falstaff—one of the few he cannot wittily dash aside: when will you "leave fighting o' days and foining o' nights, and begin to patch up thine old body for heaven?" [*II Henry IV*, II.iv.251-53].) Thrasymachus is deeply shocked at the assertion that his soul seems fairly sure of damnation: "Who a mischief put you in my way to disturb my conscience, which was very quiet before?" But he will hunt up some easygoing priest, and he hopes that "God is of a forgiving nature." Thus, in the *Colloquies* of March, 1522, Erasmus fired a well-aimed shot in the humanist effort to reshape the age's attitudes toward the noble art and trade of war. *Of a Soldier's Life*, moreover, is directed not to old and custom-hardened men but to youth. (The *Colloquia* were indeed widely read in schools for two centuries.)

While Erasmus devised this entertainingly charged medium for gaining a wide audience for humanist criticism, Vives had been busy on the *City of God*, and between January and April, 1522, he finished another section of his commentary (*EE*, 1222, 1271, 1309n.). Contemplating the tragic folly of resumed wars, he enlarged his vision and dwelt on man as man's own worst enemy and one capable of depravities no brute beasts can match. In the golden age mood of 1518, his little *Fable about Man* idealistically emphasized human dignity as godlike, since man alone, with his great gift of reason, shared "power to do all things." In the spring of 1522 he stressed man's proneness to inflict man-made evil upon his own kind. St. Augustine put forward that God foreknew that man would sin, and that he "would run on in that height of iniquity, that

brute beasts should live at more atonement and peace between themselves
. . . than men." "Any place," wrote Vives, "will hold brute-beasts without contentions, sooner than men." In support he cited Pliny's proverb,
"For man is wolf to man." He recalled Cicero's summing-up on Dicaear-
chus' book "*Of the death of men*. . . . And herein having reckoned up
inundations, plagues, burnings . . . and other external causes, he com-
pares them with the wars and seditions wherewith man hath destroyed
man," only to conclude that man is more fatal to his kind than all the
inevitable ills that flesh is heir to. Vives' terse comment indicates how
completely he had come to share the values and critical outlook of his
English friends: "This war amongst men did Christ desire to have
abolished, and for the fury of wrath to have grafted the heat of zeal
and charity. . . ." And as Erasmus had done earlier, Vives in his grim
closing pondered the possibility of some tragic flaw in human nature
which may make a life of reason and peace impossible: "Men's minds
are already too forward to shed blood, and do wickedly: they need not be
set on" (*CDV*, p. 150).

As for More, as a courtier, his ever-contracting opportunity to serve
through practical social criticism is well defined by the purely routine
role that he played publicly when, in May and June, the Emperor visited
England to cement the alliance for the war against France. Hall chron-
icled with rich detail the gorgeous pageants devised for the Emperor's
progress from Dover to London. There, outside the gates (June 6),
Charles and Henry VIII were met by the Mayor and the City Companies "in fine scarlet and well horsed." And there "one Sir Thomas More
knight, and well learned . . . made to them an eloquent oration, in the
praise of the two princes, and of the peace and love between them, and
what comfort it was to their subjects, to see them in such amity" (Hall,
p. 637). Hall tells us no more about it. Protocol evidently called for a
short, complimentary oration, and More was given the assignment. Thus
England was set to renew attack upon France.

Vives, the Emperor Charles' subject, dearly hoped to settle in Henry
VIII's England, yet these two mighty kings appeared to be deliberately
throwing away the whole achievement of peace in Christendom. The
war criticism last written (April-July, 1522) for his edition of the *City
of God* (XIX, xiii) mirrors a feeling of great social tragedy, almost of
despair (*EE*, 1303, 1309n.). Now he concentrated upon the "perverse
nature of men," but it seems evident from his reference to "their States"

that what he had in mind was the perversity and corruption of contemporary monarchs and their pro-war aides.

Vives agreed that St. Augustine proved "all things to consist by peace and concord: so that consequently, discord must needs be the fuel to all ruin and confusion." How, then, can one explain the eagerness (of princes) to create catastrophes of war? "Wherefore I wonder at the perverse nature of men that love dissensions . . . as their own very souls, hating peace, as it were a most pernicious evil." For them would not perfect happiness be total war? "Surely they had but their due, if their bosoms within, and their States without, were wholly fraught with this their so dearly affected darling, war." After St. Augustine wrote of "humane peace" as a great good, Vives remarked savagely that "men do turn all these goods nowadays into contentious uses," making a hell on earth as though there were none hereafter "where they may enjoy their damned desires forever" (CDV, p. 723).

All these criticisms by Vives were written for the work whose dedication to Henry VIII (July 7, 1522) he hoped would result in a royal invitation to live and work decently in England. Such dedications, under the circumstances, necessarily appear to be flattering. I am inclined to think, nonetheless, that, relatively speaking, Vives' letter suggests how far, for the humanists, Henry still bore the reputation, pre-eminently among the great European princes, of one who held that not the arts of war but those of learning and peace conferred the greatest true glory. Vives grants Henry's "warlike prowess," as was conventional, but his highest encomiums are for Henry's lawful acquisition of his realm (not "by arms and homicide"), for his active concern to promote growth of learning, for his recent defense of the Church against Luther, and for his evident conviction that the most enduring glory is secured by such deeds. Learned men "do not so much bewonder your wealth or your power, as . . . that you are good and gracious: not deeming it to be admired, that you are a King, since even wicked men have oft been Kings." After the defense of the Sacraments appeared, "the reputation of your mind's goodness . . . was now infixed in the minds of all . . . yea, even those that place riches above all things, and . . . beauty, brawny strength, and agility; and that are students in the art of war, as if war were the omnipotent commander of all things." [13]

While the City of God was in Froben's press, Vives renewed his project to settle in England (August 15), and two weeks later Erasmus warmly recommended him to Bishop John Fisher.[14] Not until early May of 1523, however, was he to arrive at his humanistic promised land, and then, ironically, to take his place as one actor in a developing social tragedy.

The kind of war devised and sanctioned by Henry VIII and Wolsey, and waged by their commanders in 1522-23, must be characterized if the humanist social criticism in response to these events is to be made intelligible. According to Brewer (I, 24), "war had not then [1513] lost all traces of its chivalrous aspect. It was the chosen field for the display of personal skill, courage, and gallantry;—tournament on a grander scale." Or: "War was, in fact, at that time [1523] little more than an aristocratic amusement . . ." (II, 1). The evidence cited elsewhere even by this historian, together with a wealth of records, suggests a cruelly different picture. In fact in these wars virtually all vestiges of the chivalric code, which the humanist critics had often satirized as little more in their day than a cloak for legalized tyranny, were deliberately scrapped.

It is not surprising to find outrage upon common humanity the usual thing in Renaissance France. As the criticism of Sir John Fortescue, followed by that of More in Book I of *Utopia*, made clear, the French people had long been brutalized by their kings. Francis I at this time, if anything, surpassed his predecessors in the ruthless exactions and oppressions inflicted to maintain his armies. Nothing was sacred, not even holy relics escaped the royal depredator, until, as a French spy wrote to England, "his people are eaten up to the bones, and, with the Church, cry for vengeance upon him" (*LP*, III, p. 1141). Wolsey, with grim joy, observed that in Francis I's wartime "base and exile poor estate" he had "molten the garnishing of St. Martin's corpse, and founded [melted for coin] the twelve apostles, with other jewels and sacred ornaments of the churches" (*LP*, III, p. 1091). It was during such events that Erasmus wrote to Pope Adrian VI (August 1, 1522) to plead that he do his utmost to compose the "tumult" among the impious within the Christian world (*EE*, 1304.335).

The sullen, deliberate barbarity of the English invaders, however, far exceeded the less efficient spoliation of the French king. The method of war devised in 1522 for France (and in 1523 for Scotland) was one of total, indiscriminate, even senseless destruction, inflicted indifferently upon noncombatants and combatants alike. The objective was not speedy, decisive victory but rather to plunder and devastate until (it was hoped) the enemy collapsed through utter exhaustion. Henry's treaty with Charles V called for three months of war in France in 1522, during which Boulogne would be besieged, if practicable, but otherwise the commanders "are at liberty to devise any plan, by the execution of which, in their opinion, the greatest mischief can be done . . ." (*Cal. LP Spain*, II, 442). The commander in France was Thomas Howard, the Earl of Surrey since 1514, Lord High Admiral in 1513 and leader of the English van against the Scots at Flodden. Burned indiscriminately were castles and villages, churches, and crops in the fields. To the fate of the helpless villagers, whose homes and fields were left in smoldering ruins, the invaders were completely indifferent. From France on September 12 Surrey wrote a typical report to the King, telling him that the country about Boulogne "is so burnt and pillaged that the French have good reason to be angry. . . . All the country we have passed through has been burnt. . . . When we have burnt Dorlance, Corby, Ancre, Bray, and the neighbouring country . . . in about three weeks, I cannot see that we can do much more" (*LP*, III, 2540). In happy mood, on September 16, he added that "there is universal poverty here, and great fear of this army. I trust the King's grace and you [Wolsey] will be content . . ." (*LP*, III, 2549).

They were indeed content, and the picture of Henry, receiving and rejoicing over these terrible dispatches, shows vividly how More's room for positive social criticism against such inhumanity and folly had now shrunk almost to the vanishing point. The war-infatuated Henry was vastly delighted with these optimistic reports sent him from France. More wrote to Wolsey of the hour-long dramatic scene when Henry read to the Queen Surrey's letter of September 16, and they rejoiced together "that the French king should be now toward a tutor, and his realm to have a governor." Self-intoxicated with a surfeit of glory, "the King's grace said, that he trusted in God to be their governor himself, and that they should . . . make a way for him, as king Richard did for his father." What room did this singular piece of the drama of tyranny provide for the humanist social critic in More? Only so much, as with grim discretion, he used to write to the Cardinal: "I pray God, if it be good for his grace and for this realm, that then it may prove so, and else in the stead thereof I pray God send his grace an honorable and profitable peace. . . ." [1]

No doubt it took courage, in 1522, to express this mild implied criticism even to Wolsey, if not directly to Henry VIII. [2] The measure of the change in both More and the King can perhaps be judged by comparing Colet's bold outspokenness against the French war at its outset in 1513—and Henry's toleration of the Dean's candor—with More's very "cautious and guarded" expressions to a different kind of king in 1522. In his *Utopia* (1516) More had himself written blunt satire (letting Hythlodaye be his spokesman) upon just such pretensions as Henry's to a right to the throne of France (*MUL*, pp. 45, 81-87). Ironically, More's actual role, as seen above, of war counselor to the King seems vastly more impotent than any he could imagine when he argued that Hythlodaye should join a prince's court as an adviser. Rejecting the idea, Hythlodaye said, "By this means nothing else will be brought to pass, but, whiles that I go about to remedy the madness of others, I should be even as mad as they." Not at all, replied More: let us agree that kings cannot practically use counsels of perfection, "But you must with a crafty wile . . . handle the matter wittily . . . for the purpose; and that which you cannot turn to good, so to order it that it be not very bad" (*MUL*, pp. 99-100). There were, indeed, several matters which More did not treat at all in *Utopia*'s first book, "The Dialogue of Counsel." One was what a humanist adviser should do if the good king whose service he had taken up turned into a tyrant. The other was how this adviser could be a force for good under such secret diplomacy as Wolsey's, especially after the 1518 Treaty of Universal Peace. More also urged to Hythlodaye that, once he had elected a king's service, he must not abandon the ship because he could not keep down the tempests which imperil it. By 1522, More found himself living intimately with all three conditions.

The war methods which gave Henry and Wolsey such joy in 1522 in plain fact brought about their own ironic nemesis. Triumph became futile. No one has better shown this than Brewer, who termed such war "little more than an aristocratic amusement." For the triumph of such a campaign, under existing supply conditions, was creation of a condition in which every step of the invading English armies away from the sea-coast, by which in the end they must escape, added to their difficulties and perils. At their backs smoked a barren wasteland, while all about them they carried forward a fearful solitude of their own making. In front nothing could be expected but resistance each day more desperate than before. Almost the only element of chivalric mercy lay in the campaigns' brevity, produced unintentionally, by the "practical and ignoble difficulties" met in victualing and supply.[3] Indeed, when a French spy reported that the way lay open to Paris itself (*LP*, III, 2707), the English in France dared not risk such a farther advance.

In contrast to Henry's and Wolsey's ideas on war, the English humanist critics' over-all view of their age's paramount needs appears to grow in realism and soundness. As winter brought the campaigning of 1522 to a halt, "peace," wrote Pollard (p. 135), "was growing not merely a national but a European necessity." From Louvain (October 12, 1522) Vives wrote to Pope Adrian VI his letter on war and Luther, "On the Tumultuous Condition of Europe." He urged that war between Christians was fratricide, as though parts of the same body were to fight together, and that the Pope should swiftly use his powers to pacify the princes.[4] Evidently Vives thought that the Pope still owned such powers. The Pope, by late 1522, had distractions rushing in upon him from all sides. In a brief, very important for Erasmus' support against his increasingly numerous enemies, Adrian VI stressed that, for their age, universal peace must be the aim of all Christendom, but he emphasized the benefits if Lutheran sympathizers were not permitted to spread.[5]

While Henry VIII, Wolsey, Francis, and Charles were engaged in the amusement of war in western Europe, the militant Moslem imperial forces were in cold fact battering its eastern defenses (Pollard, p. 135). Belgrade had fallen on August 29, 1521, and the Turks, able to sustain a mighty two-pronged offensive, capped this by taking surrender of the key island fortress of Rhodes, after prolonged siege, on December 28, 1522. ("And much blame put on all princes," wrote Hall [p. 655], "because they sent no succor . . . to the isle.") In 1523 "it was the firm conviction of more than half the Christian world that if Rhodes fell, Rome and the rest of Christendom must fall with it," said Brewer (I, 570). The truth and magnitude of this disaster, of course, reached western Europe slowly. On December 26 Henry VIII's ambassador to Rome wrote to congratulate him on the glory already achieved in the war upon France. Henry's "achievements and good fortune make him worthy of a double crown and double glory. It is foreseen that by his authority peace will be restored to Christendom before the spring, or that those who prefer war will perceive what it is to slight the avenging gods" (*LP*, III, 2726). In other words, next year Henry might happily anticipate that the French king would "make a way for him, as king Richard did for his father."

The image of Henry VIII as a justly avenging god had no more appeal for the English humanists than the image of a king as a tyrant—or, as in Erasmus' *Scarabeus*, an eagle preying on the entrails of lesser birds. Erasmus perhaps still hoped against hope that the princes might come to their senses, and be persuaded to rule justly. On January 5, 1523, he dedicated to Charles V's brother, Ferdinand of Austria, his *Paraphrase of John*. He recognized that such a gift might surprise those who think the only literature suitable for princes to be "matters of hunting, keeping of dogs and horses, of engines for war. . . ." But the Scriptures contain the principles of justice that no Christian prince can escape, for as God gave power for right use, so will He punish tyranny: "He that poulleth [robs] the people, that oppresseth the poor, that by war defaceth all both good and bad, he that is the occasion for many calamities, for whose vain glory so much man's blood is shed. . . ." [6]

Erasmus was very well informed about the developing pattern of these wars. As tyranny more and more clearly showed its contemporary face, he brought out (January, 1523) an edition of the *Adages* which included at least three expansions of his essay against war (*Dulce bellum*). First, to the term "great princes" he now added a bitter parenthesis: "the which, saving the shape, have no point of manhood, yet seem they in their own conceit to be gods." [7] Second, a new comment on the Old Testament war king, David, is revealing, especially if beneath the name of David we may sense covert reference to Europe's princes in general (and just possibly Henry VIII in particular). Erasmus now commented that when Solomon wished a temple built, he discarded David's example, charging him with bloody ambition. And yet, noted Erasmus, David only warred under God's command, against the impious, and in an epoch when the reformer of the Mosaic law (Christ) had not taught that he should love his enemies. [8]

In his third significant addition to *Against War* he suggested strongly that contemporary Christians, confronted by the Turkish menace, could learn much from the primitive Christian Fathers who were also endan-

Sir Thomas More. Portrait by Holbein
Copyright the Frick Collection, New York

gered by the pagans.[9] This last addition, prudently omitted by the anonymous English translator of 1533-34, is the most remarkable for its biting identification of contemporary princes as tyrannous. It began as an attack on corrupt monks (Wolsey?) who do not really teach Christ's doctrine or live a Christian life; instead they haunt courts and aid tyranny, by supporting war as "just," and so forth. He asked: how are we to convert the Turks by murder, burning, and pillage (*EDB*, l. 1059)? and said, "I prefer a true Turk to a false Christian" (l. 1065). Then:

What will come out of this great tumult of war? I do not wish to seem to guess at what is alas only too clear, too often. They [princes in church and state] use the pretext of a crusade against the Turks to rob the Christian people, and to induce them—already oppressed in so many ways—to endure more servilely the tyranny of civil and religious princes (*seruilius ferat principum utriusque generis tyrannidem*). . . . This is not to say that I absolutely oppose war against the Turks if they attack us. But any war under Christ's name should use a Christian spirit and [i.e., humane] methods. . . .[10]

Evidently Erasmus had not forgotten that the Turks had captured Belgrade on August 29, 1521, and that the supposedly impregnable island fortress of Rhodes was under siege.

The news that Rhodes had capitulated (December 28, 1522) had evidently not reached Rome when Wolsey's agent there wrote (January 13, 1523) that Adrian VI "had described Rhodes as 'the key of Christendom,' and declared that 'if that island were taken, the pope could not stay in Rome' " (*LP*, III, 2771). By January 25 rumors of a great Turkish triumph had reached Louvain (*LC*, 37.12 ff.). By February 22 the news there was certain, and Vives was appalled at the danger to Christendom (*LC*, 45.13-17).

The shock wave of this catastrophe sped through all Europe. The news would have reached England shortly after it was known at Louvain. With great urgency Pope Adrian, as a Moslem invasion hung over Italy, set about securing what the Christian humanists realistically had so long declared vital and so often to deaf ears, namely, peace among the Christian princes. He wrote to Wolsey, who appeared to be the key figure in England's participation in the renewed French war; of course Wolsey was also papal legate in England. Of Rhodes' fall, he said (*ca.* February 23), they had doubtless already heard. But did they realize its significance—even the danger to England itself? (Here the Pope seemed partly to imitate arguments made by Erasmus earlier, including those directed to the enlightened self-interest of princes.) "This [Rhodes] and Belgrade were the outworks of Christendom, and now they are lost the Turk will with greater ease conquer Hungary, Sicily, and Italy, and place the rest of Christendom and England itself in the greatest danger."

Continuing, the Pope asserted that the "dissensions of Christian princes" aided the Moslems, and that by itself an already war-exhausted Italy would offer but little resistance. "Henry should act up to his title of Defender of the Faith," and the "first step should be a general peace." But if such action "is objectionable, a truce for some years might be taken" (*LP*, III, 2849). In the papal court, wrote Campeggio (Cardinal and Bishop of Salisbury), "Wolsey was expected to turn Henry's mind to peace" (*LP*, III, 2865). Letters to Wolsey, and to the King, begging help to restore peace and sanity, streamed from Rome to England. The College of Cardinals exhorted Henry to follow the Pope's counsel, to withdraw his troops from France, and begin the work of defending Christendom (*LP*, III, 2871). "Everyone knows how much Wolsey could do to effect this," added Cardinal Ghinucci to Wolsey himself (*LP*, III, 2872-73).

Details soon followed to underline the danger to Rome, and, after Rome, to the west. Wolsey heard, in a letter of March 14, that "if the Turk come to Italy he will have it without resistance," and that the "principal men of the town are preparing to leave Rome" (*LP*, III, 2891). In Louvain, where the humanists, Vives among them, most nearly shared the ideals developed by Colet, More, and Erasmus in England, men grimly savored the *"O felices quietas"* before the expected Turkish invasion of the west (*LC*, 48.7), and Wolsey rather than Henry VIII was blamed for the endless wars and for the peril of Christendom disunited before the Turk (*LC*, 50.10-34). So staggering was the disaster that some could not for months credit the fall of the supposedly impregnable fortress of Rhodes (*LC*, 51.40). When it was common knowledge (April 17) that the Pope had proposed a truce between Henry, Francis, and Charles, to be followed by joint attack on the Turks (*LC*, 53.37), the humanists could only hope that the princes would see that sheer self-protection and self-interest made such action mandatory.

Engrossed with their glorious French war, Henry and Wolsey were deaf and blind to such appeals and to the perils even to England. A year earlier (June 21, 1522) Wolsey had declared, after the attack on Belgrade developed, that "The real Turk is he [Francis I] with whom we are occupied, and I know no other Turk" (*Cal. LP Spain*, p. 444). Now on June 11 a year later he expressed to the Pope Henry's great affection for him, but said that the King had suffered such injuries from France (i.e., from the invaded) that war was necessary, and he finished by urging the Pope to take care of himself.[11] To provide funds for further war, Parliament was summoned for the first time in eight years, and before it Wolsey promised to make in France "such war . . . as hath not been seen" (Hall, p. 655).

As nearly as I can fix the moment, it was during these French wars of 1522-23 that the once-grand medieval concept of a common Christendom finally expired and assumed the practical status of a myth. Perhaps few or no men then living were or could have been aware of it, but events speak with a clarion voice. To the Pope's anguished appeals the great Christian princes were not only indifferent, they were, as Brewer (I, 571) saw, now even incredulous.

When this great concept of a world united by common concepts of ethics, law, and religion ceased to be a reality and became a haunting myth, of course a new reality replaced it—and a new ideal. Certainly from this moment in history onward to our own day, broadly speaking, the Christian humanist concept of a good life based on reason and common justice (as in Utopia) has been submerged by a radically different and, internationally speaking, frankly anarchic form of "reason"—*raison d'État*, which was progressively substituted for the ideal of justice common to and a right of all humanity. From 1522 onward, all peaces would be, as Frederick Duval says, of iron, and the "natural" relation of states would be chronic war.[12] Wolsey has been praised, probably wrongly, for inventing something in statecraft known as the "balance of power." Now, perhaps, this so-called balance confronts all humanity in its ultimate and absolute form: the balance of terror based on mutual power for total world-wide nuclear warfare using intercontinental missiles for which, in their ideally perfected form, no defense is possible. Thus not only western Europe (and the then hardly discovered America) but all mankind may ironically be approaching the end of the road which was at last clearly opened to the future in the wars of 1522-23.

The deepening tragic irony of More's position as exponent of the good life is curiously apparent in the role he played in the Parliament of April-August, 1523. The great humanist work, from Erasmus' *Against War* to the *Utopia* and the *Christian Prince*, strove with hard realism to drive home to the monarchs in actual power the economic as well as humane fact that a king could not wage war without huge cost and injury to his own subjects. Now Henry VIII's vast inheritance from his father had all been dissipated in the insane, if chivalrically glorious, projects for the reconquest of France. Parliament, which had not met since 1515, was therefore summoned "for the first and only time in Tudor history to meet the whole cost of a war." Unfortunately, when thus confronted with the financial, if not human, bill for all this glory, "the nation began to display a stubborn preference for peace" (Pollard, pp. 132-34). Thomas More was appointed Speaker, and with loyalty and skill he led a stormy session to grant a large part of Wolsey's demands for a huge capital levy.[13] That More had long regarded such military projects as the English invasion of France as a tragic folly, we fortunately know from his earlier criticism. Certainly it would not be apparent from the records of his tight-lipped work as Speaker.

There survives from this Parliament one remarkable speech, ostensibly written (though not certainly delivered) for Henry himself to hear.[14] What is now ironic about Thomas Cromwell's piece is that so much of it reads like a digest of the earlier humanist analysis of the folly and cost of unnecessary war. Conspicuously missing from it, however, is the Christian humanist ethics and concern for the welfare of humanity. Cromwell's objections to continued war were strictly those of *realpolitik*. As Machiavelli might have done, he simply argued carefully that, however desirable, the proposed conquests were militarily and economically impracticable, as indeed events were proving them to be. Unlike the humanist critics, he granted Henry's "good and just title" to France. He agreed, moreover, that the French so richly deserved defeat that "to speak of peace . . . it is no time." But to him war was the art of the possible. For an English army to advance deeply into France while leaving uncaptured strongholds behind it would be military folly. On the other hand, the 1513-14 war had established the cost of such sieges, when to take Thérouenne "cost his Highness more than twenty such ungracious dogholes could be worth to him." Renewed war, furthermore, would exhaust the country's bullion and force the English to "coin leather again," and while no doubt patriotic Englishmen would accept leather money, on the continent only gold would buy army supplies. With the best fortune in the field, he argued, there were simply too few Englishmen ever to occupy a country as large as France. Besides, trusty allies were now lacking. And the rising national spirit of the French must be reckoned with: "there was never nation more marvellously linked together than they be amongst themselves."

Before any foreign conquests were attempted, Cromwell saw it as a natural necessity for England first to win Scotland to "join with us in one politic body" as the two nations were "joined . . . by nature all in one island." Finally, and perhaps most shrewdly of all, he touched the heart nerve of the English nation—its growing fear over the succession—in his passionate plea that "our most redoubted sovereign should in no wise pass the seas [as Henry did in 1513] in his own noble person" (Cromwell, I, 30-44).

As for the honor and glory won by Surrey's forces in the 1522 campaign, Cromwell summed them up with what is probably unintentional irony: "We have spoiled and burnt [Morlaix], and laid waste a great country, with great honor to . . . Surrey, who remained in the French dominions, with a small number of men, for six or seven weeks, when all the power of France durst not give him battle" (*LP*, III, 2958). Nevertheless, the war subsidy was granted, and Wolsey boasted (August 30) that the army which had set out for Calais under Suffolk a week before was "the largest which has passed out of this realm for a hundred years" (*LP*, III, 3281).

As for More's work as Speaker, judging by the results—the unenthusiastic approval of the grant—there is no solid reason not to accept Hall's account (p. 656): Wolsey appeared, explained the "time of necessity" and exhorted Commons to make the grant; after he departed, More, the next day, seconded the Cardinal's request. Indeed both More and Cromwell were made collectors of the war tax, whatever More's private opinions may have been.[15]

More, in the Utopian Dialogue of Counsel, argued to Hythlodaye that royal advisers should avoid impractical counsels of perfection and labor instead to make the best of things as they were. It would appear, ironically, that as the King's loyal servant in the 1523 Parliament he had virtually no choice but to plead for the extremely heavy war tax needed by his masters, whether or not it would contribute to "an honorable and profitable peace" which he devoutly wished. An undoubted letter of Cromwell, written (August 17) after the Parliament's close, gives a sardonic indication that advancing needless wars was only part of More's burden:

I amongst others have endured a Parliament which continued . . . xvii whole weeks, where we communed of war, peace, strife . . . debate, murmur, grudge, riches, poverty, penury, truth, falsehood, justice, equity, deceit, oppression, magnanimity, activity, force, intemperance, treason, murder, felony . . . and also how a commonwealth might be edified . . . and continued within our realm. Howbeit, in conclusion we have d[one] as our predecessors have been wont to do, that is to say, as well as we might, and left where we begun [Cromwell, I, (313)].

The irony is that More himself, in *Utopia*, had imaginatively projected his own vision of "how a commonwealth might be edified and continued" in England, but that was done in the golden age atmosphere of 1516.

In 1523 Henry VIII and Wolsey advanced their version of chivalric war into Scotland. Cromwell, in the Parliamentary speech prepared for the King to hear, had argued that England's first natural necessity was to win the Scots "to join with us in one politic body" as the two nations were "joined . . . by nature all in one island." Henry and Wolsey, however, seemed determined to follow a policy like that of Rome for Carthage—create a desert and call it peace. For the campaign, Henry transferred to its command his military man-of-all-work, Surrey; and Surrey transferred to the Borders the methods of total warfare which had been first developed the year before for France. Shakespeare's ideal chivalric knight, Hotspur, thought it "an easy leap / To pluck bright honor from the pale-faced moon." Under each full moon Surrey's men sought bright honor in the new style. Devastation was indiscriminate and, as far as possible, complete. "Border hate and . . . warfare recognized no distinction of age or sex, or things sacred or profane" (Brewer, I, 517). Typically, at Eccles in June, a convent of nuns met the English invaders, gave up their abbey's keys, and promised to throw its walls down within a few days. Should they fail, said Dacres, the abbey would be burnt over them (*LP*, III, 3098).

From Hampton Court at the end of August, Wolsey wrote exultantly to the English ambassadors in Spain of the splendid progress which had been made toward turning the whole Border into a smoking, sterile, impassable desert between England and Scotland. Such destruction had already been wrought upon the entire Teviot country and the March that

. . . there is left neither house, fortress, village, tree, cattle, corn, or other succor for man; insomuch as some of the people which fled from the same, and afterward returned, finding no sustentation, were compelled to come into England, begging bread, which oftentimes when they eat they die incontinently for the hunger passed; and with no imprisonment, cutting of the ears, burning them in the face, or otherwise, can be kept away.

"Such," concluded this prince of the Church, "is the punishment of the Almighty God to those that be the disturbers of good peace, rest, and quiet in Christendom" (*LP*, III, 3281). "It was the rule of the strong," said Brewer (I, 517, 456), "the justice and righteousness of which no one in those days thought of disputing"—no one, he himself added, but a few humanists such as Erasmus and More.

During the golden age of 1515-16, Erasmus, like More, usually referred to the common people as less corrupted than their princes. By 1523, however, popular disturbances were rapidly rising in Germany, and Erasmus had these in mind in June when he spoke of the populace as that "fickle, many-headed beast" (*EE*, 1365.36). Then in the August, 1523, edition of the *Colloquies* he added the mordant "Soldier and the Carthusian." [16]

The new dialogue wittily but grimly satirized both the common man turned mercenary and the idea that war is a romantic and brave adventure. Erasmus is not famous as a friend of the monastic way of life, but in this popular satire the Carthusian got much the better of things. Two old friends meet after some years and compare their ways of life. One has become a monk, the other a mercenary, now returned from the wars, heavily scarred, stooping "like a mower," and meanly dressed. The soldier makes fun of the monastic life as a poor one, but the Carthusian turns a deadly wit upon his old acquaintance. He suggests, first, that two years ago the trooper, who has a young wife and children, must have been in dire need of a "good physician." What but sickness can explain why of his own volition he " 'listed . . . for a soldier . . . and was hired for a pitiful pay to cut men's throats" at the risk of his own? So the monkish life seems unattractive? "What do you think is a more unhappy way of living, for a poor pay, to murder a fellow Christian, who never did you harm, and to run yourself body and soul into eternal damnation?" Sincerely shocked by the word "murder," the soldier exclaims, "Why, it is lawful to kill an enemy!" The Carthusian's rejoinder emphasizes one of the strongest points made in the English humanist criticism of the orthodox medieval theory of the "just" (lawful) war. "Perhaps it may be so," agreed the Carthusian, "if [the enemy] invades your native country. Nay, and it is pious too, to fight for your wife, children, your parents and friends, your religion and liberties, and the public peace." Since obviously none of the saving clauses fits the mercenary soldier, the Carthusian strikes home with, "But what is all that to your fighting for money?" and, "If you had been knocked on the head, I would not have given a rotten nut to redeem the very soul of you."

The remainder of Erasmus' dialogue satirizes romantic notions (based quite simply on lack of experience, in this instance) of war as a chivalric and "brave adventure," i.e., truly honorable. The Carthusian and the soldier compare their superiors, prior and captain. The soldier must admit that it is miserable enough to "be under the command of some barbarous officer, who often calls you out to fatiguing marches at midnight, and sends you out, and commands you back at his pleasure, exposes you to the shot of great guns, assigns you to a station where you must either kill or be killed." As for the penalty for disobedience, it is so savage that the soldier grants that it "would be a favor" to have his head cut off instead.

There must be some advantages, surely; since the soldier went off to get as rich as possible, what pay has the gallant brought home? As far as coin goes, he has none; in fact he wishes that the penniless monk would "furnish me with some money" toward his debts. Surprised, the monk inquires, "But how come you so bare?" Bitterly the soldier replies, "Do you ask that? Why, whatsoever I got of pay, plunder, sacrilege, rapine and theft, was spent in wine, whores and gaming."

As it turns out, however, the soldier *has* brought home some war trophies. There is the "trench" on his forehead—his crossbow broke when he pulled it, and the accident almost killed him! The great scar on his cheek? From a "battle"—one that "arose at dice." But the most grievous of all his physical changes is suggested by the "rubies" on his chin and by the deeply stooped walk that makes him like a man of ninety, or a "semi-reptile animal," for the pox "has contracted my nerves to that degree." He tries to comfort himself with a good old cliché: "This is the fortune of war"; but the Carthusian replies in a humanist voice: "Nay, this is the madness of your own mind."

Finally, "what spoils will you carry home to your wife and children?" The soldier sums it in one word—his "leprosie" (syphilis), and he grants that now he will infect with it those who are dearest to him. So much for his body. "But what sort of a soul do you bring back with you?" With brutal candor the soldier replies, "Just as clean as a Paris common whore in Maburtu's Road, or a common house of office." This last touch of quiet horror is as characteristic of the humanist vision of social tragedy as it is of Ibsen in *Ghosts*. Both Erasmus and Ibsen comprehend the ever widening circles in which man-made social evil creates suffering for the innocent.

Erasmus' Carthusian suggested to the soldier that he needed, before it was too late, a good physician to cure him, if possible, of the war sickness of the time. A similar metaphor, of the physician urgently needed in a sick world, figured strongly in Erasmus' dedication to Henry VIII (August 23, 1523) of his *Paraphrase of Luke*—"Luke the Physician"—offered to the King ". . . in case any vacant time of leisure may in so great unquietness and troublous state of the world be gotten." To a sick world Luke brought the "medicine" of the Gospel, for "the Lord Jesus was a physician" for the human spirit. "The pestilent diseases . . . of a common weal are evil manners." In antiquity there were wise lawgivers: Solon and Plato in Athens, the Stoics who promised "liberty, freedom, true riches," and the Epicureans who "made high words and promises of pleasure." But who ever heard of men willing to suffer death for all these precepts? In contrast, martyrdoms testify to the truth of the Christian teachings.[17] The richness and warmth of his friendships nostalgically stirred Erasmus even in the fall of 1523 to think of living and working in England again, but conditions had changed sadly since 1517—now "one is not at liberty" there (*EE*, 1386.14-15). Dared More express so much truth then?

In late August, as Wolsey boasted, there sailed for France under Suffolk the largest English army "which has passed out of this realm for a hundred years." Behind, with Thomas More as their usual go-between, waited Henry VIII, avid for double glory and a double crown, and Wolsey, no less eager for the papacy to which Charles V had promised to help him at the first opportunity. From Scotland, on the one hand, the reliable Surrey sent good news (September 12): "He is cursed by the merchants and commons for this war with Scotland. If the Scots will not give battle, more destruction shall be done to them than has been done in one journey for 100 years" (*LP*, III, 3321).

The French campaign, between September and late November of 1523, was another matter, one of slim harvest for princes so hungry for glory. Despite the huge cost of taking that "ungracious doghole," Thérouenne, in 1513, Henry had his heart set on the capture of Boulogne. More relayed Suffolk's report to Wolsey (that it was impregnable and that its siege should be abandoned), news which the King took hard (*LP*, III, 3319, 3320). Most striking of all, perhaps, is More's report of the King's desires on September 20. Suffolk, whose ambition was made of gentler stuff than Surrey's, had advised that his command was marching virtually unopposed toward Paris, and he had ordered "that the King's army shall in the marching proclaim liberty, sparing the country from burning and spoil." (At war the Utopians, it may be remembered, do not promiscuously and needlessly burn, waste, despoil, and sack either countryside or cities, and "All the weak multitude they leave untouched" [*MUL*, p. 263].) Henry would have none of Suffolk's humane (and Christian) methods.

The King's Highness thinketh [wrote More to Wolsey] that sith his army shall march in hard weather, with many sore and grievous incommodities, if they should also forbear the profit of the spoil (the bare hope whereof, though they gat little, was great encouraging to them) they shall have evil will to march forward, and their captains shall have much ado to keep them from crying, Home! Home [*MC*, p. 123]!

Here was an English Renaissance Caesar!—when would come such another? Doubtless Henry remembered his 1512 Spanish fiasco, when a mutinous English army, in defiance of his express commands, returned home—an episode which then made his youthful military pretensions the laughingstock of Europe.[18]

Despite Henry's visions of heroic conquests, of which More was an almost daily spectator, and despite the outpouring of treasure, France in 1523 seemed no nearer than a year before to making "way for Henry, as king Richard did for his father." Every dispatch from Suffolk told of military success, but each clamored for gold, more gold: "Nobody knows how money is to be got." [19] By October 17 Wolsey, ominously, had to request the King himself to furnish ten thousand pounds; it seemed the wars in France and Scotland had consumed twice as much as estimated.[20] One remembers Erasmus' grim advice to contemporary princes: before beginning war, in pure self-interest reckon the costs— and More's wistful, discreet hopes for "an honorable and profitable peace" a year earlier. Desperately Wolsey urged to Henry (November 3) that he would never have a better chance to conquer France and establish his title to be its king (*SP*, I, 144). Even as he wrote, the English army was in full retreat. Although almost unopposed on the road to Paris, Suffolk could only burn and loot as far as Montdidier, then return to Calais (November 7) for escape.[21] Ruthlessly, Henry ordered an almost unheard-of winter campaign, but the weather was so bitter that by November's end "all the foot-soldiers . . . demanded to return" (*LP*, III, 3580). Willy-nilly, the King's insane idea of the army's wintering in devastated France (like Napoleon's of wintering in Moscow) had to be abandoned.

In 1522 Henry and Wolsey had plunged into this imperially invasive war with high hopes, but their moods as 1523 drew to a close were bitter and, for Wolsey, increasingly desperate. As December began, Erasmus wrote to Francis I the epistle dedicatory to his *Paraphrase of Mark*, grimly observing that the "long season" of wars between Christian princes was bringing on "the utter decay of Christ's religion." [22] For Wolsey the news of December 6 was that, thanks to the wily Charles V, he had once more failed of election as pope, and even to the Cardinal it was now clear that, despite all the ruinous costs of the wars made under the alliance with the emperor, Charles would never help him to the papacy. Neither was there any peace in Scotland, however much Wolsey might trust that, with sufficient boldness, the faction of Albany might be "briefly extincted," i.e., exterminated to a man.[23] For what may perhaps now be called the English tyrants, it was a matter of indifference to hear from the new Pope, Clement VII, as the year ended, that he would promote a war against the Turks—something about which Henry and Wolsey could hardly have cared less. For them, whirled along now in the war storm which they had done so much to create, there were far more absorbing questions. For the King, what chivalric glory could be rescued from the débacle? For Wolsey, beneath whose feet the ground was indeed crumbling, the looming problem was not so much to secure glory as to avert ruin.[24] Gloomily he wrote to Knight in the Low Countries (January 5, 1524), "The King is rejoiced at his success, but still nothing has been done for the King's profit, and no portion of his inheritance recovered" (*LP*, IV, 8).

In the first act of our drama of ideas, John Colet searched out a novel way to solve the problem of the Gospel's meaning as an aid to peaceful reform of society. For an interlude before Henry VIII's coronation the play took on a flavor of satire. The middle acts, after

1509, offered, as it were, a form of bright romantic comedy, except for a brief burst of melodramatic violence in the 1512-13 French war. In mellow, golden-age mood, this phase lasted until a little after the Field of the Cloth of Gold (June, 1520). With the eruption of wars and spreading social violence in 1522, however, the drama changed its character. As the last acts begin, it seems more and more clear that our play is turning toward immense social tragedy which, from our vantage point in England, spreads as far as the eye can see. With the quiet arrival in England of Juan Luis Vives in May, 1523, our last major humanist actor comes on the stage.

Vives' experience in England,[25] even if taken alone instead of in its place in the whole fabric of humanist social criticism, would provide a vivid mirror for the last and most tragic act of this drama of men and ideas. His work formed, in effect, a kind of test case, showing how far the humanism developed by Colet, More, and Erasmus—all older men—might continue to live and grow as an organic part of the English Renaissance. Following Erasmus' departure in 1517, Vives was the most notable intellectual to come to England. In a way, he was almost a replacement for Erasmus after that astute scholar, failing to make suitable arrangements in 1519 when he evidently wished to return, had decided that the England of late 1523 owned too little liberty to make living there once more attractive (*EE*, 1386.14-15). He could hardly have come more highly or warmly recommended to Henry and Wolsey than he had been by More and Erasmus, who regarded him as finely equipped to carry forward their kind of new learning. The most famous humanist of the early sixteenth century, Erasmus himself, saw in Vives one who in time would overshadow his own name (*EE*, 1107.6-8). How deeply on his part, as a critic of war and peaceful reform, Vives saw eye to eye with More and Erasmus is well marked in his commentary upon the *City of God*, which they encouraged him to undertake and (I believe) to dedicate to Henry VIII. With his Utopians in mind, More himself might have said, as Vives did with conviction, that heathen in the "faithless isles of the ocean" might attain "the glory of a Christian" (*CDV*, p. 694). Or the cutting wit and realism of Erasmus might have created Vives' grim comment: "If Augustine lived nowadays, he should be held a pedant, or a petty orator, and Paul a madman or an heretic." [26]

Vives came to England, moreover, with a warm welcome from Henry

VIII and Wolsey. The dedication to Henry (July 7, 1522) of the edition of the *Civitas Dei*, finished by Froben's press on August 31, of course preceded his own arrival. During that autumn, unfortunately, Henry and Wolsey were busy with the aristocratic amusements of the French war. In any event, on January 23, 1523, Henry graciously replied and invited him to make England his scholarly home, an invitation seconded by Wolsey. The King's letter, with its generous and intelligent praise of Vives' labors, again suggests why the humanists so long regarded Henry as a great Christian prince. By Vives' learning "Saint Augustine, long time imperfect and obscure, is now at last brought from darkness to light, and restored to his ancient integrity" to the benefit of all posterity.[27] By May Vives had arrived in England, and by August Wolsey had appointed him to one of his Readerships at Oxford, then held in Bishop Fox's college of Corpus Christi, since the Cardinal's was still being formed. Thus Vives from the outset enjoyed not only the friendship of More but friendly notice by and access to the highest authorities of the realm.

Vives, furthermore, came to England at a critical time for English humanism. However warm his English friendships, from the continent Erasmus could now hope to gain royal or Wolseyan attention only through his writings. As for More, now deeply absorbed into the King's service, we have already seen how he found himself increasingly powerless to influence high policies for good, e.g., to avoid or lessen the horrors of the almost insane involvement of England in the continental wars after 1522. As early as June, 1520, when he opposed publication of his letters, More himself showed sensitivity to the sharp contraction of his opportunities to function as a wise social critic at court: he had not, he said, always been sufficiently "cautious and guarded" in his remarks upon "peace and war, upon morality, marriage, the clergy, the people." That list virtually includes all the most fiercely debated and deadly dangerous topics of the 1520's in England. Thus increasingly More stood under a self-imposed sentence of at least public silence. Vives, on the other hand, retained and used the power to express social criticism openly. When, indeed, we read his candid comments on English affairs, I think we come as near as may be to hearing also the silenced voice of More himself, once the greatest public satirist of massive social folly in his time.

Vives' royal welcome to England was indeed signally marked by the King and Queen in the late autumn of 1523. The humanist was settled at Oxford, and by a custom of long standing the kings of England had avoided entering Oxford town. Returning from Woodstock to Windsor, Henry and Catherine broke the ancient practice to pay Vives a visit and to invite him to Court for the Christmas holidays—a great mark of favor and one quite in keeping with the character of a Christian humanist prince (de Vocht, pp. 8-9).

That December Vives published his remarkable little treatise, *The Education of a Christian Woman* (*De institutione Christianae foeminae*). Through this work, before the tragedy of the last act of our drama sweeps to its close, we may bring into complete perspective the entire English humanist attack on medieval romance as potentially, for princes, an encouragement to corruption and tyranny.

Few aspects of the literary and social criticism of More, Erasmus, and Juan Luis Vives have been more frequently misunderstood than their concerted attack upon medieval romance and its imaginative world. The Elizabethan humanist, Roger Ascham (who had been the future Queen Elizabeth's tutor), did not invent the idea but only followed his great predecessors when he singled out the *Morte Darthur* of Malory as representative of the "books of Chivalry . . . the whole pleasure of which . . . standeth in two special points, in open manslaughter and bold bawdry. . . ." [1]

Consider the criticism of C. S. Lewis in his *English Literature in the Sixteenth Century*. From this readers discover that these humanists "rejected . . . chivalrous romance" with the most humorless, narrow-minded, and witless kind of contumely. They were, one is told, so obsessed with "hatred of the Middle Ages" that they "could not really bring themselves to believe" that "the poet cared about the shepherds, lovers, warriors, voyages, and battles." It is said that More, Erasmus, and Vives represent some sort of kill-joy union of "the humanist with . . . the puritan." We are reminded, correctly, that More's Utopians used military methods "mischievously devised to flout the chivalric code at every turn," that Erasmus [*Christian Prince*] would "forbid a young prince to read 'Arthurs and Lancelots' which smack of tyranny and are moreover rude, foolish, and anile" (*anilibus* really means "old-womanish"), and that Vives [*The Christian Woman*] condemned Arthurian romance as full of lies. At the same time Lewis rejoiced because "so far as the common reader was concerned, the humanists' attack on the romances was not, in the sixteenth century, very success-ful." Instead, the common readers—seemingly wiser than the human-ists—with simple joy "pressed the siege, wept with the heroine, and shuddered at the monsters." In general explanation, it is proposed that

223

these humanists were aligned against the Middle Ages in an ill-conceived rebellion which represented "not a war between ideas but against ideas." [2] This is a shrewd attack which might better have been leveled against continental neoclassicism.

Such a view seems profoundly to mistake both the humanists' intentions and their artistic accomplishments. It is, however, very true that they mounted a sustained satiric attack upon medieval romance, which forms an integral part of their analysis of and attack upon literature which stimulates tyranny, just as they denounced the romantic glamorization of tyrants either in history or in contemporary life.

More and his friends were actually engaged in a fateful war both against and between some of the most significant ideas of modern times. Indeed, until the nature of this war of ideas is better understood, their literary and social criticism hardly makes whole and complete sense. To bring the humanist attack on romances into full perspective, the ideas involved may be grouped under four main headings. These have to do with: (1) tyrants versus just kings; (2) a war-ridden and disintegrating late-medieval society versus a concept of a possible Renaissance social order of peace and Christian justice; (3) a conflict between two codes of value (ethical, political, economic, and esthetic) involving radically different ideas of honor, glory, and human greatness; and (4) opposed ideas of woman's nature and potential role in modern society.

It may, however, be useful to summarize here some of the ideas that More, Erasmus, and Vives *were* against. They were, above all, against tyrants and tyranny in all forms. They were against the idea that a king can do no wrong and that the right of a ruling class *is* its might. They were against the flattering of tyrants in either history or romance. They were against the idea that romance, history, or biography should be admired when it represents imperial despots and conquerors (such as Alexander the Great or Caesar) as great and good men, worthy to be imitated by modern princes.

Being not merely sentimental but rather based firmly on a reasoned view of the common welfare of all men, this hatred of tyranny carried over logically (e.g., in *Utopia, Christian Prince, Christian Woman*) into constructive criticism of plans for the education of those destined to wield great power over society, either for good or for ill. These humanists did not regard a future (or present) prince as a "common reader." They were against the idea that because kings (and fools, said Erasmus' bitter adage) are born such, they need not undertake seriously to learn a just and Christian art of ruling from literature, history, or life. They were against the idea that if a future prince reads at all, it need only be "amusing" stories. They were against the idea that habituation to vicious pleasures in youth is harmless to future rulers. They were against the idea that a young prince's earliest and most impressionable years should be used to fill his mind with glamorized images of tyrants and military conquerors as truly great or heroic men, worthy of imitation. They were against the idea that romance fictions which from a Christian viewpoint were obviously immoral, if not amoral, or history as written to flatter tyrants, should be seriously admired for their truth to human nature and their value in providing future rulers with sound models to imitate. They were against the idea that medieval romance ("Arthurs and Lancelots") is credible as history (or what the Elizabethans called "mirrors for magistrates") or that writers of history should be lauded for imitating the literary technique of the romances. They were against the idea that the supermen heroes and heroics of romance fiction should be taken seriously when they run counter to the verifiable facts of human physiology, psychology, or natural law (in the modern scientific sense, as it is partly used in the state of Utopia).

A second cluster of ideas which the English humanists opposed have to do with their concepts of a desirable and practicable social order— a good life. While these are here stated in terms of what they opposed, their criticism in breadth aimed to be positive and constructive. To a high degree they were against the idea that a good life can be reconciled with chronic warfare of Christians upon each other. They were against the idea that anarchy and violence, however romantic, are, for the common people, preferable to a social order founded upon reason and Christian justice. They were against the idea that a pagan society which glorifies unreason, passion, and sensuality may be accepted as essentially Christian if only, as in many medieval romances, it is thinly veneered with pseudo-Christian trappings. They were against the idea that, in any good society, admiration should be heaped on the individual, regardless of his social status, who gratifies his passions at the expense of reason and the rights of others.

In the third place—using late 1523 as our location in time—More and his humanist circle were against certain traditional ideas, whether found in medieval romance or in classical writers, centered on the codes of value which, embodied in custom, powerfully affect men's motivations. They were against the idea that true glory can be derived from depraved pleasures, from wanton brutality, violence or bloodshed, or from their socially ritualized form, war. They were against the idea that unnecessary wars (e.g., most wars of invasion, such as Henry VIII's imperialist ventures into France) can rightly, or even sanely, be called glorious, or that manslaughter is ever such. They were against the idea that true human greatness is to be found in the tyrants or conquerors of history or romance. They were against the idea that mere possession of power, wealth, or title to great dominion makes the possessor automatically a great man. They were against the idea that moral, esthetic, or other basic values can be determined by corrupt custom or changed at will by these alleged supermen. As to "honor," that shibboleth of the decadent chivalric world, the humanist social critics were against all ideas of honor which, however superficially appealing in their manifold literary disguises, had in life evidently become largely euphemisms, pretexts, or mere masks used to justify and to quasi-legalize the exploitation of the commonwealth by a ruling and war-loving class of corrupt and mercenary men who were virtually devoid of any sense or responsibility to the human race or even to the people of their own nation.

Finally, these humanists, especially More and Vives, were against certain traditional concepts of woman's nature and role in society. They were against the idea that the heroine of romance (e.g., Guinevere) or history (e.g., in the epic, Helen of Troy; or in history, Cleopatra), should be admired or imitated any more than the hero for sensualities and adulteries, however spectacular, at the expense of ideals of Christian marriage. The humanists' efforts to further the education of women suggest that they were implicitly against the idea, evidently common to the imaginative world of medieval romance, that the necessary social role of women is to serve as precious sex symbols or as objects of lawless passion, and the idea that women are almost congenitally incapable of education and of disciplined intelligence. They were therefore against the idea that women (e.g., the Princess Mary, for whom Vives wrote *The Christian Woman*—and consider the humanist education gained by the Princess Elizabeth) could not or should not be educated for mature and civilized roles in marriage and society.

The kind of attack on medieval romance found in Vives' *Christian Woman* of 1523 began at least eighteen years earlier. When Erasmus visited England in 1505-6, he and More made some translations from Lucian, particularly from his satires on tyrants, conquerors, and pompous generals, and upon the trifling pretexts so often used as excuses for starting wars and for the pursuit of military glory. There are indeed no Renaissance translations of Lucian's *Tyrannicida* recorded before those by More and Erasmus. As for heroines whose beauty might launch whole fleets and topple Ilium's towers, Lucian's *Menippus* (translated by More) takes us to Hades to view the ghost of Helen of Troy. No surge of lush romanticism greets her vision, however. Instead Menippus is inspired to ironic and cynical astonishment that a mere bare skull should have caused so great a war and the deaths of so many thousands.[3] Erasmus' *Praise of Folly* (1509) aimed a critically selective wit against a kaleidoscopic range of human follies and forms of unreason, including the pursuit of martial glory by churchmen. More, in his epigrams against Brixius and his literary superman-hero, the naval captain Hervé (1513), mocked such figures as bogus elements of the romance-epic tradition, as falsehoods and absurdities, and in effect called their author a liar and a fool for attempting to perpetuate them. More's *Richard III* is no less a mordant disclosure of a tyrant than are his most distinctive epigrams of 1509-19. Although Henry VIII and many of his courtiers regarded the invasion of France in 1512-14 as a romantic adventure filled with chivalric glory, John Colet, in two of the most remarkable of pre-Reformation sermons known in Renaissance England, attacked the war between Christians as basically unethical and contrary to Christ's teaching. Writing from England in 1513, Erasmus held up to scorn the contemporary military conqueror Pope Julius II himself, in his blistering *Julius Excluded from Heaven*.

In his imaginary state of Utopia (1516), More ironically represented the Utopians as acting purely by the light of natural reason, since they know nothing of Christian ethics, and of course nothing directly of the world of decadent medieval chivalry. In his witty picture of the Utopian art of war, he shows these rational people everywhere concerned for the lives and welfare of the sane Utopians and also the oppressed common people of neighbor nations. The Utopians are rational humanitarians; they regard nothing as more vilely corrupt than to take pleasure or to find true glory or honor in butchery, hunting, manslaughter, or war. They "flout the chivalric code at every turn" because they find such codes gratify a corrupt warmaking class at the expense of humanity and decency. Their aim is to live a good life, not to expire romantically on a battlefield or in a love death. Hence the Utopians think it to be nobly reasonable to cut short war's bloodshed by purchasing the capture or assassination of the war-mad princes of chivalry whom they regard as primarily responsible for driving the common people to war in the first place. Instead of feeling delight at the idea of the kind of head-on pitched battle customary in medieval romances, the Utopians think such behavior stupid and "beastly" (subhuman); they prefer to use their wits and to triumph, if possible, through some crafty and life-saving stratagem. As we know, More wrote *Utopia* with England in mind, while reflecting upon the good life that might, beginning in his own lifetime, come to be possible there, if the powers of reason were aided by those of a peacefully reformed Church.

In the adverse criticism quoted above, Erasmus was attacked for characterizing "Arthurs and Lancelots," i.e., Arthurian romance generally, and the sixteenth-century "common readers" were admired for having better sense than the humanist. When the matter is examined more closely, in its original context, it appears that Erasmus' remarks, in *The Christian Prince*, were written directly as a guide for the education of the sixteen-year-old Prince Charles, who three years later (1519), as Charles V, became Emperor and the most powerful man in Europe, ruling Spain and the Netherlands. By what stretch of the imagination could he be called a "common reader"? Erasmus, who had then been appointed a councilor to Charles, was, like the other English humanists, above all practically concerned with the beneficial or corrupting effects of literature upon the very men, such as Charles or Henry VIII, in whose hands lay actual power.

Erasmus' remarks on Arthurian romance, indeed, appeared in a chapter whose theme was the problem that a wise prince must face if he is to avoid being duped by adulation and self-seeking flattery. At once the humanist realistically, if obviously, observed that "everyone flatters princes" (*omnes adulantur Principes*). That is, no prudent man holding the highest powers in the state dares ever forget that inevitably, in the nature of things, he will be surrounded by many dissimulators who seek their own selfish ends, who seek to "use" the prince. Hence a well-educated king should know this universal truth, the better to discount flattery and not easily be led into rash actions, or led to imitate tyrants. In any man's education, however, the time of youth is the time of greatest impressionability and malleability—this to the sixteen-year-old Charles. One who desires to learn from history how a naturally high-spirited and impetuous youth (*puer natura ferox ac violentus*) becomes a tyrant, unless some antidote is applied in time, can study the examples of Achilles, Alexander the Great, or Julius Caesar. (Clearly Erasmus meant that the ideas formed in youth as to what constitutes true greatness and glory are of immense importance in shaping the motivations and character of the future ruler.)

But Erasmus also noted, in *The Christian Prince*, that books may be powerful flatterers. Books, no less powerfully than any self-seeking courtier, may present to the young prince, if he is not well guided, lying and corrupt images of greatness for him to imitate. Therefore Erasmus reasoned that Charles should not *begin*, as a largely inexperienced youth, by absorbing literature which flatters tyrants and men of war, or which by inference offers truly vicious concepts of glory but shows them as attractive.

It was at about this point in his argument that he introduced his hostile criticism of medieval romance. In these days, he said, we see "Arthurs and Lancelots" and similar "amusing fables" aplenty—stories that not only favor tyranny (*non solum tyrannicis*) but are "unlearned, foolish, and old-womanish" (*ineruditis, stultis, & anilibus*) (*EO*, IV, 587D). These, in Erasmus' opinion, were better read in the form of satiric comedy in which the author for an hour sets up an obviously ridiculous fable.

Erasmus did not suggest, however, that even romances should be wholly prohibited in the education of the young prince, any more than he (or the other English humanists) held that ancient or more recent history should go unstudied because in fact frightful tyrannies have existed. In this light, after attacking careless romance reading, he put forward positively a list of antityrannical writers whom a prince should come to know and respect first. "Since his destiny is to rule, he must learn the art of ruling" (*Regno destinatus est, hic regnandi docet artem*) (*EO*, IV, 587E). His basic list of literature against tyranny included the Scriptures, Stoics such as Plutarch, Cicero, and Seneca, Aristotle's *Politics*, and various historians. As Erasmus' reasoning goes, only *after* thus forming clear, right-minded, and objective concepts of what tyranny truly is, should the young prince study its history more broadly. For then he will not readily be duped by the tyrant's "great" names and false prestige. Instead he will see them truly, like Seneca, as raging mad robbers (*furiosi latrones*) (*EO*, IV, 587B). It would, moreover, Erasmus thought, be extreme madness (*extremae dementiae*) for Charles to imitate Alexander and Julius Caesar in all things simply because in a few respects they were undoubtedly superior to such Old Testament kings as David or Solomon. Such, restored to its rightful context, is Erasmus' attack upon the medieval romances. His intentions and critical method are fairly typical of those developed by More and Vives as well.

Erasmus was consistent when writing what now appears as a farewell to England—his letter (September 9, 1517) to Henry VIII, which I take to be a similar criticism of romances and in a similar context. He congratulated Henry as one "far from agreeing with persons who think that princes of the highest rank ought of all things, to keep clear of serious or philosophic study [i.e., statecraft], and that, if books are taken in hand at all, nothing should be read but amusing stories, scarcely good enough for women, or mere incitements to folly and vice" (*EN*, III, 45-6). Erasmus, who had a famous sense of humor, did not object to the King's amusing himself. His point was simply that the prince who reads nothing but such idle tales gains thereby no skill for his great duty of ruling justly. Similarly, he attacked the romantic glamorizing of tyrants and would-be world conquerors in ostensibly truthful and nonfictional, but actually lying and deceptive, history or biography, such as Quintus Curtius' account of Alexander the Great. He viewed Alexander (November 4, 1517), not (in late-medieval fashion) as a romantic hero, but as on the whole a frightful example of a "world-robber," "drunk with ambition," and a "disaster to humanity" like Homer's Achilles. What good was it to "this solid globe," asked Erasmus, to be thrown into slaughterous confusion "to please one young madman" (*EN*, III, 129-30)?

Although all the above points were touched on earlier, the principled continuity of the criticism is most readily apparent when it is seen as a progressively unified whole. The English humanists worked, not in isolation, but in warmly friendly association, each adding to the total structure of ideas on man and society. This quick résumé, moreover, brings Vives' attack on medieval romance and tyranny, in his

Christian Woman of December, 1523, into focus as the climax of this total effort.

Vives composed his *Education of a Christian Woman* at the request of Queen Catherine and it became (like his *De ratione studii* of October, 1523) part of the plan of education for the Princess Mary.[4] At the age of seven the Princess—hardly a "common reader"—was, as a result of treaties for war and peace, affianced to the Emperor Charles V. Theoretically, at least, she was therefore to be the future Empress of Europe's most powerful sovereign. As Colet, More, and Erasmus had done earlier, Vives confronted this practical situation and sought to devise the most effective possible ways by which his humanist ideals could be brought into the closest harmony with the original Christian ethics. The *Christian Woman* has so many crossties to Erasmus' *Christian Prince* that the two are virtually companion pieces, rounding out each other.

First, Vives attacked the reading of medieval romance on the ground that it would be a corrupting influence upon the princess. He found that there were currently popular many books, essentially pagan in spirit, written in the vernacular, which "have none other matter but of war and love"—books designed for "idle men and women to read." [5] For Christians, at least, he found the mischief of such literature to be like the quick flare of fire when "straw and dry wood" are heaped upon it. (His fire image is not trifling, coming, as it does, from a day when out-of-hand conflagrations were a perpetual terror of city and country alike.) But are not romances harmless enough because they are "written . . . for idle folk"? His reply was, that if idleness is a vice in itself, it is doubly foolish to add "firebrands" to it "wherewith the fire may catch a man altogether."

It is almost true that Vives rather sharply satirized Arthurian romance as "full of lies." More exactly, he ridiculed romances as full of childish, incredible, and absurd fictions about the nature of man, of human physiology and psychology, and of war. Like More (and, one might add, Rabelais, Shakespeare, and Cervantes), Vives found the medieval romances' typical representation of heroic combat to be hilariously funny, that is, if one was supposed to take such narratives seriously, and to "press the siege, weep with the heroine, and shudder at the monsters." If one presumes the Princess Mary at seven to have possssed fairly normal intelligence, even she might have seen the humor as Vives presented the picture:

And when they [romances] tell ought, what delight can be in those things, that be so plain and foolish lies? One killeth xx himself alone, another xxx; another wounded with 100 wounds and left dead riseth up again, and on the next day made whole and strong, overcometh ii giants, and then goeth away loaden with gold, and silver, and precious stones, more than a galley would carry away. What madness is it of folks, to have pleasure in these books [*VCW*, sig. D3ʳ]?

in fact, Vives' bright mockery of such romance elements is of the same breed as More's, which produced his satire upon the seriously heroic romance figure which the French poet Brixius drew of the luckless naval captain, Hervé, after a 1512 sea fight.[6]

In the *Christian Woman* Vives did not stop with satire upon romance's absurd physical heroics. Perhaps more serious in their corrupting effects upon the inexperienced woman, because more subtle in the establishment of vicious patterns of thought and feeling which in chivalric custom were presented as glorious or honorable, he found to be the highly fashionable war games (so dear to Henry VIII!) and tournaments of the day, in which men acted out seriously the colorful rituals of chivalric make-believe. (Probably these spectacles were never more elaborately staged than at the Field of the Cloth of Gold, near Calais in mid-June of 1520. There, while the sovereigns and the nobility vied in friendly tournaments and in professions of perpetual amity, behind the scenes were conducted the Machiavellian schemes aimed at renewing English invasions of France—since Henry VIII was so enamored of the chivalric glory won by Henry V at Agincourt a century earlier.)

Was it wise, Vives asked, for a young gentlewoman (the Princess Mary) to learn to delight in the "plays and joustings of armed men"? Many such women, true, by socially approved custom "behold marvelous busily" such war games and "give sentence and judgement of them: and . . . the men . . . set more by their judgements than the men's."

Evidently to Vives, as to More's Utopians, false pleasure is objectively knowable as a corrupting power through observation of its social effects. The worst of such pleasures are those by which sane men and women gradually habituate themselves to enjoy cruelty. From Vives' viewpoint, such pleasures are unquestionably debauching to character. Indeed he thought sexual chastity itself endangered for the woman who thus learns to love masculine cruelty and violence. "It cannot lightly be a chaste maid, that is occupied with thinking on armour, and tourney, and men's valiance. . . . A woman that useth [accustoms herself to] those feats, drinketh poison in her heart. . . ." Considering that the ethical rightness of war for Christian men is by no means undoubted, how can such corrupting joys be morally healthy for a woman? "When I cannot tell, whether it is meet for a Christian man to handle armour, how should it be lawful for a woman to look upon them, yea though she handle them not, yet to be conversant with them with heart and mind, which is worse?" Since such pleasure is in effect a "deadly sickness," he thought it none of his business to describe it in detail, lest it either "hurt . . . with the smell . . . or defile . . . with the infection" (*VCW*, sigs. Di^v-D2^r).

Quite clearly the views on romance of More and his circle represent a conscious and radical change in critical temper which their kind of humanism brought into England. Consider, in contrast, the ideas—all well-worn clichés—held by Caxton as recently as 1485 when he printed the *Morte Darthur*. To him that wondrous romance stood as a version of history, not as the purely poetic fiction which a twentieth-century reader, with a different esthetic, may find harmlessly amusing. Caxton saw in Malory's pages—and nostalgically hoped that the young and old knights of England would both see and imitate—a splendid mirror of the "noble acts, feats of arms, of chivalry, prowess, hardiness, humanity, love, courtesy, and very [true] gentleness with many wonderful histories and adventures." [7]

Vives, on the other hand, had read many romances "but . . . never found in them one step either of goodness or wit." In his opinion, indeed, the romances appealed especially to those who knew nothing of Cicero, Seneca, St. Jerome, or the Scriptures (*VCW*, sig. D3^r)—i.e., the writers (adding St. Jerome, praised by these humanists for holding to Christ's original antiwar teachings) who appear on Erasmus' list of authors who show tyranny in a true light. In a word, the humanist new critics sought to develop and apply a unified Christian humanist esthetic to *both* history and romance.

Here is a brief résumé of the intentions and methods underlying the London Reformers' attack on the world of medieval romance. More and his friends were indeed engaged in a war between and for, as well as against, ideas, one of the earliest and most important for human welfare of such struggles in the English Renaissance. Above all they were against tyranny in all its forms. In the romance world they found the glorification of passion and unreason, carried over into the glamorization of tyrants, of conquerors, and of a militarism which in hard fact resulted in unmeasurable suffering to the commonwealth. With satire as their chief weapon, they attacked this complex of ideas. At the same time they undertook a sustained and diversified effort to make clear to their day's most powerful rulers a Christian humanist concept of a just king, and to persuade them (or at least the most promising, Henry VIII) to accept the practical wisdom and necessity for just rule. To these humanists, the end proposed for such a just kingship should be the rational and peaceful reform (in England, at least) of a medieval society which was evidently fast disintegrating and sinking into chronic war and international anarchy.

In the romances they found, typically, a thinly disguised pagan social order which glorified injustice, violence, and war, and they sought to expose it as both unchristian and absurd. To them the romances glamorized, and the vogue of romances helped to perpetuate, inhuman and antisocial ideals of the superman-hero, together with equally false and dangerous notions of honor, of glory, and of the greatness, not to say the dignity, of man. They attacked these false ideals and sought to replace them with more rational and Christian views, as essential to the achievement of any good life for their age. The English humanists agreed in setting a high value on Christian marriage. Therefore they satirized the romances for their generally attractive treatment of blind and adulterous passion. In general the romance world represents woman as a sort of mindless sex symbol or lure. In contrast, More and Vives set about educating daughters no less well than sons.[8] (One might perhaps say that, in this new humanist ideal of the woman who is both feminine and witty— in no way the intellectual inferior of the men in her circle—there first appeared an English prototype for the Shakespearean comic heroine, that dazzling figure of a new and unmedieval kind of romance.) But above all, the humanists' great aim was to oppose tyranny and to help create just rule. To do so, they had to make clear to their age what tyrants and tyranny really were, beneath their many traditional disguises. Hence the sustained attack on open manslaughter and bold bawdry.[9]

The height of the humanist achievement in the golden age from 1509 to 1520 was the triumphant vision of the "genius of this island," perhaps best of all expressed in More's representation of the Utopian common-wealth. As realistic men (but not revolutionaries), Colet, More, Erasmus, and Vives all knew full well that the practical achievement of a good life, through peaceful progress and social reform, would require the full pow-ers of the ablest of executives. And with the achievement of Wolsey's and Henry's 1518 Treaty of Universal Peace, the humanists might well re-joice in England's great fortune, at a critical moment in Renaissance his-tory, in owning not one but two Christian princes of the highest ability. With these princes' exultant plunge into the French war in 1522, how-ever, the humanist hopes were first imperiled, then crushed, as a tremen-dous storm of violence began to rise in the heart of European civilization. As if the princes' insane pursuit of chivalric glory were not enough, at the same time the Lutheran agitations were beginning to overflow Germany, while from the Middle East, virtually unopposed, the Turks were mov-ing to invade the vital center of Christendom. Of all this the English humanists were realistically aware as 1524 began.

In 1523, after his arrival in England in May, Vives had done much more than round out climactically the humanist attack on medieval ro-mance and certain forms of history writing as incentives to tyranny. At the request of Queen Catherine, he had prepared a *Plan of Study (De ratione studii)*, dedicated from Oxford on October 7 and including a pro-gram for the education of the seven-year-old Princess Mary, then affi-anced to the Emperor Charles V but destined to be Queen of England briefly. At the request of the imperial ambassador to England Vives set forward in his *De consultatione* his ideas on conciliation between princes as a highly practical method of adjusting their differences in the light of their common self-interests, as well as on grounds of Christian ethics. The humanists felt certain that modern rulers, if they would so choose, could benefit from ancient statecraft, especially from work produced in times of conflict and crisis resembling the early sixteenth century, e.g., Athens with its Peloponnesian wars, or the Roman experience with tyranny and mercenary war. Like Erasmus, Vives therefore translated Isocrates, and on December 15, 1523, in appreciation of his appointment to Oxford, he inscribed to Wolsey two translations, the *Areopagitica oratio* and *Ad Nicocles,* the one setting forth a just monarch's duty to his subjects, the other dealing with first steps needed for a reform of morals (in the Athens of *ca.* 355 B.C.). To Wolsey, Vives expressed his sense that England was fortunate to have so able a man as Chancellor.[1] This was not mere flattery: no one, I think, has ever questioned Wolsey's extraordinary abilities as an executive.

The Christian princes, however, wished to continue their aristocratic amusement of war. From Oxford, on January 25, 1524, Vives declared to a friend the hope that Pope Clement VII might effect some change for the better, yet he considered the Pope himself to be the head and author of the "tragedies" impending over Christendom. Already to him the actions of Henry VIII seemed wonderfully unpredictable—"the heart of the King is in the hands of God" (*LC,* 90.62-68). Erasmus had predicted widespread destruction of the cultural revival if wars were not arrested; in January his friends recalled his work as prophetic, while at the same time they were inclined to regard the tempests in Church and state as too vast for any but divine powers to quiet (*LC,* 85.211-31). Henry VIII was eager enough to resume the war with France, but English power appeared to be exhausted. Bitterly Wolsey wrote that the King "cannot bear the whole burden alone," and rumors spread of Wolsey's desire for a face-saving peace.[2] In March Wolsey's agents in Rome wrote that the season for continuing the war was at hand, yet "matters are too raw to speak of peace," and a commission was even appointed to seek at least a French truce.[3] That Vives was not unrealistic in his estimate of the Pope's rule in perpetuating conflict is fairly clear. Clement VII "is so called upon for peace," wrote Clerk to Wolsey, "and is so expected to promote it, that he cannot openly show himself against France for a season. . . . There is as much craft and policy in him as in any man." [4]

By way of comment upon the folly and shiftiness of all such "holy war" diplomacy, as it were, Erasmus in March, 1524, added to his *Col-*

loquies one newly composed since the previous August, *The Old Men's Dialogue*. In this piece the satire was concentrated upon the absurd figure of Pamperius ("Try-all-things"). After beginning life as an honest merchant, he first ruined himself with gambling, then became a monk, and last of all turned mercenary soldier in a "holy war . . . as indeed they gave out at that time. . . . Pope Julius the Second made war upon the French." But Pamperius found nothing of Christianity in the war and now, after some forty years of largely wasted life, he was desperately looking for religion again. Nowhere had he found it more difficult, not to say impossible, to live a good life than in the army (*ECF*, pp. 228-41). The tone of the dialogue is rather grim and bitter, suitable to the new age of iron and seemingly perpetual war. Quite absent now is the infectious but earlier Erasmian optimism, as in the *Praise of Folly*, or even the more cautious hope sounded at the end of the *Utopia*. But, to be sure, in that happier time the humanists could still believe it at least possible that in their own age the forces of reason and humanity might well triumph over those of decay and aggressive destruction.

In an explosive atmosphere the humanists worked forward. April brought a vain hope that the Turks would not advance farther into Hungary (*LC*, 97.8-12). Erasmus, sharpest of critics of princely war folly, may have thought of coming again to England. "Your presence . . ." Vives wrote in June, "will be very acceptable to the King, the Cardinal, and all the nobility." But war had changed England, and Vives warned that appearances were deceptive: "you must prepare measures beforehand, or you will meet with frowns where you ought to have smiles; but no doubt More has written to you on all this . . ." (*EE*, 1455; *LP*, IV, 419).

Savage reality underlying conventional symbols of noble respectability was a theme in Vives' little companion or guide to emblems (*Satellitium siue symbola*), composed at the Queen's request and dedicated to the Princess Mary on July 1, 1524 (de Vocht, pp. 9-12). One remembers Erasmus' adage, *Scarabeus*. Vives thought that "Their Ferocities" was the term most aptly descriptive of princes who used, as was customary, figures of wild beasts in their heraldic emblems. This custom he found to be one of "stolid arrogance," unworthy not only of Christians but of pagans, for a just king's emblem should be rather a symbol of humanity and kindness than beastly savagery. As things stood, however, the brutal insignia were exactly appropriate:

It will be understood about whom I am speaking, nor is it necessary for me to name them more explicitly. Their ferocities take upon them the insignia of lions, bears, panthers, wolves, snakes, dragons, hounds, eagles, vultures, swords, fires, and things of that kind; as if it were beautiful, magnificent and truly worthy in a king to be of a mind which imitates what is savage, greedy, cruel, bloodthirsty. How will a man show his excellence more in assuming an ensign? Will it be by choosing such as allures and invites him away from humanity, gentleness, mildness, and sweetness, or by choosing an ensign which deters him from greatness, majesty, dignity and excellence? [5]

Perhaps not long after he went to the Low Countries in April, 1524, Vives had printed at Antwerp his little *Introduction to Wisdom*.[6] What astonishes one is its essential simplicity and clarity of vision and, after that, its gracious, kindly tone. (Controversy, like finance, seems to have its Gresham's Law; and by the mid-1520's, as the Lutheran debates grew almost daily more rawly violent on both sides, such an approach and such a tone become increasingly hard to find.) Vives aimed to make no egotistical display of abstruse learning, no intellectually aristocratic amusement. His spirit is like that of Erasmus' *Christian Knight* (1504), of which in 1518 Erasmus said that he desired to present in plain language a brief, simple, and clear guide on essential Christian principles for the "unlearned and rude multitude" (*ECK*, A4ᵛ). "Unlearned" should not be read with a misleading connotation. After all Vives wrote in Latin for the commonly educated literate man of the Renaissance, who was no more a scholar than that Shakespeare whom the learned Ben Jonson disparaged for having "little Latin and less Greek." All such terms are relative. There is, indeed, in the *Introduction to Wisdom* nothing that a bright boy or girl (like the Princess Mary) should fail to understand.

The basic question which, in essence, he raises, might be put as this: from what sources and by what means do true and false happiness in this life come to be? He is content to consider three essential comparisons: between true and false (or corrupt) honor, true and false beauty or strength, true and false human love. Everywhere Vives shows realistically his awareness, characteristic of the English humanist critics, of the ways by which, in everyday practice, evil customs learned in youth come to tyrannize over men until, too late, they discover the terrible cost of basing action upon self-ruinous values, a process of which war is the supreme example.

First, then, Vives compared true and corrupt honor (*VIW*, B8ᵛ-Ciᵛ).

True honor he found to be based on virtue, i.e., virtue which enhances both individual and mutual happiness. But he observed how many, as their world went, had risen to place or power

. . . of causes sometime foolish, sometime very naughty [evil]. Oft times he cometh up a pace, that can play well at tennis, oft times he waxeth honorable that leaves honesty, spending his patrimony upon junkets, minstrels and scoffers. But war—that is to say, robbery without punishment—is a great advancer of men to honor, such is the madness of foolish people.

Speaking of true and corrupt beauty or strength, Vives, like More in his picture of Utopia, suggests that happiness is best based on what is naturally necessary, with both past and current experience of the ruins brought on by pride kept in mind (*VIW*, C6ʳ-C8ᵛ). "The nature of man is such, and so ordained, that it needeth very few things." Thus apparel may be held to the "necessary," and food as well: "Nature teacheth us things necessary, which be but few, and soon prepared: foolishness hath invented things superfluous, which are without number and hard to come by." False pride blinds men to the fact that youthful beauty and strength "vanish away," but many men, desiring these things, are led to progressively ruinous vices: "What will you now say, when those things which so many men do highly desire, be occasions of great vices, as of insolent arrogance, of luskishness [lustiness], of fickleness, of envy, of privy hatred, of strife, of debate, of battle, murder and manslaughter?"

In the third place, Vives agrees wholly with More's and Erasmus' view of human nature and the power of love. Virtually everything in uncorrupted Nature as well as the true (original) Christian teaching shows that man was made for and is capable of peace and harmony with his own species. But, as contemporary war clearly indicates, many men have become quite accustomed to the subbeastliness of war, essentially a crime against both Nature and God:

The highest point wherein a man passeth the fierceness of all wild beasts is battle, a thing more agreeing to beasts unreasonable, than to man. . . . How much doth Nature herself abhor from war, which brought forth man into this world, naked without armor, shaping him to meekness and lovely society of life? God also abhorreth the same, which [wills] and commandeth mutual love between man and man. One of us may not war with another, nor hurt one the other, without grievous offense [*VIW*, H2ᵛ-8ʳ].

Vives closed the *Introduction to Wisdom* by urging again the practicality of men settling their differences by conciliation, compromise, and mutual agreement rather than resorting to violence.

As 1524 moved on, the humanists kept alive the hope that conciliation might yet arrest the age's drift toward chaos. In early July, Vives wrote to John, Bishop of Lincoln, to reason that continued war "is against the wishes of all concerned in it," i.e., as I understand him, that at a delicate impasse a voice of reason for peace might be effective, if that voice were of a man in power fired with a vision of peaceful, not chivalric, glory. As in *Utopia* More's imagination was stirred by the New World discoveries, so with Vives. "The Spaniards say that in the islands of the New World, when war breaks out, he is considered to be the most deserving of distinction who desires peace, and he the least who refuses it" (*LP*, IV, 481). It would seem that, in thus writing to the King's Confessor, Vives hoped indirectly to reach the ear of the King himself and, as the Pope had futilely sought to do, to suggest a sufficiently triumphant peacemaking role to inspire the "Defender of the Faith."

Underneath the hope for conciliation to which the humanists stubbornly clung, however, can be seen working a tone of increasing despair. In More this seems apparent in most cautious and guarded communications which were certain not to reach either the King or Wolsey. On August 10, 1524, he wrote to his friend Francis Cranevelt, a Louvain humanist and a counselor to the Emperor Charles, that in England war and public affairs had now become almost synonymous, while for want of "leisure" (Henry's and Wolsey's) domestic problems were forgotten in the universal calamity: "But the minds of all are so fully occupied with public affairs now that war begins everywhere to rage so fiercely, that no one has leisure to attend to domestic matters. If hitherto a man has had family troubles, they are now quite forgotten in the general calamity" (*MC*, 135.23-28). Grimly he cut off with, "But of this, enough."

Yet More himself, as a delightful companion, had perhaps never stood higher in Henry's curious favor. It was perhaps about this time, in 1524, after More bought his place at Chelsea, that, all unlooked for, the King (as Roper tells) "suddenly came home" to More's house, to "be merry with him." After dinner Henry walked in the garden with his arm affectionately about More's neck, an incident which aroused Roper's, but not More's, wonder and delight. " 'Howbeit, son Roper,' he said, 'I may tell thee I have no cause to be proud thereof, for if my head [could] win him a castle in France (for then was there wars between us) it should not fail to go.' " [7] What innocent anecdote could better suggest the feeling of precariousness under tyranny? "The heart of the king," Vives

240

wrote with similar irony in January of that year, "is in the hands of God." The royal "ferocities" remarked by Vives remained largely behind the mask of merriment, and humanist hopes for peace rested in Henry and Wolsey, if anywhere.

As the unrests of war added to the rising Lutheran tumults in the last two months of 1524, some arrest of humanism became unmistakably clear simply in the book markets. On November 13 Vives wrote to Erasmus that he had been made a "champion" (against Luther) whether he liked it or not: the King had read a few pages of Erasmus' *De libero arbitrio*, liked what he read on free will, and wished "also for a conversation with Erasmus" (in England), which More could arrange, for he was "very popular with the King and is much with him." Unhappily, however, Vives also wrote that "The Lutheran controversy has put a stop to the production of ancient books in Germany." [8] (Great older English humanist figures were passing; in October died Linacre, the physician, friend of all in More's circle.) However books went in Germany, Vives had printed in November, probably in England, and we know at the urging of his friends, the essay on *War and the Lutherans* which in 1522 he had directed to the Pope.[9] With ironic memories of his own experience of slim English patronage, Erasmus replied to Vives in late December, finding it pleasant that Vives was in "such favor with the King and Queen . . . but that will not keep soul and body together." Froben, he added, was not inclined to print Vives' works, "as nothing sells but [books] on the Lutheran controversy." In fact not one copy of Vives' edition of the *De Civitas Dei* had been bought that year at the great Frankfort book market (*EE*, 1531; *LP*, IV, 941)! In the rising social tumult, voices of conciliation found fewer and fewer who could or would hear.

Amidst the deepening pessimism widely felt by the humanists late in 1524, Vives advanced the realistic idea that perhaps the most practical measure toward peace would be to use wisely the point at which (as then appeared when Charles V seemed to be losing ground to Francis I) opposed war powers were nearly in an equilibrium. While the plague raged in Oxford, he went down to London, and from there on December 2 he expressed the hope that, before human nature was burdened unendurably, such a fair peace between equal combatants might be made. Although he was not sanguine about the prospects for *any* peace, he foresaw the precariousness of one-sided treaties (*LC*, 128.15-31). If Vives' letters at this time fairly indicate the tenor of English humanism, late in 1524 and early the next year the humanists alternately hoped for and despaired of a peace honorable and profitable to all Christian nations. His continental friends frequently mention his hopes for such a settlement.[10] Shrewd Louvain observers, however, suspected all English good faith or even sense (*"Britannu[s] caudam trahit"*) in the treaty with Charles, and believed that the English and the French might together try to compose a most unjust peace.[11] From Oxford in late January, 1525, Vives advanced to a friend the idea that sheer self-interest as well as Christian ethics seemed to necessitate an end to these mad wars. How could they more profitably be terminated than through a Christian concord? In all reason, more than a nominal and transient peace would now be practical between national groups of nearly equal power.[12] Meanwhile general humanist opinion held Wolsey more than Henry VIII responsible for the continuation of the war in France in 1524-25 (*LC*, 191.7-8).

Reasonable as such a peace of mutual self-interest might seem to the English humanists and their friends, Henry and Wolsey had quite different ideas. They were still bent on heaping up imperial and martial glory. In 1524, by sending (despite their treaty) no English army into France, they had caused some initial reverses to Charles. And now arose a fateful new motive in diplomacy, the first signs of the waning of Henry's affection for Catherine of Aragon, the aunt of Charles V, and the first suggestions of an annulment or divorce. The alteration in Henry's affections coincided with signs of France's getting the upper hand in the war with the Emperor. Although Wolsey dared not risk a complete breach with Spain, he now seized—or manufactured—an ingenious opportunity to turn English policy toward France.[13] The Spanish ambassador in England, a *"fortissimus patronus"* of Erasmus and Vives, was Louis de Praet. (It was at de Praet's suggestion that, in the autumn of 1524 at Oxford, Vives composed his essay *De consultatione*, on conciliation based on mutual self-interest as a practical means for adjustment of princes' disputes.) On Wolsey's orders, in the best (or most insane) cloak-and-dagger style, the ambassador's messenger, "riding after midnight to Bryneford" on February 11, was arrested and his diplomatic pouch broken open. His letters were then brought to Thomas More, who passed them on to Wolsey. Wolsey in turn virtually imprisoned de Praet in his own house on the pretext that he had written false reports.[14]

The Machiavellian madness of Wolsey's action was not instantly apparent. On March 7 Vives could again write from Oxford expressing to friends hope for a just and equal peace (*LC*, 144.14-22). Swiftly then came one of the many catastrophes which mark the last act of the English humanist struggle for peace. On March 9 the news reached England of the battle of Pavia. There, on his twenty-fifth birthday (February 24, 1525), in utter desperation the Emperor Charles V rallied his forces, almost annihilated the French army, and took Francis I himself prisoner (Pollard, pp. 138-40). By his accumulated follies capped with the midnight arrest of the Emperor's ambassador, Wolsey had nearly provoked war between England and the most powerful prince in Europe, even if Charles chose to overlook the occasion while seeking for " 'some good means . . . to punish the Cardinal' " (*LC*, 150 pref. b).

Boldly, at this time when More's critical voice was virtually silenced, Vives spoke for all the humanists. (Those who wonder at More's comparative silence may consider what he wrote *circa* 1522 on the fate meted out to Buckingham's wife and children after his execution in 1521. As Bacon might say, More had "given hostages to fortune." Vives' bride had remained in the Low Countries.) [15] From Oxford, on March 12, Vives sent directly to Henry VIII a memoir, *De Francisco Galliae rege a Caesare capto*. (It is ironic to observe that by capturing Francis, Charles V had in effect accomplished one of the major objectives in the Utopian art of war—capture alive, if possible, of the enemy leader whose mad folly caused the war in the first place.) Vives exhorted Henry and Charles to make a moderate and magnanimous use of their victory—not to devastate the "most flourishing realm in Christendom" nor "to pluck out one of the eyes of all Europe." He wrote frankly that it was not the fault of the common people that Francis made war against the will of his council, and the humanist openly deplored the fact that a king's folly could so plunge his people into misery. He urged that if both victorious princes would "send ambassadors to comfort the people, and assure them they will allow of no violence, both Princes will be gladly received." [16]

What is most distinctly the English Christian humanist note in this letter to Henry is the assertion of the implicit rights of the common people as, on humanitarian and just grounds, superior to the legalistic rights of princes. Vives is as toughly realistic, in his understanding of the savage facts of contemporary war, with its mercenary soldiers, as was Erasmus when, in June of 1514, he advised (without knowing it) the papal nuncio to England that what was essential was an immediate truce, not prolonged negotiations during which, at the very smell of peace (*odorem pacis*) such soldiery was quite eager to commit worse deeds than in open war itself. Evidently Vives' concern was not so much for the personal welfare of Francis I, who drove his nation to war in pursuit of chivalrous glory, as it was for the welfare of the common people, lest after Pavia both Henry and Charles should tacitly or overtly permit, or take no steps whatever to hinder, general pillage and massacre in France—i.e., in part of Christendom.

It seems ironic that, on March 15, 1525, only three days after his appeal to Henry VIII, Vives reported to Wolsey on his work toward humanist reshaping of the curriculum at Oxford (*LP*, IV, 1187). Evidently Vives felt that the Cardinal was concerned about these advances of the new learning. To Vives, indeed, wrote de Vocht (pp. 17-18), "is ascribed in large measure the changes in the studies at Oxford, where ... the useless abstractions of a degenerate scholasticism were abandoned for more beneficial knowledge and pursuits, grammar, rhetoric and poetry being again put in honour and the degrees in those sciences revived." Since in 1524 More was appointed High Steward of Oxford, and in July, 1525, of Cambridge, he was in a stronger position than ever before to aid in such humanist reforms (Chambers, pp. 214-15). These great friends, I take it, were essentially in agreement with the founders of Corpus Christi at Oxford—" 'that we should have care for the increase of learning, and for such as who by their learning shall do good in the church and commonwealth.' " It appears that, like Fox and Oldham, they were intent on realizing designs for the best practicable form of a new society, not continuing "houses and livelihoods" simply "for a company of bussing monks, whose end and fall we ourselves may live to see."

The battle of Pavia, and its consequences for the English Renaissance, could not have been foreseen by Henry or Wolsey. "It was thought surely," wrote Hall (pp. 692-93), "that the King of England would have had peace with the French King, if this chance had not happened. . . ." But to both the King and the Cardinal, Pavia seemed to present an incredibly fortunate opportunity to realize—by (in Vives' phrase) "plucking out one of the eyes of all Europe"—Henry's wildest dreams of chivalric glory. Neither was minded to accept humanist advice to comfort the French common people and to prevent victorious troops from committing outrages. Only thirteen days before the battle of Pavia, Wolsey had ordered the strong-arm arrest of the Emperor's ambassador in England.

Nevertheless, his first thought after it was to enlist Charles V's aid to gratify Henry's insatiate ambition to complete the ruin of France "by deposing the Valois dynasty and restoring to Henry VIII the provinces conquered by Edward III and Henry V"; and he even hoped for the future to exclude "all French-born kings of France." [17] Roper (pp. 19-21) relates that Wolsey wished More to go to Spain (after the death of the ambassador, Wingfield) to help in these war projects, but that More evaded this mission on grounds of health. Spain was sufficiently unhealthy, but it is a fair surmise that More wished to avoid giving active aid to increased English military folly: the aim of this embassy was to stir Charles to "make the joint invasion [of France] which 'Providence had postponed' in 1524." [18] Charles' frigid reception of the English ambassadors, however, made it clear that Henry would be forced to invade France alone if he wished more war in 1525, and on March 26 the Emperor wrote that he left to the English the responsibility for any war they chose to wage.[19]

Five days before these English ambassadors departed, Wolsey set about raising money and patriotic enthusiasm for a renewed French war. Thomas More had been named one tax collector for the war subsidy grudgingly granted by Parliament in 1523, a levy not yet fully paid in. Now what Wolsey termed an "Amicable and Loving Grant" was to be demanded of the nation. It was probably "the most violent financial exaction in English history." On Wolsey's secret instructions, without sanction from Parliament or custom, the commissioners were ordered to collect capital levies and taxes amounting to over one sixth on all laity, over one third on all clergy (Pollard, pp. 140-42). The King's orders to Wolsey were to stress to the people his intent to go into France personally to accomplish its complete conquest, the priceless opportunity for which " 'by the purveyance of God, and in manner, the consent of the World' was offered to him." [20]

Collection from the English people of the monstrous war subsidy now demanded of them was an experience less happy than this ecstatic royal contemplation of the imperial plum which God had purveyed and the world (i.e., as he then thought, Charles V and the Pope) had consented to offer, ripe for the plucking. All during the month of April, when Wolsey's collectors were, as he commanded, "practicing" on the people, Vives was staying with Thomas More in London, "in the most intimate familiarity." Vives, moreover, was about to begin his treatise *On Aid to* the Poor (*De subventione pauperum*) whose composition occupied him from June to December, 1525 (de Vocht, pp. 19-20). No man of the age had surpassed hitherto More's own penetrating analysis of chronic poverty and resulting social violence (Book I of *Utopia*), shown as the man-made outcome of economic and princely injustice and infatuation with chivalric war, based, as far as the monarch was concerned, upon the conviction (or delusion) that the king can do no wrong. Neither More nor Vives, perhaps, could have had a better vantage point from which to observe the workings of this newest example of a maturing tyranny in England.

When More wrote *Utopia*, in the brief decade of early humanism's golden age, the examples he cited of contemporary misrule were mostly readily recognizable as continental, particularly French—and with some justice, for Tudor history would have offered no such acute examples of persistent royal folly, to use the mildest possible term for it. In the Utopian Dialogue of Counsel, Hythlodaye (More's alter ego) asked how the king of France would welcome advice "that all this busy preparance to war, whereby so many nations for his sake should be brought into a troublesome hurley-burley, when all his coffers were emptied, his treasures wasted and his people destroyed, should at the length be in vain and to none effect"—and that the King should content himself with seeking to rule his own kingdom wisely, "seeing that which he hath already is even enough for him, yea and more than he can well turn him to?" The More of 1515-16 could only answer candidly that such advice would be received in France, "So God help me, not very thankfully" (*MUL*, p. 87).

Wolsey could and did appoint "discreet persons to declare to the people the great overthrow of the French king" and order bonfires lit in celebration (April 1) (*LP*, IV, 1235, 1261). Four days later, Archbishop Warham, once Erasmus' best patron, reported grimly from Kent in Norfolk, for "Wolsey's secret ear," on the temper of the English people, confronted with these latest war demands. Men spoke "cursedly . . . reckoning themselves, their children, and wives as desperates, and not greatly caring what they do or what become of them," declaring that "they shall never have rest of [war] payments as long as some [i.e., Wolsey] liveth." "Too much English coin is already exported to Flanders" (i.e., in wars to date), and "it would be the greatest means of enriching France to have all money spent there . . . ; and if the King win

France, he will be obliged to spend his time and revenues there." "They are sorry, rather than otherwise, at the captivity of Francis I," and "all the sums already spent on the invasion of France have not gained a foot more land in it than his father had, 'which lacked no riches or wisdom to win the kingdom of France if he had thought it expedient.' " (It is highly ironic, at this time when More was almost silenced as a critic, to find the common people thus speaking in the very tone and almost the words of Hythlodaye in *Utopia*.) Warham, no less loyal than More, did his best under an impossible situation. But he did tell Wolsey that he could wish "that this practicing with the people for so great sums might have been spared 'til the Cuckoo time—and the hot weather (at which time mad brains be wont to be most busy) had been overpassed. . . ." [21]

In the Discourse of Utopia, the French common people are generally represented as supine victims of monarchic outrage. On the other hand, Sir John Fortescue, More's most probable ancestor as a social critic, almost exulted over robbery's prevalence in England as proof that there the people had a spirit higher than the French or Scots. Now in 1525, as Wolsey's demands for a kind of official robbery were pressed, the resistance in some shires exploded into rebellion, something apparently unlooked for by either Wolsey or Henry, for whom, as Pollard (p. 148) said, "insurrection was then a novel experience." On May 8 the King was warned that in Suffolk there was "insurrection" which might well spread (*LP*, IV, 1319), and which indeed armed force was needed to put down three days later (*LP*, IV, 1324). Cambridge scholars combined with the town, reportedly twenty thousand strong, to resist, " 'while other countries are looking out for a stir that they may do the same.' " [22]

By May, moreover, reports had certainly reached England of the peasants' revolt raging in Germany.[23] The reports appalled humanist circles, and, whatever their causes, they were enough to trouble even English authorities. Indeed by late May, not without some substance, word was circulated "throughout France . . . that the English had mutinied and had too much to do at home to think of invading their neighbour." [24]

English humanist criticism in the 1509-20 period usually spoke of the common people as saner than their rulers, and the humanists desired far-reaching but peaceful social reform in church and state. By 1523, however, as popular disturbances rose in Germany, Erasmus spoke of the populace as that "fickle, many-headed beast." These humanists were not revolutionaries, and realistically they regarded social anarchy as perhaps the worst of human conditions. All this was caught up by an addition which Erasmus made to his adage, *Scarabeus*. This theme prompted earlier one of his fiercest denunciations of the archetypal corrupt monarch who "makes the whole people tremble, the senate subservient, the nobility obedient, the judges obsequious, the theologians silent" as he beats down just laws, customs, and the rights of humanity. With hard realism he added in 1525: "But princes must be endured, lest tyranny give way to anarchy, a still greater evil. This has been demonstrated by the experience of many states; and lately the insurrection of the German peasants has taught us that the cruelty of kings is better than the universal confusion of anarchy." [25] As for More, in his *Utopia*, while men might quietly advocate any conceivable social change, violent sedition was sternly punishable by banishment or bondage (*MUL*, p. 272). On May 14, Pope Clement VII wrote that he refused to help Wolsey to renew the war on France. He spoke of Germany, distracted and ruined by the peasants' revolt and by schism, and told Wolsey's agent "that this continuance of war is to the utter subversion of Christ's faith . . . and . . . that if the wars continued, we should see a new world shortly" (*LP*, IV, 1336).

When mutterings of English mutiny reached Henry, he once again showed the face of a just, humane ruler. Wolsey's demands were much softened, and even ringleaders of insurrections were to be pardoned. " 'Poverty,' said one of them in East Anglia, 'was their captain, for he and his cousin Necessity, had brought them to this doing.' " [26]

Another aspect of the chivalric glory Henry had already won in France showed itself when, in latter July, after Pavia, the President of Rouen came to sue for peace, saying (according to Hall [p. 704]): "if we have offended, you have punished, for you have burnt our towns, slain our people, destroyed our country, so that you have brought the low parties [common people] to a long misery without recovery. . . ."

Between the capture of Francis I at Pavia (February 24, 1525) and the Treaty of Madrid early in the next January, the English humanists, like the "low parties" or common people, remained, as it were, suspended in an unstable solution of mingled hopes and fears. On August 14 Erasmus wrote the dedicatory epistle to his book *On the Use and Abuse of the Human Tongue* (the *Lingua* [Basel, August, 1525]). Somberly he compared the abuses of language in recent times to the emergence of such violent, relatively new diseases as syphilis in its later forms, as though man were not already subject to calamities enough (*EE*, 1593.1-130). Digressing from his immediate subject, as he often did, he also put forward a brief sketch of an ideal state, in which the rights of the people, of ecclesiastical authority, and of the prince would all be in a healthy, moderate balance.

As for More, he and the Bishop of Ely were sent that summer to make a peace arrangement, since an impoverished and mutinous England was for the moment unwilling or unable to pay to help win more castles in France (*LC*, 156 pref. c.), despite Bishop Tunstall's urgent warnings from Toledo against the perils of a separate treaty which, made while Francis I was Charles V's captive, might well lead Spain and France to combine forces against England. Nevertheless, such a separate pact was concluded on August 30, with More as one signer.[27]

Months of tension and danger ensued, and during this time once again Vives appears as the boldest voice in England humanist social criticism. In March, soon after Pavia, he had written to urge that Henry VIII do all in his power to make a just and moderate use of this unexpected opportunity for a general peace settlement. Now on October 8 he wrote to the King a second critical letter on war and peace. As a born Spaniard, he praised his great patron for treating relative strangers like himself with the same courtesy as his own subjects. Then he again urged Henry to use his vast authority, as the world expected he would, to bring the peace thus begun to a successful completion. He suggested that no possible course of action could win more glory or more nobly befit the "Defender of the Faith." [28] Simple as this may appear, it won his dismissal from his Oxford Readership early the next year.

The English humanists, one would say in general, had a more accurate and realistic appreciation of the needs of their society than did the King and the Cardinal who repeatedly led England into idiotic attempts to revive the triumphs of medieval chivalry or to seize imperial footholds on the continent. This may be inferred in part from the celebration of Agincourt day (October 25) with the army. In April, Warham reported to Wolsey how desperately unwilling the common people were to give further aid toward French conquests. Crowds could readily enough be gathered, on the other hand, to delight in military glories out of the romantic past—to thrill to the magic of Henry V's valor:

For the victory that God gave to your valiant predecessor, King Henry the Fifth, with so little number of our countrymen against so great a multitude of the Frenchmen at the battle of Agincourt, your retinue at . . . Calais, and others there, once yearly, make a solemn triumph, going in procession, lauding God, shooting guns, with the noise and melody of trumpets and other instruments, to the great rejoicing of your subjects being aged, the comfort of them that be able men, the encouraging of young children.[29]

The spectacle of England and Europe, potentially rich and at peace, but in which man-made war and massive poverty were chronic, made a profound impression upon Vives, as upon More and Erasmus, and his insights were expressed in his *On Aid to the Poor* (*De subventione pauperum*). After visiting More in April, he had rejoined his family in Bruges and he worked on this little treatise off and on from June to December, 1525 (de Vocht, p. 20). Although dedicated January 6, 1526, to the Senators of Bruges, it is, I think, a direct outgrowth of the English humanist criticism of man and society. He had evidently begun to shape his ideas on the subject when he mentioned greed as one great motive for modern war (May 27) and, soon after, that he saw poverty itself as one of war's basic causes (i.e., as in the vicious circle of poverty-crime-war discussed in Book I of *Utopia*) (*LC*, 153.9-14, 157.10-24).

The agreement between Vives and his English humanist friends is evident throughout *On Aid to the Poor*. He accepts the view of More and Erasmus especially on the theory of human nature, of obligation owed by man to man, and the concept of human dignity (which underlies, for example, the idea of citizenship in Utopia). He agrees in seeing such a social evil as poverty as man-made.[30] One of its great causes he does find to be war,[31] another the oppressions of wealth which in the past have often angered the desperate multitude of poor to violent attacks upon the rich (*VRP*, p. 6). (One may perhaps hear an echo from England of the previous April, when Archbishop Warham found so many who "spoke cursedly . . . reckoning themselves, their children, and wives as desperates, and not greatly caring what they do or what become of them," declaring that "they shall never have rest of payments as long as some liveth." And the Senators of Bruges would surely have heard of the terrible events of the peasants' rebellion in Germany earlier that year.)

Thomas More has, with at least some seeming justice, been marked as an ineffective thinker because, after brilliantly exposing the corruption of contemporary Christian culture, he offered no idea how "it can be transformed into the Good Society" (Hexter, pp. 59, 98). Actually More suggested that the initial reforms which started Utopia on its 1760 years of gradual evolution—i.e., to the condition in which it was described to us —came from an original wise, benevolent, absolute monarch, Prince Utopus. Understandably, the poor, living in Bruges on January 6, 1526, might find even a modest fraction of such a period a little too long to wait.

Where Vives goes beyond More, therefore, is in his very practical proposals to the Senators of Bruges for immediate action. If work is essential to human dignity (wherein he agrees with More's Utopians), then Vives proposes that it is the duty of the Senate to provide, as a matter of human right, work for all the poor who are able-bodied, useful employment suitable to each man's age and health. In brief, public works when private may not be available. Vives has no quarrel with charity which (in the old sense) still applies to those unable to toil, but who do not thereby lose their rights as members of the human race. Vives also proposed that the Senators of Bruges, as representatives of the commonwealth or city, must recognize the same obligation toward any victim (cf. today's international refugees) of catastrophe: "But if they are from villages or towns afflicted with war, then the teachings of Paul must be borne in mind, that among those baptized in the blood of Christ, there is neither Greek nor Barbarian nor Gaul nor Flamand, but a new creature; and they must be treated even as if they were native born" (*VRP*, p. 14).

It is clear that while Vives thus worked out his practical ideas for the realization of at least a small part of the humanist good life, More had been drawn, as an expert diplomat, ever deeper into Henry's and Wolsey's Machiavellian schemes looking to imperial aggrandizement. He can scarcely now have been unaware of their true intent. When opposing Hythlodaye in Book I of *Utopia*, More himself said that a king's councilor must be practical, avoid perfectionist advice, and work "to handle the matter wittily and handsomely for the purpose, and that which you cannot turn to good, so to order it that it be not very bad" (*MUL*, p. 100). The passage has been noted as showing More's "open-eyed realism" (Hexter, p. 131). I have been unable to discover one clear instance when More, engaged on tortuous war-peace embassies, was in fact able to shape affairs toward that "honorable and profitable peace" which he profoundly craved as the prerequisite to any good life for England.

Erasmus' ideas on the condition of Europe during the explosively dangerous year after Pavia, and before its consequences for war or peace were quite apparent, are best revealed in three dialogues newly written for the *Colloquies* and in comments added for the first time to his essay "Against War" in the *Adages,* both for editions of February, 1526. In them his vision rises by degrees to present a broad view of social tragedy which, like that suggested in the heath scenes of *King Lear,* seems to have passed the bounds of sane comprehension or remedy.

The simplest of these is *The Funeral,*[32] which reflects the time of precarious interruption of war after Pavia. The dialogue's basic contrast is between the death of a truly Christian man and that of a typically corrupt Renaissance general, one George Balearicus. Marcolphus has heard that the general, now on his deathbed, is very rich "with ill-gotten gains, as it happens, from robberies, sacrileges, and extortions." "Of course," agrees Phaedrus with quiet force, "that's the custom for generals. . . . If I knew the man well, however, he grew rich by his wits rather than by violence." Phaedrus explains that General Balearicus had perfected his art of war in terms of "scientific" business management:

"He was clever at accounting. . . . He reported 30,000 troops to his commander when there were scarcely 7,000. Next, to many soldiers he paid nothing at all. . . . Then he waged war scientifically. He used to contract for monthly payments at the same time by villages and towns of both friend and foe: from the enemy, so fighting wouldn't break out; from friends, for allowing them to trade with the enemy" [*ETC*, pp. 99-100].

"I'm familiar with the common practice of military men," observes Marcolphus with grimly satiric realism.

Bright humor of the kind so often produced during the humanist golden age is hard to find in the violent 1520's, but in *The Funeral* Erasmus produced one fine example when he let his imagination play over the elaborately vulgar funerary art which is to be executed for this robber-general's bier and tomb. A symbol of Christian love, the pelican, will be worked in, plus boar's heads and a leopard indicative, with the profusion of gold, of his vocation of beastly rapacity:

On the top of the tomb was to be George's effigy carved in Parian marble, in full armor from head to foot. His helmet was to have his crest (a pelican's neck), and his left arm a shield bearing as insignia three boar's heads [see *Richard III*] of gold in a field of silver. Nor was his sword with the golden hilt to be missing from his side, nor his gold baldric decorated with jeweled studs, nor his gold spurs from his feet; for he was a gilded knight. At his feet he was to have a leopard. The borders of the tomb were to have an inscription worthy of such a man [*ETC*, p. 103].

In the dialogue *On Fish-Eating* Erasmus rallied his powers of constructive criticism and desperate hope. (In some respects this colloquy prefigures Swift's debate of the Big- and Little-Endians [i.e., two phases of Christian truth] in *Gulliver's Travels*.) The flow of thought seems to reflect currents of Christian humanist response to the war before Pavia, to the challenging opportunity for peace that Pavia created, and to realistic fears lest the outcome of peace negotiations be simply a prelude to an even wider tragedy for common humanity (*ECF*, pp. 366-78).

Ostensibly the principals speaking are a Butcher and a Fishmonger, but in the dialogue's heart they often speak like humanists who largely agree in their common concern for the welfare of war-imperiled Christendom. At first, arguing which is the better, they heap insanitarily comic abuse on each other, as though mankind might well starve before they agreed that both were necessary. From reflecting on how mankind has eaten since the Golden Age, they pause in their flow of billingsgate to muse on conditions in the New World, which the Butcher "lately saw . . . described in a large map," making him think "how much of barbarian and how little of Christianity was in it." His rival, too, had seen it, noting especially the "Southern Shore, and the Christian Island [America?]." "I saw 'em," says the Butcher, "and learned that there were great spoils brought out of them, but no Christianity carried into them" (*ECF*, pp. 366-75). (Evidently the New World stirred Erasmus' imagination, as it had More's and Vives', to compare cultures and barbarisms.) Laying aside their strife at the sobering thought of this immense, unchristianized world of opportunity, both pondered war-torn Europe.

There they found "the whole world in a flame" of "deadly contentions" over seeming trifles—"spiteful calumnies upon account of a garment differently tied," and so forth. Wistfully they hoped that Pope Clement would somehow be able to bring all Christians to "live in greater concord." Were the Christian nations able to settle their differences quietly, they thought that Christianity would extend itself to the "barbarous nations," which "would of their own accord offer us more than the utmost violence can extort from them." But how could such agreement be hoped for as long as some hellish spirit of Discord, like the goddess Ate in Homer, "engaged the two most mighty monarchs in the world in a bloody war?" (This much reflects conditions before Pavia.)

Then both puzzled over why a good peace had proved so difficult to achieve (i.e., after Pavia), considering that each monarch (Francis and Charles) "taken separately is an admirable prince." And what of the fate of common humanity, friend and foe, while the lawyers argue over terms? Is it fit, asks the Butcher:

"that because of the contentions and delays of lawyers, in relation to contracts, the whole world should be kept in pain? For as matters are now, there is no safety anywhere, and the worst of men [mercenary soldiers] take advantage of the opportunity, while there is neither peace nor war" [*ECF*, p. 375].

The concluding part of the war criticism in *On Fish-Eating* touched on the roles for peace still potentially open to Charles V and the Pope, and on widespread fears of a vindictive treaty as only a prelude to further war (*ECF*, pp. 375-78). This humanist Fishmonger told what he would do, were he Caesar. He would freely release Francis I, without any vengeful conditions or extortions, and in the future would compete with him, not to see "which shall govern the largest dominions, but who shall govern his own with the greatest justice . . . ," for, "The fame of this clemency will get me more true glory than if I had added all France to my dominion. And in you [Francis] a grateful mind will be more to your praise than if you had drove me quite out of Italy." [33]

What both speakers above all feared was an outrageous treaty which would destroy the opportunity to lance properly the sick condition in monarchy which caused the war in the first place: " 'For if this ulcer should happen to be skinned over, rather than thoroughly healed, by unequal terms, I am afraid that upon the first opportunity, the skin being broken, abundance of corrupt matter would issue out, and that with more dangerous consequences.' " Erasmus has his Fishmonger say what he would do, were he pope: " 'I would so demean myself that the whole world should see that there was a prince of the Church that aspired after nothing but the glory of Christ and the salvation of mankind. That would infallibly take away all invidiousness from the name of Pope, and gain him solid and lasting glory.' "

In the unfolding structure of Erasmus' ideas, we place here the three main additions which he made to the February, 1526, version of his *Against War*. The first and briefest of these was one pungent sentence, enlarging "They [those whose Christianity is infected with civil law] praise war as a noble thing, so it be just." The addition was simply: "They define as just what has been declared so by the prince, be he child or idiot" (*Iustum autem esse definiunt quod indictum sit a principe, quamlibet puero aut stulto*).[34]

A second addition (some nineteen lines) amplified and sharpened his original attack on Church authorities who have justified war by corrupting Christ's teaching, which was, as Colet said in 1496, that Christians may rightly use only the sword of the spirit, not military weapons. These orthodox doctors, Erasmus now added, propose a rabbinical distinction: according to trade regulations, one is permitted to take up the trade of soldier just as one is permitted to slaughter beasts. Men may make war, so it be "just"; and if declared "just" it matters not what the war, against whom, or under what prince. Sycophants of power in church and state have now so warped Christ's doctrine as to support the will of the prince, whatever it may be. "Where is he whose cause does not seem just to him?" If a man now preaches strongly against war, he is suspected of heresy; but those who interpret the Scriptures so as to give princes the pretexts to satisfy their desires are orthodox teachers of Christian piety. But a truly Christian teacher never approves war; he may perhaps permit it under certain circumstances, but against his will and in grief.[35] In a word, Erasmus declared that, as things were, the Church aided and abetted tyranny.

The attack upon tyranny is even more powerfully made in the longest and most interesting of these additions to *Against War*. Originally Erasmus had represented such ancient tyrant-imperialists as Xerxes and Alexander the Great as insane world robbers but still, in their war methods, more humane and honorable than their Renaissance apes. The amplified comparisons were even more bitterly unfavorable to the modern tyrants; yet at the same time they suggested a more humane art of war which the moderns might imitate—if they were not so utterly daft about "glory." The passage, too long to quote, may be summed up to suggest Erasmus' ideas on how wars should be fought, if conciliation fails:

Pagan history often shows how princes avoided war by admirable means, or overcame by good actions rather than force of arms. Some even chose to renounce power rather than risk war. But we—false Christians—never miss an occasion for war. Before taking up arms, the pagan princes exhausted diplomacy. The Romans, after all conciliations had failed, sent a chief religious leader, who took over final negotiations (preparatory to a declaration of war). He searched carefully for means to moderate the fury of the war itself. No one was allowed to begin fighting before the signal, which was given in such fashion that the ignorant soldier must understand it. And after this signal, all soldiers were bound by the military oath to pursue and attack only the enemy [i.e., were forbidden to attack noncombatants].

As the signal for combat gave permission to fight only to soldiers bound by the military oath, so likewise that for retreat took away all authority to kill. Cyrus praised a soldier who had overcome an enemy and had his sword raised (for the kill), but who sheathed it when he heard "retreat" (cease fire) sound. Thanks to these controls, no one believed that he was permitted to kill a man except when compelled by dire military necessity.

In our time, among Christians, they hold a man to be brave who— meeting in a wood an unarmed enemy who has gold and who does not want to fight but only to quit the war—has killed this man and afterward looted the body! Now they term "soldiers" those who, in hopes of a meager profit, hurry to war and take part, on either side, like gladiators, so that brother fights brother and holds this right because a prince authorized it (i.e., not necessarily even the prince of their own country). The battles over, these men return to their own people, tell their doings as though they were true soldiers, and are not punished (quite the contrary!) as thieves, assassins of their country, and deserters of their own prince.

We feel toward the executioner a horror although he butchers those condemned as guilty, even though he is paid to do it and so commanded by legal authority. But those who abandon parents, wives, and children, to hurry of their own free will to war, not to fulfill pledges but as desiring to take part in an unholy butchery, are more congratulated when they return than those who refused to take part in it. They (the mercenary soldiers) believe that from their crimes they reap a certain glory (*nobilitatis*). This would be an atrocity (*infamis*) if done stealthily without a uniform; but when it is part of military service, they acquit themselves and return, after having despoiled many innocents, into the number of honest citizens. Those soldiers who have behaved with the greatest cruelty are considered worthy to become commanders in the next war.

When you study ancient military discipline, you perceive that among Christians war is not war but brigandage (*latrocinium*). If you compare pagan and Christian monarchs, ours are the worse, for their only ambition is for "glory" (*gloriam*).[36]

Such were the criticisms added to the February, 1526, version of *Against*

War. They sharply reflect ideas matured since the edition of January, 1523.

The last of the three colloquies new in the February, 1526, printing was *The Childbearer*. Here Erasmus' tragic vision reached out to take in all Europe—a panorama of violence marked by chronic wars in France, the peasants' revolt in Germany, the menace of the looming Turkish invasion, in fact by the apparently imminent prospect of a civilization falling into bloody anarchy. In the dialogue a simple soul asks what else God has to do but to "preserve . . . what he has founded by creation?" The critic's voice replies:

Francis, King of France, is a sojourner in Spain [i.e., still captive after Pavia]. . . . Charles labours with might and main to enlarge the territories of his monarchy. And Ferdinand is mightily taken up with his affairs in Germany. And the Courtiers everywhere are almost famished with hunger after money. The very farmers raise dangerous commotions, nor are deterred from their attempts by so many slaughters of men, that have been made already. The people are setting up for an anarchy, and the Church goes to ruin with dangerous factions . . . and do you ask what else God has to do [*ECF*, pp. 319-20]?

CHAPTER FIFTEEN

THIS CRUEL TURK SHALL SWALLOW THEM ALL (1526-27)

After the battle of Pavia and before the nature of the Treaty of Madrid (January 14, 1526) was widely known, it seemed to the English humanist circle that, on the brink of widespread catastrophe, Europe had one more chance for peace. At the least, for England there was a priceless opportunity to cease its mad involvement with imperialist war ventures on the continent. In December of 1525, Wolsey had claimed that England now wanted "perpetual" peace with France, and of course he claimed to be its chief author.[1] Perhaps England's impoverishment through needless wars, and Francis I's capture by Charles, were, or might be used as, blessings in disguise. That some such desperate hope stirred Erasmus is evident in the *Colloquies* written during Francis' captivity. England had unquestionably, in these storms of war, been greatly ruffled, but its Renaissance world, though endangered, had not yet fallen in a wildness.

Unmistakably, nevertheless, currents, rip tides, and winds of social violence were converging from many directions. Never in the Renaissance had the need for great captainship in the state been more acute, and from the humanists' viewpoint the great kings had rarely if ever been more unaware of the extent and nature of the crisis. The Lutheran agitations were spreading fiercely, but complacency could remember that in its long history the Church had weathered many reform crises and divers schisms. In England, behind the royal scenes, some sort of marriage crisis might be emerging, but why should anyone relate this to Church-reform agitation or imagine that two such forces would exert a combined effect on English society? As far as I am aware, no English humanist or statesman foresaw the course these great events actually took.

But the catastrophes which the humanists most clearly saw, and thought they understood best, were those imminent in early 1526:

258

first, that with renewed national wars, Europe would fall "in a wildness," that is, into bloody anarchy; and, second, that for lack of any unified military resistance, the Christian nations would be devoured piecemeal by the relentlessly advancing Turkish armies. Already the Turks had moved deeply into Hungary, and, after the fall of Rhodes, their invasion of a helpless Italy was regarded as inevitable. To the humanists, the overwhelming danger to all Christendom was perfectly obvious, just as was the historical parallel of the danger to ancient Rome before its collapse beneath the pagan forces of its time. The Turkish danger towered above all others, for it meant survival of Christian culture or its engulfment in pagan tyranny. Vives in 1526, More in 1528, and Erasmus in 1530 were to express essentially similar ideas on it. Indeed, one of More's last writings, done while he was in the Tower, was his *Dialogue of Comfort against Tribulation* (1534), an imagined translation of a Latin essay by a Hungarian, on how Christians should behave under the expected Turkish tyranny. In 1526 and after, the English humanists no longer mentioned hope for a golden age of peaceful social reform and progress. Rather they desperately hoped that such massive and pending calamities might be averted before too late.

As the vengeful nature of the Madrid Treaty became rumored, even while Francis (until March 17, 1526) remained a prisoner of the Emperor,[2] pessimistic realism appeared among the humanists, both in England and in sympathetic circles at Louvain. On February 14, as Vives was about to return to England, he wrote to Erasmus that the peace seemed joyful insofar as there was at least a respite from war's shameful crimes, if only by way of intermission. Would that one dared hope for a Christian peace! But, torn apart by factions as the Christian world is, many seem to applaud catastrophe (*EE*, 1665.22-7; VI, 260n.). Three days later the humanist historian, Polydore Vergil, wrote to Erasmus from London (with his usual ironic understatement) that he doubted this peace would last many years (*EE*, 1666.7-9). Back in England by late February, Vives found what it now meant to be an outspoken critic against Henry's and Wolsey's current imperialist war ventures. In the previous October he had openly addressed to the King a memoir, following up one of March, 1525, in which he urged Henry to use his power for peace after Pavia. Since then, Wolsey's policy had secretly turned to oppose Charles V and to aid France. Hence

Vives' humanist criticism had made him an enemy, and during his three-months' visit to his family at Bruges, Wolsey had removed him from his Oxford Readership.[3] (Not only did Vives personally suffer; so did the renaissance of learning in England. As late as 1534 the University Council at Oxford somewhat wistfully desired such professors "from beyond the sea, as was Mr. Vives" [*LP*, VII, 308].)

In April of 1526 we find Wolsey inviting Erasmus himself to come again to England, perhaps to his Cardinal College, perhaps as successor to Vives at Corpus;[4] but news of such treatment as Vives' travels fast, and Erasmus (pleading inability to stand cold drafts) was too shrewd to enter such a trap situation. Other continental scholars, after checking with Erasmus, were equally wary (*EE*, 1765.22n.). More befriended Vives as best he might but could do little (de Vocht, pp. 20-22). Very grimly, More wrote to Cranevelt on February 22 that "Peace has been made between the monarchs, but God knows how long it will last." Hoping "perpetually," he did not despair. The princes are fully informed of war's evils and have seen enough of the thing itself not to need its repetition. He could not expect tranquillity (*securius*), however, unless somewhat softer conditions than those known so far were made the basis of concord.[5]

Indeed, Charles V's liberation of Francis on March 17 was simply the signal to Wolsey to intensify secret diplomacy aimed at renewed wars (now, madly, against the most powerful prince of Europe, the Emperor).[6] Soon that skillful diplomat, Thomas More, was engaged as one of Wolsey's tools in the tortuous intrigues designed to produce an anti-imperial alliance between Henry VIII and his recent enemy, France.[7] A shrewd humanist friend of Vives, analyzing the likelihood of further wars, observed that England, by attempting to play both sides in the conflict between Charles and Francis, had gained only the reputation for complete untrustworthiness: the British make magnificent promises to their allies but never keep them (*LC*, 182.21-23). While expressing his ceaseless hope for peace among the Christian princes and union against the invading Turks, Vives noted quietly (April 13) that in England he was "sailing against the stream" (*LC*, 185.22).

The defeat (or arrest) of the early English humanism more and more merged with the general tragedy of an age whose princes seemed insanely addicted to national wars. On April 25, as Erasmus declined Wolsey's invitation to return to England, while saying that he had been cheered by the Cardinal's loving letters (these are not extant), he now felt it wise to defend his *Colloquies* (presumably the edition of February, 1526) against anonymous charges that they contained matter "indecent, impious, or seditious." [8] The last two elements, as the tragic violence of the 1520's opened out, tended to become fused, especially as the Lutheran agitations rose in their intensity. Against the importation of Lutheran books into England, old Bishop Tunstall had begun a fresh campaign on October 12, 1524. On December 22, 1525, perhaps in hope of keeping out Tyndale's New Testament in English, More himself had begun more stringent proceedings against German merchants residing in London; and one result of all this was a second book burning by Wolsey at Paul's Cross in February, 1526 (*EE*, 1697. 23n.).

Five days after defending his *Colloquies* to Wolsey, Erasmus wrote in rather similar vein to John, Bishop of Lincoln, the King's Confessor. Some learned English friends, he said, "think highly" of them, but others "are of so vinegar a disposition as to dislike everything playful." The Bishop, he thought, would find in them "much . . . serviceable for the education of the young." But the situation confronted by the humanist social critics was squarely indicated when Erasmus said that in these times it was now impossible to write anything not open to slander, no matter how circumspect the author, and both sides are offended, for on both sides there are those who seem seized with insanity.[9] In fact, as Erasmus perceived, the times had now produced a climate of opinion fatal to humor, to tolerance, and perhaps to all rational social criticism. Writing the same day (April 30) to Polydore Vergil, Erasmus remarked grimly that he heard many rumors of peace but saw no festivals of thanksgiving: either the rumors of it were void or the peace was not quite worthy of applause.[10]

How unworthy of applause was this brief "perpetual peace" (accompanied by Henrician maneuvers for renewal of war, of which More must almost certainly now have known) is ironically implied in the role played by More himself on April 28. Then, before the King and the Cardinal, the President of Rouen paid a second visit seeking peace. He spoke, reported Hall, to show:

. . . how dreadful the wars had been between . . . England and France, what great loss . . . France had sustained . . . what power the King of England was of and what conquest he might have made in France, [Francis] being prisoner . . . & knowledged the King of England's right in the wars, and . . . thanked him . . . that he would consent to peace.

Of course the only reason Henry and Wolsey suspended further devastations in France was that the English people stubbornly refused to pay Wolsey's infamous "Amicable and Loving Grant." Thomas More, ironically, had the duty to reply, and he said "that it much rejoiced the King, that they first considered, how by his power he might have oppressed, and how by his pity he had relieved them" (Hall, p. 711). Once again Henry VIII enjoyed the delights of power and pity (even if fictitious), while (through his subtle irony) we may again perhaps see More's own stubbornly persistent hope, as four years earlier, for an "honorable and profitable peace."

After returning to Bruges in late May, 1526, Vives wrote to intimates on the deteriorating world situation with a candor apparently too dangerous for More in England. To de Fevyn he said frankly that while the blame for leading England on to war was Wolsey's, the real responsibility was Henry VIII's, for without the King's support the Cardinal could do nothing.[11] Although the massive Turkish invasion was moving forward in Hungary, the great Christian princes of the west seemed preoccupied with their own wars as usual. In Italy, by the end of April, hostilities had been renewed, although the failure of the English to supply money or the French effective aid served to restrict destruction.[12] On June 10 Vives said bitterly that neither God nor man could approve the open eastern (Turkish) threat to the peace of the entire Christian world—but see how unhindered the Turks bring down their troops (*LC*, 193.24-32)! As summer advanced, Louvain humanists were appalled to see how, as the Turks moved nearer in Hungary, they met with no serious opposition because of the engrossing quarrels and "unaccountable negligence" of the three leading princes of Europe (Charles V, Henry VIII, Francis I) (*LC*, 198.61). Marching on from Belgrade, the forces under Suleiman the Magnificent, at Mohács on August 29, 1526, scored a stunning triumph. Louis II was killed and his army annihilated, and consequently Budapest fell to the Turks.

Against this tragic spectacle of a world falling in a wildness, Vives, in October, 1526, while on leave from England, put his major social criticism into one volume (*De Europae dissidiis, & republica* [Bruges, December, 1526]) and added a new piece "On Europe Divided and the Turkish War" (*De Europae dissidiis et bello Turcico dialogus*).[13]

Dominating Vives' mind was the idea of culture versus anarchy, of Europe torn with dissensions and confronted with the Turkish menace. Swiftly the speakers in *On Europe Divided* agree that everywhere in Europe there is now dissension, strife, and war between the princes. The most baffling of questions is why, when the princes are all confronted with the Turkish invasion, in sheer self-interest and desire for survival they do not bury their feuds and jointly resist? It should be obvious that if the Turk succeeds in the seemingly imminent invasion of Italy (i.e., as well as of all Hungary), all Christendom may be overthrown. Savagely one speaker observed that the princes are possessed or insane with greed or sensuality (*odia, voluptates, cupidines prauae dementarunt nos*). All the speakers are concerned over the safety of Italy and Rome (*On Europe Divided*, Di^v-3^v).

But all realize that the popes themselves have greatly contributed to the state of prevailing violence. Julius II actively aided war, which his death did somewhat lessen. His successor, Leo, inherited an evil situation in which the kings of Spain, England, France, and Scotland were tangled in war. But fake peace treaties hardly produce the genuine article. (Says one speaker, sardonically: *"Ex discordia confoederatorum pax nascitur"* [*On Europe Divided*, $D5^v$].) They find that greed in high places has helped produce these wars ($C7^r$).

The speakers have heard that after crossing the Danube, the Turks will invade Europe from the east, and they hope against hope that the warring princes will bury their differences in time and come to the aid of Italy, i.e., the papacy. But Tiresias, who seems nearest to Vives' own voice in the dialogue, thinks the afflictions overhanging Europe now so great that only God's wisdom may be able to alleviate them (*Deus ipse sapientia & beneficio suo opem ac subsidium afferat rebus tam afflictis*). Some ask, says Minos, whether between Christians war is "war" (i.e., "just") or merely outrage (*latrocinium*). To him the correct answer is that it is not war but insanity (*Insanias mihi narrasti, non bella*). All feel sure that the danger of Turkish invasion is real and formidable (*On Europe Divided*, $D5^v$-6^v).

Tiresias speculates as to what has become of "humanity" in Europe, so that from being truly men, so many have degenerated into savage wolves, not rightly to be called Christians. True Christians would rather conquer the Turks by Christianity itself than fight among themselves. From the familiar humanist point that in peace all good arts flourish,

263

while war produces corruption, arson, and poverty, the speakers move to the question: what evil dementia prompts men to go long distances to fight with each other? The princes, says Basilius bitterly, seek "glory" in war (*Bello queritur gloria*), such as that gained by Alexander the Great, Julius Caesar, or Pompey; to which Tiresias says bluntly that such men were thieves (*latrones*) (*On Europe Divided*, E2ʳ-5ʳ).

Vives' most characteristic constructive proposal is the obvious one that reason would suggest. Confronted by a common peril, the princes should make a common peace, then appoint one commander over all the armies of Christendom to oppose the Turks. Confronted by a united Christian commonwealth (*republica*), the Turks would lose much of their interest in attacking the west. The only question is, whether between Christians there remains a basis for such an agreement, without which victory and Europe's preservation is impossible (. . . *si maneat inter Christianos firma & solida concordiae, sine qua invicti & salui esse non possunt*) (*On Europe Divided*, F3ʳ-4ʳ).

If one understands Vives, he recognized that under existing conditions such an alliance, based on a commonwealth-of-Europe idea, could not be produced by the power of the papacy. It could be produced only by statesmanlike collaboration between the princes, joined for the interest that even they might have in practical survival. Thus perhaps the Christian nations might escape a Turkish tyranny. Was he born four centuries too soon?

Vives wrote *On Europe Divided* while on leave from England but with it much in mind. In a letter of December 31, 1526, he commented caustically on the insensate apathy of the English rulers. Although most other Christian princes were making at least token preparation to resist the Turks after their latest and ominous victories, the English send neither men nor money—indeed they seem to think it all an old wives' tale (*Britannus sensim subducit se a fabula*) (*LC*, 217.18-31).

The rough treatment received from Wolsey made Vives in no hurry to return to England. From Bruges on January 27, 1527, he wrote somberly that while peace is best, he expected renewed wars (*LC*, 223.13-16). In mid-March he offered Erasmus (always looking out for safe messengers) delivery of anything he wished sent to England, and by about mid-April he had returned. While Wolsey was ill-disposed toward the humanist, Henry and the Queen were outwardly as cordial as before. Indeed, the King valued Vives highly enough to ask his collaboration on a little book (*Opusculum*) to answer Luther's letter of September 1, 1525; and by July Vives' work on it was done, ready for Henry's annotations.[14] Called back to the continent by family illness, he was only permitted to go in June on condition that he return by October 1, to teach Latin to the Princess Mary that next winter.[15] One might almost be lulled into thinking life to be peaceful at the English court.

If Vives hoped for conversation with More, he was disappointed; for between April 30 and August 17, Wolsey, with More among his train of negotiators, was in France. This embassy's objectives were characteristic of Henry and Wolsey. Spurning peace, they wanted more and more glorious war. Wolsey aimed to ratify the French treaty of the previous April, to scheme for war against Charles V, and, fatefully, if possible to get himself designated Vicar-General for the Pope.[16] The whole sinister summer's work was wound up with grandly solemn services in the cathedral at Amiens and with plenty of the pompous peace celebrations which could delight Wolsey's heart.

Back in Bruges by June 13, Vives wrote keenly of the situation in England and indeed all Europe, as the princely tyrants schemed only for more wars. Lack of gold does not deter them when they have the needed wrath, power, and compulsive desire for war (*LC*, 237.11-23)! Just a month later he wrote to Henry VIII, praised him for always finding time for study however busy with Europe's affairs, sent over a copy of Erasmus' *Adagia* not to be found in London, and discreetly expressed hope that Wolsey's current mission to France would "settle the affairs of Christendom" by achieving "full success in the shape of universal peace." [17] This should be read, I think, as a profoundly ironic humanist prayer for a cause doubly tragic and almost doubly lost. For one secret intent in Wolsey's latest venture was to advance Henry VIII's divorce from Catherine (or the annulment of the marriage); and as a confidant of the Queen, Vives very probably knew as much.[18]

Wolsey's vain efforts to secure appointment as the Pope's Vicar-General, during the summer of 1527, had a peculiar urgency and, indeed, fateful effects upon the English Renaissance. For while the Cardinal was taking some first steps secretly in Henry's endeavor to secure a divorce from the Emperor's aunt, the Pope himself had become Charles' prisoner. Probably this was not exactly intentional. Even while the Turk invaded Hungary and seemed about to descend on Italy, the armies of Francis I and Charles V there had continued merrily to destroy each other's wealth and to gain glory but no enduring settlement. A fantastic disaster capped these wars and had direct repercussions upon England. After months of preliminary terror in the city, on May 6, 1527, the Emperor's Christian troops (including his Lutheran mercenaries)—hungry, unpaid, and mutinous—began the terrible sack of Rome itself.[19] And as a result, just when for Henry and Wolsey it was vital that the Pope should be most independent of the Emperor, he fell into Charles' hands. Hence Wolsey's need to become the Pope's Vicar-General during his captivity, so he might manage Henry's "great matter."

The peculiar importance of Rome as a symbol in English humanist eyes, and the horror at these events, did not simply depend on its being the heart center of Christendom. For the fall of ancient Rome to the Gothic barbarians was also the final collapse of antique culture before a storm of subbeastly human passions loosed in war, coming as the climax of long abuse of power by decadent Roman rulers. Thus to the humanists these two falls of Rome stood in tragic parallel. In Vives' comments on St. Augustine's *City of God,* dedicated to Henry VIII, and used as his passport to England, he had called to mind "what manner of people the Goths were, and how they took Rome" (*CDV* [1610], A2^r-A5^v). The brutalities of Alaric and his mere barbarians some eleven centuries earlier, as described by Vives, paled before those of the modern Christians whose crimes were inflicted upon fellow Christians.

Words like "terrible" and "horror" tend to lose concrete meaning. To comprehend this event one needs the evidence, as apparent to English eyes. One account is credited to Wolsey, the other is More's own—and they will be given without elisions. (Wolsey, like Henry himself, one remembers, rejoiced at the inhumanities inflicted by English soldiers in France and Scotland in 1522-23.) Now Wolsey, outraged and ready for war with the Emperor, is reported by Hall (p. 744):

". . . and farther in the Church, they violated virgins, and stupid matrons, and despoiled the holy relics of the city of Rome. And like as the King in hunting time hath slain 300 deer, and the garbage and paunches be cast round about, in every quarter of the park, so (said the Cardinal) every street lay full of the privy members and genitures of the Cardinals and holy prelates: the whole history were too abominable to tell."

Thomas More's narrative in *A Dialogue Concernynge Heresyes* (1528) is longer and more appalling, but there is no reason to doubt that he told the truth as he knew it. Of course he cast heavy blame upon the mercenary Lutheran *Landsknechte* in Charles V's forces:

Of this sect ["those uplandish Lutherans"] was the great part of those ungracious people also, which late entered into Rome with the Duke of Bourbon, not only robbing and spoiling the city, as well their own friends as the contrary part, but like very beasts did also violate the wives in the sight of their husbands, slew the children in the sight of the fathers. And to extort the discovering of more money, when men had brought out all that ever they had to save them further business, then the wretched tyrants and cruel tormentors, as though all that stood for nothing, ceased not to put them eftsoons to intolerable torments. And old ancient honorable men, those fierce heretics letted not to hang up by the privy members, and from many they pulled them off & cast them in the street. And some brought out naked with his hands bound behind him, and a cord tied fast unto his privy members. Then would they set before him in his way other of those tyrants with their moorishpikes, the points toward the breasts of these poor naked men. And then one or two of those wretches would stand behind those moorishpikes and draw the poor souls by the members toward them. Now then was all their cruel sport and laughter, either to see the silly naked men in shrinking from the pikes to tear off their members, or for pain of that pulling, to run their naked bodies in deep upon the pikes. Too piteous and abominable were it, to rehearse the villainous pains and torments that they devised on the silly women, to whom after that they had beastly abused them, wives in the sight of their husbands, and the maidens in the sight of their fathers, they were reckoned for piteous, that did no more but cut their throats.

For good measure More added also a description of the soldiers' technique for extracting more gold from penniless folk whose misfortune it was to be parents. Bound to a "broach" (spit), children were roasted in the parents' sight. When no more money was forthcoming, "Then would they let the child roast to death." Finally, however, a fearful plague came and left hardly a third of these men of arms alive (*MEW*, pp. 258-9). Thus did More record this great triumph of the Renaissance art of war.[20]

Vives—I think ironically—had praised Henry VIII in mid-July, 1527, for always finding time for serious study, i.e., of statecraft and just rule. As the humanist doubtless knew, the King at that time was otherwise occupied. The *Letters and Papers* for the period are filled with love letters to Anne Boleyn (*LP*, IV, 3218-21) as well as with divorce matters. Writing candidly to friends, Vives showed that he was not much deceived. When referring to English affairs on August 14, he spoke of no golden age of peaceful progress and reform. For him, everything in that reeling world (*orbis motibus*) was unstable; he was sticking to a slippery path rather than standing on it, and he had no hope whatever for even the next day.[21] Writing two days later, plainly with reference to the sack of Rome itself, his pessimism for Europe's future suggested that only God could pacify the fearful storms of violence apparently rising from every source (*LC*, 246.2-37).

Even amidst such tempests, which Henry and Wolsey had done so much to stir and so little to calm, the King could find time and pleasure for the outward gestures appropriate to a Christian humanist prince. Thus, ironically, it appears that on September 18, 1527, he once again grandly invited Erasmus to return to England and make it his scholarly home. Five years before, Erasmus and More had supported Vives in his move to England, hoping thereby to strengthen the revival of learning, but that was before the renewed Henrician folly of war with France, not to speak of the lunatic schemes for war with Charles V. Nor was Erasmus unaware of the harsh treatment Vives had received at the hands of Wolsey while the King stood idly by. When Erasmus left England in 1517 it was in large part because war preparations had for the worse altered "the genius of the island" and made it "partly resemble a prison." Even in English humanism's golden age after 1509, royal patronage had in cold fact been erratic if not downright niggardly; yet now in 1527, as ever, Henry promised Erasmus rich rewards! Almost the only touch of realism in the King's letter seems to be a reference to the state of Christendom as more and more troubled by the Lutherans. Apparently he meant to offer the age's greatest scholar a dignified old age in England, with full liberty to work in freedom from cares. One can only wonder at such euphoria and such a fantastic vision of a world which the humanists all too clearly saw was falling in a wildness. Erasmus wisely hesitated to enter again the den of such a dubious lion, of one who might soon become his patron the Emperor's open enemy. He delayed, explored the situation, and finally refused to return to the England which Henry VIII and Wolsey had so far transformed from what Erasmus envisioned in 1509, when he hoped to find there "an age that was really golden and isles that were happy." [22]

As our Renaissance play of men and ideas draws toward its close in the early 1530's, More, Vives, and Erasmus increasingly have parts as choral commentators upon a tragic process as wide as their world. In some ways they resemble Shakespeare's Enobarbus in *Antony and Cleopatra*, one who but too well understands that enormous catastrophe is expanding around him but also that he cannot avert it or even save himself from the general wreck. When a world order collapses, there is no place to hide. One cannot escape mankind in volcanic eruption. Trapped in the machinery of English court life, More and Vives were caught up in its calamities. From his personal magic mountain in Basel, Erasmus sent out occasional discourses upon tyranny, war, and the débacle of the age. Lucky to escape from England, even in dire poverty, Vives spoke from the Low Countries.

Essential clarity of vision, when what it reveals is a wilderness of glorious lost opportunities, is a tragic burden. In their last years, all three men stand as ever more lonely figures. To them was denied the warm, crazy joy of the returned trooper in Erasmus' colloquy, *The Soldier and the Carthusian*—the pleasure of being mad with so many of mankind, or, more crucially, with so many great and noble princes in state and church alike.

Although the latest humanist criticisms on man and society are profoundly pessimistic—and with intensely realistic warrant—More and his friends stubbornly refused to "hang up philosophy," in Romeo's wild phrase. They refused, heroically, to embrace misanthropic cynicism and despair for mankind, present and to come. Evidently the long-sustained struggle to induce Henry VIII and Wolsey to use their talents and powers to bring about peaceful reform and progress toward a good life for their England had failed. The most obvious prospect was that their world of Christendom, fallen in a wildness of anarchy and tyranny of man-made creation, would soon go under the oncoming Turkish tyranny. Yet the grand struggle for freedom and just rule never ends. Even with such desolate prospects confronting their world order, even after the fall and sack of Rome by the modern barbarians, one humanist voice or another is heard now and then, attempting to set down the best practicable wisdom for the use of men coming after, just in case Christian civilization should somehow survive its own best efforts to commit suicide.

Vives' fifth stay in England (October, 1527, to April, 1528) furnishes a grim epitome of humanist criticism in its last phase. Dismissed by Wolsey from his place in Oxford, he tutored the Princess Mary. But the agonizing question dominating these months was the one the humanists called *"de Jove et Junone"*—the great matter of the King's divorce. With dignity and considerable courage the Spaniard Vives stood up for the despised and lonely Queen, giving her such aid as he might by word and writing. Meanwhile, rumors of impending war were continual (*EE*, 1932.64-65; de Vocht, p. 28). Few men living under the emerging English tyranny would perhaps have dared do as much. Hated by Wolsey and his party, he was in deep danger. His actions and writings were spied upon. For some thirty-eight days (*ca.* February 25—April 4, 1528) he was indeed under house arrest, from which he was released on condition that he never again put foot in Court.[1]

While Vives was thus incarcerated, a startling glimpse of More's desperately slight ability to influence the King or Wolsey toward a just and profitable peace appeared, when on March 16 More wrote to Wolsey the word on Henry's ideas for war against the Emperor Charles V. "The King sent for More and expressed his unwillingness to have war with the Low Countries [i.e., the Emperor]," although he had readied armed companies. The day before, reported More, Henry said that "no one was more loath than he to have war, but as the Emperor had shown himself intractable [in the divorce matter, and so forth], he was resolved to defend his cause. . . ." Then "When I [More] was about to tell him my mind, he said 'this gear could not be done so suddenly,' but that he and you [Wolsey] must first speak together" (*LP*, IV, 4080).

Released from domestic jail, Vives, on the secret advice of the Queen, who evidently feared for his safety, quickly left England. Even now he was not in complete disfavor; a few days later he was informed that his royal pension would be continued. In Bruges by May 15, Vives remarked at first only that Henry was "too little removed, as it were, from folly or love madness" (*stultitia, aut amore vesano*) (*LC*, 260.14-21). A week later, however, as he viewed the European scene broadly on the eve of Henry's divorce, he found it so miserable that peace seemed possible only through divine aid, for men (i.e., princes) let no occasion for war pass without combat (*LC*, 261.16-23). If Vives suggested, as seems likely, that Erasmus use his voice to the King for good purposes, Erasmus replied sharply (September 2) that he was keeping out of the Jove-and-Juno affair (*EE*, 2040.41-49).

Detached from the fierce storm center in England, Erasmus, finding his social criticism almost deliberately misinterpreted in those mad times, clarified in August what he had said upon war and its justice. Rightly he repeated that he had not condemned *all* wars, for some are "necessary," but he found that "wherever there is war, there is crime on one side or the other, if not both" (*EE*, 2032.452-53). Thus he still opposed the idea dear to the Christian princes of the age, that in war both sides could presume the cause to be justly Christian, an idea preposterous on its face but conventionally accepted.

By the time of Vives' sixth and last visit to England, in November, 1528, the King's divorce had come to dominate English minds almost so far as to exclude, if temporarily, thought on further aristocratic amusements of war. In October the hapless Queen was allowed to send to Flanders for two advocates and for "Lodovico Vives, whom she herself nominates, and who was formerly in this kingdom, and read lectures at Oxford" (*LP*, IV, 4875). Without hesitation he took the Queen's side. He seems, indeed, to have well understood that her trial had a foregone conclusion and was only intended to induce the nation to believe that she had enjoyed a fair chance to make her defense. His advice (first resented, later taken) was, as de Vocht said (p. 35), not to play a "part in that sinister comedy . . . to desist from every defence, and to rely merely on her right and guiltlessness. . . ." While under house arrest—such is tyranny—Vives was forced not only to reveal the Queen's private confidences but to write for Wolsey a memoir giving his opinion on the validity of the marriage. Vives staunchly supported the Queen, at his real peril. He was a remarkable man. Under the Queen's first displeasure at his advice, he left England forever. Although his pension was now cut off, leaving him in bitter poverty, he continued for years not only to praise the Queen but to speak kindly of Henry himself! [2]

More, Erasmus, and Vives no longer hoped seriously for a golden age of peaceful progress. Sir Thomas More's famous three wishes of *ca.* 1528 represent the best but desperate hopes of English Christian humanism toward the end of a rather frightful decade. No longer was there enough optimism surviving to produce even modestly revised visions of a utopia, of a potentially practicable good life lived according to reason. Realistically confronted with the existence of anarchy and misrule spreading throughout Europe, and of tyranny as the visible alternative, More, like Vives, could now at best hope that within the battered framework of existing states, laws, and princes, enough basis for agreement could be found to prevent even greater catastrophes. Otherwise, as he put it to Roper with tragic understatement, one might expect "a disturbance to a great part of Christendom." All More wanted was peace between the Christian princes, now at "mortal wars," peaceful reform of the Church, and a "good conclusion" of Henry VIII's marriage problem. Given these, "Now would to God . . . I were put in a sack, and here presently cast into the Thames" (Roper, pp. 24-25).

What the English humanists regarded as a good conclusion of the marriage problem, itself a grave danger to the peace of England, is perhaps indicated by the memoir which Wolsey obliged Vives to write while under arrest and which he sent to the King three years later, since through the Cardinal it might not have reached him. He sent it as one "moved to write by his duty to the King, love to England, where he was so kindly received, and anxiety for the quiet of Christendom." The gist of his advice was that "if he [the king] were to marry another wife, there is no certainty that he would have a son, or that a son would live. A new marriage would leave the succession doubtful, and afford grounds for civil war." [3] If in the spring of 1528 Wolsey ever showed the Vives' critique of the marriage to the King, which is doubtful, it went to one, as the humanist himself had said, "too little removed . . . from folly or love-madness." What hero of chivalric romance would be turned back by such sane considerations as Vives put forward?

Doubtless implied in More's first great wish—that the Christian princes, at "mortal wars," should come to peace together—is one of the English humanists' greatest concerns in late 1528. This of course was

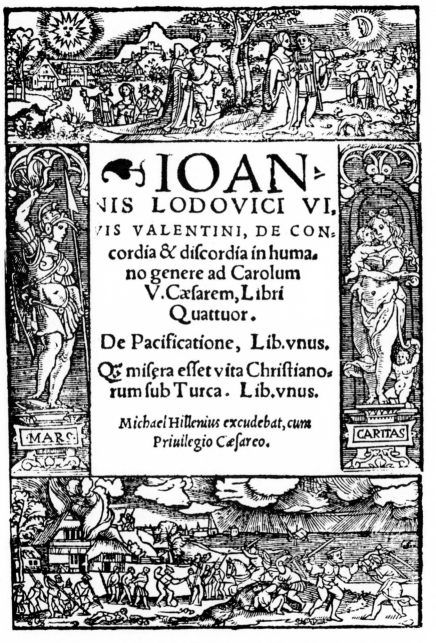

IOAN·
NIS LODOVICI VI,
VIS VALENTINI, DE CON,
cordia & diſcordia in huma,
no genere ad Carolum
V. Cæſarem, Libri
Quattuor.

De Pacificatione, Lib.vnus.

Qʒ miſera eſſet vita Chriſtiano,
rum ſub Turca. Lib.vnus.

Michael Hillenius excudebat, cum
Priuilegio Cæſareo.

MARS

CARITAS

Title page of Vives' *Of Concord and Discord in Mankind*

for the preservation of Christendom against the rising surge of Turkish military invasion. By an imaginary analogy, it may be possible to suggest to twentieth-century readers a comparable situation. One need but conceive, in mid-century, that while the relatively free western powers in Europe brawled among themselves, in response to relentless military pressures, the Iron Curtain advanced year by year toward the Atlantic shores and toward England.

In the 1520's, while Charles V, Henry VIII, and Francis I were ever more insanely preoccupied with the wars of ambition and revenge, the Turkish menace rose continually. Slowly a vast pincers strategy of land and sea operations took form. On August 29, 1521, Belgrade fell. On December 28 of the next year the legendarily impregnable island fortress of Rhodes, blocking one invasion route, capitulated. The Pope termed this loss that of the "key of Christendom." Thereafter the invasion of a helpless Italy seemed merely a matter of time and the Turk's convenience. Promptly the papal legate to England pointed out to Henry and Wolsey that Rhodes and Belgrade were the "outworks of Christendom" and that, after their collapse, all Hungary or, alternately, Sicily and Italy lay open to conquest. Indeed he said that "the rest of Christendom and England itself are in the greatest danger." He spoke but common sense.

The English humanists, and others, strove to arouse the three great princes of Europe to form a common cause against this common peril, to which otherwise they would become, one by one, vulnerable. What were the results of these rational pleas for Christian union, if only in self-interest? Henry VIII (seeking chivalric glory plus castles in France) and Wolsey (seeking the papacy) rather renewed war on France and Scotland (1522-23). Indeed they desisted only when confronted by the impossibility of extorting more gold from the English people. Wolsey held that the "Turk" as far as he was concerned was the French king. As for Charles V and Francis I, they busily drove their armies to destroy each other's wealth until, in the battle of Pavia (February 24, 1525), Francis was unexpectedly taken prisoner and so remained until after the vengeful Treaty of Madrid (January 14, 1526). Did Henry and Wolsey, despite England's financial exhaustion, use the lull after Pavia (as the humanists urged) to seek a compromise peace between the Christian princes? Not at all: instead they did their utmost to insure renewal of the English invasion of France. Thus the Christian princes pursued chivalric glory and honor.

Meanwhile the Turkish military machine had not been idle. By August 29, 1526, it had annihilated the Christian armies at Mohács in Hungary. With the last major barrier to the invasion of Austria thus removed, the Turks on September 20, 1529, laid siege to Vienna. Between 1526 and 1530, Vives, More, and Erasmus in succession treated this real and present peril to the continued existence of "free" Europe (in the analogous twentieth-century phrase).

More's views on the Turkish-invasion crisis appeared best in his *Dialogue Concerning Tyndale* (1528). There they were bound up with an attack on what More understood Luther to have said, namely, that the Turkish invasion represented a visitation of divine wrath upon the sins of rulers and peoples alike and that as such it could not rightly be resisted by Church leaders.[4]

More attacked what he incorrectly took to be Luther's ideas—e.g., that to resist the divinely appointed instrument, the Turk, was sinful—not because they were dangerous to the existence of the German nation (or of England itself, for that matter), but because they were "dangerous to the peace, unity, and existence of all Christendom" (Chambers, p. 266). Clear light on More as a critic of war comes when we follow his reasoning. The Lutherans, said More, hold it wrong for Christians to resist the invading Turks, and defend this as observance of the "counsels of Christ," even though the Turks "invaded us and did us all the harm they possibl[y] could": "And in this opinion is Luther and his followers which . . . hold for a plain conclusion, that it is not lawful to any Christian man to fight against the Turk, or to make against him any resistance, though he come into Christendom with a great army and labour to destroy all." [5]

Then More examined the argument put forward in support of this view: namely, that the medieval Christian use of war against the Turks (the Crusades) was the *cause* of the decay of Christendom. For since such armed resistance began, Christendom has "always minished and decayed. So that at this day the Turk hath estraited us very near, and brought it [Christendom] within a right narrow compass, and narrower shall do, say they [Lutherans], as long as we go about to defend Christendom by the sword." Thus the only rightly Christian way to oppose

the Turkish invasion would be to accept the proffered tyranny or martyr-
dom.

More attacked this Lutheran argument from two points, one of hypocrisy, the other of elementary logic. First, while the Lutherans say it
is impious for Christians to war against the Turks, with what evident
alacrity they take arms against their fellow Christians! Obviously the
horrors of the sack of Rome, credited in part to the Lutheran *Landsknechte*, were in mind: "And where they may not fight against the
Turk, [they] arise up in great plumps [*sic*] to fight against their even
Christian [fellow Christians]." In other words, More satirized a hideous
discrepancy between Lutheran theory and practice. Accordingly he
judged it highly probable, if the "Turk happen to come in," that the
two-faced men would take the invaders' part "and that Christian people
be like to find none so cruel Turks as them." With deadly sarcasm he
said:

It is a gentle holiness to abstain for devotion from resisting the Turk, and in
the meanwhile to rise up in routs and fight against Christian men, and
destroy as that sect hath done, many a good religious house, spoiled, maimed,
and slain many a good virtuous man, robbed, polluted, and pulled down
many a goodly church of Christ.

Second, More ridiculed Luther's argument as childishly illogical—
a use of *post hoc ergo propter hoc* reasoning. And here, rare enough in
these passion-torn years after 1527, came a touch of More's old delightful humor. He mocked the idea that God's discontent with armed
Christian resistance to the invading infidels was proved because in fact
there had been "loss and minishment of Christendom since that guise
began." He brought the absurdity of such reasoning home to Englishmen
by recalling an inquiry held into the causes why Sandwich Haven, once
a good harbor, had silted up to become useless. One key witness was a
"good old father" whose intellect resembles that of a blundering Shakespearean constable, such as Dogberry in *Much Ado About Nothing*. This
gaffer was unshakably positive that the "cause" was building Tenterden
Steeple ("by the mass, cholde t'were a fair fish pole!"), for after its
erection, the haven "never throve since."

More's kind of English humanism appeared best of all in his positive
treatment of the causes of decay in the Christian world, of which he,
like Colet, Erasmus, and Vives, was acutely conscious. Luther, as
More understood it, harked back to St. Augustine and found the

cause of the Turkish invasion to be sin, hence the militant Turks stood for divine wrath. More did not absolutely deny this reasoning. He did, however, strongly tend to find the causes to lie in a historical process in which man-made, especially princely, follies and crimes against humanity had cumulatively produced the presently dangerous situation for Christendom. If the Lutherans "had any reason in their heads," they would blame the internal divisions and strife (i.e., nationalist conflicts) of Christian against Christian. When Christian princes in the past were solidly united, they were well able to prevent such calamities as the current invasion of Europe. In fact, to More, the most immediate cause why the "Turk doth prosper against Christendom" was the "ambition of Christian rulers, desiring each other's dominion." Since this war process began, with these princes "at war and deadly dissension among themselves, whereby each hath aspired to the enhancing of his own, they [the princes] have little forced [troubled] what became of the common corps of Christendom."

Characteristically, where Luther saw the invasions as God's punishment for the sins of the people *and* their rulers, More located the responsibility primarily in the rulers, not the people or "common corps." To More, then, God's purposes were evident in the Turkish attack but not in the same way as Luther saw them. So God, "for the revenging of their [the princes'] inordinate appetites," has allowed princes and peoples to suffer. As in Book I of *Utopia*, and generally in the humanist social criticism, the people are saner than their rulers. Thus while each prince of Europe labors "to eat up other," the Turks prosper; and if the princes' "blind affections [passions] look not thereto the sooner, [the Turk] shall not fail (which our Lord forbid) within short process to swallow them all" (*MDT*, p. 307). Thus in the *Dialogue Concerning Tyndale*, More once again mounted the humanist attack upon typical contemporary tyranny, including implicitly that of Henry VIII.

During the explosively uneasy lull in the Christian princes' wars after Pavia (February 24, 1525), it was still possible for the humanists to hope that the princes would see the light of reason and abandon their senseless wars. This desperate hope had gone by when Erasmus wrote three new pieces for the *Colloquies* of March, 1529: "Cyclops, or, The Gospel-Carrier," "The False Knight," and the most brilliant of all, "Charon." In these (of which I place "Charon," with its Turkish references, last) the tragic vision successively deepens, and about them there is a strange odor of *fin de siècle*. A great early movement of renaissance was coming to its end.

Simplest, and relatively most charitable, is the *Cyclops* (i.e., the clergy). In this dialogue Erasmus, in his old age, was content to expose and ridicule dissipated priests whose hypocrisy and lack of true Christian religion is illustrated not only by their foul ways of living but especially by the support they lend to war.[6]

The False [or would-be] *Knight* is both more biting and a good deal funnier reading nowadays. Here once again Erasmus turned his wit to expose to sane laughter various persistent frauds carried over from the rotten world of chivalry. Harpalus, the would-be knight, consults Nestor. His question is: if I am not born noble but want the reputation of "nobility," how can I get it as quickly and as cheaply as possible? Nestor advises freely, if with tongue in cheek, in a dialogue full of lively pointers which Shakespeare or Ben Jonson very likely enjoyed when they came to draw their stage epitomes of corrupted nobility and fake chivalry, Falstaff and Bobadil. And through Nestor's shrewd counsel, which is taken with alacrity, the reader may see how far chivalric knighthood had degenerated (*ECF*, pp. 465-72). This was Erasmus' latest and most mordant satire on the criminal fakery that often now stood for chivalric nobility. The would-be knight blithely undertakes to become in turn liar, bully, highwayman, whoremaster, dicer, church robber, and atheist—all this in the name of knighthood.

The colloquy *Charon*,[7] however, is Erasmus' most triumphant and sinister masterpiece. Even in old age he could still bring to criticism of man at war a power of comic invention and a racy verve both amazing and delightful. He even had the humor to include himself in the composition, where fun is made of the peacemongering Polygraphus. Beneath its packed ironies, however, the dialogue conveys a tone approaching despair, an acute consciousness that civilized man seems determined to bring himself and his world to mass suicide—a "glorious destruction of mankind," says Charon gaily, especially when well assured that he has "no reason to fear a peace for these ten years."

When we first encounter Charon, ferryboatman for ghosts bound for Hades, he is dripping wet. His ancient ghostly ferry has just sunk under him, and he has swum ashore to get a stout new one to be ready to carry over the River Styx the hordes of ghosts of those new-slain in Europe's wars and due any minute. Charon encounters a cheerful, evil genius, one

Alastor, bringing the happy word: great crowds are coming, for the entire earth has become infected with "hellish calamities, seditions, wars, robberies, and plagues." With fine savage humor, Charon and Alastor review the world situation and outlook for Christian civilization's survival. Where one lacks a point of information, the other can usually supply it. Thus the dialogue swiftly built up a panoramic view of the obsession with war and violence which, by 1529, seemed to be the most fatal European disease of the age. Charon first gives the broad picture:

[He hears:] "That the three monarchs of the world [Henry VIII, Charles V, and Francis I] were bent upon one another's destruction with a mortal hatred, and that there was no part of Christendom free from the rage of war; for these three have drawn all the rest to be engaged in the war with them [Danes, Poles, Scots, and so forth]. Nor are the Turks at quiet, but are preparing to make a dreadful havoc."

As if such man-made evils were not enough, the plague "rages everywhere." And to add further to humanity's woes, there has sprung up a hideous "variety of [religious] opinions" which now corrupt men's minds with the speed of fire. So "that there is no such thing as sincere friendship anywhere; but brother is at enmity with brother, and husband and wife cannot agree. And it is to be hoped that this distraction will be a glorious destruction of mankind, if these controversies, that now are managed by the tongue and pen, come once to be decided by arms" (i.e., in wars of religion). Brightly, Alastor agrees that Charon has the scene very well in mind; the Furies who inspired mass insanity were never worthier of their name than now.

But what causes it all? And is not Charon rash in counting his ghosts before the souls are out of the bodies? On this point Charon and Alastor lay their heads together. Charon is slightly worried: "But there is danger, lest some good spirit should start up, and of a sudden exhort them to peace: and men's minds are variable, for I have heard that among the living there is one *Polygraphus* [Erasmus] who is continually, by his writing, inveighing against wars and exhorting to peace."

Alastor stoutly reassures the ferryman: Polygraphus might as well be talking to the deaf. Besides, to make conflicts more certain, there are great numbers of "animals in black and white vestments" (clergy) who are always hanging around the princes' courts and fomenting what they call "just, holy, and religious war." In addition, a new form of insanity is now accepted as wisdom. For most marvelously, says Alastor, the priests in the various nations nowadays always claim that "God is on the French side"—or the English, or the Spanish! This kind of idiocy is almost more than even the disillusioned Charon can swallow. Alastor reassures him with a thrust of satire: "What can't a well-dissembled religion do?"

"And that which would make you stand in admiration at the confidence of these men [clergy], is the cry of both parties. In France they preach it up, that God is on the French side, and they can never be overcome that have God for their protector. In England and Spain the cry is, the war is not the King's, but God's; therefore if they do but fight like men, they depend upon getting the victory. And if any one should chance to fall in the battle, he will not die but fly directly up to heaven, arms and all."

Grimly Charon, who clearly detests wars between Christians, wishes for a suitable opportunity to "do these animals [corrupt clergy] a good turn with all my heart."

But Charon is still a bit puzzled as to the motives of these priests who so hotly whip up wars. Alastor enlightens him—their motives are greed and ambition to climb the ladders of preferment. "Because they get more by those that die than those that live. . . . They had rather live in a camp than in their cells. War breeds a great many bishops, who were never thought good for any thing in a time of peace."

A discussion of the new ferryboat which Charon plans to build leads these friends to the subject of "just" war and the fate of its victims. Why does Charon need a new, stronger craft when he ferries only disembodied spirits? He explains that some shades weigh more than others, the heaviest of all being those "that are torn of a sudden out of gross bodies; such as are sent hither by apoplexies . . . pestilence, and especially by war." In fact Charon anticipates with pleasure a heavy payload of "fat lords, Hectors, and bullies."

Charon is stung by Alastor's sly insinuation that business may not turn out to be quite as good as expected: "As for those that die in a just war, I suppose none of them will come to you; for they [clergy] say, they fly bolt upright into Heaven." Charon's reply has even more intensity than that which in 1513 animated Erasmus' strongly satiric picture of the war-mad Pope Julius II, in full armor, arriving at Heaven's gates only to be rejected with withering contempt. Charon intimates that the conventionally accepted just war idea is a myth and a fake; all he knows is that, come war in Europe, business is terrifically good:

279

"I can't tell where they fly to; but this I am sure of, as often as there is a war, there come so many wounded and cripples to me, that I admire that there should be one soul left above ground; and they come over-charged [loaded], not only with surfeits and paunch bellies, but with bulls, benefices, and a great many other things. . . ."

But Charon is still a bit worried lest peace break out, for things are rarely as certain as they seem. He has been saving up for three thousand years for this new boat and would hate to lose on his investment. True, he sees that, left to themselves, the princes of Europe, aided by corrupt clergy and greedy men, should certainly create a perfectly splendid and comprehensive slaughter of the peoples. But suppose some of the gods interfere! "If any deity should start up, and make peace among the princes, all this goodly expectation of mine is knocked on the head at once."

All Charon's residual doubts are overwhelmed by Alastor's gaily confident assurances. The opportunity is golden. From these wars Charon should make his fortune. As one who gets around and is well informed, Alastor finds that for at least ten years there is no reason to "fear a peace." It is true that here and there murmur a few subversive critics (the English humanists and their circle) who find it "unreasonable" that the whole world should be in an uproar, and that so many should die, just to please the private desires of two or three persons (Henry, Francis, and Charles). But Charon need have no fears—the spirit of mass madness is abroad. Those reliable Furies will see to it that these wild wars will proceed:

"I'll be your security, so that you may set your heart at rest. You have no reason to fear a peace for these ten years. The Pope is the only man that persuades them [princes] to come to an agreement amongst themselves, but he had as good keep his breath to cool his porridge. The cities murmur at the load of calamities they lie under; and some there are—I can't tell who— that whisper it about, that it is an unreasonable thing, that the whole world should be turned upside down, for the private piques and ambitions of two or three persons. But for all this, take my word for it, the Furies will get the better of it, let these occasions be as promising as they will."

Vastly cheered and comforted, Charon departs for earth to get boat-builders' wood, since all the nearby Elysian forests have been destroyed with building fires to burn heretics' ghosts, "so that of late, for fuel we have been forced to dig for coals." Alastor urges all possible haste in construction. Already the wars in Europe have sent over 200,000 shades to the bank of the Styx, ready to be ferried over to Hades.

The humanist criticism of man and society climaxed in *Charon* presents a deeply tragic view of Renaissance civilization on the eve of what we now coolly term the Reformation. Erasmus saw all Europe deeply infected with a drive toward a kind of cultural mass suicide. Means aplenty lay ready to hand, and all were in use. Some, like the plague, mankind could not help. As though the onmoving Turkish invasion were not enough, the great princes, distracted with the fascinations of mutual destruction—a man-made calamity—seemed irresistibly drawn to anticipate the Turks and hurl their nations into a wildness of nationalist wars for revenge and glory. Cynical realists like the "False Knight" well understood that under the mask of chivalric nobility it was now fairly easy to commit crimes against the citizenry without serious fear of punishment. The corrupt elements in the clergy found their own greed and ambition most readily satisfied by whipping up the war spirit and terming their own prince's wars to be just and Christian. The princes might possibly be insane; their elemental incapacity even to act in rational self-interest would suggest as much. But the greedy, corrupt clergy are not: "They know their business" says Charon savagely.

Generally the English humanists agreed that war could be just when fought against invasion of one's own country. Clearly More would add, when fought by Christians in common against invasion of Christendom by the Turks. In Charon's view, however, the number of truly just wars was now so trifling as to be of no account. The overwhelming majority of those who die in the princes' wars are no better than common murderers. The humanists once hoped that the people had better sense than their rulers, but the anarchy accompanying the peasants' revolt in Germany moved Erasmus to think that in comparison even the tyranny of a prince was preferable. Henry VIII, Charles V, and Francis I—up to the time he wrote—seemed, however, incompetent even to maintain tolerable tyranny over their own people. Here and there cities "murmur" at the "load of calamities" laid on them by the mad folly of the princes. By listening very carefully amidst all these tumults, one might hear a rare voice saying that it was "unreasonable" that so many should suffer for the "private piques and ambitions of two or three persons." But one might safely conclude that no one in real power now heard such voices of reason and humanity.

As for the common people, they had now widely caught a contagion of madness once reserved to theological disputation and were fiercely at loggerheads over religious opinions. Might not deity at this late hour "start up and make peace"? Recent European history made this seem unlikely. Either by intent or indifference deity had left Christendom to its own mortal devices. The present Pope urged peace, but the popes themselves had too long shared intrigues for war to be heard now. Charon had indeed no "reason to fear a peace for these ten years" and might happily anticipate a "glorious destruction of mankind," i.e., of western civilization. Not being interested in the preservation of that Renaissance world, the Turks might confidently be expected to do their part, as needed, "to make a dreadful havoc."

To the English humanists the only adequate parallel was that presented in history when Rome, the symbol of ancient cultural achievement, mankind's highest before their own time, was overwhelmed, first by decadence within, then by external barbarism. Most tragically ironic of all it was for these humanists to perceive that modern man, or his literate rulers, possessed what ancient Rome lacked—its own fall as a process and precedent. Thomas More caught up this tragic vision in a single sentence in 1528: "After that it were once come to that point, and the world once ruffled and fallen in a wildness, how long would it be, and what heaps of heavy mischiefs would there fall, ere the way were founden to set the world in order and peace again" (*MEW*, p. 274).

Although probably the age was incapable of producing successful revolution against its tyrants, some highly placed ears caught dangerous overtones in such criticism as that of Erasmus. In Spain, for instance, his satire provoked by way of reply a sort of imperial "white book." This was intended to place the responsibility for war among Charles' *enemies*, whereas the humanist left no doubt that he considered Europe's three great princes all to be guilty.[8] And in 1528 Vives was forbidden to translate into Spanish eight of Erasmus' colloquies.[9] Perhaps even so late the humanists were not talking only to one another.

From the early months of 1529, during which Erasmus' *Charon* appeared in print, events moved with a swiftness no narrative can hope to equal. From the viewpoints of More in England, of Vives at Bruges, and of Erasmus at Basel or Freiburg, the European stage exhibited one immense climactic scene of tragedy. Writing to Ferdinand of Hungary, the brother of Charles V, on January 27, 1529, Erasmus once more touched on the fatal folly of continued war among the three great Christian princes. What sorrows Europe has recently suffered from the divisions of Charles and Francis! And how clear it is that between them, "victory" can at best be but Cadmean (*EE*, 2090.17-72)!

At the English court during early 1529 two fateful and intertwined events-in-motion dominated all else. These were the matters of the King's divorce and of a rumored possible separate peace between Charles and Francis. In both Thomas More was to be deeply involved. Vives and Erasmus, meanwhile, had, as it were, box seats from which to observe and comment upon the drama of men and ideas in England. And during the early months of 1529 Vives was at work upon an enlarged form of his 1526 essay on war.

During that sinister spring in England, moreover, the dynamic pattern of events swept toward the fall of Wolsey. Under his direction primarily, England's foreign policy after Pavia (1525) had been to play both sides, but essentially to back French power in Italy as a counterpoise to that of the Emperor Charles V. More's viewpoint had been that England should stay out of the war of fools but Wolsey's was to involve England in the continental strife lest the fools combine to attack. Now Wolsey's mad schemes came to wreck. As early as January, 1529, word reached England not only of the rising danger of Turkish invasion of Germany but of a private peace to be made between Charles and Francis, with England left out in the cold.[1] Wolsey, megalomaniac and desperate, apparently could not or would not believe that any peace was possible without his active support. By January 28 the King had the Cardinal's assurances, "on pain of his head" (one of his favorite phrases), that such separate-peace reports were "an invention of the enemy" (*LP*, IV, 5138, 5231). In mid-February Wolsey could arrogantly declare that "if the Pope wishes for peace, he must first settle the King's matter [divorce]," which the Emperor should see as also to his interest (*LP*, IV, 5314). Strangely unrealistic, the infatuated King and Cardinal still thought they were in a position to make demands, to indicate to Pope and Emperor what "must" be done as the price of peace. On May 21, still unable to credit that a separate peace with England left out of the negotiations could be brewing, Henry even issued a commission for ambassadors to treat for peace with Charles V "in conjunction" with the French (*LP*, IV, 5577). On June 23 Wolsey could still write to assure the Pope that he himself expected to go to Cambrai "to meet the two ladies [Louise of Savoy, mother of Francis I, and Margaret of Austria, aunt of Charles V] . . . to talk of universal peace," confident that "unless Wolsey is there, no such peace will be concluded" (*LP*, IV, 5710).

Was it ignorance or a colossal bluff on the part of the desperate Cardinal? All during that spring he had made little headway in securing the King's divorce with papal sanctions and imperial agreement. Now swiftly the ground crumbled under Wolsey's feet, as the wreck of the entire English pro-war foreign policy of the 1520's, which the humanists had persistently opposed as a huge folly, became unconcealable. On the very next day (June 24, 1529) the mask cracked wide open, for now Wolsey wrote to Casale the truth, that he now feared his "ruin," with loss of "authority, reputation, and life itself" for failure to gain success in the divorce matter (*LP*, IV, 5711). It had become inescapably clear, even to a king "too little removed, as it were, from folly or love-madness," as Vives had said, that unless the English acted with the greatest speed, not to say humility, Charles and Francis were but too likely to conclude an agreement which would leave England quite outside. And since the total effect of Henry's and Wolsey's war policy of 1522-29 had been to secure for England not merely the loss of its wealth but the hearty hatred of both sides, this meant the probability of combined attack in revenge by France and the Emperor. On top of all this, stronger and stronger reports kept coming from the east where the Turks were advancing toward Vienna (*LP*, IV, 5722, 5723). Only narrowly, indeed, did the English escape having Charles and Francis conclude a treaty without English knowledge or participation.

With extreme and unseemly dispatch, English ambassadors had to be sent to Cambrai to make the best they could of a very bad matter indeed. On June 30, 1529, Thomas More and his old friend Bishop Cuthbert Tunstall were commissioned to go, instead of Wolsey, to treat for peace with the French and Imperial ambassadors (*LP*, IV, 5744; *MC*, 169). As events were to turn out, it was More's last foreign embassy. But in Italy, nine days before this commission was issued, and of course too soon for the news to have reached London, the decisive battle of Landriano took place. It established the complete superiority of the imperial forces, thus confirming Pavia four years earlier. Not as spectacular, it was more final, for it completed the education of Francis I, so long insanely in pursuit of chivalric honor and glory; and Francis thereafter accepted the decision as a fact of life.

Throughout that spring, and during the negotiations which stretched through the summer, rumors of peacemaking had of course reached humanist circles. By 1529, however, more than the most temporary and make-believe harmony between Europe's three great princes was almost too much to swallow. Yet still within More's circle there persisted the desperate hope, the ideal, now almost fantastic, of a "universal" peace settlement.[2] Leaving Thomas More (for the first time more or less out from under Wolsey's thumb) busy with his Cambrai negotiations between late June and early August, 1529, we may find the English humanists' view of the anarchic world situation best reflected in the last major work to be considered here.

This is Vives' *On Concord and Discord in Mankind* (July, 1529).[3] In this essay, in effect, he brought to a climactic summary the constructive idealism and criticism developed by the early Tudor group centered around Colet, More, and Erasmus. It was written with a deep awareness that Renaissance civilization stood at a crossroads of history, that its continued existence and very survival were extremely precarious, and that only truly great statesmanship could preserve it from destruction through cumulative man-made folly. He addressed the work to the Emperor Charles V as the only monarch now capable of exerting such crucial leadership. Evidently he had written off Henry VIII and Wolsey as lost in their own special forms of folly and love madness. The fateful question, unanswered when he wrote, was whether or no even Charles could extricate himself from the senseless wars of princely ambition and revenge which promised to create total anarchy and leave all Europe wide open and helpless to the Turkish tyranny.

The humanist's vision shows a lofty understanding of the cultural rebirth which stood in the direst peril. In broad terms the dedicatory epistle outlined to Charles the nature of the social crisis:

> Because the wonderfully fertile renascence in all Europe [*incredibili foecunditate renascentium*] suffers disaster by the continuation of these wars, and moreover almost all great things, and the all but universal renewal [*quasi vniuersali instauratione*] are in want, nothing is as vital as to work for peace and to spread concord throughout mankind [*VCD*, A2ʳ].

Vividly he pictured the broad panorama of Europe in early 1529, after decades of warfare between the great Christian princes:

> We see fields destroyed and unpeopled, buildings razed, cities equally desert or wholly plundered and abandoned, food scarce and dear, scholarly work [*studia litterarum*] sluggish and almost abandoned, manners depraved, justice almost wholly corrupted, and evil received as though it were good [*VCD*, A2ʳ⁻ᵛ].

Thus far in recent times it appears that the kings have made no serious effort to create conditions of stable peace. Treaties have become simply cynical mockeries and deceptions: "Kings and nations conspire together to protect the political authority [i.e., *status quo*], constructing treaties with grandiose and dreadful [*horribilis*] conditions, which the treatymakers themselves do not believe [i.e., which they merely pretend to accept]" (*VCD*, A3ᵛ).

In Vives' view the time and the condition of Europe alike called for a truly great statesman, a political Hercules, one able to perform heroic labors, if necessary to carry the world on his shoulders. Such a leader could rise to the mighty challenge of history and break out of the mutually suicidal patterns of the princely wars. Using existing and effective power, and motivated by a sense of the fateful urgency of the need, he might still create a tolerable state of law and order between the presently warring nations. "When almost the whole world has begun a great cultural renewal or renaissance [*qui orbem pene vniuersum suscepit instaurandam*], but when at the same time there is a collapse of social conduct, what is so necessary as to correct and to reconstruct [society]" (*VCD*, A7ʳ)?

In a word Vives' effort was to arouse the Emperor to rise and meet a challenge of leadership which makes Machiavelli's advice to his prince on how to be a locally successful Italian tyrant seem petty and provincial. Vives rather emphasized than minimized the tremendous difficulties of the world situation when he spoke of the "frenzy of men" (*rabie homines*) as now one great source of war. And he granted that to sustain a "tottering world" was a labor of which Hercules himself wearied. Yet such a leader as Charles really has no choice but to shoulder the burden, for no one else can do so. Vives proposed to treat broadly, first, the social sources of concord (or peace) on the one hand and of discord (or war) on the other. After that his intent was to explain ways by which concord between men can be built and preserved (*VCD*, A7^r-8^r).

The essay which followed this epistle to Charles V is a singular example of Christian humanist, as opposed to Machiavellian, realism. As Foster Watson observed, "It is . . . characterized by the enthusiasm for humanity, rising beyond national interests, or rather identifying national and international with human and cosmopolitan aims." [4]

Vives made no attempt to offer the Emperor localized advice on tactics or strategy. His central argument was made from ethics and history. On the one side he carefully represented that from the cause-and-effect patterns of human behavior and history there would be no escape. He sought to prove not only the decisive reality of the Renaissance crisis but the active possibilities for just rule which still remained. (Evidently he accepted, like More, the idea that if the Christian princes could be reasonably united, the calamity of the Turkish invasion could be prevented.)

Part of his problem was to make clear that leadership decisions could no longer be deferred. (He was aware, I take it, that he worked under formidable difficulties in this desperate effort to influence the Emperor. Sheer custom, as the English humanists were keenly aware, blinds men and lulls them into complacency. For how long had popes and princes practiced such aristocratic and chivalric amusements of revengeful war as those of 1512-29? Why should they not continue them indefinitely? There was abroad, moreover, a powerful pessimism, expressed in the idea that the natural condition of man was war.) Hence Vives is found restating the English humanist conviction that wars are largely man-made evils, thus conceivably within men's power to correct and alleviate.

His basic argument throughout was the one of fateful parallels between the historical situation of Renaissance civilization in 1529 and that of the ancient Roman state just before its irretrievable collapse. In a way his effort was like that of Cassius to Brutus at the outset of Shakespeare's *Julius Caesar,* to persuade him to act wisely before the passage of an opportunity never to return: "Men at some time are masters of their fates." In effect Vives' *On Concord and Discord* sums up the positive side of the entire English humanist movement in social criticism.

To put the matter most briefly, the choices placed before Charles were suggested by the anonymous artist whose woodcuts adorned Vives' title page. To left and right, symbolic figures confront each other. The one is of Mars, helmeted, his left hand holding a spear, his right a torch. Opposed to him is the figure of humane love, Caritas, cradling a child in her arms. Below is a panorama of war. From the left two soldiers stroll away from a great country house left in flames. The foreground offers episodes of battle. A fallen man is about to be run through with pikes. Against a knot of infantry a mounted knight rides with upraised sword. Nearby a trooper chops at a falling enemy while others hack at each other. In the background we see abandoned fields beneath a sullen sky.

Above, the artist offered a panorama of idyllic peace. In the left distance appears a prosperous city on which the sun shines. Front and center stroll men and women at their ease, with a pet dog romping nearby. To the right are fields under cultivation. The basic contrast intended is clearly that between human savagery and destruction in war, and human sanity and dignity at peace.

Vives' first book basically outlines his main arguments. In the three which follow he then proceeds to support them with what amounts to a brief from human experience as recorded in history and literature.

The prince who seeks counsel may well have difficulty deciding the nature and limits of the problem of peace and war. Some perversely witty advisers, indeed, flatter rulers by defending war's evils as merely usual. But the spread of vice's infections is now so rapid that there is no use pretending the situation to be better than it is. Clearly a monstrous strife now infects mankind seized by discord without visible limits. Though peace is a primary need of humanity, we now have endless strife. The arts, sciences, and all the age's great accomplishments are endangered. The civilized gains thus imperiled are remarkable. A literary revival such as few ages have seen has taken place; the remote oceans are now navigated; languages are binding men into a common life. Right-minded men want peace; only the idiots (*hominis imbecillitas*) prefer war. Human sanity and dignity alike make peace a necessity. And to emphasize the point, as Erasmus had done earlier, he described in contrast the idealized figures of the good Christian (*Christianus homo perfectus*) and the depraved figure cut by men of war. The ruler's problem, then, is which to encourage by wise action (*VCD*, Bi^r-7^v).

The rest of Vives' first book analyzes two opposing views of war's causes in human nature. One, which he swiftly rejects, is that chronic war is inevitable in the nature of man, inherent in "the egg" (*VCD*, C2^v). His view, like that of More's Utopians, is that men who live rightly according to nature (*sub legibus naturae*) live in harmony. In fact the theory that war arises inevitably from the nature of man serves tyranny (Ci^v). The argument is old; both sides have been supported in the past. For Vives the important thing is that man has choice (free will); he is not necessarily doomed to live in perpetual strife. Yet obviously in history mankind has been far more at war than at peace. The rest of his Book I seeks answers why.

Anyone who, like Vives, asserts that war is not inherently the natural state of man, undertakes a frightening task when he confronts human history. To what periods of peace could the critic refer? At best, perhaps, only to the mythical Golden Age, to the Augustan peace of Rome, or to the *Pax ecclesiae* which in hard fact the medieval Church was rarely able to bring about.

Vives' answer to the problem, like the answers of More and Erasmus, depended upon a theory of the ways by which "false" and "true" ideals are established and perpetuated in human society. What emerges is an analysis of self-love (*amor sui*). The humanist found it not inevitable but amazing how often men have been dominated by false ideas of "honor," "virtue," and "glory"—all to him variant forms of false pride (*superbia*). Hence men came to admire things neither good in themselves nor even neuter but either "frivolous, stupid, criminal, immodest, or vicious" (*ex friuolis, ac ineptis, ex noxiis, ex pudendis ex viciis*) (*VCD*, C3^r). Once accepted as true, these false ideas led to robberies, extortions, adulteries, frauds, and impostures, as we see in "nobility" nowadays. As true, moreover, they were transmitted to posterity, so we see how warriors get noble reputations. This false pride is indeed a madness which refuses men belief in evidence seen with their own eyes (*ipsorum oculis*). Nor are the learned exempt. Hence they have often praised [tyrannic] emperors, called avarice generosity, and men of war good and virtuous instead of the thieves (*latrones*) which they are. Indeed the men who were not thus duped (like Seneca) were rare (C3ʳ-6ʳ).

Vives asserts in contrast that there is a right kind of self-love (*ille rectus & justus amor*) (*VCD*, C7ᵛ). One terrible example of the false form is the pride which, in their ferocity, conquerors have taken in the great extent of the destruction they have wrought, their pride as well in revenging every injury. But true self-love would rather arbitrate than destroy (C7ʳ-8ʳ).

From this view of corrupt self-love in antiquity he proceeded to examine its more recent and Renaissance forms (*VCD*, D2ʳ ff.). Generally speaking, the corrupt ideas now rule. Among the Christian nations men think they must fight over every real or imagined injury. Even the learned war about rules of grammar and pronunciation! To Vives all this is ignoble, pagan, or vile. Similarly the national princes fight among themselves, though their victories are but Pyrrhic and cannot rightly be called honorable or glorious. But ancient tyrants were likewise prompted by love of false virtue—and he gives a long list. Even so, some, like Alcibiades in Athens, opposed war. Vives declines to yield to sheer weight of precedent. How vast, then, is the folly of the ancient tyrants' modern imitators! They seize on any pretext to throw the world into war. Certainly the princes who have avoided such war and have ruled justly have been rare, but nevertheless tyranny and just rule are radically different (*VCD*, D2ʳ-7ᵛ).

Woven into social tradition, however, these false ideals encourage tyranny and war. Thus in England the Henrys, father and son, sing over how glorious were the wars of Greece and Troy. Much better, in Vives' view, were the ancients who traced the Trojan war to its causes and demanded that Paris return Helen to her husband, for such private strife was no just excuse for a general war. Nor should such women as Cleopatra be admired (*VCD*, D7ᵛ-Ei⁴).

To Vives, one of the most extraordinary forms assumed by false ideals was the power of "mine" and "yours" as interpreted by princes. After two such princes, obsessed by *meum* and *tuum*, have fought together for several years, the lands of one are a little enlarged. This, despite all the losses, he calls "glorious." To such folly has false glory led him! Specifically he cites recent events and the trivial pretexts used for war by England against France and Scotland, by France and Spain, by Helvetia and Germany. Why did they not conciliate their differences? From these the known benefits are few, the harms immortal (*Brevis est beneficii recordatio, immortalis iniuriae*). In fact what is nowadays considered odious between individuals is somehow considered correct between nations (*VCD*, E2ʳ—end Book I).

Having thus outlined the problem of choice before the Emperor Charles, Vives then developed an extensive historical and literary "brief" on all these points. In sum, in *On Concord and Discord*, he proposed to Charles that peace was possible, that it was not inherently contrary to human nature, and that its achievement in Europe would be truly heroic and glorious (*VCD*, Dd8ʳ). The great problem to Vives, then, was to stir the Emperor to abandon false and suicidal goals and instead to use his utmost powers not to destroy but to preserve European civilization. Nor would a mere truce and inactivity suffice, for in the prevailing state of advanced social disintegration this would amount to handing Europe to the Turks on their own terms. As Vives finished *On Concord and Discord*, in June, 1529, reliable reports were reaching Wolsey from Venice and Rome that already the Turks were marching westward in Hungary (*LP*, IV, 5722-23). Published with the desperate appeal to Charles V was Vives' somber little essay on the conditions of life which Christians might expect under a Turkish tyranny. Since it might soon be useful for Christians to know what to expect and how earlier men had endured such oppression, he reviewed some histories of the martyrs.

While Vives thus constructed a last, desperate humanist appeal to Charles V, Thomas More and Bishop Tunstall were negotiating for peace at Cambrai. The problem confronting them, now immensely aggravated by twenty years of Henry's and Wolsey's megalomaniac and chivalric follies, was somewhat like that which had first been met by More's Prince Utopus when that worthy began the good life for Utopia. This was to separate Utopian affairs (Utopus physically created Utopia as an island by cutting off the continent) from those of the corrupt, war-ravaged mainland states. Thereafter, militarily speaking, the Utopians adopted an island-fortress or essentially defensive concept. After that they cultivated their own garden. The first problem of More and Tunstall was "to get out of the European cockpit with only financial losses" (Pollard, p. 224). As the Turkish invasion rolled on during the summer of 1529, Erasmus' letters mirror desperate humanist hopes and fears for Cambrai. By mid-August, in Freiburg, he had heard merely rumors and only hoped that the long-sought "universal" peace had been made (*EE*, 2205.147-64, 2207.12-15).

For twenty years Henry and Wolsey, like their continental rivals, had constructed only mock treaties whose grandiose and dreadful conditions, as Vives said, they merely pretended to believe. The humanists had sensibly come to expect the worst, almost to fear seeming good news. Finally on September 5 the information reaching Erasmus had convinced him that, just a month earlier, a great and good peace had apparently been made, and that day he wrote to congratulate More. He would like to expect the best from this agreement among the world's most powerful kings. Certainly More merits high praise for his faithful work toward a stable agreement to restore law and order. But he had heard so many rumors that the Cambrai peace seemed too good to be true, like help coming when sorrows are at their peak, or as when in tragedies, at the last ditch, help comes from the *deus ex machina* (*deo quopiam repente de machina semet ostendente*). He had also warm praise for Henry VIII, with whose help and wisdom discord among the princes at last seemed giving way to concord. How he yearned for a perpetual peace, though knowing that in mortal affairs nothing *is* perpetual. With the Turkish invasion under way (*imminentes*), at last the princes are showing some signs of uniting to resist it. And at least some measures of reform in the Church had been put into effect (January–February, 1529). Given moderation, he hoped for good things, yet signs of tumult were appearing (*EE*, 2211).

Three days later (September 8) Erasmus wrote in similar vein to his old English patron, Lord Mountjoy, in a letter also obviously intended to reach the distracted King if possible. He emphasized grimly that the Turkish peril was great and real, that invasion from Hungary was on, and that Italy might be next (*EE*, 2215). By mid-September news of the Cambrai peace had arrived but was scarcely yet believed in Erasmus' circles in Freiburg. How he wished that such a peace had been concluded earlier! For the Turks threaten all Europe with a terrible war from which victory, if any, is likely to be but Cadmean (*EE*, 2217.13-21). As he thus wrote to More in England, neither knew that the Turkish siege of Vienna had already begun (September 20, 1529).[5] The dreaded invasion of Europe's heart, which the humanists had so long foreseen, was a reality. While this tremendous external danger to Renaissance civilization rose in the 1520's, More's circle of social critics had labored to the utmost to warn the princely fools that their senseless wars were bringing on their common peril. But the princes were too happy with their wars and glory to heed even arguments of sheer self-interest in survival. Now, after Cambrai, had the fools come to their senses—too late?

For Thomas More, not the writing of the *Utopia,* but his share in making peace for England at Cambrai was almost certainly the greatest achievement of his entire public life. Aeschylus hoped to be remembered for his military services rather, it seems, than his achievements in the art of tragedy. After resigning the Chancellorship in the summer of 1532, More wrote his own "epitaphy" (as Rastell called it) for the tomb he had recently "made in his parish church of Chelsey . . . three small miles from London." The public offices he had held were merely enumerated. The *Utopia* went unmentioned. And the only public action of his life which he chose to remember was the embassy for peace at Cambrai:

> . . . and last of all at Cambrai (joined fellow and companion with Cuthbert Tunstall) . . . he [More] both joyfully saw & was present ambassador when the leagues between the chief Princes of Christendom were renewed again and peace so long looked for restored to Christendom. Which peace our lord stable and make perpetual [*MEW*, p. 1421].

This epitaph is as near to public boasting as More ever came. And actually the Cambrai treaty was the basis for the longest period of peace— almost a decade and a half—in Henry VIII's reign. (It became known as the "women's peace" [Hall, p. 762], since Louise of Savoy, mother of Francis I, and Margaret of Austria, aunt of Charles V, concluded it for their sovereigns.) To the hardheaded chief of embassy and friend of humanism, Tunstall, as to More himself, the vital thing was not to cover themselves with glory but to re-establish the unromantic but essential commercial relations of England and Flanders on their prewar basis. All this was as different from the empty theatrics of the Field of the Cloth of Gold of June, 1520, as night from day. Offered a temporary plan, these Englishmen refused it "for six years and for six hundred years after" (*LP,* IV, 5822). Bargaining from a terribly weak position, they won on their only point of strength; and Margaret's negotiators sensibly agreed, because for the Flemish to lose the English trade would have been too great a disaster.[6]

As More's Utopians, who made no written treaties, were well aware, no agreement is better than the intentions of its signers. Ironically, the

293

Cambrai peace, on which More rightly prided himself, was no better or worse than the other perpetual peace treaties made earlier by Henry and Wolsey. It did not end the wars of France and the Emperor. Nor did it stop Henry VIII from resuming war against France when he chose to find a pretext. It did nothing toward meeting the Turkish menace. One might say it was for a time the basis for foreign peace because Henry temporarily had more than enough of his and Wolsey's demented pursuit of martial glory. Or that for the folly of war madness he exchanged that of love?

Foreign disasters were soon made unnecessary by the surfeit of those at home. Wolsey's fall on October 17, 1529, and More's designation as Chancellor eight days later were merely transitional motions in statecraft. If the Cambrai peace served to extricate England from the European cockpit with merely financial losses, these had been immense and such as to create a desperate need of ready wealth for those in power or ambitious to be so. It is easy to agree with Pollard (p. 224) that Henry VIII and England were glad now to "revert to domestic problems which had been burked by . . . [Wolsey] but now claimed the attention of the first long Parliament in English history." Vives, in his *On Concord and Discord*, hoped to find in Charles V a political Hercules, capable of sustaining a tottering world. With Wolsey's fall a similar role became More's for England. Whatever need for reforms he could declare as Parliament opened on November 3, 1529 (*LP*, IV, 6043), probably no man with his firm ideal of justice could have succeeded in preventing further débacle.

The staggering folly of twenty years' wasted opportunities for just rule under Henry and Wolsey is suggested in what amounts to a kind of mock legacy to England, written as though done by Wolsey. Actually the piece was the work of one of More's humanist friends, John Palsgrave, an educator who had encountered difficulties not unlike those of Vives.[7] This English humanist document, seized in a rather mysterious search of Palsgrave's rooms, was evidently not intended for publication because it is almost as much an indictment of the King as of Wolsey. (As Vives had written to discreet friends, without the King's sanction the Cardinal could do nothing.) Our excerpts concentrate on war accomplishments. Palsgrave sarcastically imagined what Wolsey might have said with terrible accuracy:

Here followeth a brief remembrance how the affairs of this realm have been conducted since it pleased our Sovereign to make my lord Cardinal's grace his chiefest and only councillor:

We have begun a general league . . . of peace between the Pope, the Emperor elect, and the French king and us [1518].

We have won [Thérouenne] and Tournay [1513].

We have killed the king of Scots, and almost all his nobles, spiritual and temporal [Flodden, 1513].

We have gotten Navarre for the king of Arragon . . . [1522-23].

We have begun war with France for the defence of the Church; and for want of good conduct, notwithstanding the great substance of bullion . . . left . . . by king Henry the VIIth, we were constrained to give our Prince's sister to him we moved war against, to make an honorable peace [1522+].

[Another item admits that of sums raised for these wars, £1,300,000 are unaccounted for, though Wolsey grants it "came out of the Tower . . . employed at our disposition."]

We have defended the Church, against the French king, to our great impoverishing and enriching of his . . . subjects.

We have begun to pull down [Thérouenne], which is now stronger than ever it was.

We have begun to set up a chargeable garrison at [Tournay].

We have begun to make a sumptuous castle there.

We have now again begun just war with France, provoked by many notable injuries . . . [1522——].

We have spoiled and burnt [Morlaix], and bidden seven weeks in the realm of France unfoughten with, notwithstanding any provocation we could give in burning and spoiling the countries as we went . . . [1522-23].

We triumphed at our encountering at Calais [Field of the Cloth of Gold, 1520], to the great impoverishing of the noblemen of England, and prodigal dispending of the King's treasure, as well in the sumptuous building made there only to that use, and not to endure, as in mummeries, banquets, jousts, and tourneys . . . [*LP*, IV, pp. 2555-62].

If Palsgrave had possessed Vives' sharp critical powers he might have gone beyond this tragic accounting. In Vives' July, 1529, epistle to Charles V, in *On Concord and Discord*, he not only summed up the vast material loss from the princes' wars for glory but stressed also the pervasive moral corruption which accompanied the war process. "We see . . . scholarship sluggish and almost abandoned, manners depraved, justice almost wholly corrupted, and evil received as though it were good." In 1522-23 Wolsey and Henry rejoiced to hear how under Francis I, as the war with the English proceeded, nothing remained sacred. Not even the holiest relics escaped the royal depredator, until "his people are eaten up to the bones, and, with the Church, cry for vengeance upon him." And the great English depredators observed with grim joy that in Francis' "base and exile poor estate" he had "molten the garnishing of St. Martin's corpse, and founded [melted for coin] the twelve apostles, with other jewels and sacred ornaments of the churches" (*LP*, III, pp. 1141, 1091). Between 1509 and 1529 at least a powerful minority of an entire English generation had completed a practical education for ruthless outrage abroad. What might be expected if such sinister talents, given the highest sanction, were turned upon the Church in England itself?

As long as the Turkish invasions hung over Europe, the very future of its Renaissance civilization stood in doubt. Such fatal circumstances make looking to coming generations difficult. Yet the humanists still considered the education of the young. Fifteenth-century Italian humanist educators conventionally debated the choice of a career in arms or letters, usually with agreement that glory and honor were to be won through either and that a nobleman's or prince's education should be as thorough in the arts of war as of peace.[8] Erasmus, in various adages (1513-15) most frequently dwelt on the corrupt education he found usual for princes, who were almost invariably trained not to govern wisely in peace but to destroy in war. His *Christian Prince* (1516) stressed training in the arts of peace and deliberately omitted the customary chapter on those of war. In the state of Utopia children were carefully conditioned to abhor cruelty and war as base, vile, and subhuman.

Now in the gloomy months of 1529 Erasmus summed up his thought *Concerning the Aim and Method of Education.*[9] Characteristic of the English humanists is his simultaneous idealization of peace and of man as a teachable, reasonable creature distinguished above all other animals by capacity for "philosophy and right conduct" (*ECE*, p. 190). His educational views resemble those of More's Utopians. Since reason is man's distinctive gift, what can be worse than to see him blinded to his right duty to nature, man, and God (pp. 186, 190)?

Thus, for instance, Erasmus decried the frequent contemporary practice of determining in infancy that a child should become a soldier and therefore training him to no other service. A future soldier should be well trained, but no less should he be equipped to serve the state in peace. "Why then refuse to provide not less early that the boy may be worthily prepared to fill [his future career]: so that he grow up not only to be a captain of a troop, but a fit and reputable officer of the commonwealth" (*ECE*, p. 185). Particularly he attacked children's early acquaintance with adult vices and especially breeding into them an evilly precocious love of war:

I would also denounce those who bring up their sons to a love of war. Straight from their mother's arms they are bidden to finger swords and shield, to thrust and strike. With such tastes, already deeply rooted with years, they are handed over to a master, who is blamed for their indifference to worthy interests. If it be urged that parents find some pleasure in this evil precocity of their children, let me ask if any true father will rather that his son pick up gross speech . . . than to hear him . . . utter something worthy and true [*ECE*, pp. 185-89]?

He deplored as well the mad error of those who think practical experience provides sufficient education, as though a prince can learn to rule in peace only through war's disasters: "It is an unhappy education which teaches the master mariner the rudiments of navigation by shipwrecks; or the Prince the true way to kingship by revolutions, invasions or slaughter" (*ECE*, p. 192). Nowhere do the English humanists praise a career in arms for its own sake. Their great effort was to reshape education, as essential to any good life, toward peace. As Vives put it in 1531, "the State has for its scope the preparation of quiet, peaceful living, so that its citizens may help one another to live in a generous and benevolent manner." [10]

Vives' *On Education* (1531) consistently followed out the philosophy he shared with his English humanist friends. He gave a very acute analysis of many psychological factors in history, designed to show how rulers can gain from its study valuable insights into the passions' effects in everyday life. "So history serves as the example of what we should follow and what we should avoid." No instance described is given more weight than that of war as represented in history. He held that most historians had placed exaggerated emphasis on war and warriors and that these, as evil examples, should be quickly passed over. Instead the student's major attention should be concentrated upon the practical examples found in peaceful affairs:

Wars and battles need not be studied closely, for they merely equip the mind with examples for the performance of evil, and show the ways in which we may inflict injuries, one on another. Yet we cannot help noticing briefly, who took up arms, who were the leaders on either side . . . who were beaten, and what happened to them. But whatever is said or read in history, wars should be regarded not otherwise than as cases of theft, as indeed they usually were, excepting perhaps when undertaken against thieves. But even amongst Christians other causes less justifiable, are only too often the grounds of war. Let the student then give his attention to peaceful affairs, a far more satisfactory and fruitful study, so that he may realize the glory and wisdom which have been gathered by virtuous acts, and the disgrace which has followed on horrid crimes . . . [*VOE*, p. 236].

Useful truth in history, to Vives, meant predominantly truth which is the basis of a good, peaceful life. He regretted that while generals' evil deeds have been recorded with care, many works of holy men were never recorded at all (*VOE*, p. 248). Speaking of specific books then often read by students, he, like Erasmus, found Suetonius too prone to praise virtue and overlook vice even in the worst of emperors. Tacitus, on the other hand, appealed to Vives as more valuable "because he is concerned with domestic politics rather than with warfare" (p. 243). He condemned the famous *Cyropaedia* of Xenophon, despite Cicero's praise of it, because "it appears to me . . . to have too much of military matters in it" (p. 260). And he thought wretchedly misguided the use of human wit in inventions whose only obvious purpose is to destroy human life: "The goal of knowledge is sometimes harmful to piety, e.g., in arts which aim at injuring men, of which kind are . . . that part of the military art which belongs to the attacking and slaughtering of men; and the whole class of war-machines . . ." (*VOE*, p. 31).

Set against the dominant events of 1529-34, of a world falling in a wildness, these relatively sane remarks on education take on an aspect of fantasy. So perhaps for that matter do many of the long-overdue reform proposals made by Chancellor Thomas More to the first long Parliament in English history, opened in November, 1529. Hanging by a thread over English society was the sword of the King's great matter, the divorce. But hanging over all the Renaissance world was the even greater matter, in humanist eyes, of the active Turkish invasion. In the week before Wolsey's fall on October 17, 1529, the Turks drew back from the siege of Vienna. But then Suleiman the Magnificent simply prepared an invasion of Germany designed to force Charles V to a grand test of powers for survival. The whole tremendous question, whether or no Renaissance civilization was doomed to disappear under a Turkish tyranny, remained in suspense when More went to the Tower.

Under heavy pressure but doing his best to avoid embroilment in the Lutheran controversy, Erasmus expressed his views on war with the Turks in 1530. Contemplating apparently the last act in a great social tragedy, his mood as he surveyed the human scene was almost one of despair. "We are so accustomed to wars, civil uproars, factions, plunderings, plagues, poverty, and famine that we do not now hold them to be evils." As though these were not enough, the courts rush to war. God alone may have the remedies but we men bear the guilt. Both the secular princes and the Church are included in his grim indictment. The Turks have made immense gains against the west in recent years. And what have the Christian princes done but war among themselves, though all Europe is threatened? Only Charles V may take leadership against the Turks; this would be legitimate resistance. Erasmus repeated that he had not condemned all wars, for defensive war against the Turks may be justified. He *had* said that war in itself was by nature so atrocious that the most just prince, with the most just motives, may reap more evil than good from it. And he recalled Bernardus, who wittily equated *"militiam"* (soldiers) with *"malitiam"* (evil men), which Erasmus thought generally true. He rejected what he, like More, took to be Luther's teaching on war against the Turks. That war *can* be just for Christians Erasmus thought was clear, since the Bible gave princes the power and right to punish. To make himself clear to his age, what he, like the other English humanists, had opposed as unethical were wars of private princely ambition, greed, or revenge. These are not "just" wars but robberies (*latrocinium esse constat non bellum*). If "just" wars must be fought, a truly Christian prince will seek the consent of his people and conduct them with the least possible bloodshed and destruction. As for the European scene, in which most princes seemed everywhere preoccupied with private greed, what was needed was a new Moses. The only hope he, like Vives, saw was in Charles V.[11]

That Hercules, the Emperor, more than any one man at this historic crisis, did finally provide modern European civilization with an opportunity for survival and new growth. Certainly this great prince gained little enough help from England. Indeed, on December 28, 1529, Chapuys, the imperial ambassador in England, received very secret warnings, probably from the disgraced Wolsey, that Henry VIII and Francis I of France were now laying their heads together to scheme up aid to the Lutheran princes *against* Charles (Pollard, p. 285)! Marching into Germany, the Turks ravaged several provinces, while Charles V withdrew his forces from before the invader.[12]

Could any appeal to reason, let alone faith, have reached through to the distracted Henry VIII? On January 13, 1531, Vives wrote to the King, appealing to him not to plunge England into possible war with the Emperor, "now that the Turk is victorious." He had not heard from the King for three years, nor from the Queen for a long time, but warmly desired to see them both. He sent to Henry the books he had written three years before, giving his adverse opinion on the proposed divorce, lest Wolsey had at that time kept them from the King. And Vives said that he was "moved to write by his duty to the King, love to England, where he was so kindly received, and anxiety for the quiet of Christendom" (*LP*, V, 46). This was not only warm and candid humanist criticism; it was realistic. But Henry could no longer hear; the storm over England was too loud.

Only Charles V, with such allies as he could desperately rally, then stood—as the humanists saw it—as barrier to ward off the ultimate calamity of a world collapsing beneath invasive barbarism. At court More's friendliness to the Emperor's cause in defense of Christendom made him in Chapuys' eyes "justly called the father and protector of Your Majesty's [Charles V's] subjects." [13] What he had heard by April 11, 1531, convinced the ambassador "that these people desire above all things the arrival of the Turk in Germany." But this sinister group did not include More: "The Chancellor [More] himself complained some days ago . . . in a very piteous tone, of the blindness of those princes [including Henry VIII] who refused to assist Your Majesty [Charles] against so cruel and implacable an enemy." On the other hand, More assured Chapuys bitterly that there was no likelihood of an English attack on Charles either, not because of lack of evil will but because "there were no preparations or power to do so." [14]

Chapuys gave a telling glimpse of the distracted Henry and of More as well on April 16, 1532, just a month before More resigned as Chancellor. Muttering "half between his teeth," the King threatened to take the English trade "elsewhere" and damage the Low Countries irreparably unless their demands were made less exorbitant. He was still sane enough, however, to admit that there *was* no elsewhere. Nor was Henry at all displeased with reports "that the Turk had made great preparations for invading the dominions of the Emperor." Norfolk, who brought the reports to court, implied comfortably that "the Emperor would have too much to do elsewhere to wish to be a bad neighbour." And at the same time, ironically, one of More's later official actions was to propose new war taxes from Commons. In other words, Henry was again preparing for war, now against the Emperor, though the shrewd ambassador wrote to Charles V that "many think the exaction of the [war] tax will cause mutiny" in England (*LP*, V, 941). Mutiny or no, as English humanist hopes for a good life in England were overwhelmed in the common catastrophe, there were still men in England (as Chapuys could hear making incredible murmurs) who even now spoke out as candidly as had Vives in his letter of January, 1531, to the King. For Vives had boldly touched the political heartstring of all good Englishmen's fears: that "a new marriage would leave the succession doubtful, and afford grounds for civil war." Having already destroyed almost all else of his father's inheritance, the mad King was about to destroy a legacy rare indeed in English medieval history, that of lawful succession.

More had built his tomb at Chelsey while he was Chancellor. I suspect that this English Socrates surmised with a good deal of clarity the most probable course of events still to come. Hence in the summer of 1532, like any prudent man foreseeing death and setting his affairs in their best possible order, he wrote the epitaph mentioned earlier and now had it inscribed on the waiting stone. "The readiness," as Hamlet would say, "is all." Commend me to my friends in England (i.e., above all, More), wrote Vives to Erasmus on June 12, 1531, apparently with recognition that since he was regarded as an enemy, this way was safer for his friends (*EE*, 2502.6-7).

At times life assumes almost the proportions of tragic art. With such a condition of affairs our early Tudor drama of humanists seeking a good life for England comes to its end. Always, as truly tragic catastrophes surge toward their close, the only safe way compatible with human dignity leads toward death of the hero. Such death may not be certain, but it must be confronted face to face. Perhaps, however, no perception is more essential to great English tragedy than that the personal death of the hero implies the potential survival of what is noblest in his vision of life as it should be lived.

So with More. Thus, in the Tower in 1534 awaiting the executioner's blow, he occupied himself—not with vainglorious visions like Shakespeare's King Richard II—but with writing in English his *Dialogue of*

Comfort against Tribulation. Fictionally it was a translation of a Latin work by a Hungarian, i.e., one already acquainted with the expected Turkish tyranny. Its purpose, like that of Vives' similar but briefer 1529 essay, was to suggest how Christian men might endure what was to come. Such a work now perhaps seems both archaic and fantastic, since hindsight comfortably assures us that western civilization was not thus destroyed and especially since our vision of the early Tudor age tends to be blinded by the dazzle of the Elizabethan cultural renaissance. When More wrote, however, he dealt with urgently present realities. His intent as always was not to provide an age with Platonic counsels of escapist perfection but to bend philosophy to the practical aid of mankind.

The imagined setting of More's *Dialogue* is a conquered Hungary. Brought before us are old Antony, near a natural death, and a would-be comforter, the younger Vincent. Ironically, however, Vincent envies age its privileges: "But now . . . the world is here waren [become] such, and so great perils appear here at hand, that me thinketh the greatest comfort that a man can have is, when he may see that he shall soon be gone" (*MEW*, p. 1139). But old Antony, twice a Turkish prisoner, quietly assures him that the difference between them is really small. Young men may die, too. It is best to have trust in God.

Digesting this stoic counsel, Vincent asks specific advice on how to bear up best under the imminent Turkish tyranny. No naïve optimist, he has already formed a fairly realistic vision of terrors to come. More wrote primarily now with Englishmen in mind:

Both I and mine are sore beaten already, and now upon the coming of this cruel Turke fear to fall in far moe [*sic*]. . . . And now since these tidings have come hither so brim, of the great Turk's enterprise into these parts here, we can almost neither talk nor think of any other thing else than of his might and our mischief [*MEW*, p. 1140].

The image Vincent has already formed of the expected tyranny is different from, but no prettier than, that which any careful, free, twentieth-century reader may have formed of totalitarian rule, at least before it became fairly plain that any future world war would lead to universal nuclear destruction and the probable end of civilization as now known.

There falleth so continually before the eyes of our heart a fearful imagination of this terrible thing: his mighty strength and power, his high malice and hatred, and his incomparable cruelty, with robbing, spoiling, burning, and laying waste all the way that his army cometh; then killing or carrying away the people far thence from home, and there sever the couples and the kindred asunder, everyone far from other: some kept in thralldom, and some kept in prison, and some for a triumph tormented and killed in his presence [*MEW*, p. 1140].

Moreover, the Turk brings his "false faith" with him, so that men must either lose all or accept it. But the worst of Vincent's fears are of the Christians who will pliably agree with the Turks to save their hides and property, for such are, if possible, worse than the Turks themselves (*MEW*, pp. 1140-1). Clearly, Vincent could do with some advice. In the rest of the piece his Uncle Antony, relying on classic Christian doctrines, does his best to provide some comfort.

On this note of restrained tragedy our narrative closes.

Chapter One

1. Quincy Wright, *A Study of War* (Chicago, 1942), I, 396.
2. Pierre Mesnard, *L'Essor de la philosophie politique au XVI*ᵉ *siècle* (Paris, 1936), p. 675 (cited hereafter as Mesnard).
3. Of general works which at least touch on this humanist social criticism, the best is C. L. Lange, *Histoire de l'internationalisme* (New York, 1919), pp. 146-87 (cited hereafter as Lange). See also Hanz Prutz, *Die Friedensidee* (Munich, 1917), pp. 62-107, 136-53. For period studies, see: Francis Gasquet, *The Eve of the Reformation* (London, 1905), pp. 137 ff.; Lewis Einstein, *The Italian Renaissance in England* (New York, 1903), pp. 45, 286-315 *passim*; J. N. Figgis, *Studies in Political Thought . . . 1414-1625* (Cambridge, Eng., 1907), *passim*; H. O. Taylor, *Thought and Expression in the Sixteenth Century* (New York, 1920), I, 167-76; J. W. Allen, *A History of Political Thought in the Sixteenth Century* (New York, 1928), Part II, *passim*. Quaker scholars have touched the Renaissance but little: e.g., P. S. Belasco, *Authority in Church and State* (London, 1928), pp. 58-67. Studies of humanist education are better but spotty: see W. H. Woodward, *Vittorino da Feltre* (Cambridge, Eng., 1897), pp. 115, 138; W. H. Woodward, *Studies in Education . . . 1400-1600* (Cambridge, Eng., 1906), chaps. vi, x, *passim* (cited hereafter as Woodward); Foster Watson, *The English Grammar Schools to 1660* (Cambridge, Eng., 1908), chap. vi *passim*; F. Watson, *The Beginnings of the Teaching of Modern Subjects in England* (London, 1909), pp. xxix-xxx, 45-86 *passim*; F. Watson, *Vives: On Education* (Cambridge, Eng., 1913), pp. cxlvii ff. (cited hereafter as *VOE*). See also D. Nisard, *Études sur la renaissance et réformé, Érasmus—Thomas Morus* (Paris, 1855), pp. 37-42; Frederick Seebohm, *The Oxford Reformers* (London, 1887), *passim*; Ernest Nys, "Quâtre utopistes au XVIᵉ siécle," *Revue de droit international et de législation comparée*, XXI (1889), 65-76; John W. Mackail, *Erasmus Against War* (Boston, 1907), pp. ix-xxiv; L. Einstein, *Tudor Ideals* (New York, 1921), pp. 230-33.
4. Lange, pp. 19-131; James Bryce, *International Relations* (New York, 1922), pp. 1-19; A. O. Lovejoy and G. Boas, *Primitivism and Related*

Ideas in Antiquity (Baltimore, Md., 1935), especially pp. 23-102 (cited hereafter as LB).

5. For the Israelites, see: Isaiah 2:4, 11:6-9; Micah 4:3-4; for the Greeks, see the eighth century B.C. tradition in *Works of Hesiod,* trans. J. Banks (London, 1856), pp. 80-81. See W. E. Caldwell, *Hellenic Conceptions of Peace* (New York, 1919); H. Schulte-Vaerting, *Die Friedenspolitik des Pericles* (Munich, 1919); C. H. McIlwain, *The Growth of Political Thought in the West from the Greeks to the End of the Middle Ages* (New York, 1932), chaps. i-iv; Wright, *A Study of War,* I, 163.

6. Lucretius *De rerum natura* v.989-1009 and 1113-42 (in LB, pp. 228, 233). On man's misuse of the winds to aid warfare, see L. A. Seneca, *Physical Science in the Time of Nero . . . the Quaestiones naturales,* trans. J. Clarke (London, 1910), pp. 212-17. For Pythagoras, see Ovid's *Metamorphoses* xv.75-142 (in LB, pp. 61-62). For Ovid's own account, *Metamorphoses* i.76-215 (in LB, pp. 47-48). The Ovidian version was historically "probably more potent than any other" (LB, p. 49), for it was widely known in medieval Europe when the Greek poets were "largely forgotten." For Seneca, see *Epistulae morales* 90 (in LB, pp. 263-79), 91.17-18, 94.61-69, 113.27-31, and his *Quaestiones naturales,* Book III *passim* (in trans. by Tho. Lodge [1614], pp. 805-7). On Plutarch, see especially "Of Eating Flesh . . ." [*Moralia*] *The Morals,* trans. P. Holland (London, 1603), pp. 572-77. On Pliny see *The Naturall Historie,* trans. P. Holland (London, 1601), Book VII, pp. 152-53 (in LB, pp. 401-3). Citations are illustrative, not at all exhaustive.

7. Woodward, pp. 111-12.

8. Lange, pp. 28-30, 47-66 (on antimilitarist sects, including Wycliffites); E. V. Arnold, *Roman Stoicism* (Cambridge, Eng., 1911), pp. 408-36; G. T. Buckley, *Atheism in the English Renaissance* (Chicago, 1932), p. 17; A. J. Carlyle, *A History of Mediaeval Political Theory in the West* (Edinburgh, 1903-28), especially Vol. I, Part I, chaps. i, ii, and pp. 81 ff.; Vol. III, pp. 1-18; and Vol. V, Part III, pp. 441-74 *passim.* For similarities between the moral and political teachings of St. Paul and Seneca, see Seneca, *On Benefits,* trans. A. Stewart (London, 1887), pp. vii ff., and especially *De ben.* i.15, iii.18, and his *Epistulae morales* 41 and 116. Arnold collects a wealth of such parallels.

9. Augustine, *Contra Faustum* (*Patrologia Latina,* Vol. XLII), Book XII, chaps. lxxiv-lxxvi; *De civitate Dei,* and Book I, chap. xxi; Book III, chap. xxvi; Book IV, chaps. iv, vi, xv; and Book XIX, chap. vii (see further the documents given in John Eppstein, *The Catholic Tradition of the Law of Nations* [London, 1935], pp. 68-81). Augustine did, however, denounce the wars motivated by material ambition which extended Roman rule. See also *The Decretals* of Gratian, Pars Secunda, Causa XXIII, Quaestiones I-V *passim,* VIII; St. Thomas Aquinas, *Summa,* Secunda Secundae, Q. XL. See also F. M. Russell, *Theories of International Relations* (New York,

1936), pp. 90-115; C. Van Vollenhoven, *The Law of Peace*, trans. W. Carter (London, 1936), pp. 1-56; W. Ballis, *The Legal Position of War* (The Hague, 1937), pp. 40-59; Herschel Baker, *The Dignity of Man* (Cambridge, Mass., 1947), chap. xi; Robert P. Adams, "Pre-Renaissance Courtly Propaganda for Peace in English Literature," *Papers of the Michigan Academy*, XXXII (1948 [for 1946]), 431-38 (cited hereafter as Adams [1948]).

10. The ideas of primitive Churchmen on war and peace are summed up by J. Moffat, *s.v.* "War," *Dictionary of the Apostolic Church* (Edinburgh, 1918), II, 646-72. For texts see C. J. Cadoux (ed.), *The Early Christian Attitude Toward War* (London, 1919), and J. Eppstein, *The Catholic Tradition of the Law of Nations*, Parts I, II. Cf. Wright, *A Study of War*, I, 101-65.

11. See, e.g., the lament on the miseries and prevalence of war (conventionally attributed to greed [sin]) by the medieval Pope Innocentius III, in *The Mirror of Mans Lyfe*, trans. H. Kirton (London, 1576), Vol. I, chaps. xvii, xxvii; Vol. II, chap. ii. See also Bryce, *International Relations*, p. 15; R. W. Church, *Dante* (London, 1878), *passim*; W. H. Ramsay, *The Imperial Peace, an Ideal in European History* (Oxford, 1913); Bede Jarrett, *Social Theories of the Middle Ages 1200-1500* (London, 1926), pp. 181-213; the fine work by R. F. Wright, *Medieval Internationalism* (London, 1930), pp. 18-51, 109-16, 133-81; J. K. Ryan, *Modern War and Base Ethics* (Washington, D. C., 1933), pp. 5-24; J. N. Figgis, *The Political Aspects of St. Augustine's "City of God"* (London, 1921), *passim*.

12. O. Gierke, *Natural Law and the Theory of Society 1500-1800*, with *The Ideas of Natural Law and Humanity* by Ernst Troeltsch, trans. E. Barker (Cambridge, Eng., 1934), I, 201 *et passim*; O. Gierke, *Political Theories of the Middle Age*, trans. F. Maitland (Cambridge, Eng., 1900), *passim*; for Wycliffe's position, see E. Troeltsch, *The Social Teaching of the Christian Churches*, trans. O. Wyon (New York, 1931), I, 359, 306-27 *passim*.

13. Alan Gewirth, *Marsilius of Padua and Medieval Political Philosophy* (New York, 1951), pp. 91-97 *passim*; Ernest Baker, "Mediaeval Political Thought," in *The Social and Political Ideas of Some Great Mediaeval Thinkers*, ed. F. Hearnshaw (London, 1923), pp. 30-33.

14. J. W. Allen, "Politics," in *Mediaeval Contributions to Modern Civilization*, ed. F. Hearnshaw (London, 1921), p. 267; Fréderick Duval, *De la paix de Dieu à la paix de fer* (Paris, 1923), p. 98.

Chapter Two

1. J. G. Nichols (ed.), *The Boke of Noblesse* (London, 1860), pp. 1-82 *passim*. This is the first known publication. Nichols (p. iv) found it done mostly by 1460 but with additions near 1475.

2. Dame Juliana Berners, *The Boke of Saint Albans,* ed. W. Blades (London, 1901), p. 24.

3. *The Prologues and Epilogues of William Caxton,* ed. W. Crotch (London, 1928), p. 48.

4. *The Book of the Ordre of Chyualry,* ed. A. Byles (London, 1926), pp. 121-25; *Prologues of Caxton,* ed. Crotch, p. 77. Lull's work was widely known; on the MSS see Byles's edition, pp. xvi-xix.

5. *Le Morte Darthur,* ed. H. O. Sommer (London, 1889), pp. 3-5; Ascham, *The Scholemaster* (1570), in *English Works,* ed. W. Wright (Cambridge, Eng., 1904), p. 231. On chivalry regarded as a "civilizing influence," see E. Prestage (ed.), *Chivalry,* (London, 1928), especially pp. 183-228.

6. Christine de Pisan, *The Book of Fayttes of Armes and of Chyualrye,* trans. W. Caxton, ed. A. Byles (London, 1932), pp. 291-92.

7. *Ibid.,* pp. xlvi, xlii-li, 10-12.

8. *Ibid.,* p. xlix, 213, 217, 224 ff., 247-48, 282.

9. *Ibid.,* pp. xlii-xliii, 13, 20, 128. Curiously, Christine (and Caxton) made no use of one of Bonet's most daring passages, in which he extended to non-Christians a humane consideration rare in the Middle Ages. He held that wanton warfare against Saracens, Jews, or other unbelievers was unlawful. Against them war should be waged only to recover formerly Christian lands or to redress injuries done to Christians or to the faith. For while love may not be lost between Christian and Jew, persecution is wrong: instead, let conversion of the Jews be attempted, for the Scriptures say that in the future all peoples will be one (*ibid.,* pp. xlviii-xlix).

10. *The Governance of England,* ed. C. Plummer (Oxford, 1926), pp. 8, 82 ff.

11. For *De natura legis naturae,* see *The Works of Sir John Fortescue,* ed. Lord Clermont (London, 1869), I, 63 ff.; for *De laudibus* see the edition and translation by S. Chrimes (Cambridge, Eng., 1949). Only *De laudibus* (1537) was printed before 1714.

12. Mesnard, pp. 141-77 *passim.* One of Fortescue's last works shows a rising English revulsion from the chronic injustice, the "pain and anguish," of the civil wars, which destroyed "many men of honest living" but often enriched the "naughty"; see Fortescue's "Dialogue between Understanding and Faith," *Works,* I, 483-90, and *The Governance of England,* p. 79. Fortescue is not mentioned in R. W. Chambers' *Thomas More* (London, 1935) (cited hereafter as Chambers).

Chapter Three

1. P. A. Duhamel, "The Oxford Lectures of John Colet," *JHI,* XIV (1953), 494.

2. Cf. P. O. Kristeller, *The Classics and Renaissance Thought* (Cambridge, Mass., 1955), pp. 78-79.

3. Erasmus, *The Lives of Vitrier . . . and Colet*, trans. J. H. Lupton (London, 1883), pp. 21-33 *passim* (cited hereafter as *EC*); *Opus epistolarum Des. Erasmi*, ed. P. S. and H. M. Allen (Oxford, 1906-47), 1211 (cited hereafter as *EE*).

4. John Colet, *An Exposition of St. Paul's Epistle to the Romans,* trans. J. H. Lupton (London, 1873), pp. 86-89, 92-93 (on warmakers as madmen), xl, 95.

5. Duhamel, "The Oxford Lectures of John Colet," p. 494; J. W. H. Atkins, *English Literary Criticism: The Renascence* (London, 1947), pp. 57-59, 34-65 *passim;* P. Kristeller, *The Classics and Renaissance Thought,* p. 82; Douglas Bush, *Classical Influences in Renaissance Literature* (Cambridge, Mass., 1952), pp. 13-15; A. L. Rowse, "Erasmus and England," in *The English Spirit* (New York, 1945), pp. 75-76; R. P. McKeon, "Renaissance and Method in Philosophy," in *Columbia Studies in the History of Ideas* (New York, 1935), III, 47. In contrast, one view holds that there was nothing new in Colet's study of St. Paul, who had been studied often in the Middle Ages; as for Erasmus, what was new and unconventional was his mention of "Jesus and Paul . . . in the same breath with Achilles and Hercules," often, "long before 1501" (A. Hyma, "Erasmus and the Oxford Reformers [1495-1503]," *Nederlandsch Archief voor Kerkgeschiedenis,* N.S., XXV [1932], 129).

6. Ficino: during his Italian visit (*ca.* 1493-96), Colet may have been inspired by Ficino, with whom he had some correspondence; see R. Marcel, "Les 'découvertes' d'Érasme en Angleterre," *Bibliothèque d'humanisme et renaissance,* XIV (1952), 117-23. Moreover the latest extant work of Ficino (d. 1499) was an incomplete commentary upon St. Paul's Epistle to the Romans, probably done in the 1490's although not printed until 1561; see P. O. Kristeller, *The Philosophy of Marsilio Ficino,* trans. V. Conant (New York, 1943), p. 18, and E. Cassirer *et al.* (eds.), *The Renaissance Philosophy of Man* (Chicago, 1948), pp. 185-212 *passim.* If, however, Ficino was "not interested in political problems" but was interested in a speculative, metaphysical treatment of morals, art, and religion (Kristeller, *The Philosophy* . . . , pp. 12, 15, 288n.), it is not easy through him to account for the intense concern with practical social reform characteristic of Colet and of More, Erasmus, and Vives as well. (M. de Wulf regrets that these men were *not,* for instance, interested in the complete Stoic philosophy but instead in *practical* ethics and rhetoric [*History of Medieval Philosophy,* trans. P. Coffey (3rd ed.; London, 1909), pp. 466, 475]).

Colet has been placed in Rome (April 1, 1493), where he was interested in the work of the humanist Aeneas Sylvius (1405-64), later Pope Pius II, like Colet an educational reformer; see W. K. Ferguson, "An Unpublished Letter of John Colet . . . ," *AHR,* XXXIX (1934), 696-99; see also

TLS correspondence by V. Flynn (September 12, 1935) and R. Weiss (September 26, 1935), which shows that, in addition, Thomas More's patron, Archbishop Morton, was in Rome in 1495. That Colet may have visited Florence about 1495 is apparently pure surmise: see Frederick Seebohm, *The Oxford Reformers* (London, 1887), p. 21, and the "presumption" that Colet heard Savonarola, by W. E. Campbell, *Erasmus* (London, 1949), pp. 19-20. Savonarola preached peace but was also known to exhort to violence on behalf of reform: see P. Villari, *Life and Times of Savonarola*, trans. L. Villari (New York, 1893), I, 278-98 *passim*.

Lollards: this argument, first made by Seebohm (*The Oxford Reformers*, pp. 258-67), then cautiously enlarged by J. H. Lupton (*A Life of John Colet* [London, 1887], p. viii), was stressed (without new evidence) as probable by Ernest Nys, "Quâtre utopistes au XVIe siècle," *Revue de droit international et de législation comparée*, XXI (1889), 65-76. At best it seems a bare hypothesis: see Lange, pp. 148-49. The idea is unsupported by evidence on Lollard popular preaching, although some such preachers dwelt satirically on the gloriousness of England's military past as contrasted with the degenerate present: see G. R. Owst, *Literature and Pulpit in Medieval England* (Cambridge, Eng., 1933), pp. 70, 330-38 *passim*. Lollard preachers were, however, likely to express doubts as to the justice of military campaigns, "very probably on religious grounds": see G. R. Owst, *Preaching in Medieval England* (Cambridge, Eng., 1926), p. 205. These scattered allusions can hardly prove that a chain of Lollard antiwar ideas reached directly to Colet.

7. A. Hyma, "Erasmus and the Oxford Reformers (1495-1503)," *passim*.

8. A. Hyma, "The Continental Origins of English Humanism," *HLQ*, IV (1940), 4, 22.

9. Erasmus' biographers tend to offer only notes on his thought concerning war: e.g., Preserved Smith, *Erasmus* (New York, 1923), pp. 108, 194-96 (cited hereafter as Smith); A. Hyma, *The Youth of Erasmus* (Ann Arbor, Mich., 1930), pp. 216-17. Hyma asserted that Erasmus' mature attitudes toward toleration and peace were "natural" in a follower of Wessel Gansfort, a leader in the Brethren of the Common Life (*The Christian Renaissance* [New York, (1935)], p. 230); see P. Duhamel, "The Oxford Lectures of John Colet," pp. 494 f. Political historians do not often relate his ideas on war closely to Tudor humanism: e.g., P. S. Allen, *The Age of Erasmus* (Oxford, 1914), pp. 164-66; A. Renaudet, *Érasme* (Paris, 1926), p. 29; W. K. Ferguson, "The Attitude of Erasmus Toward Toleration," in *Persecution and Liberty* (New York, 1931), pp. 171-81; L. K. Born, "Erasmus on Political Ethics," *Pol. Sci. Quart.*, XLIII (1928), 520-43 *passim*; A. Renaudet, *Machiavel* (Paris, 1942), pp. 75-79; A. Renaudet, *Érasme et l'Italie* (Geneva, 1954), pp. 176-86. See, in contrast, Fritz Caspari, "Erasmus on the Social Functions of Christian Humanism," *JHI*,

VIII (1947), 78-106 *passim*, and Caspari's *Humanism and the Social Order in Tudor England* (Chicago, 1954), pp. 28-49 *passim* (cited hereafter as Caspari).

10. Allen, *The Age of Erasmus*, p. 164.

11. *The Epistles of Erasmus*, trans. F. M. Nichols (London, 1901-18), I, 82 (cited hereafter as *EN*); *EE*, 39.125-38.

12. Erasmus, *Opera omnia*, ed. J. Clericus (Leiden, 1703-6), V. 1239-62 (cited hereafter as *EO*); Smith, p. 14.

13. *EE*, 39.35-50; Hyma, *Youth of Erasmus*, pp. 207-17 *passim*; see *EN*, I, 65.

14. Bush, *Classical Influences in Renaissance Literature*, p. 7.

15. *EN*, I, 71; *EE*, 29.35-38; *Letters of Cicero*, trans. E. Shuckburgh (London, 1904), I, 102.

16. *EO*, VIII, 545E-552B, trans. Hyma, in *Youth of Erasmus*, pp. 216-17. See Pico della Mirandola, "Oration on the Dignity of Man," in *The Renaissance Philosophy of Man*, ed. Cassirer *et al.*, pp. 215-56; H. Baker, *The Dignity of Man* (Cambridge, Mass., 1947), p. 273.

17. Hyma, *Youth of Erasmus*, pp. 216-17.

18. See C. R. Thompson, *The Translations of Lucian by Erasmus and St. Thomas More* (Ithaca, N. Y., 1940), and Mesnard, pp. 128 ff.

19. J. W. Mackail, *Erasmus Against War* (Boston, 1907), p. xxiii (cited hereafter as *EAW*); T. C. Appelt, *Studies in the Contents and Sources of Erasmus' "Adagia"* (Chicago, 1942), pp. 48-64 *passim*. Even in the 1513 edition Erasmus' comment filled only four lines (*Adagiorum chiliades tres* [Basel, August, 1513], p. 150).

20. Hyma, "Erasmus and the Oxford Reformers (1495-1503)," p. 71.

21. Renaudet, *Érasme et l'Italie*, p. 32. Cf. Hyma, *The Christian Renaissance*, p. 230; in contrast see E. F. Rice, Jr., "Erasmus and the Religious Tradition, 1495-1499," *JHI*, XI (1950), 387-411; Robert P. Adams, "Erasmus' Ideas of his Rôle as a Social Critic *ca.* 1480-1500," *Renaissance News*, XI (1958), 11-16.

Chapter Four

1. A. Salomon, "Democracy and Religion in the Work of Erasmus," *Review of Religion*, XIV (1950), 228. Erasmus' more mature thought on war and peace has received attention, but few have tried to relate it to his over-all English relationship. See: H. Durand de Laur, *Érasme précurseur et initiateur de l'esprit moderne* (Paris, 1872), I, 106; II, 459-528 *passim*; L. Enthoven, "Erasmus Weltburger oder Patriot?" *Neue Jahrbücher für das klassische Altertum*, XV (1912), 205-15; P. S. Allen, *The Age of Erasmus* (Oxford, 1914), pp. 164-66; Lange, pp. 146-76; R. H. Murray, *Erasmus and Luther* (London, 1920), *passim*; E. T. Kuiper, "Erasmus als politiek Propagandist," *Tijdschrift voor Geschiedenis*, XXXVII (1922),

147-67; A. de Iongh, *Erasmus' Denkbeelden over Staat en Rageering* (Amsterdam, 1927), pp. 93-110, 149-69 *passim;* L. K. Born, "Some Notes on the Political Theories of Erasmus," *JMH*, II (1930), 226-36; Erasmus' *The Education of a Christian Prince,* trans. L. K. Born (New York, 1936), pp. 15-23 (cited hereafter as *ECP*); C. R. Thompson, "Erasmus as Internationalist and Cosmopolitan," *Archiv für Reformationsgeschichte,* XLVI (1955), 167-95 *passim.* Caspari to date best establishes Erasmus' English contributions to the new learning and the social order in the sixteenth century.

2. See A. Renaudet, *Machiavel* (Paris, 1942), pp. 141 ff., 247-65, and Thompson, "Erasmus as Internationalist and Cosmopolitan," *passim.*

3. *EE*, 152.33-38. Allen dates it 1501 though it is marked May 4, 1498; it was clearly intended to preface the Cicero but was first printed in 1520; see Cicero, *De officiis* (Paris, 1535), sig. Aii^v.

4. E.g., *EN*, III, 129-30; See also in 1517 *EE*, 586.194-97. How sharply these humanists were turning against dominant medieval traditions can be seen by contrasting George Cary, *The Medieval Alexander* (New York, 1956), pp. 95-98, 227.

5. First edition, Antwerp, 1503; editions in 1509, 1515; after this new editions almost every year; translated into seven languages by 1536. See Smith, pp. 57-58.

6. *Enchiridion militis Christiani* [trans. Wm. Tyndale?] (London, 1905), pp. 47, 54 (cited hereafter as *EMC*).

7. Emerton, *Erasmus* (New York, 1889), pp. 118-19.

8. *EO*, IV, 507-52. He had worked on it since September 28, [1503] (*EN*, I, 355-58); printed at Antwerp, February, 1504, it was reprinted *ca.* 1506 and in many editions of the *Institutio principis Christiani* from April, 1516, on (*EE*, 179).

9. *EN*, I, 363 ff.; see Caspari, p. 45, on Erasmus' use of flattery.

10. See Chambers, pp. 58-74.

11. A. W. Reed, "Sir Thomas More," in *The Social and Political Ideas of Some Great Thinkers of the Renaissance and the Reformation,* ed. F. Hearnshaw (London, 1925), p. 138; Sidney Lee in *DNB*, XIII (1888), 877.

12. *Utopia,* ed. J. H. Lupton, (Oxford, 1895), pp. xlix-li (cited hereafter as *MUL*); *Civitas Dei,* Book XIX, chap. xiv; Book XXII, chap. xxx.

13. Thomas Stapleton, *The Life . . . of Sir Thomas More* (1588), trans. P. E. Hallett (London, 1928), pp. 8-9; on his sources see Chambers, pp. 38-39.

14. F. Seebohm, *The Oxford Reformers* (London, 1887), p. 143.

15. *The English Works of Sir Thomas More,* ed. W. E. Campbell *et al.* (London, 1931), I, 345-62 (cited hereafter as *MEW-C*); Chambers, pp. 92-93.

16. G. R. Owst, *Preaching in Medieval England* (Cambridge, Eng., 1926), pp. 206-8.

17. J. H. Lupton, *A Life of John Colet* (London, 1887), p. viii.

18. Thomas More, *The Latin Epigrams*, ed. and trans. L. Bradner and C. Lynch (Chicago, 1953), p. xi (cited hereafter as *MLE*).

19. J. A. K. Thompson, "Erasmus in England," Bibliothek Warburg, *Vorträge, 1930-1931* (Leipzig, 1932), p. 67; C. R. Thompson, *The Translations of Lucian by Erasmus and St. Thomas More* (Ithaca, N. Y., 1940), p. 44. See also Mesnard, pp. 128 ff.

20. *Lucian's Dialogues*, trans. H. Williams (London, 1888), iv, pp. 92-93.

21. *Ibid.*, x, pp. 112-14.

22. *Ibid.*, xiii, pp. 120-23; see also xii and xiv, which satirize conquerors, and xviii and xix, which ridicule usual motives of great wars.

23. Trans. in LB, p. 144.

24. *Lucian's Dialogues*, trans. Williams, p. xviii.

25. Thomas More, *The Dialogue Concerning Tyndale*, ed. W. Campbell (London, 1927), p. 5 (cited hereafter as *MDT*).

26. C. R. Thompson, *The Translations of Lucian by Erasmus and . . . More*, p. 44.

27. *EE*, 999 *passim*. Many cannot be specifically dated; those pinned down fall within 1509-19 (*MLE*, p. xii).

28. *MLE*, pp. xxvii-xxviii; see, e.g., No. 1.23-38 and 89-102 (pp. 138-43), plus the comments on tyrannical kings in No. 62 (p. 162).

29. Russell Ames, *Citizen Thomas More and his Utopia* (Princeton, N. J., 1949), pp. 181-84 (cited hereafter as Ames).

30. Other classic satirists of war and its follies were widely known by some humanists of the Renaissance, the Latin perhaps better than the Greek. Horace did praise the Romans' "martial courage" and victories of loyal over seditious troops (*Odes*, trans. C. Bennett [Loeb Classical Library], Ode iii.3.5 and Epode ix). But the fratricidal folly of Roman civil war prompted most somber lyrics (*ibid.*, ii.1.29-38); it is worse than strife of wild beasts: "Does some blind frenzy drive us on? . . ." (*ibid.*, Epode vii). Civil war more than northern barbarians endangers Rome (*ibid.*, Epode xvi). And Horace mourned departure of the great *Pax Romana*, during which at least there was peace at the empire's heart (*ibid.*, Ode iv.5, 15).

Juvenal denounced his time, asserting that "in these days there is more amity among serpents than among men . . . ," that man is inferior to beasts in virtue because of his addiction to warfare, and he attacked the abuse of reason to invent weapons (*Juvenal and Persius*, trans. G. Ramsey [Loeb Classical Library], Satire xv.145-74). Bitterly he attacked the vain thirst for military "glory" and the power lusts of Hannibal: "What then was his [Hannibal's] end? Alas for glory! A conquered man, he flees headlong into exile, and there he sits, a mighty and marvellous suppliant. . . . On! On!

thou madman, and race over the wintry Alps, that thou mayst be the delight of schoolboys and supply declaimers with a theme!" (*ibid.*, Satire x.136-89 *passim*). Both Juvenal and Persius satirized the ignorance and coarseness of the professional soldiery (*ibid.*, Juvenal, Satire xvi; Persius, Satire iii.77-87).

31. Smith, pp. 64-65; A. Renaudet, *Érasme et l'Italie* (Geneva, 1954), pp. 41-109.

32. November 16, 1506; *EN*, I, 420; Smith, p. 106. See also the descriptive passages in Erasmus' Novum Testamentum (on Acta, V, 14), *EO*, VI, 455; and W. K. Ferguson (ed.), *Erasmi opuscula* (The Hague, 1933), p. 85.

33. With Caesar in mind, Cicero approved tyrannicide on grounds that it is morally right to exterminate a human monster who is destroying the basic bond of "nature" in human society (*De officiis* iii.6.32 and iii.21.83). Livy, who sought to display the ideal Rome of the Augustan *Pax Romana*, grimly asked whether more good or harm came to the state from the birth of Julius Caesar (cited by Seneca, *Quaest. nat.*, trans. Clarke [1910], v.18, pp. 212 ff.; *Livy*, trans. B. Foster [Loeb Classical Library], I, xiv). On Renaissance enthusiasm for Livy see *Livy*, Foster trans., I, xxix ff. Pliny, though admiring Caesar's "extreme vigour and quickness of spirit," admitted that the carnage caused by Caesar in the civil wars was "no special glory" to Caesar but in reality a very great injury to mankind. Pliny pointed out that Caesar himself in part realized as much, for he did not record his triumphs in that sanguinary strife, in which Pliny estimated that 1,192,000 (*sic*) Roman citizens died (Pliny, *The Naturall Historie*, trans. P. Holland [London, 1601], vii.25, p. 168L). Lucan painted Caesar as a "bloodthirsty ogre" (Lucan, *The Civil War*, trans. J. Duff [Loeb Classical Library], pp. xii-xiii). Classical accounts of war's horrors, including Lucan's, were often repeated in medieval epics and used by educators to teach the dangers of civil war: see J. Crosland, "Lucan in the Middle Ages," *MLR*, XXV (1930), 41-43.

34. Smith, p. 106; *Opera Hutteni* (Munich, 1859-70), I, 267, in H. Milman, *Savonarola, Erasmus, and Other Essays* (London, 1870), pp. 98-99.

35. Erasmus, *Adagiorum chiliades tres* (1508), I, xxxi, fol. 12r/v, cited in Dora and Erwin Panofsky, *Pandora's Box* (New York, 1956), pp. 14-18, as part of Erasmus' comment on "The fool gets wise after having been hurt."

36. May 27, 1509: *EN*, I, 456-59; for the story of Erasmus' first meeting with Henry, in 1499, when he was introduced by More, see *EN*, I, 201 ff. On Henry's early favors to Erasmus, see *EE*, I, 6.5-26. On the optimism in 1509, see Chambers, p. 100, and H. Fisher, *The History of England from the Accession of Henry VII to the Death of Henry VIII (1485-1547)* (London, 1934), pp. 158-60 (cited hereafter as Fisher).

37. *EE*, 215.68-69; Panofsky, *Pandora's Box*, p. 15.

38. R. Brown (ed.), *Calendar of State Papers . . . Venice,* (London, 1867), II, 11 (cited hereafter as *Cal. SP Ven.*).

39. See J. A. Williamson, *The Tudor Age* (London, 1953), pp. 62 ff.

40. [Edward] Hall, *Hall's Chronicle,* ed. Henry Ellis (London, 1809), pp. 493, 499 (cited hereafter as Hall).

41. "The Note . . . of . . . Ladie Kateryne," in *The Antiquarian Repertory,* ed. F. Grose *et al.* (London, 1808), II, 249-51.

42. *The English Works of John Fisher,* ed. J. Mayor (London, 1876), p. 269.

43. *Ibid.,* pp. 301, 303. Lady Margaret founded Christ's College and St. John's at Cambridge, and she helped to place friends of humanism in what became the peace party in Henry VIII's first councils (*DNB,* II, 48-49).

44. See *DNB;* also *Letters of Richard Fox 1485-1527,* ed. P. S. and H. M. Allen (Oxford, 1929); Thomas Fowler, *History of Corpus Christi College* (Oxford, 1893); *EE,* I, 416n.

45. Edmund Dudley, *The Tree of Commonwealth,* ed. D. Brodie (Cambridge, Eng., 1948), pp. 16, 50, 60-64. *The Tree* was written between July 18, 1509, and Dudley's execution, August 17, 1510.

46. *MLE,* pp. 141, 143n. Allen did not find that this ode was printed; the original copy presented to Henry VIII may be that in the B. M. Cotton MSS (Tit. D. IV) (*EE,* IV, 222n.).

47. E.g., A. Hyma, "Erasmus and the Oxford Reformers (1495-1503)," *Nederlandsch Archief voor Kerkgeschiedenis,* N.S., XXV (1932), 69-92, 97-134; Hyma, "Erasmus and the Oxford Reformers (1503-1519)," *Nederlandsch Archief voor Kerkgeschiedenis,* N.S., XXXVIII (1951), 65-85 *passim;* Hyma, "The Continental Origins of English Humanism," *HLQ,* IV (1940-41), 1-26 *passim.*

48. E.g., R. H. Tawney, *Religion and the Rise of Capitalism* (London, 1927), pp. 72-73.

49. C. R. Thompson, "Erasmus as Internationalist and Cosmopolitan," p. 167.

50. A. L. Rowse, *The English Spirit* (New York, 1945), p. 75.

51. H. H. Hudson in his edition of *The Praise of Folly* (Princeton, N. J., 1941), p. 130 (cited hereafter as *EPF*). As satirist of inventors, Folly of course seems to mock the Prometheus myth, in which invention is the key to "progress." Though more literally accurate, Hudson's translation lacks the vivid energy of the 1549 version by Sir Thomas Chaloner: *The Praise of Folly,* trans. Sir Thomas Chaloner, ed. J. Ashbee, London, 1921 (cited hereafter as *EPF-C*). See also *Encomium Moriae* (1515), facsimile edition by H. Schmid (Basel, 1931).

52. See Lucretius *De rerum natura* v.988-1009; Ovid *Metamorphoses* i.76-215, and Pythagoras' account, given by Ovid, *ibid.* xv.75-142; Seneca *Epistulae morales* 90.4-16 etc.; Plutarch, "Of Eating Flesh (whether it be

lawful or no)," *The Philosophie . . . called, the Morals,* trans. P. Holland (London, 1603), pp. 572-74 *passim.* For these texts and other classical parallels see LB, pp. 23-102, 263-79. In the essay cited, Plutarch treats the beginning of bloodshed as dating from rupture of a presumed primitive peace between men and beasts, after which men became progressively brutalized, ending by enjoying what at first seemed cruel or "unnatural." Erasmus' whole process of reasoning could easily be derived from Seneca: *Ep. mor.* 90.41, 108.17-20, 75.11-12; "A Treatise of Anger," *Workes,* trans. Lodge (London, 1614), pp. 510-30 *passim; Ep. mor.* 94.61-66. Much similar reasoning appears in Seneca's *De beneficiis.*

53. W. E. Campbell, *Erasmus, Tyndale and More* (London, 1949), pp. 52-54.

54. L. von Ranke, *The History of the Popes,* trans. E. Foster (London, 1889), I, 40-41.

55. *EPF,* pp. 111-13 *passim;* Matthew 26:52, Mark 14:47, Luke 22:50.

56. See C. A. Beard, *The Devil Theory of War* (New York, 1936).

57. See Leonard Dean in his translation of *The Praise of Folly* (Chicago, 1946), pp. 16-30.

Chapter Five

1. See Robert P. Adams, "Designs by More and Erasmus for a New Social Order," *Studies in Philology,* XLII (1945), 131-45 (cited hereafter as Adams [1945]); D. Bush, *Classical Influences in Renaissance Literature* (Cambridge, Mass., 1952), p. 7.

2. J. M. Berdan, *Early Tudor Poetry* (New York, 1920), pp. 43-45; see the 1531 praise in *Cal. SP Ven.,* IV, 293.

3. A. F. Pollard, *Wolsey* (London, 1929), pp. 10-11 (cited hereafter as Pollard).

4. *MUL,* p. xxxviii; A. W. Reed, *Early Tudor Drama* (London, 1926), pp. 11-12; Chambers, pp. 139-40.

5. Fisher, p. 140; Chambers, pp. 103-8.

6. See Pollard, *passim.* Fox, diplomat and friend of the new learning, executed many peace missions under Henry VII. In November, 1487, he helped negotiate a truce between Henry VII and James III of Scotland. Five years later he is mentioned first among English ambassadors making the treaty of Étaples which ended the siege of Boulogne and the war with Charles VIII of France. He was a prime executive of Henry VII's most notable act of diplomacy, the treaty (1498-1503) for permanent peace and an intermarriage between the crowns of England and Scotland, although this union was only completed in 1603. Warham was Chancellor of Oxford University from 1506 until his death in 1532.

7. December 6, 1514, G. A. Bergenroth (ed.), *Calendar of the Letters . . . and State Papers . . . between England and Spain* (London, 1866——), II, 249 (cited hereafter as *Cal. LP Spain*).

8. J. H. Lupton, *A Life of John Colet* (London, 1909), *passim; EE*, I, 459; *EN*, II, 8; Chambers, pp. 7, 102.

9. A. F. Pollard, *Encyclopaedia Britannica* (11th ed.), XXVIII, 779.

10. *De rerum inuenteribus* (Basel, 1532), pp. 111-12. First edition 1499. Polydore Vergil said of the unknown inventor that "he might for this Abominable device, have been evil spoken of and cursed, whilst the World lasts" (*A Pleasant . . . History of the First Inventers,* trans. anon. [London, 1685], p. 42).

11. Polydore Vergil, *The Anglica historia . . . 1485-1537,* trans. D. Hay (London, 1950), pp. 161-63 *passim* (cited hereafter as Polydore Vergil).

12. Pollard, *Encyclopaedia Britannica* (11th ed.), XXVIII, 779.

13. George Cavendish, *The Life and Death of Cardinal Wolsey* (Boston, 1905), p. 11. The work was done between 1527 and 1557. On the other hand, G. A. Bergenroth viewed Henry's advisers as notoriously corrupt and of slight aid to a self-indulgent, inexperienced prince (*Cal. LP Spain,* II, xviii-li *passim*).

14. *The Tree of Commonwealth,* ed. D. Brodie (Cambridge, Eng., 1948), p. 50.

15. Published at Paris, June 9, 1511, the *Moriae encomium* became an enormous best-seller, with five editions within a year of its first publication, one (July, 1512) revised by Erasmus. The Holbein illustrations and Lystrius' notes were added in 1515. By 1522 more than 20,000 copies had been sold. Forty editions appeared before Erasmus' death in 1536, and the satire was reprinted often in the sixteenth century, including translations into French (1517, printed first in 1520), German (1520), Italian (1539), English (1549), and Dutch (1560). See *Bibliotheca Belgica,* 2nd Ser., Vol. XIII (Ghent, 1891-1923); Smith, pp. 123-26.

16. *EN*, II, 24. The *De ratione studii,* written before December, 1508, was printed in 1511 without Erasmus' consent. In it he considered *inter alia* the educational value of study on wars of antiquity for students seeking understanding of classical poets and orators. He held that there is "no discipline . . . whether music, architecture, agriculture, or war—which may not prove of use to the teacher" who expounds the classics. The ancient art of war may also illuminate geography and history. Neither in 1508 nor later did he praise study of the art of war for its own sake. See *Erasmus Concerning the Aim of Education,* trans. W. H. Woodward (Cambridge, Eng., 1904), p. 168 (cited hereafter as *ECE*); *EE*, I, 121n., 193n.

17. (London, May 15, 1515), *EE*, 333.56-58. Erasmus seems to find that Henry VIII was as taken by surprise at war's outbreak as he was: "*. . . siquidem cum reliquos amicos, tum Regem ipsum, aurei saeculi parentem, mox secuta bellorum procella Musis omnibus praeripuit. . . .*" See Pollard, p. 17.

18. *Journals of the House of Lords* (n.p., n.d.), I (1509-77), 10; Pollard, p. 17. Hall (p. 526), usually sure that what Henry wants is right if

he says so, thought Warham showed how correct the King was: Warham "declared how Justice was put by, and peace turned into war. And there upon he showed, how the French king would do no Justice, in restoring the King [Henry] his right inheritance, wherefore, for lack of Justice, peace of necessity must turn to war."

19. "Machiavelli and the Elizabethans," *Proceedings of the British Academy*, XIV (1928), 56; M. Praz, *The Flaming Heart* (New York, 1958), p. 97.

20. Lupton, *A Life of John Colet*, pp. 178-88 *passim*.

21. "The Sermon of Doctor Colete," in *ibid.*, pp. 293-304. Pynson printed it (1512 N.S. [*STC* 5545]). Lupton (p. 293n.) thought the English translation Colet's own work (printed 1530 [*STC* 5550]); other editions in 1534, 1577.

22. Lupton, *A Life of John Colet*, p. 178; see James Gairdner, *Lollardy and the Reformation in England (1300-1555)* (London, 1908-13), III, 282; F. Seebohm, *The Oxford Reformers* (London, 1887), p. 242.

23. Lupton, *A Life of John Colet*, pp. 189-203 *passim*. Though aiding Colet, Warham even so did not promptly vindicate him but apparently let a three-month suspension from preaching go by: see P. S. Allen, "Dean Colet and Archbishop Warham," *EHR*, XVII (1902), 303-6; Colet to Erasmus (October 20, [1514]), *EE*, 314. This sermon has apparently not survived.

24. *EC*, pp. 41-43.

25. Pollard, p. 18; see also J. S. Brewer, *The Reign of Henry VIII from His Accession to the Death of Wolsey*, ed. J. Gairdner (London, 1884), I, 12-22 (cited hereafter as Brewer).

26. (September 9, 1517), *EN*, III, 46; similarly to Wolsey, *EN*, III, 50.

27. Polydore Vergil, p. 199; Brewer, I, 24; Fisher, pp. 178-79; Pollard, p. 18.

28. This exists only in Erasmus' epitome of June 13, 1521, *EE*, 1211; citations are to *EC*.

29. On this (and Henry VIII's worry about the "rough soldiers"), cf. "The Soldier and the Carthusian," *The Colloquies of Erasmus*, trans. H. Bailey, ed. E. Johnson (London, 1878), I, 261.

30. J. S. Brewer (ed.), *Letters and Papers . . . of the Reign of Henry VIII* (London, 1862———), I, 1677 (*ca.* March 11, 1513) (cited hereafter as *LP*).

31. C. S. Lewis, *English Literature in the Sixteenth Century, Excluding Drama* (Oxford, 1954), p. 159 (cited hereafter as Lewis). The myth seems based on a note in Bishop Matthew Parker's *De antiquitate Britannicae ecclesiae* (n.p., 1572), pp. 353.38-354.15 (*STC* 19292). If Parker had the story from contemporary witnesses, he names none. From later editions of Parker the story got into Samuel Knight, *The Life of Dr. John Colet* (London, 1724), p. 207, and thence has been rather uncritically repeated to

date. I think no close student of the Oxford Reformers credits the story: see Lupton, *A Life of John Colet*, p. 192; Seebohm, *The Oxford Reformers*, pp. 266-67; Chambers, p. 113.

32. (Mainz, April 26, 1520), *Epistolae aliquot eruditorum virorum* (Basel, 1520), pp. 139-41. Erasmus is praised for making known throughout Europe the great talents of English humanists—Colet, More, Mountjoy, Linacre, and Tunstall. The letter shows contemporary German recognition that before 1520 English humanism had a golden age.

33. *Erasmi opuscula,* ed. W. K. Ferguson (The Hague, 1933), pp. 35-37. Ferguson thinks it done in England before the Pope's death.

34. A. L. Rowse, *The English Spirit* (New York, 1945), p. 77.

35. *Erasmi opuscula,* pp. 38-124; trans. J. A. Froude, *Life and Letters of Erasmus* (London, 1894), pp. 140-60. The argument for Erasmus' authorship (which he never acknowledged) seems solid: see Ferguson, *Erasmi opuscula,* pp. 41-45; C. Thompson, "Erasmus as Internationalist and Cosmopolitan," *Archiv für Reformations geschichte,* XLVI (1955), 167-95 *passim.* Erasmus apparently passed copies around among intimate friends, like More (*EE,* 502.9-12), but was either unwilling or afraid to have it printed. Yet it was known in Basel Erasmus circles by August, 1516, and was first heard of as printed early in 1517, with many later editions, almost all n.p., n.d. When it was in print, Erasmus characteristically expressed annoyance that people attributed it to him (*EN,* II, 610-12; *EE,* 622.12-30). A. Renaudet, *Érasme et l'Italie* (Geneva, 1954), pp. 112, 122n., argues against Erasmus' authorship but concedes that echoes of the satire appear in Erasmus' acknowledged later work.

36. See *Epistolae obscurorum virorum,* trans. F. G. Stokes (London, 1925), pp. xv, xlv-xlviii *passim,* and the casual satiric remarks on wars on pp. 371, 405-9, 423-24, 490.

37. (*Ca.* March 11, 1513), *LP,* I, 1677; see also *ibid.,* 1682, 1718, 1719, 1738.

38. Polydore Vergil, p. 199; Fisher, p. 179.

39. Polydore Vergil, pp. 209-15; Pollard, p. 19; Brewer, I, 24-32. *LP,* I, 2053, shows "Master Almoner" (Wolsey) commanding 200, Fox and Ruthal 100 each. Fox became a casualty: "much hurt by the kick of his mule; for some days he could neither sit nor stand" (*LP,* I, 2391). The *Erasymus of London* was among the hired ships (*LP,* I, 2304).

40. See *Poetical Works,* ed. A. Dyce (London, 1843), I, 182-90, as well as his verses patriotically cheering victory over the French (I, 191).

41. *The Poems of . . . Erasmus,* ed. C. Reedijk (Leiden, 1956), p. 304. First edition in *Erasmi epigrammata* (Basel, 1518), p. 353; see C. Butler, *The Life of Erasmus* (London, 1875), pp. 116-17.

42. *MLE,* No. 228; Hoyt Hudson, *The Epigram in the English Renaissance* (Princeton, N. J., 1947), pp. 49-52 (cited hereafter as Hudson).

43. Polydore Vergil, p. 187; *Letters and Papers Relating to the War with France 1512-1513*, ed. A. Spont (London, 1897), pp. xxv-xxvi, Documents 30, 33, 36, 39; Fisher, p. 177.

44. Bush, *Classical Influences in Renaissance Literature*, p. 11.

45. *Ibid.*, p. 7.

46. *Holinshed's Chronicles*, ed. H. Ellis (London, 1808), III, 573; Fisher, pp. 191-93; Pollard, p. 19.

47. See A. L. Rowse, *The English Spirit* (New York, 1945), pp. 48-51.

48. *MLE*, No. 124; see also Nos. 14, 62, 92, 96, 102, 103, 144, 185, 211, 222, 227. There are twenty-three epigrams on kings and government (*MLE*, pp. xxvii ff.). The datable epigrams fall between 1509 and 1519 (*MLE*, p. xii).

49. E.g., Chambers, pp. 115-18; R. W. Chambers, "On the Continuity of English Prose . . . ," in Nicholas Harpsfield, *The Life and Death of Sr Thomas Moore*, ed. E. V. Hitchcock (London, 1932), pp. xlv-clxxiv *passim* (cited hereafter as Harpsfield). With More, contrast the anonymous historian who in 1513 encouraged Henry VIII to emulate Henry V in French conquests: see *The First English Life of King Henry the Fifth*, ed. C. Kingsford (Oxford, 1911), pp. ix-x.

50. *MEW-C*, I, 42-53; Chambers, p. 116.

51. Polydore Vergil (p. 251) tells how Wolsey, when in 1518 it suited him to make peace and to relinquish Calais, went out of his way "when various discussions took place, as they do, at lunch and dinner," deliberately turned the conversation to overseas topics, and often said, "Why should we value so much that little continental place Calais, which is more loss to us than profit? Would God . . . that we might be dispossessed of the place!" See also the comments of the Venetian ambassador on Henry VIII in 1519: "His father left him ten millions of ready money in gold, of which he was supposed to have spent one half in the war against France . . ." (*Cal. SP Ven.*, II, p. 559).

52. *EN*, II, 122-23. After the capture of Thérouenne, the first French town taken by the English since 1453, by Henry VIII's orders the walls were leveled, to strip the city of protection "lest they [the English] themselves should be compelled to restore" and garrison it. "But at the same time that it lost its walls, the unhappy place was almost entirely destroyed by fire" (Polydore Vergil, p. 215; see also Fisher, p. 183).

53. (1532), *EE*, 2599.1-27. Allen dates the conversation in early June, 1514 (*EE*, 294n.).

54. See Adams (1945), pp. 131-45.

55. J. S. Phillimore, "The Arrest of Humanism in England," *Dublin Review*, 153 (1913), 1-26; Chambers, pp. 351-400 *passim*. The Phillimore-Chambers thesis of "arrest" is vigorously disputed by Douglas Bush, "Tudor Humanism and Henry VIII," *Toronto University Quarterly*, VII

(1937-38), 162-77, and his *The Renaissance and English Humanism* (Toronto, 1939), pp. 73 ff.

56. *EE*, 333.55-59; see also Pollard, p. 17.

Chapter Six

1. P. S. Allen, *Erasmus* (Oxford, 1934), pp. 62-66 (cited hereafter as Allen [1934]).

2. *Ibid.*; J. W. Mackail's introduction to his edition of *EAW*, pp. ix-xxiv. *EAW* gives a modernized *Bellum Erasmi*, [trans. Richard Taverner?] (London, 1533-[34]) (*STC* 10449). For the letter (London, January 5, 1513) prefatory to the 1515 Basel edition, see *EE*, 269; here Erasmus speaks of the *Adages'* development and praises Warham, almost the only English patron who gave him substantial aid; *Bibliotheca Erasmiana*, comp. F. Vander Haeghen *et al.* (Ghent, 1897-1907), *Adagia*, pp. 91-92 (cited hereafter as *BE-A*). Translations used for adages are variously by Allen (1934), p. 64; Smith, p. 200; and from H. Durand de Laur, *Érasme précurseur et initiateur de l'esprit moderne* (Paris, 1872), II, 525-26.

3. *EO*, II, 775D-E. See Lange, pp. 158-59. Cf. the very similar statement by Hythlodaye at the end of *Utopia*, Book I. See *STC* 10507: *A Scorneful Image or Monstrus Shape . . . called, Sileni alcibiadis* [London, 154?], sigs. A8ʳ, B5ʳ-6ʳ, Ciʳ-2ᵛ, D5ʳ-7ʳ.

4. *Adagiorum chiliades tres* [Basel, August, 1513], p. 150; *BE-A*, pp. 90-91; 1515 text in *EO*, II, 951-70. See Pindar *Isthmian* 7.110 and Wallace Caldwell, *Hellenic Conceptions of Peace* (New York, 1919), p. 78.

5. *EE*, I, 37; in *EAW*, p. 57, he mentions this "Antipolemus," written at Rome (*ca.* 1509) for Pope Julius II.

6. See R. W. Battenhouse, "Hamlet's Apostrophe on Man," *PMLA*, LXVI (1951), 1073-1113 *passim*.

7. The idea that social calamity may be man-made obviously involves the question: has man free will? Erasmus' attitude indicates his answer: yes. See Smith, pp. 337-56. Erasmus' 1524 book on free will, of course, by then involved controversy with Luther.

8. That the "true Christian writers" are those like Jerome and Tertullian may be inferred from the fact that the subsequent authority of Augustine (A.D. 354-430), who declared that war might be "just" for Christians, became decisive for the later church: see R. F. Wright, *Medieval Internationalism* (London, 1930), pp. 133-81.

9. See Guillaume Budé's similar remarks in the letters to Thomas Lupset which prefaced both 1518 editions of *Utopia* (*MUL*, pp. lxxxiv-lxxxvi).

10. See Cicero's main argument against Caesar, *De officiis* iii.

11. *EN*, II, 183-90 *passim*; *EE*, 334.45-61 and 84-85.

12. More's royal commision, dated May 7, 1515 (*The Correspondence of Sir Thomas More*, ed. E. F. Rogers [Princeton, N. J., 1947], No. 10;

[cited hereafter as *MC*]). On May 8 the Court of Aldermen gave More leave for a deputy to serve for him as undersheriff during the embassy. Chambers thought More probably began work on *Utopia* in 1513-14. The best analysis of its scheme of composition is that of J. H. Hexter, *More's Utopia* (Princeton, N. J., 1952) (cited hereafter as Hexter), who finds (p. 26) that most of Book II was done in Flanders, "probably while More was waiting . . . for Charles' councilors to make the decisions on which his mission depended," the rest "later in London some time after More's return. . . ." See also Chambers, pp. 115-20.

13. *EN*, II, 199 and 241-42 (February [18], [1516]).

14. J. Huizinga, *Erasmus*, trans. F. Hopman (New York, 1924), pp. 121 f.

15. See the 1520 letter by Hattstein, in *Epistolae aliquot eruditorum virorum* (Basel, 1520), pp. 139-41.

16. *EE*, 304.54-55; *MC*, No. 15 (October 21, [1515]); Chambers, pp. 253-54.

17. (June 19, [1516]), *EN*, II, 282; *EE*, 421.79-93. From Paris on July 7 Budé wrote that in Parisian literary circles the "*Sileni* passage and some others" were the "most talked about" (*EN*, II, 301).

18. See *BE-A, passim*. The complete *Adagiorum chiliades* had thirty-five editions, 1537-1603. As a pamphlet, *Bellum Erasmi* was printed only twice between 1536 and 1600. In the *Adages* both "Dulce bellum inexpertis" and "Sileni Alcibiadis" were frequently censored, especially during 1575-1600 (*BE-A*, pp. 155, 180). The extent of censoring between 1515-36 is not fully clear (*BE-A*, pp. 90-119). After 1517 Froben and others produced "diverse editions" of the *Sileni* and the *Scarabaeus* (*EE*, II, 254n.).

Chapter Seven

1. See Ruth Kelso, *The Doctrine of the English Gentleman* (Urbana, Ill., 1929) (cited hereafter as Kelso).

2. See P. S. Allen's ambiguous criticism of Erasmus' statements on the time of composition: e.g., it may have been written by May, 1515 (*EE*, II, 161n.), or between January and March, 1516 (*EE*, II, 205n.). When Erasmus said he had the work "*in manibus*" by the earlier date, I think he meant that he had it finished or nearly so. This inference gains strength from the fact that the work makes no reference to Marignano (September 13, 1515). And the first proposal that he become councilor to Charles, to whom the work is dedicated, "had perhaps been made in May, 1515" (*EE*, II, 161n.).

3. E.g., Hexter, pp. 62-64. Erasmus' pursuit of the ideal of "humanity" is treated as a key to his thinking by Caspari, pp. 32-49; he finds (p. 36) Erasmus' humanism directly opposed to the *realpolitik* characteristic of Machiavelli's *Prince*.

4. *EN*, II, 250. See also *ECP*, pp. 133-36.

5. "Glory," in J. Burckhardt, *The Civilization of the Renaissance in Italy*, trans. S. Middlemore (2nd ed.; London, 1928), Part II, chap. ii.

6. *Ibid.*, pp. 4-128 *passim*; J. W. Allen, *A History of Political Thought in the Sixteenth Century* (New York, 1928), Part IV; M. Cockle, *A Bibliography of English Military Books up to 1642 and of Contemporary Foreign Works*, ed. H. Cockle (London, 1900); see also the military items in Kelso. One recalls ironically how much of his career Leonardo da Vinci devoted to military engineering.

7. *EN*, II, 247-48; *EE*, 396.377-81; Chambers, p. 121.

8. Pollard, pp. 111-24, is here used for facts on diplomatic-military affairs. Personal details on Francis are from Jules Isaac, *Encyclopaedia Britannica* (11th ed.).

9. Sebastian Giustinian, *Four Years at the Court of Henry VIII. Selection of Despatches Written by the Venetian Ambassador, Sebastian Giustinian . . . to the Signory of Venice, January 12th, 1515, to July 26th, 1519*, trans. Rawdon Brown (London, 1854), I, 212 (cited hereafter as Giustinian).

Chapter Eight

1. *MUL*, pp. 45-56 *passim*; Fortescue, *De laudibus legum Angliae*, chap. xiii, in which Fortescue "positively exults in the greater prevalence of robbery in England as compared with France and Scotland as a proof of the high spirit of the people" (C. Plummer in his edition of *The Governance of England* [Oxford, 1885], p. 100). On Fortescue and More's criticism of monarchy, see Mesnard, pp. 144 ff.

2. *MUL*, p. 47; see John Colet, *An Exposition*, trans. J. Lupton (London, 1873), p. 87n.: "In June, 1497, there was fought the battle of Blackheath. In September . . . [1497] Perkin Warbeck landed in Cornwall, and was joined by many thousands who had lost relations and friends in the fierce fight at Blackheath, and who were anxious for revenge. In the winter, and, it is possible, whilst these Lectures were being delivered, the prisoners taken after . . . Taunton were being tried by Commissioners, of whom . . . [the] then Dean of St. Paul's was one."

3. Mario Praz, "Machiavelli and the Elizabethans," *Proceedings of the British Academy*, XIV (1928), 56. Some scientific aspects of More's thought are more fully set forward in Robert P. Adams, "The Social Responsibilities of Science in *Utopia*, *New Atlantis* and After," *JHI*, X (1949), 374-98 (cited hereafter as Adams [1949]), with focus on the different ideas of progress held by More and Bacon.

4. Henry S. Lucas, *The Renaissance and the Reformation* (New York, 1934), p. 398.

5. E.g., *The Utopia*, ed. H. Goitein (London, 1925), pp. 3-11, 18-20.

6. E.g., *Utopia*, ed. J. St. John (London, 1850), pp. iv-vi; *Utopia*, ed. J. C. Collins (Oxford, 1904), p. 125, 1.21.

7. *MUL*, pp. xlvii and 117n. See generally F. L. Baumann in *JMH*, IV (1932), 604-10.

8. See Karl Kautsky, *Thomas More and His Utopia* (1907), trans. H. Stenning (London, 1927); or Ames (1949), who treats *Utopia* largely as a "republican, bourgeois, and democratic" critique of decadent feudalism, done in "the interests of the 'best' aspects of rising capitalism" (pp. 6, 21, *et passim*); see R. H. Tawney, *Religion and the Rise of Capitalism* (1922) (London, 1927), pp. 72-73.

9. In F. Hearnshaw (ed.), *The Social and Political Ideas of some Great Thinkers of the Renaissance and the Reformation*, (London, 1925), pp. 139 ff., with concern especially for toleration of heretics.

10. Robert P. Adams, "The Philosophic Unity of More's *Utopia*," *Studies in Philology*, XXXVIII (1941), 45-65 (cited hereafter as Adams [1941]).

11. H. W. Donner, *Introduction to Utopia* (London, 1945), pp. 5, 11, *et passim* (cited hereafter as Donner).

12. Hexter, p. 80. He himself suggested serious difficulties: "More does not explicitly speak of pride very often in *Utopia*," (p. 80), although the Discourse is remarkable for its "intellectual coherence, . . . sureness of thought, . . . and the sense of clear purpose" (pp. 77, 80). To Hexter the medieval unity of Christendom was "largely mythological" (p. 76). One may agree but observe that the London Reformers were unaware of this, a perception of modern scholarship.

13. Caspari, pp. 50-75 *passim*. I cannot unqualifiedly agree that More's "moral justification of war . . . [follows and develops] the teachings of Aristotle and the Schoolmen." See Caspari's "Sir Thomas More and *Justum Bellum*," *Ethics*, LVI (1946), 306.

14. Edward Surtz, *The Praise of Wisdom* (Chicago, 1957), pp. 2, 13, 293 (cited hereafter as Surtz *PW*). By paralleling passages, he seeks to show More's continuity of the Schoolmen's teaching. He assumes on grounds of faith that More's works written after the *Utopia* may surely be used to throw light on it (p. 16). See also his *The Praise of Pleasure* (Cambridge, Mass., 1957), *passim*.

15. Adams (1949), pp. 381-82; Chambers, p. 125.

16. E.g., *MUL*, pp. li-liii; Hexter, pp. 83-84; Donner, p. 15 *et passim*; Caspari, pp. 58-61.

17. Adams (1941), pp. 45-48.

18. *MUL*, pp. xlix-li; *Civitas Dei*, Book XIX, chap. xiv; Book XXII, chap. xxx.

19. See *MUL*, p. xxxvii; Donner, pp. 27, 46.

20. *Amerigo Vespucci Letter to Piero Soderini . . . (1504)*, trans. G. Northup (Princeton, N. J., 1916) (cited hereafter as *AVS*).

21. *Mundus novus Letter to Lorenzo . . . de Medici*, trans. G. Northup

(Princeton, N. J., 1916), p. 6 (cited hereafter as *AVM*). On More's voyage reading, see Donner, pp. 27-29, 38, 46.

22. *AVM*, p. 7. For a contemporary woodcut showing these "beast-like" war practices, see leaf 6ʳ in *The "Dutch Vespucius." . . . the Letter of Vespucius . . . Describing His Third Voyage* [1501] (Providence, R. I., 1874).

23. Hexter, pp. 50-51. While I agree that More's irony and his chosen form (an imaginary travel) make it "unresolvably uncertain" what More's "own" opinions are in Book II of *Utopia*, I do not agree that therefore it becomes impossible to estimate his intentions in creating the satire. As evidence there remains the continuity of humanist thought which the present study seeks to represent as a unified whole.

24. See Boies Penrose, *Travel and Discovery in the Renaissance 1420-1620* (Cambridge, Mass., 1955), p. 78, and pp. 1-20 on medieval backgrounds.

25. For details, with an attempt to define the key word "nature" as More used it, see Adams (1941), *passim*.

26. *MUL*, p. 190n.; see Adams (1941), p. 62, n. 53.

27. *De finibus* iii.33.117. Compare Plutarch's essay, argued in Stoical terms, "That a man cannot live pleasantly according to the doctrine of Epicurus" (*Morals*, trans. P. Holland [London, 1603], pp. 580-605). Plutarch derided the Epicureans as anti-intellectuals who foolishly deprived themselves of the highest human pleasure (and that which the Utopians most enjoy)—full use of the natural gift of reason. Seneca's onslaught upon the Epicureans (*De beneficiis*, Book IV) would probably have been known to any humanist. For further classical parallels, see Adams (1945), pp. 136-39.

28. J. B. Bury, *The Idea of Progress* (London, 1920), p. 5.

29. See Richard F. Jones, *Ancients and Moderns* (St. Louis, 1936), pp. 23-42; George Williamson, "Mutability, Decay, and Seventeenth-Century Melancholy," *English Literary History*, II (1935), 121-51; Don C. Allen, "The Degeneration of Man and Renaissance Pessimism," *Studies in Philology*, XXV (1938), 202-7; Arnold Williams, "A Note on Pessimism in the Renaissance," *Studies in Philology*, XXXVI (1939), 243-46.

30. *MUL*, p. 217; Basil Willey, *The Seventeenth Century Background* (London, 1934), p. 35.

Chapter Ten

1. E.g., Esmé Wingfield-Stratford, *The Foundations of British Patriotism* (London, 1939), pp. 136-38.

2. *EN*, II, 499-500. On the pursuit of fame, see Ralph Roeder, *The Man of the Renaissance* (New York, 1933).

3. *LP*, II, 2, 2988; Chambers, pp. 154-67 *passim*.

4. *EN*, II, 559-61; *EE*, 584.25-37 (Allen thought the "puppet-show" meant the duties of following Maximilian in the Netherlands).

5. J. A. Gee, *The Life and Works of Thomas Lupset* (New Haven, Conn., 1928), p. 87 (cited hereafter as Gee); on Erasmus' gratification, see Thomas Fowler, *Corpus Christi* (London, 1898), p. 48.

6. *Letters of Richard Fox 1486-1527*, ed. P. S. and H. M. Allen (Oxford, 1929), pp. xii-xiii.

7. Hall, in *Holinshed's Chronicles* (London, 1808), III, 617. Allen accepted the account as true (*Letters of Richard Fox* . . . , p. xiv); see also Thomas Fowler, *The History of Corpus Christi College* (Oxford, 1893), p. 21.

8. (April 30, [1517]), *Letters of Richard Fox* . . . , No. 57. Allen (p. 92) argues solidly for the 1517 date instead of [1522] as in *LP*, III, 2207.

9. *Letters of Richard Fox* . . . , pp. xii-xiii.

10. *EE*, 586—the preface to Suetonius as edited by Erasmus (Basel, June, 1518).

11. Woodward, pp. 111-12.

12. For this dating, see Allen (1934), p. x. Argument for composition in part as early as April, 1515, is made by Lange, pp. 166-67, and by Élise Bagdat, *La "Querela pacis" d'Érasme* (Paris, 1924), pp. 1-8. Its composition seems to fall between September, 1516 (when More was finishing *Utopia*), and July, 1517. See W. J. Hirten (ed.), *The Complaint of Peace* (New York, 1946), pp. v-xxvii.

13. See Bagdat, *La "Querela pacis" d'Érasme*, pp. 44-55.

14. Erasmus, *The Complaint of Peace*, trans. anon. (Chicago, 1917), pp. 2, 9, 33 (cited hereafter as *EQP*), in *EO*, IV, 625-42. First edition at Basel, December, 1517. On sources see R. Bainton, "The *Querela pacis* of Erasmus, Classical and Christian Sources," *Archiv für Reformationsgeschichte*, XLII (1951), 32-47.

15. See Roy Battenhouse, "Hamlet's Apostrophe to Man," *PMLA*, LXVI (1951), 1073-1113.

16. *EN*, III, 129-30; *EE*, 703.25-35. The preface was for the edition of June, 1518. To see how the English humanists had turned against dominant medieval idealization of Alexander, cf. George Cary, *The Medieval Alexander* (New York, 1956), *passim*.

17. *EN*, III, 289-90. See his similar letter to John Colet (*ca.* March 5, 1518), *EE*, 786.24-29; and Pollard, p. 115.

18. *EN*, III, 312. Pollard (p. 115) observed that "Leo X wanted a crusade against the Turk, or at least financial contributions which, failing a crusade, might perhaps be spent on building St. Peter's." See Pollard also on the complex motives which in 1518 conspired momentarily to make Europe's men of power want peace.

19. *Letters of Richard Fox* . . . , p. 111; *LP*, II, 3952.

20. Hexter, pp. 103-32; *MEW-C*, I, 27; E. Routh, *Sir Thomas More and His Friends 1477-1535* (London, 1934), p. 91; Chambers, pp. 156-

67; More's *English Works* (London, 1557), p. 1224 (cited hereafter as *MEW*).

21. Routh, *Sir Thomas More* . . . , pp. 103 ff. But Pollard (p. 114) finds generally that "English diplomatists—Tunstal [*sic*], West, Knight, and More—seem to have been unanimous in urging Wolsey . . . that patience and peace would serve England better than passion and war. . . ." See Hexter, pp. 132-55.

22. [*The Christian Knight*, trans. anon. (London, 1541)], sig. A7^v, Ci^r (*STC* 10482) (cited hereafter as *ECK); EE*, 858 (the preface to the new edition of Basel, July, 1518).

23. *Foedera*, ed. T. Rymer and R. Sanderson (London, 1704-35), XIII, 624; *LP*, II, 4469; Fisher, pp. 203-4. Giustinian (II, 229) summarized it thus: "First, peace and alliance are made between this most serene King [Henry], and his most Christian Majesty [Francis I], to last for ever; his Holiness [Leo X], the Emperor, and his Catholic Majesty [Charles], being included therein as principal confederates, being bound to ratify said peace . . . within . . . four months. . . ."

24. *Oratio Richardi Pacei in pace* [London: Pynson, 1518] (*STC* 19081a), Sigs. A2^v-A5^v. Paces' earlier "little book" on the Turkish war and upon papal pardons is lost (*EN*, III, 290; *EE*, III, 239).

25. *Letters of Richard Fox* . . . , pp. 111-14 *passim*.

26. See *EE*, 961, 962, 964-67; also Erasmus' letter to Pace (April 22, 1518), *EN*, III, 345, on the humanistic brilliance of Henry's court; similarly on July 26, *EN*, III, 421-22.

27. *EN*, III, 379. Allen (*EE*, III, 517n.) sums up the relations of Erasmus and Luther to March 28, 1519, when Erasmus still knew him "only by repute. . . . As the years went on, [Erasmus] more and more looked on Luther as retarding the progress of a movement for peaceful reform, which, impelled in no small measure by his own writings and influence, had seemed well upon its way."

28. Giustinian, I, 237. Pollard (p. 119n.) argued that, except for the 1544 expedition against France, Henry's reign was pacific, and that the policies leading to war were mainly Wolsey's.

29. *EE*, 1026 (to Lupset); *EE*, 1211 (June 13, 1521) for Erasmus' short biography of Colet.

30. *EN*, II, 578; *EE*, 620. Brixius later said that he never saw Erasmus' placative letter until its printing in late October—in a book Erasmus did not see until late November (*EE*, IV, 119n.), too late to head off the *Antimorus*.

31. Brixius, *Antimorus*, f°.B^{3}v, cited by Allen, *EE*, IV, 222n.

32. *Thomae Mori Epistola ad Germanum Brixium* (London, [April], 1520) (*STC* 18088), title page translated in Hudson, p. 56.

33. *MLE*, Nos. 250-53; Hudson, pp. 56-57. More's satire on vainglory may be reflected in Rabelais' mockery of Brixius' Hervé. Panurge, when the

ship seems near to foundering in a great storm, suggests letting it go and making a will. Even if he drowns, the will may wash ashore and gain for his memory "a stately cenotaph . . . [as] Germain of Brie to Hervé, the Breton tarpawlin" (*Pantagruel*, IV, chap. xxi [trans. Urquhart and Motter]).

34. The Field was vividly described by eyewitnesses: *LP*, III, 869; *Cal. SP Ven.*, III, 119; *LP*, III, i, pp. 303 ff.; Hall, p. 604.

35. A. F. Pollard, *Henry VIII* (London, 1902), p. 104.

36. *Cal. SP Ven.*, III, 33, 55, 84.

37. *Ibid.*, p. 29. Pace was made a reader in Greek at Cambridge in April, 1520, although there is no evidence that he ever discharged such duties. J. H. Lupton thought it largely owing to the "representations of Pace and More that Greek chairs were now founded at Cambridge and Oxford" (*DNB*, XV, 23).

38. John Fisher, *Two Fruytfull Sermons* (London, 1532) (*STC* 10909), Sigs. A2^{rv}, Bi^v; Hall, p. 621; T. E. Bridgett, *Life of Blessed John Fisher* (London, 1888), p. 82.

Chapter Eleven

1. *MC*, p. 246.13-22; T. Stapleton, *The Life . . . of Sir Thomas More*, trans. P. E. Hallett (London, 1928), p. 86. Only in a general way earlier was Erasmus aware that More might want to delete "unsuitable" passages (March 5, 1518; *EN*, III, 288; *EE*, 785.13). More may have found Budé sympathetic partly because Budé had satirized soldiery in his *Annotations aux Pandectes* (1508) and *De asse;* see L. Delaruelle, *Études sur l'humanisme Français: Guillaume Budé* (Paris, 1907), pp. 110-25, 161-62 *passim*. More never published his letters in his lifetime (*MC*, preface).

2. *MLE*, pp. xv-xvi; *EE*, 1087.182-86.

3. *Repertory of the Court of Aldermen*, Vol. V, folio 204b, in Chambers, p. 192.

4. *Literae virorum eruditorum ad Franciscum Craneveldium 1522-1528*, ed. H. de Vocht (Louvain, 1928), p. xlix (cited hereafter as *LC*). On Vives (but with surprisingly little on his social criticism in England) see: J. B. Mullinger, *DNB*; Adolfo Bonilla y San Martin, *Luis Vives . . .* (Madrid, 1903), II, 291-304; G. D. du Dezert's review of San Martin in *Revue hispanique*, XII (1905), 373-412; F. Watson, "J. L. Vives and St. Augustine's *Civitas Dei*," *Church Quarterly Review* (London), LXXVI (1913), 145-47; F. Watson, *Luis Vives* (Oxford, 1922), chaps. iii-iv; F. Watson, "The Influence of Valencia . . . on . . . Vives," *Aberystwyth Studies*, IX (1927), 47-103 *passim;* L. Thorndike, "John Louis Vives . . .," in *Essays . . . Dedicated to James Harvey Robinson* (New York, 1929), pp. 341-42; Henry de Vocht, *Monumenta humanistica Lovaniensia* (Louvain, 1934), pp. 1-60 (cited hereafter as de Vocht); P. S. Allen in *EE*, III, 508n.

5. Watson, *Luis Vives*, pp. 24-25; *Vivis* . . . *opera* (Basel, 1555), II, 131-37 (cited hereafter as *VO*).

6. P. S. Allen surmised that in 1517 Vives went to England "seeking employment but without success" (*EE*, III, 508n., and Ep. 545.15). De Vocht (pp. 1-6) explodes the idea that there was any such visit.

7. Translated by Nancy Leskeith in *The Renaissance Philosophy of Man*, ed. E. Cassirer *et al.* (Chicago, 1937), pp. 385-96.

8. Watson, *Luis Vives*, pp. 29-33; *MUL*, pp. 184-86; *MC*, 60 (March 29, [1518]); *EE*, 1106.69.

9. *Saint Augustine, of the Citie of God: With . . . comments of Io. L. Vives*, trans. J. H[ealey] (London, 1620), p. 11 (*STC* 917) (cited hereafter as *CDV*). See *VOE*, p. cxlvii.

10. *State Papers . . . I, King Henry VIII* ([London], 1830), No. XIV, p. 20 (cited hereafter as *SP*); *LP*, III, 1437.

11. Erasmus, *The First Tome . . . of the Paraphrase . . . upon the Newe Testamente* (London, 1548) (*STC* 2854), sig. C3ʳ-4ᵛ (cited hereafter as *EP*).

12. *The Familiar Colloquies*, trans. N. Bailey (London, 1725), pp. 318-34 *passim* (cited hereafter as *ECF*); *EO*, I, 641-43. For dating, see P. Smith, *A Key to the Colloquies of Erasmus* (Cambridge, Mass., 1927), pp. 17-18; *Bibliotheca Erasmiana*, comp. F. Vander Haeghen *et al.* (Ghent, 1897-1908), *Colloquia*, pp. 145-46 (cited hereafter as *BE-C*).

13. *CDV* (1610), sig. A4ʳ-Aiʳ.

14. *EE*, 1306.37-43, 1311.40-43. Froben finished the edition on August 31, but Vives had been ill and is quite unlikely (contrary to P. S. Allen's surmise, *EE*, III, 508) to have visited England that autumn (de Vocht, pp. 1-6).

Chapter Twelve

1. *LP*, III, 2555; *MC*, 110, p. 263n.; see E. Routh, *Sir Thomas More and His Friends* . . . (London, 1934), p. 113. With More's attitude contrast John Skelton's exultation (see Brewer, I, 485).

2. Chambers, p. 199; Brewer, I, 498.

3. Brewer, I, 455-58. Speaking of the scheme to reconquer France, Brewer defends Henry VIII's competence; he then points out that the King heartily approved all Wolsey's actions designed to bring about the war. He also declares the project "chimerical" and a pursuit of "barren honour" (I, 416)!

4. *LC*, p. 352; *VO*, V, 164-74; de Vocht, p. 3.

5. *EE*, 1324.55-58; *LC*, 28.25, 45-46, 60-63.

6. *EP*, sigs. o.2ʳ-(∴)4ʳ *passim*.

7. *Érasme Dulce bellum inexpertis*, ed. and trans. Yvonne Remy and

René Dunil-Marquebreucq (Berchem-Brussels, 1953), p. 40, ll.338-39 (cited hereafter as *EDB*); cf. *EAW*, p. 23, par. 3, end of sentence 3.

8. *EDB*, pp. 52-54, ll.539-43; omitted in *EAW*, p. 35 (just before "At the birth . . .").

9. *EDB*, p. 86, ll.996-1004 *passim*; partly omitted in *EAW*, p. 56 (just before "Succor the Turks . . .").

10. *EDB*, p. 93, ll.1006-85 *passim*; omitted in *EAW*, p. 57 (just before "But of all these things . . .").

11. *LP*, III, 3093; Pollard, pp. 135-36.

12. F. Duval, *De la paix de Dieu à la paix de fer* (Paris, 1923), p. 98.

13. William Roper relates that More incurred Wolsey's displeasure by indirect resistance to the grant (*The Lyfe of Sir Thomas Moore*, ed. E. V. Hitchcock [London, 1935], pp. 12-20 [cited hereafter as Roper]). Chambers (pp. 200-6), largely accepting Roper's story, thought More's "dislike of war" was probably intensified by the onerous duty of helping to finance it. But Roper's account seems to be "either fictitious or much exaggerated" (Pollard, p. 133n.). See More's acknowledgments to Wolsey (*LP*, III, 3302, 3270, 3291, 3363). And Wolsey secured for More an extra fee for his work (*LP*, III, 3267).

On slight evidence it has been surmised that More acted under "compulsion" and similarly that "Wolsey himself did not want war, but instead it was the king and the great lords" (Ames, pp. 66-67, citing only Brewer, II, 50). Against these surmises, see Hexter, pp. 103-55, especially p. 141. On Wolsey's role Brewer blew hot and cold: he claimed that Wolsey opposed the 1513 war but documented that Wolsey became its "directing genius" (1, 22), and he rather asserted than proved that in all his vastly active work for the 1522-23 wars Wolsey did "violence to his best convictions" when he departed from his own peace policy of 1517-18. Ames (p. 67n.) thinks Wolsey's opposition to the 1523 war "definitely indicated" because "his servant Cromwell" wrote "a speech against the tax and the war." While, however, Cromwell knew Wolsey in 1523, he did not enter Wolsey's service until 1524 (Roger Merriman, *Life and Letters of Thomas Cromwell* [Oxford, 1902], I, 15, 46 [cited hereafter as Cromwell]).

14. Probably on April 15, when the King was present (*LP*, III, 2958); Cromwell, I, 30.

15. Cromwell, I, 15, 46; *LP*, III, 3282, and IV, 547.

16. *ECF*, pp. 172-77 *passim*; *EO*, I, 708-10; Smith, *A Key to the Colloquies of Erasmus* (Cambridge, Mass., 1927), pp. 17-18.

17. *STC* 2854, sigs. (∴)i^r-(∴)4^v *passim*. It was sent to both the Pope and Henry VIII (*EE*, V, 312n., and Ep. 1385).

18. *LP*, I, 3356, 3451; Brewer, I, 19-21.

19. (October 23), *LP*, III, 3462; see also 3319, 3346, 3371, 3516, etc.

20. *SP*, I, 144; *LP*, III, 3433; Pollard, p. 136.

21. *LP*, III, 3516, 3462, 3485; Brewer, I, 504-9.

22. *EP*, sig. a2ʳ. Erasmus sharply criticized both Pope and princes, whose houses need cleaning. Some say that the Pope's dominion extends even to hell; he wished only that the world might see the papal powers used to effect peace among Christian princes, "which have a long season with no less dishonor than slaughter and effusion of Christian blood, warred against one another to the utter decay of Christ's religion."

23. *LP*, III, 2974, 3058, 3114, 3281, 3321.

24. Pollard, pp. 127-37 *passim*; *LP*, III, 3664; *LC*, Ep. 84 preface.

25. De Vocht gives the best account of Vives' visits to England and is the source of all facts not otherwise documented.

26. *CDV*, p. 469. These last two opinions were among those later condemned by the Church; see F. Watson, "J. L. Vives and St. Augustine's 'Civitas Dei,'" *Church Quarterly Review* (London), LXXVI (1913), 150.

27. *CDV* (1610 ed.), sig. A4ʳ; de Vocht, p. 5n.; *EE*, 927 preface. As Paul O. Kristeller observes: "Thus, as the whole humanistic movement had claimed to achieve a revival of ancient literature and civilization, Vives is here credited with having 'revived' the work of Augustine" ("Augustine and the Early Renaissance," *Review of Religion*, VIII [1943], 351).

Chapter Thirteen

1. *The Scholemaster* [1570], in *English Works*, ed. W. Wright (Cambridge, Eng., 1904), p. 231.

2. C. S. Lewis, *English Literature in the Sixteenth Century* . . . , (Oxford, 1954), pp. 28-30.

3. C. R. Thompson, *The Translations of Lucian by Erasmus and St. Thomas More* (Ithaca, N. Y., 1940), *passim*; Mesnard, pp. 128 ff.

4. De Vocht, pp. 1-12 *passim*. He had the work finished by April 23, i.e., after receiving Henry VIII's invitation to England.

5. *The Instruction of a Christen Woman*, trans. Richarde Hyrde (London, 1541), sigs. Diᵛ-D2ʳ (*STC* 24858) (cited hereafter as *VCW*). See F. Watson, *Vives and the Renascence Education of Women* (New York, 1912), pp. 56-59. Vives' 1523 work was cited as "perhaps the earliest attack" on romance reading, by R. S. Crane, "The Vogue of *Guy of Warwick* . . . ," *PMLA*, XXX (1915), 136.

6. *MLE*, Nos. 172-75. See, similarly, the Morean mockery of romance's absurdities in an anecdote told by Richard Pace, More's friend and fellow humanist. The youthful More is supposed to have met two learned Scotists, who affirmed that, from the beards of giants he had slain, King Arthur made himself a toga. More asked how this was possible. Very gravely he was told: "My lad, the reason is manifest and the cause evident—the skin of a dead man stretches wonderfully." The younger of the theologians applauded this

explanation as both subtle and Scotistic. In the anecdote More admitted that hitherto he had been totally ignorant of this phenomenon. He did, however, contribute his own bit of pseudoscientific lore: "This, nevertheless, is very well-known; one of you milks a he-goat and the other holds a sieve beneath to catch the milk." Seeing that the two Scotists did not comprehend his ironic treatment of their romantic Arthurianism, More departed chuckling to himself (*De fructu qui ex doctrina percipitur* [Basel, October, 1517], p. 83). (This incident was called to my attention by E. L. Surtz, S.J.)

7. *Le Morte Darthur*, ed. H. O. Sommer (London, 1889), I, 3-5.

8. See the first defense in English of the education of women, by Richarde Hyrde, tutor in More's house, given in Erasmus, *Treatise upon the Paternoster*, [trans. Margaret More (London, 1526?)], sigs. A2ʳ-B3ᵛ (*STC* 10477). Against the many men who will not even try to teach women, Hyrde vigorously defends a solid humanistic education for them (quite clearly with Margaret More in mind as a fine example). For women, no less than for men, good books show "the image and ways of good living, even right as a mirror showeth the . . . body" (A4ᵛ). Without a trained mind a man is "worse than an unreasonable beast" (Biᵛ), and so is a woman. Hyrde stresses especially the value of learning matters good and true while one is young: then learning will be "delectable in youth, comfortable in age, and profitable in all seasons" (Biʳ). And a woman of such a mind will get and keep more love, for she will not have to depend solely on bodily beauty which declines inevitably with age. He seems to imply that if Helen of Troy had been better educated instead of merely a dazzling beauty, she would have been able to resist Paris' seductions (for which in any case Paris was the more to blame) (A3ʳ).

9. See also chap. lxiv, "Of Bawdry," in Cornelius Agrippa's work of *ca.* 1527, *Of the Vanitie and Uncertaintie of Artes and Sciences*, trans. Ja[mes] San[ford] (London, 1575) (*STC* 205), especially folio 98 on Lancelot, Tristram, etc. In 1510 Agrippa studied under John Colet (H. Morley, *Cornelius Agrippa* [London, 1856], pp. 226-53 *passim*). Parts of this chapter appeared in Robert P. Adams, "Bold Bawdry and Open Manslaughter: The English New Humanist Attack on Medieval Romance," *HLQ*, XXIII (November, 1959), 33-48.

Chapter Fourteen

1. De Vocht, pp. 6-12; *VO*, I, 308-20. Erasmus himself followed the text of the *Christian Prince*, in the quarto of May, 1516, with his translation of Isocrates' *De regno administrando* (*EE*, II, 249).

2. (January 24, 1524), *LP*, IV, 61; (March 1, 1524), *ibid.*, 138.

3. (March 21, 1524), *ibid.*, 170 (p. 67); (March 23), *ibid.*, 177.

4. *Ibid.*, III, 3584; see also *ibid.*, 3651. Pollard (p. 137): Clement VII's "Medicean and Machiavellian principle was to begin treating with a foe as

soon as he had contracted with a friend; and he has better claims than Wolsey to whatever credit attaches to the invention of the doctrine of the balance of power."

5. Translated in F. Watson, *Vives and the Renascence Education of Women* (New York, 1912), p. 153.

6. J. L. Vives, *An Introduction to Wysedome*, trans. Rycharde Morysine [London, 1540] (*STC* 24847) (cited hereafter as *VIW*); *VO*, II, 70-95.

7. Roper, pp. 20-21; Harpsfield, pp. 24-26, 319n.

8. *EE*, 1513; *LP*, IV, 828, 1760.

9. *LC*, 130.14-18, 128.4 and notes.

10. [January 15-17, 1525], *ibid.*, 134.36-46; see *ibid.*, 112.32-34, 137.18-19.

11. [February 18, 1525], *ibid.*, 133.14; and *ibid.*, 142, on the growing French power at the English court.

12. (January 25, 1525), *ibid.*, 136.40-50. As de Vocht said (p. 17): through these letters at this time runs tragic awareness "that war was causing misery and havoc to nations which should have been united as brothers." See *LC*, 128.27-28, 130.21, 134.37, 136.47, 142.20, 146.4 (March 26).

13. *LC*, 191.7n.; Chambers, pp. 223-30.

14. *LC*, 150, preface b; *LP*, IV, 1148-49, 1154. Wolsey even complained about de Praet through his ambassadors in Spain and Brabant; Margaret of Austria chose to ignore the event's real meaning and to apologize. Cf. Ames, p. 68. (For "Bryneford" Pollard noted "Brantford" in his copy of *LP*, now in the Folger Library.)

15. De Vocht, pp. 1-6; *MEW-C*, I, 21-22, 482-83. On More's loss of even the "freedom of silence," see Hexter, p. 156.

16. *LP*, IV, 1177; *VO*, II, 939-41; see also Pollard, p. 142, and Chambers, p. 213.

17. *LP*, IV, 1212, 1301 (p. 572); Pollard, p. 138.

18. *LP*, IV, 1378-80; see *ibid.*, 1190; Pollard, p. 139; Ames, p. 68.

19. *LP*, IV, 1213, 1378 (p. 615).

20. *Ibid.*, 1199, 1200 (both March 21); *Original Letters*, ed. H. Ellis, 3rd Ser. (London, 1846———), I, 367-75 *passim;* Hall, pp. 694-97.

21. *LP*, IV, 1243; *Original Letters*, III, 367-75 *passim.*

22. *LP*, IV, 1321, 1323; Pollard, pp. 145-47.

23. See *LC*, 150.55-86 (March, 1525), 156.2, 158.19, 160.16 etc.

24. *LP*, IV, 1364, 1401, 1464.

25. Translated in Smith, p. 201; *EO*, II, 871.

26. *LP*, IV, 1324, 1317; Hall, p. 700.

27. *LP*, IV, 1600 (3), 1555, 1557, 1570.

28. "De pace inter Caes. et Franciscum Galliarum regem: deque optimo regni statu," *VO*, II, 941-47; *LP*, IV, 1689.

29. Anon., "An Address to King Henry the Eighth," MS Reg. Brit. Mus. 18 A. IV, cited in *Original Letters*, I, 368-69.

30. J. L. Vives, *Concerning the Relief of the Poor*, trans. M. M. Sherwood (New York, 1917), p. 6 (cited hereafter as *VRP*).

31. J. L. Vives, *De subventione pauperum* (Leiden, 1532), sig. A6ʳ.

32. *Ten Colloquies of Erasmus*, trans. C. R. Thompson (New York, 1957), pp. 92-107 (cited hereafter as *ETC*). For dating, see Smith, *A Key to the Colloquies of Erasmus* (Cambridge, Mass., 1927), pp. 39-42.

33. In November, 1528, Charles V commented to Henry VIII that, after Pavia, he *had* shown clemency to Francis but without eliciting gratitude (*LP*, IV, 4991).

34. *EDB*, ll.638-40 (this is omitted in *EAW*, p. 40, after "so it be just").

35. *EDB*, ll.791-820 (this is omitted in *EAW*, p. 46.15, after "defence").

36. *EDB*, ll.692-736 (this is omitted in *EAW*, p. 43.13, after "as we Christian men do").

Chapter Fifteen

1. *LP*, IV, 2726, 2728; Pollard, pp. 151-52.

2. *LP*, IV, 1891; Pollard, p. 149.

3. De Vocht, p. 21; *LC*, 182.17-23, 156, 158.22, 163.15.

4. *EE*, 1697.95-97; *LP*, IV, 2121.

5. *MC*, 142.6-10; *LC*, 177.6-10.

6. *LP*, IV, 1648, 2032, 2036.

7. *LP*, IV, 1570, 1600, 2382, 3619; *Foedera*, ed. T. Rymer and R. Sanderson (London, 1704-35), XIV, 48, 185; Chambers, p. 214.

8. *EE*, 1697.23-126; *LP*, IV, 2121. No trace of an English inhibition against the *Colloquies* has been found (*EE*, 1697.23n.).

9. *LP*, IV, 2128; *EE*, 1704.22-42 *passim*.

10. *LP*, IV, 2129; *EE*, 1702.24-25.

11. (June 2, [1526]), *LC*, 191; de Vocht, p. 22.

12. *LP*, IV, 2144, 2173, 2209, 2213, 2227, 2237 (June 10); de Vocht, p. 22.

13. This volume included the two epistles of 1525 to Henry VIII (for which Wolsey fired Vives from his Oxford post), the 1524 letter to the Bishop of Lincoln, and the 1522 letter to Pope Adrian VI, on war and the Lutherans.

14. *LC*, p. 614n.; *LP*, IV, 1614, 2446. Apparently the *Opusculum* was never printed.

15. De Vocht, pp. 22-28; *EE*, 1792.29-30; *LP*, IV, 4990.

16. *LP*, IV, 3080; Chambers, pp. 229-30; Ames, p. 69.

17. *LC*, pp. 24-26; *LP*, IV, 3261.

18. De Vocht, pp. 26-27; *LC*, 241.22-28, 243.11 and 56-59, 248.7-8. The divorce scheme was already known to Charles V (*LC*, p. 624).

19. On the time of terror as seen through humanist eyes, see *LC*, 220 and note; cf. Pollard, pp. 152 f.; Ames, p. 69.

20. See the views on war expressed *ca.* 1527 by a former student of Colet, Cornelius Agrippa, *Of the Vanitie and Uncertaintie of Artes and Sciences* (London, 1575) (*STC* 205), folios 31-32, 76-77, 89-90, 127. See also Lange, pp. 197-99.

21. "Clarorum Hispaniensium epistolae ineditae," *Revue hispanique*, VIII (1901), 263-64.

22. *EE*, 1816.35-38, 1878, 1955.5; *LC*, 266.22n.; *EE*, 1998.

Chapter Sixteen

1. *LC*, 251.5-15, 252.15, 254.19; de Vocht, pp. 28n., 33.

2. *LP*, IV, 4990; de Vocht, pp. 34-37; *LC*, pp. 670-72. On the evidence of one undated letter (*EE*, 2777), Mrs. H. M. Allen and H. W. Garrod thought Vives visited England in both 1532 and 1533. De Vocht (pp. 43-58) shows good reasons why no such visits took place.

3. (January 13, 1531), *LP*, V, 46; *Vivis opera* (Valencia, 1783), VII, 134; F. Watson, *Luis Vives* (Oxford, 1922), p. 93.

4. Close to the time at which More wrote, Luther himself worked out his "On War Against the Turk" (dedicated October 9, 1528, published April, 1529). Here he had no real objection to defensive war against the Turks, provided only that it was no crusade and was not under papal direction. To him, warfare was in no way the business or duty of the church, only of the state. The Emperor's duty to conduct such defense came purely because he was the Emperor, not "because he was a Christian or defender of the faith" (*Luther's Works*, trans. C. M. Jacobs [Philadelphia, 1915], V, 77. Jacobs gives its press date as April 23, 1529; a Huntington Library copy bears the date April 16, 1529).

5. See *MDT*, pp. 305-8 *passim*.

6. *ECF*, pp. 458-63; *EO*, I, 831-33; for the dating, P. Smith, *A Key to the Colloquies of Erasmus* (Cambridge, Mass., 1927), pp. 44-50.

7. *ECF*, pp. 437-41; *ETC*, pp. 113-19.

8. See Smith, *A Key to the Colloquies of Erasmus*, p. 45; and E. W. Nelson, "Recent Literature on Erasmus," *JMH*, I (1929), 98.

9. *EE*, 1684; M. Bataillon, "Encore Érasme," *Bulletin hispanique*, XXVII (1925), 238-42.

Chapter Seventeen

1. *LP*, IV, 5133, 5139, 5166, 5192, 5208.

2. E.g., *EE*, 2167.30-37 (May 27), 2168.30n., 2205.147-64, 2207.12-

16 (August 20). Although the Cambrai peace was concluded on August 5, only rumors had reached Erasmus in Freiburg two weeks later.

3. J. L. Vives, *De concordia & discordia in humano genere* [Antwerp, July, 1529] (cited hereafter as *VCD*). The volume (Folger copy) also included the essay *De pacificatione* (written in England in 1524) and another on the anticipated wretchedness of life for Christians under the coming Turkish tyranny: *Que miseret esset vita Christianorum sub Turca.*

4. Foster Watson, *Luis Vives* (Oxford, 1922), pp. 99-100.

5. *EE*, 2230.23n., 2231.23.

6. *LP*, IV, 5830 and note; see Charles Sturge, *Cuthbert Tunstall* (London, 1938), pp. 108-9.

7. See Palsgrave's letter to More (*ca.* July 30, 1529: *LP*, IV, 5806; *MC*, 168), which suggests problems met by humanists who tried to reshape traditional education for noblemen. He asked More's help to induce the King to say that his pupil, the young Duke of Richmond, should be "brought up in learning." Opposed were many "high-shaven folk" who frankly held "that learning is a great hindrance and displeasure to a noble man. . . ." The context suggests that, like the great English humanists, Palsgrave thought education should be more for letters than for arms. Pollard (p. 226) dismissed Palsgrave's indictment of Wolsey as mere "satirical jottings . . . certainly never intended for publication," while granting them, though "less bitter" than Darcy's public charges, to be nevertheless "far more comprehensive."

8. See, e.g., Petrus Vergerius, *De ingenuis moribus (ca.* 1404), translated in W. H. Woodward, *Vittorino da Feltre . . .* (Cambridge, Eng., 1897), pp. 103-15. Vittorino himself aimed rather at good health than at special premilitary training (*ibid.*, pp. 65-66). Palmieri (*La vita civile* [1435-40]) more typically held universal military training essential to development of patriotic virtues (see translations in Woodward, pp. 66-71, 255-58 *passim*). Both Vittorino and Guarino urged military exercises for children, frequently with military training beginning at the age of ten (*ibid.*, pp. 23, 37, 246). Indeed Woodward (*ibid.*, p. 65) found this emphasis on military training to be typical of Renaissance treatises on education, and he cites examples from Vergerius (*ca.* 1404) to Castiglione's *Courtier* (*ca.* 1528) and Milton's *Of Education* (1644). Commonly humanist study of history aimed to furnish moral precepts and political examples which would make costly trial and error less necessary to future leaders of society (Woodward, pp. 17-18).

9. *ECE.*

10. *Vives: On Education. A translation of the "De tradendis disciplinis"* (1531) by F. Watson (Cambridge, Eng., 1913), p. 258.

11. "De bello Turcis . . . ," *EO*, V, 346C-367A.

12. *Encyclopaedia Britannica* (11th ed.), XXVII, 447.

13. (March 1, 1531), *Cal. LP Spain*, IV, ii, p. 80.

14. *Cal. LP Spain*, IV, ii, p. 114; *LP*, V, 187.

Adams, Robert P. "Designs by More and Erasmus for a New Social Order," *Studies in Philology*, XLII (1945), 131-45.

————. "Erasmus' Ideas of His Rôle as a Social Critic *ca.* 1480-1500," *Renaissance News*, XI (1958), 11-16.

————. "The Philosophic Unity of More's *Utopia*" *Studies in Philology*, XXXVIII (1941), 45-65.

————. "Pre-Renaissance Courtly Propaganda for Peace in English Literature," *Papers of the Michigan Academy*, XXXII ([1946]-48), 431-46.

————. "The Social Responsibilities of Science in *Utopia, New Atlantis* and After," *Journal of the History of Ideas*, X (1949), 374-98.

Agrippa, Cornelius. *Of the Vanitie and Uncertaintie of Artes and Sciences*, trans. Ja[mes] San[ford]. London, 1575.

Allen, Don C. "The Degeneration of Man and Renaissance Pessimism," *Studies in Philology*, XXV (1938), 202-27.

Allen, J. W. *A History of Political Thought in the Sixteenth Century*. New York, 1928.

Allen, P. S. *The Age of Erasmus*. Oxford, 1914.

————. "Dean Colet and Archbishop Warham," *English Historical Review*, XVII (1902), 303-6.

————. *Erasmus*. Oxford, 1934.

Ames, Russell. *Citizen Thomas More*. Princeton, N. J., 1949.

Appelt, T. C. *Studies in the Contents and Sources of Erasmus' "Adagia."* Chicago, 1942.

Arnold, E. V. *Roman Stoicism*. Cambridge, Eng., 1911.

Ascham, Roger. *English Works*, ed. W. Wright. Cambridge, Eng., 1904.

Atkins, J. W. H. *English Literary Criticism: The Renascence*. London, 1947.

Augustine, St. *Saint Augustine, of the Citie of God: With . . . comments of Io. L. Vives*, trans. J. H[ealey]. London, 1620.

Bagdat, Élise. *La "Querela pacis" d'Érasme*. Paris, 1924.

Bainton, R. "The *Querela Pacis* of Erasmus, Classical and Christian Sources," *Archiv für Reformationsgeschichte*, XLII (1951), 32-47.

Baker, Herschel. *The Dignity of Man*. Cambridge, Mass., 1947.

Ballis, W. *The Legal Position of War*. The Hague, 1937.

Bataillon, M. "Encore Érasme," *Bulletin hispanique*, XXVII (1925), 238-42.

Battenhouse, R. W. "Hamlet's Apostrophe on Man," *Publications of the Modern Language Association*, LXVI (1951), 1073-1113.

Baumann, Frederick L. "Sir Thomas More," *Journal of Modern History*, IV (1932), 604-15.

Beard, C. A. *The Devil Theory of War*. New York, 1936.

Belasco, P. S. *Authority in Church and State*. London, 1928.

Berdan, J. M. *Early Tudor Poetry*. New York, 1920.

Bergenroth, G. A. (ed.). *Calendar of the Letters . . . and State Papers between England and Spain*. London, 1866——.

Berners, Juliana. *The Boke of Saint Albans*, ed. W. Blades. London, 1901.

Bibliotheca Belgica. 2nd Ser., Vol. XIII. Ghent, 1891-1923.

Bibliotheca Erasmiana, comp. F. Vander Haeghen *et al*. Ghent, 1897-1908.

Bonilla y San Martin, Adolfo. *Luis Vives*. Madrid, 1903.

Born, L. K. "Erasmus on Political Ethics: The *Institutio Principis Christiani*," *Political Science Quarterly*, XLIII (1928), 520-43.

——. "Some Notes on the Political Theories of Erasmus," *Journal of Modern History*, II (1930), 226-36.

Brewer, J. S. (ed.). *Letters and Papers of Henry VIII*. London, 1862——.

——. *The Reign of Henry VIII from His Accession to the Death of Wolsey*, ed. J. Gairdner. London, 1884.

Bridgett, T. E. *Life of Blessed John Fisher*. London, 1888.

Brown, R. (ed.). *Calendar of State Papers and Manuscripts, Relating to English Affairs, Existing in . . . Venice*. London, 1871.

Bryce, James. *International Relations*. New York, 1922.

Buckley, G. T. *Atheism in the English Renaissance*. Chicago, 1932.

Burckhardt, J. *The Civilization of the Renaissance in Italy*, trans. S. Middlemore. 2nd ed. London, 1928.

Bury, J. B. *The Idea of Progress*. London, 1920.

Bush, Douglas. *Classical Influences in Renaissance Literature*. Cambridge, Mass., 1952.

——. *The Renaissance and English Humanism*. Toronto, 1939.

——. "Tudor Humanism and Henry VIII," *Toronto University Quarterly*, VII (1937-38), 162-77.

Butler, C. *The Life of Érasmus*. London, 1875.

Cadoux, C. J. (ed.). *The Early Christian Attitude Toward War*. London, 1919.

Caldwell, W. E. *Hellenic Conceptions of Peace*. New York, 1919.

Campbell, W. E. *Erasmus, Tyndale and More*. London, 1949.

Carlyle, A. J. *A History of Mediaeval Political Theory in the West*. Edinburgh, 1903-28.

Cary, George. *The Medieval Alexander*. New York, 1956.

Caspari, Fritz. "Erasmus on the Social Functions of Christian Humanism," *Journal of the History of Ideas*, VIII (1947), 78-106.

———. *Humanism and the Social Order in Tudor England*. Chicago, 1954.

———. "Sir Thomas More and *Justum Bellum*," *Ethics*, LVI (1946), 303-8.

Cassirer, E., et al. (eds.). *The Renaissance Philosophy of Man*. Chicago, 1948.

Cavendish, George. *The Life and Death of Cardinal Wolsey*. Boston, 1905.

Caxton, William. *The Prologues and Epilogues of William Caxton*, ed. W. Crotch. London, 1928.

Chambers, R. W. *Thomas More*. London, 1935.

Church, R. W. *Dante*. London, 1878.

Cicero. *De officiis*. Paris, 1535.

———. *Letters of Cicero*, trans. E. Shuckburgh. London, 1904.

Cockle, M. *A Bibliography of English Military Books up to 1642 and of Contemporary Foreign Works*, ed. H. Cockle. London, 1900.

Colet, John. *An Exposition of St. Paul's Epistle to the Romans*, trans. J. H. Lupton. London, 1873.

Columbia Studies in the History of Ideas, Vol. III. New York, 1935.

Crane, R. S. "The Vogue of *Guy of Warwick* from the Close of the Middle Ages to the Romantic Revival," *PMLA*, XXXIII (1915), 125-94.

Crosland, J. "Lucan in the Middle Ages," *Modern Language Review*, XXV (1930), 41-43.

Dictionary of the Apostolic Church. Edinburgh, 1918.

Delaruelle, L. *Études sur l'humanisme Français: Guillaume Budé*. Paris, 1907.

Desdevises du Dezert, G. "Luis Vives," *Revue hispanique*, XII (1905), 373-412.

De Vocht, Henry. See Vocht, Henry de.

Donner, H. W. *Introduction to Utopia*. London, 1945.

Dudley, Edmund. *The Tree of Commonwealth*, ed. D. Brodie. Cambridge, Eng., 1948.

Duhamel, P. A. "The Oxford Lectures of John Colet," *Journal of the History of Ideas*, XIV (1953), 493-510.

Durand de Laur, H. *Érasme précurseur et initiateur de l'esprit moderne*. Paris, 1872.

Duval, Fréderick. *De la paix de Dieu à la paix de fer*. Paris, 1923.

Einstein, Lewis. *The Italian Renaissance in England*. New York, 1903.

———. *Tudor Ideals*. New York, 1921.

Ellis, H. (ed.). *Original Letters*. 3rd Ser. London, 1846.

Emerton, E. *Erasmus*. New York, 1889.

Enthoven, L. "Erasmus Weltburger oder Patriot?" *Neue Jahrbücher für das klassische Altertum*, XV (1912), 205-15.

Epistolae aliquot eruditorum virorum. Basel, 1520.

339

Eppstein, John. *The Catholic Tradition of the Law of Nations.* London, 1935.

Erasmus. *Adagiorum chiliades tres.* [Basel, 1513].

——. *Erasmus Against War,* ed. J. W. Mackail. Boston, 1907.

——. *Bellum Erasmi* [trans. Richard Taverner?] London, 1533-[34].

——. [*The Christian Knight,* trans. anon. London, 1541.] STC 10482.

——. *The Colloquies,* trans. H. Bailey, ed. E. Johnson. London, 1878.

——. *The Complaint of Peace,* trans. anon. Chicago, 1917.

——. *The Complaint of Peace,* ed. W. J. Hirten. New York, 1946.

——. *Erasmus Concerning the Aim and Method of Education,* trans. W. H. Woodward. Cambridge, Eng., 1904.

——. *Encomium Moriae* (1515), facsimile edition by H. Schmid. Basel, 1931.

——. *Dulce bellum inexpertis,* ed. and trans. Y. Remy and R. Dunil-Marquebreucq. Berchem-Brussels, 1953.

——. *The Education of a Christian Prince,* trans. L. K. Born. New York, 1936.

——. *Enchiridion militis Christiani,* [trans. Wm. Tyndale?]. [London, 1905].

——. *Erasmi epigrammata.* Basel, 1518.

——. *The Epistles of Erasmus,* trans. F. M. Nichols. London, 1901-18.

——. *The Familiar Colloquies,* trans. N. Bailey. London, 1725.

——. *The Lives of Vitrier . . . and John Colet,* trans. J. H. Lupton. London, 1883.

——. *Opera omnia,* ed. J. Clericus. Leiden, 1703-6.

——. *Opus epistolarum Des. Erasmi,* ed. P. S. and H. M. Allen. Oxford, 1906-47.

——. *Erasmi opuscula,* ed. W. K. Ferguson. The Hague, 1933.

——. *The First Tome of the Paraphrase . . . upon the Newe Testamente.* London, 1548.

——. *The Poems of Erasmus,* ed. C. Reedijk. Leiden, 1956.

——. *The Praise of Folly,* trans. Sir Thomas Chaloner (1549), ed. J. Ashbee. London, 1921.

——. *The Praise of Folly,* trans. Leonard Dean. Chicago, 1946.

——. *The Praise of Folly,* trans. H. H. Hudson. Princeton, N. J., 1941.

——. *A Scorneful Image . . . called Sileni alcibiadis.* [London, 154?]. STC 10507.

——. *Ten Colloquies of Erasmus,* trans. C. R. Thompson. New York, 1957.

——. *Treatise upon the Paternoster,* [trans. Margaret More. London, 1526?] STC 10477.

Ferguson, W. K. "The Attitude of Erasmus Toward Toleration," in *Persecution and Liberty,* pp. 171-81. New York, 1931.

340

————. "An Unpublished Letter of John Colet," *American Historical Review*, XXXIX (1934), 696-99.

Figgis, J. N. *The Political Aspects of St. Augustine's "City of God."* London, 1921.

————. *Studies in Political Thought . . . 1414-1625.* Cambridge, Eng., 1907.

Fisher, H. *The History of England (1485-1547).* London, 1934.

Fisher, John. *The English Works of John Fisher,* ed. J. Mayor. London, 1876.

————. *Two Fruytfull Sermons.* London, 1532.

Fortescue, Sir John. *The Governance of England,* ed. C. Plummer. Oxford, 1926.

————. *De laudibus legum Anglie,* ed. S. Chrimes. Cambridge, Eng., 1949.

————. *The Works of Sir John Fortescue,* ed. Lord Clermont. London, 1869.

Fowler, Thomas. *Corpus Christi.* London, 1898.

————. *The History of Corpus Christi College.* Oxford, 1893.

Fox, Richard. *Letters of Richard Fox 1486-1527,* ed. P. S. and H. M. Allen. Oxford, 1929.

Froude, J. A. *Life and Letters of Erasmus.* London, 1894.

Gairdner, James. *Lollardy and the Reformation in England (1300-1555).* London, 1908-13.

Gasquet, Francis. *The Eve of the Reformation.* London, 1905.

Gee, John A. *The Life and Works of Thomas Lupset.* New Haven, 1928.

Gierke, O. *Natural Law and the Theory of Society 1500-1800.* Cambridge, Eng., 1934.

————. *Political Theories of the Middle Age,* trans. F. Maitland. Cambridge, Eng., 1900.

Gewirth, Alan. *Marsilius of Padua and Medieval Political Philosophy.* New York, 1951.

Giustinian, Sebastian. *Sebastian Giustinian, Four Years at the Court of Henry VIII,* trans. Rawdon Brown. London, 1854.

Hall, Edward. *Hall's Chronicle,* ed. H. Ellis. London, 1809.

Harpsfield, Nicholas. *The Life and Death of Sr Thomas Moore,* ed. E. V. Hitchcock. London, 1932.

Hearnshaw, F. (ed.). *Mediaeval Contributions to Modern Civilization.* London, 1921.

————. (ed.). *The Social and Political Ideas of Some Great Mediaeval Thinkers.* London, 1923.

————. (ed.). *The Social and Political Ideas of Some Great Thinkers of the Renaissance and the Reformation.* London, 1925.

Hesiod. *Works of Hesiod,* trans. J. Banks. London, 1856.

Hexter, J. H. *More's Utopia.* Princeton, N. J., 1952.

Holinshed, Raphael. *Holinshed's Chronicles,* ed. H. Ellis. London, 1808.

Horace. *The Odes and Epodes,* trans. Charles Edwin Bennett. Loeb Classical Library. Cambridge, Mass., 1914.

Hudson, Hoyt. *The Epigram in the English Renaissance.* Princeton, N. J., 1947.

Huizinga, J. *Erasmus,* trans. F. Hopman. New York, 1924.

Hyma, A. *The Christian Renaissance.* New York, 1935.

————. "The Continental Origins of English Humanism," *Huntington Library Quarterly,* IV (1940), 1-26.

————. "Erasmus and the Oxford Reformers (1495-1503)," *Nederlandsch Archief voor Kerkgeschiedenis,* N.S., XXV (1932), 69-92, 97-134.

————. "Erasmus and the Oxford Reformers (1503-1519)," *Nederlandsch Archief voor Kerkgeschiedenis,* N.S., XXXVIII (1951), 65-85.

————. *The Youth of Erasmus.* Ann Arbor, Mich., 1930.

Innocentius III. *The Mirror of Mans Lyfe,* trans. H. Kirton. London, 1576.

Iongh, A. de, *Erasmus' Denkbeelden over Staat en Regeering.* Amsterdam, 1927.

Jarrett, Bede. *Social Theories of the Middle Ages 1200-1500.* London, 1926.

Jones, Richard F. *Ancients and Moderns.* St. Louis, Mo., 1936.

Journals of the House of Lords. N.p., n.d.

Juvenal. *Juvenal and Persius,* trans. George Gilbert Ramsey. Loeb Classical Library. Cambridge, Mass., 1928.

Kautsky, Karl. *Thomas More and His Utopia,* trans. H. Stenning. London, 1927.

Kelso, Ruth. *The Doctrine of the English Gentleman.* Urbana, Ill., 1929.

Kingsford, C. (ed.). *The First English Life of King Henry the Fifth.* Oxford, 1911.

Knight, Samuel. *The Life of Dr. John Colet.* London, 1724.

Kristeller, Paul Oskar. "Augustine and the Early Renaissance," *Review of Religion,* VIII (1943), 339-58.

————. *The Classics and Renaissance Thought.* Cambridge, Mass., 1955.

————. *The Philosophy of Marsilio Ficino,* trans. V. Conant. New York, 1943.

Kuiper, E. T. "Erasmus als politiek Propagandist," *Tijdschrift voor Geschiedenis,* XXXVII (1922), 147-67.

Lange, C. L. *Histoire de l'internationalisme.* New York, 1919.

Lewis, C. S. *English Literature in the Sixteenth Century, Excluding Drama.* Oxford, 1954.

Livy, trans. Benjamin O. Foster. Loeb Classical Library. Cambridge, Mass., 1929.

Lovejoy, A. O., and G. Boas. *Primitivism and Related Ideas in Antiquity.* Baltimore, 1935.

Lucan. *The Civil War* [*The Pharsalia*], trans. James. D. Duff. Loeb Classical Library. Cambridge, Mass., 1928.

Lucas, Henry S. *The Renaissance and the Reformation.* New York, 1934.

Lucian. *Lucian's Dialogues,* trans. H. Williams. London, 1888.

Lull, Ramon. *The Book of the Ordre of Chyualry,* ed. A. Byles. London, 1926.

Lupton, J. H. *A Life of John Colet.* London, 1887.

Luther, Martin. *Luther's Works,* trans. C. M. Jacobs. Philadelphia, 1915.

Malory, Sir Thomas. *Le Morte Darthur,* ed. H. O. Sommer. London, 1889.

Marcel, R. "Les 'découvertes' d'Érasme en Angleterre," *Bibliothèque d'humanisme et renaissance,* XIV (1952), 117-23.

McIlwain, C. H. *The Growth of Political Thought in the West from the Greeks to the End of the Middle Ages.* New York, 1932.

Merriman, Roger. *Life and Letters of Thomas Cromwell.* Oxford, 1902.

Mesnard, Pierre. *L'Essor de la philosophie politique au XVIe siècle.* Paris, 1936.

Milman, H. *Savonarola.* London, 1870.

More, Sir Thomas. *The Correspondence of Sir Thomas More,* ed. E. F. Rogers. Princeton, N. J., 1947.

————. *The Dialogue Concerning Tyndale,* ed. W. Campbell. London, 1927.

————. *English Works.* London, 1557.

————. *The English Works,* ed. W. E. Campbell *et al.* London, 1931-39.

————. *Epistola ad Germanum Brixium.* London, 1520.

————. *The Latin Epigrams,* ed. L. Bradner and C. Lynch. Chicago, 1953.

————. *Utopia,* ed. J. C. Collins. Oxford, 1904.

————. *The Utopia,* ed. H. Goitein. London, 1925.

————. *Utopia,* ed. J. H. Lupton. Oxford, 1895.

————. *Utopia,* ed. J. St. John. London, 1850.

Morley, H. *Cornelius Agrippa.* London, 1856.

Murray, R. H. *Erasmus and Luther.* London, 1920.

Nelson, E. W. "Recent Literature on Erasmus," *Journal of Modern History,* I (1929), 88-102.

Nichols, G. (ed.). *The Boke of Noblesse.* London, 1860.

Nisard, D. *Études sur la renaissance et réformé, Erasmus—Thomas Morus.* Paris, 1855.

"The Note . . . of . . . Ladie Kateryne," in *The Antiquarian Repertory,* ed. F. Grose *et al.,* II, 249-51. London, 1808.

Nys, Ernest. "Quâtre utopistes au XVIe siècle," *Revue de droit international et de législation comparée,* XXI (1889), 65-76.

Ovid. *Metamorphoses,* trans. Frank Justus Miller. Loeb Classical Library. Cambridge, Mass., 1929.

Owst, G. R. *Literature and Pulpit in Medieval England.* Cambridge, Eng., 1933.

————. *Preaching in Medieval England.* Cambridge, Eng., 1926.

Pace, Richard. *De fructu qui ex doctrina percipitur*. Basel, 1517.

———. *Oratio Richardi Pacei in pace*. [London, 1518]. *STC* 19081a.

Panofsky, Dora and Erwin. *Pandora's Box*. New York, 1956.

Parker, Matthew. *De antiquitate Britannicae ecclesiae*. N.p., 1572.

Penrose, Boies. *Travel and Discovery in the Renaissance 1420-1620*. Cambridge, Mass., 1955.

Phillimore, J. S. "The Arrest of Humanism in England," *Dublin Review*, CLIII (1913), 1-26.

Pisan, Christine de, *The Book of Fayttes of Armes and of Chyualrye*, trans. W. Caxton, ed. A. Byles. London, 1932.

Pliny. *The Naturall Historie*, trans. P. Holland. London, 1601.

Plutarch. *Morals*, trans. P. Holland. London, 1603.

Pollard, A. F. *Henry VIII*. London, 1902.

———. *Wolsey*. London, 1929.

Praz, Mario. *The Flaming Heart*. New York, 1958.

———. "Machiavelli and the Elizabethans," *Proceedings of the British Academy*, XIV (1928).

Prestage, E. (ed.). *Chivalry*. London, 1928.

Prutz, Hanz. *Die Friedensidee*. Munich, 1917.

Ranke, L. von. *The History of the Popes*, trans. E. Foster. London, 1889.

Ramsey, W. H. *The Imperial Peace, an Ideal in European History*. Oxford, 1913.

Reed, A. W. *Early Tudor Drama*. London, 1926.

Renaudet, A. *Érasme*. Paris, 1926.

———. *Érasme et l'Italie*. Geneva, 1954.

———. *Machiavel*. Paris, 1942.

Rice, E. F., Jr. "Erasmus and the Religious Tradition, 1495-1499," *Journal of the History of Ideas*, XI (1950), 387-411.

Roeder, Ralph. *The Man of the Renaissance*. New York, 1933.

Roper, William. *The Lyfe of Sir Thomas Moore*, ed. E. V. Hitchcock. London, 1935.

Routh, E. *Sir Thomas More and his Friends 1477-1535*. London, 1934.

Rowse, A. L. *The English Spirit*. New York, 1945.

Russell, F. M. *Theories of International Relations*. New York, 1936.

Ryan, J. K. *Modern War and Base Ethics*. Washington, D. C., 1933.

Rymer, T., and R. Sanderson (eds.). *Foedera*. London, 1704-35.

Salomon, A. "Democracy and Religion in the Work of Erasmus," *Review of Religion*, XIV (1950), 227-49.

Schulte-Vaerting, H. *Die Friedenspolitik des Pericles*. Munich, 1919.

Seebohm, Frederick. *The Oxford Reformers*. London, 1887.

Seneca. *On Benefits*, trans. A. Stewart. London, 1887.

———. *Physical Science in the Time of Nero . . . the Quaestiones naturales*, trans. J. Clarke. London, 1910.

———. *Workes*, trans. T. Lodge. London, 1614.

Skelton, John. *Poetical Works*, ed. A. Dyce. London, 1843.

Smith, Preserved. *Erasmus*. New York, 1923.

———. *A Key to the Colloquies of Erasmus*. Cambridge, Mass., 1927.

Spont, A. (ed.). *Letters and Papers Relating to the War with France 1512-1513*. [London], 1897.

Stapleton, Thomas. *The Life . . . of Sir Thomas More*, trans. P. E. Hallett. London, 1928.

State Papers . . . I, King Henry VIII. [London], 1830.

Stokes, F. G. (trans.). *Epistolae obscurorum virorum*. London, 1925.

Sturge, Charles. *Cuthbert Tunstall*. London, 1938.

Surtz, Edward. *The Praise of Pleasure*. Cambridge, Mass., 1957.

———. *The Praise of Wisdom*. Chicago, 1957.

Tawney, R. H. *Religion and the Rise of Capitalism*. London, 1927.

Taylor, H. O. *Thought and Expression in the Sixteenth Century*. New York, 1920.

Thompson, C. R. "Erasmus as Internationalist and Cosmopolitan," *Archiv für Reformationsgeschichte*, XLVI (1955), 167-95.

———. *The Translations of Lucian by Erasmus and St. Thomas More*. Ithaca, N. Y., 1940.

Thompson, J. A. K. "Erasmus in England," Bibliothek Warburg, *Vorträge, 1930-1931*, pp. 64-82. Leipzig, 1932.

Thorndike, L. "John Louis Vives," in *Essays . . . Dedicated to James Harvey Robinson*, pp. 327-42. New York, 1929.

Troeltsch, E. *The Social Teaching of the Christian Churches*, trans. O. Wyon. New York, 1931.

Van Vollenhoven, C. *The Law of Peace*, trans. W. Carter. London, 1936.

Vergil, Polydore. *The Anglica historia 1485-1537*, trans. D. Hay. London, 1950.

———. *A . . . History of the First Inventers*, trans. anon. London, 1685.

———. *De rerum inuenteribus*. Basel, 1532.

Vespucci, Amerigo. *The "Dutch Vespuccius" . . . the Letter of Vespuccius Describing His Third Voyage*. Providence, R. I., 1864.

———. *Letter to Lorenzo . . . de Medici*, trans. G. Northup. Princeton, N. J., 1916.

———. *Letter to Piero Soderini*, trans. G. Northup. Princeton, N. J., 1916.

Villari, P. *Life and Times of Savonarola*, trans. L. Villari. New York, 1893.

Vives, J. L. "Clarorum Hispaniensium epistolae ineditae," *Revue hispanique*, VIII (1901), 263-64.

———. *Concerning Relief of the Poor*, trans. M. M. Sherwood. New York, 1917.

———. *De concordia & discordia in humano genere*. [Antwerp, 1529].

———. *On Education. A Translation of the "De tradendis disciplinis"* by F. Watson. Cambridge, Eng., 1913.

————. *The Instruction of a Christen Woman*, trans. R. Hyrde. London, 1541.

————. *An Introduction to Wysedome*, trans. R. Morysine. London, 1540.

————. *Opera*. Basel, 1555.

————. *Opera*. Valencia, 1783.

————. *De subventione pauperum*. Leiden, 1532.

Vocht, Henry de. *Monumenta humanistica Lovaniensia*. Louvain, 1934.

———— (ed.). *Literae virorum eruditorum ad Franciscum Craneveldium 1522-1528*. Louvain, 1929.

Watson, F. *The Beginnings of the Teaching of Modern Subjects in England*. London, 1909.

————. *The English Grammar Schools to 1660*. Cambridge, Eng., 1908.

————. "The Influence of Valencia . . . on . . . Vives," *Aberystwyth Studies*, XI (1927), 47-103.

————. "J. L. Vives and St. Augustine's *Civitas Dei*," *Church Quarterly Review* (London), LXXVI (1913), 145-47.

————. *Luis Vives*. [Oxford], 1922.

————. *Vives and the Renascence Education of Women*. New York, 1912.

Willey, B. *The Seventeneth Century Background*. London, 1934.

Williams, Arnold. "A Note on Pessimism in the Renaissance," *Studies in Philology*, XXXVI (1939), 243-46.

Williamson, George. "Mutability, Decay, and Seventeenth-Century Melancholy," *English Literary History*, II (1935), 121-51.

Williamson, J. A. *The Tudor Age*. London, 1953.

Wingfield-Stratford, Esmé. *The Foundations of British Patriotism*. London, 1939.

Woodward, W. H. *Studies in Education . . . 1400-1600*. Cambridge, Eng., 1906.

————. *Vittorino da Feltre*. Cambridge, Eng., 1897.

Wright, R. F. *Medieval Internationalism*. London, 1930.

Wright, Quincy. *A Study of War*. Chicago, 1942.

Wulf, M. de. *History of Medieval Philosophy*, trans. P. Coffey. 3rd ed. London, 1909.

INDEX